SCOUNDREL

ALSO BY SARAH WEINMAN

The Real Lolita: A Lost Girl,
an Unthinkable Crime, and a Scandalous Masterpiece

Unspeakable Acts: True Tales of Crime,
Murder, Deceit, and Obsession

SCOUNDREL

How a Convicted Murderer Persuaded the Women Who Loved Him, the Conservative Establishment, and the Courts to Set Him Free

SARAH WEINMAN

An Imprint of HarperCollins*Publishers*

FIRST EDITION

Background art by Nik Merkulov/ Shutterstock, Inc.

Designed by Michelle Crowe

Library of Congress Cataloging-in-Publication Data
Names: Weinman, Sarah, author.
Title: Scoundrel : how a convicted murderer persuaded the women who loved him, the conservative establishment, and the courts to set him free / Sarah Weinman.
Description: First edition. | New York, NY : Ecco, an imprint of HarperCollins Publishers, [2022] |Includes bibliographical references and index. |
Identifiers: LCCN 2021044151 (print) | LCCN 2021044152 (ebook) | ISBN 9780062899767 (hardcover) | ISBN 9780062899798 (ebook)
Subjects: LCSH: Smith, Edgar, 1934-2017. | Murderers--New Jersey--Biography. | Swindlers and swindling--New Jersey--Biography.
Classification: LCC HV6248.S578 W45 2022 (print) | LCC HV6248.S578 (ebook) | DDC 364.152/3092--dc23
LC record available at https://lccn.loc.gov/2021044151
LC ebook record available at https://lccn.loc.gov/2021044152

22 23 24 25 26 LSC 10 9 8 7 6 5 4 3 2 1

To Jaime

There is nothing in the world more difficult than candor, and nothing easier than flattery.

—FYODOR DOSTOEVSKY, *Crime and Punishment*

Jonathan's view was that Edgar Smith was guilty, but deserved his freedom. Fourteen years constituted a life sentence today, and he had rehabilitated and educated himself in a grisly cell on Death Row.

—MARY HIGGINS CLARK, *Where Are the Children?*

CONTENTS

INTRODUCTION   1

Part I: The Sand Pit (1957)

1. "Where Is Vickie?"   11
2. The Mercury   19
3. "If You're Looking for a Fall Guy . . ."   27
4. Openings   41
5. "I Just Threw It Out the Window"   51
6. "Eddie and Don Aren't Friends Anymore"   59
7. "It Can't Be"   69

Part II: The Death House (1958–1962)

8. Patricia   75
9. Divorces   89

Part III: The Conservative (1962–1966)

10. A "Lifetime" Subscription   99
11. "My God, I Wish I Could Be Absolutely Certain"   111
12. Meeting in Trenton   119
13. Waiting for Death   129

Part IV: Making the Brief (1967–1968)

14. Lunch at Paone's   143
15. "They Must Think I Am Houdini"   149
16. Blood, Nerves, Vibrations   159
17. Hatkic   165
18. March to Publication   173

19. The Breach   189
20. *Brief Against Death*   199

Part V: Reasonable Doubts (1969–1971)

21. Rogue's Wake   209
22. *A Reasonable Doubt*   223
23. Bid for a New Trial   231
24. Conviction Overturned   241

Part VI: Getting Out (1971–1976)

25. *Non Vult*   253
26. Freedom's First Dawn   261
27. The Celebrity Convict   269
28. *Counterpoint*   277
29. Paige   283

Part VII: Boiling Over (1976–1979)

30. Rage, Revived   297
31. On the Run   303
32. Arrested Again   311
33. "The Saga of a Bad Man"   317
34. "Used and Betrayed"   325

Part VIII: Staying In (1980–2017)

35. A Strange Triangle   335
36. Vacaville   341
CODA: 1948   353

ACKNOWLEDGMENTS   361
NOTES   365
BIBLIOGRAPHY   423
INDEX   427

SCOUNDREL

Introduction

EDGAR SMITH died on March 20, 2017, just over a month after his eighty-third birthday. He spent almost forty years in California's state penitentiary system, much of his last decade in health so poor that it was a surprise he survived so long. He was hard of hearing and barely able to walk more than a quarter mile, and even that short distance required a cane. A weak heart necessitating six bypass surgeries didn't kill him, either.

That Smith lived into his eighties is all the more remarkable because he was supposed to die nearly six decades earlier, executed by the state of New Jersey for the 1957 murder of fifteen-year-old Victoria Zielinski. At one time Smith was perhaps the most famous convict in America, counting William F. Buckley, Jr., founder of *National Review* and one of the key architects of the neoconservative movement, as his closest friend.

Scoundrel tells the true, almost too bizarre tale of a man saved from death row thanks to the years-long advocacy, through financial and creative means, of a most unlikely source. When police brutality and mass incarceration are perennially under a national microscope, when the lives of countless Black and Brown boys and men are permanently altered by the criminal justice system, the transformation of Edgar Smith into a national cause more than half a century ago raises uncomfortable questions about who merits such a spotlight and who does not. His story, and the involvement of the many people who helped fashion it, complicates the larger narrative of incarcerated people who proclaim their innocence and of prisoners—on death row and elsewhere—exonerated and freed thanks to newly discovered or long-suppressed evidence.

This book is, in effect, a story of a wrongful conviction in reverse.

As a result of Buckley's advocacy, Edgar Smith vaulted from prison to the country's highest intellectual echelons as a best-selling author, an expert on prison reform, and a minor celebrity—only to fall, spectacularly, to earth when his murderous impulses prevailed again. Though the relationship between Norman Mailer and the convict and author Jack Henry Abbott is well known, the comparable one between Buckley and Smith has received far less attention despite the resulting heinous fallout.

Buckley at first took up the Edgar Smith case out of righteous indignation on behalf of Smith, a man whom he believed to be wrongfully convicted and whose literary gifts, which transformed him from underachieving blue-collar worker to curious intellectual, made him worth saving. As Buckley came to regard Smith as a genuine friend, he also operated out of loyalty. As the lawyer and former *National Review* correspondent Donald G. M. Coxe told me, "We were taken in, I suspect, in part by our unwillingness to believe that anyone who loved *NR* could be a savage killer."

Even after it was clear that his faith in Edgar was severely misguided, Buckley concluded, "Edgar Smith has done enough damage in his lifetime without underwriting the doctrine that the verdict of a court is infallible." That unshakable belief exonerated a psychopath, elevating Smith to prominence and some power at the expense of the women he harmed, injured, and murdered. Buckley fell into the trap described in Fyodor Dostoevsky's *Crime and Punishment*: "An honest and sensitive man opens his heart, and the man of business listens and goes on eating—and then he eats you up."

———

IN MARCH 1957, Edgar Smith seemed like a typical young man living in New Jersey's Bergen County: married, the father of a newborn baby, a veteran of the marines, discharged because of partial deafness in his left ear, in between jobs. Victoria Zielinski, fifteen years old at the time, was murdered in the small town of Mahwah, her head bashed in by a baseball bat and a couple of large rocks. It didn't take long for authorities to find and arrest Smith: Zielinski's blood was on a pair of his pants and in the car he'd borrowed that day. He also admitted to the police that he had given her a ride, though he claimed that she was still alive when they had parted.

The trial lasted two weeks and was a standing-room-only sensation. (Mary Higgins Clark, years before writing the novels that immortalized her as "the Queen of Suspense," attended every day and dated the beginning of her career as a crime writer to the case.) Smith testified in his own defense, and the resulting inconsistencies were noticed even by trial attendees as young as ten years old. It took less than two hours for the jury to convict him and the judge to sentence him to death. Smith kept appealing his execution and avoiding the electric chair. And since he was staying alive, he decided to better himself, enrolling in college classes, reading history books, and keeping up with current affairs through magazines.

Fate played a hand when William F. Buckley learned of a 1962 newspaper story about Smith in which the convict praised *National Review* as one of his favorite periodicals. Buckley and the *National Review*'s intellectual stock were rising among conservatives, but he had only just begun to write his syndicated newspaper column, On the Right, and he was still several years away from his quixotic run for New York City mayor and the first broadcast of his interview show, *Firing Line*.

Buckley would later learn that Smith's access to *National Review* had been cut off after the prison official who lent him copies had been transferred away from the Death House. Sensing a story, feeling some pang of sympathy, or both, Buckley wrote Smith to ensure the prisoner would always receive a copy of *National Review*. Over the next nine years, through an exchange of more than 1,500 pages of correspondence, the two men became friends—and Buckley became convinced that Smith was not Zielinski's killer.

Buckley wrote about the case, and his belief in Edgar Smith's innocence, in several columns and in a 1965 story for *Esquire*; he used the fee he earned for the story to seed the Death House inmate's defense fund. Smith had been acting as his own jailhouse lawyer; now Buckley found Smith several lawyers to work on his appeals. Buckley also set Smith up with Sophie Wilkins, a dynamic and vivacious editor at the New York–based book-publishing firm Alfred A. Knopf. She worked closely with Smith on his 1968 book, *Brief Against Death*, which argued that the state of New Jersey's case against him was riddled with holes and attempted, above all, to persuade the reader that he had not killed Vickie Zielinski.

Wilkins, as I discovered while working in her archives at Columbia University, became more than Smith's editor. Their correspondence, which she preserved nearly in full, began in strictly professional fashion, with her recommending books to read and offering encouragement on the manuscript that became *Brief Against Death*. Then it devolved into something more.

They exchanged declarations of love, gifts and artwork, and mutual pornographic fantasies, his smuggled out through third parties to avoid the prying eyes of the Death House censors. He called her "Red"; she called him "Ilya." Their fights about editorial changes quickly spiraled out of control, and then they made up, lovers' quarrel style. Wilkins would, in subsequent correspondence with Buckley, express rage and embarrassment at how besotted she had become with Smith and how foolishly she'd behaved.

But that was only after *Brief Against Death* became a critical and commercial success that prompted many conversations about the necessity of the death penalty, conversations that had been brewing throughout the decade as capital punishment began losing support among the American public. It made Smith a literary star. William F. Buckley promoted his advocacy on *The Tonight Show*, the *Today* show, and other major venues in support of the book, and Smith eventually became the first convicted murderer nominated to join PEN America. The book was chosen as an alternate pick of the Literary Guild and was reviewed by every major publication (including a glowing review by the crime novelist Ross Macdonald in the *New York Times Book Review*). Two years later, in 1970, his novel *A Reasonable Doubt* garnered similar acclaim, including praise from the hard-boiled writer James M. Cain.

By the end of 1971, the tide had turned fully in Smith's favor. A federal court of appeals threw out his confession and ordered a new trial. After a seesaw battle between state and federal powers, Smith walked out of court a free man. Officially, he had pleaded guilty to second-degree murder, and he was credited with nearly fifteen years of time served. Immediately after the guilty plea and the final ruling, Smith climbed into a limousine, Buckley took the seat next to him, and they went straight to the television studio to record two riveting hours of *Firing Line*, which aired on consecutive weeks.

Edgar Smith became a go-to guy on all things prison related. He published book reviews in *Playboy* and a self-interview in *Esquire*, appeared on *The Mike Douglas Show* and many radio programs, and returned home to Bergen County, ignoring and at times openly mocking the cloud of suspicion emanating from his neighbors. He published a thriller, *71 Hours*, under the pseudonym Michael Mason and then another book of nonfiction under his own name, *Getting Out*. He met and married a much younger woman who believed in his innocence and moved with her to California. Then his celebrity status dissipated, and the gigs dried up. His wife became the breadwinner.

In October 1976, an old pattern asserted itself. Having been turned down for a job at the *San Diego Union-Tribune*, Smith lay in wait in a supermarket parking lot, where he dragged thirty-three-year-old Lefteriya Lisa Ozbun into his car and, while driving with one hand, attempted to stab her to death with the other. He came close to committing his second murder, but Ozbun struggled mightily, kicked a hole in the windshield, and managed to pull the car over, alerting a nearby motorist. Spooked, Smith fled in the damaged car, dumped it for another, and spent the next two weeks as a fugitive, tapping his family for help and money. When those sources dried up, he called Buckley's office, reaching his secretary. She learned that Smith was in Las Vegas under an assumed name. She told Buckley, who promptly called the FBI and turned Smith in.

The following year at trial, Smith confessed to killing Victoria Zielinski: "I recognized that the devil I had been looking at for the last forty-three years was me," he told the court. "It was at that time I recognized that my life had reached a point at which I had a choice of doing two things: I could kill myself or I could return to San Diego and face what I was." He received a life sentence for the attempted murder of Lisa Ozbun and spent the rest of his days behind bars. He died at the California Medical Facility in Vacaville, California, seven years before he was next eligible for parole, in 2024, by which time he would have turned ninety.

———

HUMANS ARE HARDWIRED to believe what other humans tell them. Most people merit that belief and, when they breach it, try to atone for their mistakes. Then there are those humans who are able to manipulate, obfuscate, and make a mockery of well-meaning people, causing harm that takes years, if ever, to fully overcome. Writing *Scoundrel* was a way for me to comprehend what can seem like the incomprehensible: how Edgar Smith was able to fool so many who entered his orbit, be they intimates or strangers, and bend the American criminal justice system to his will. What I came to realize is that this story is a forgotten part of American history at the nexus of justice, prison reform, civil rights, neoconservatism, and literary culture.

William F. Buckley's attempt to free Edgar Smith resulted in catastrophic collateral damage to women: Smith's victims. Edgar had already robbed Victoria Zielinski of her chance to grow up before Buckley became involved with him. Lisa Ozbun came close to death, surviving only through happenstance and her own tenacious will to live. Smith's wives and many of his paramours and female friends suffered psychological damage that lasted the rest of their lives.

The relationship between Smith, the convict, and Buckley, the conservative, was fascinating and complex. But it is the voices of the women, sacrificed on the altar of the literary talent of a murderer, that animate the narrative of this book. The nonfiction crime genre increasingly makes greater room for the stories of women, embodying their full spectrum as human beings rather than flattening them into by-products of seductive killers. I hope *Scoundrel* adds to this growing body of nuanced, psychologically perceptive work.

On several occasions, Sophie Wilkins likened the Edgar Smith case to a work by Dostoevsky. Her son Adam told me that he found himself thinking the story, had it not been true, "would have made a wonderful novel or a wonderfully trashy one. The three key characters—the celebrity political columnist (rich, Catholic, but culturally upper-class WASP); the brilliant psychopathic jailhouse lawyer, working class, Protestant; and the sparkling bright articulate Jewish woman editor—could hardly have been more different in background and personality, but they came together in a most amazing interaction."

Edgar Smith's horrible acts, like so many other horrible acts of atrocious men then and now, were overlooked, explained away, or ignored because of his talent—and because women are expendable. The shared belief in one man's innocence and his literary acumen forged that unlikely intellectual triangle. It was undone when the totality of his violence against women revealed that his talent was a paper tiger, that brilliant people can be conned, and that the effects of betrayal ripple across generations.

PART I

THE SAND PIT

(1957)

1

"Where Is Vickie?"

MARCH 1957

FIRST, VICKIE.

She was the Zielinskis' second child. Mary Faye was the eldest, given the same first name as her mother and grandmother. Victoria Ann arrived three years after her sister, born on September 6, 1941. Then came Myrna, two years later, and finally, a couple of years after that, Anthony Jr. The Zielinskis met, married, and started their family in Honesdale, Pennsylvania, and had moved to Ramsey, New Jersey—after a short stint in Hoboken—when Vickie was seven or eight. Anthony's and Mary's ancestors had come from Poland and Austria, respectively, earlier in the twentieth century.

A nuclear family, yes. A happy one? The record says otherwise. Vickie complained about her father to her friends, usually about his curfew enforcement—always 11:00 p.m., and she had to call home if she was to be late—and sometimes about his constant drinking. Her complaints occasionally carried whispers of familial violence. That more disturbing undertone would prove important later, as would so much about what Vickie did or didn't do, what she thought or didn't think, what she wanted or didn't want.

Strip all those suppositions away, and what's left is an adolescent girl faring well by 1950s standards. "Just a kid," insisted her best friend, Barbara Nixon, describing Vickie more than 6 decades later. Which, at age 15, a shade over 5 feet and a little more than 110 pounds, was almost certainly true.

Vickie was an honor roll student in her freshman year at Ramsey High School. She took her studies seriously and was particularly keen on learning German. The summer before her sophomore year, she split her time between Ramsey and her birthplace of Honesdale, staying with her aunt Anna, her mother's sister.

In tenth grade, Vickie's marks started to slide. She seemed bored and distracted in class and was often late because she loved to socialize with her friends during the breaks. Vickie's homeroom teacher, Emily Gloekler, found none of those things too worrying, though. She told the *Paterson Evening News* that Vickie's grade drop had been "typical of sophomores, who like to enjoy themselves." Charles Schanz, the vice principal at Ramsey High, added, "She was the type who—when they say hello . . . really meant it and are happy to say it."

And Vickie did enjoy herself. Friday nights she spent at the roller rink in Paramus or at the Corral, a hangout for Ramsey teenagers to dance to jukebox tunes. She did not shy away from having fun, though weekend dates with boys and young men never went past her strict curfew. She might flirt with boys she knew, tease them and kid around with them, but she wasn't known to behave that way with strangers. In early February 1957, Vickie went out with a boy who had a bottle of beer in his car. "I won't go with you unless you break that thing," Vickie admonished him. He proceeded to smash the bottle.

One unnamed girlfriend complicated the picture with what she told the Bergen *Record* after Vickie was killed. The friend said

Vickie had changed somewhat since the beginning of the year, suggesting that she was "wilder than she used to be"—not wild enough to get into a car with a stranger, of course, but out of step with her earlier self. The kind of girl who became the subject of lurid rumors that she fooled around with older boys.

One of the last photos of Vickie shows her standing in front of a white door. The camera peers up at her from a low angle. She holds a pair of figure skates in her left hand, the wrist adorned with a white gold Wittnauer watch. Her right hand rests on her hip—a typical pose, evident in other photos taken in Vickie's teen years—while her left leg is bent slightly at the knee. She is clad in dark penny loafers, white socks that stop halfway up her shins, a white turtleneck sweater and a dark skirt whose flared hem brushes against her thighs; her expression is a Rorschach test for whatever one wishes to read into it.

She could be defiant or playful. Coy or confident. Childlike or dangerously mature. The gap between her front teeth, plainly visible in photos from earlier in her childhood, is harder to see, and so she seems to teeter on the edge between self-conscious and assured. In the photo, at least, she radiates promise of something far larger than whatever future seemed possible within the walls of her yellow-painted home at 496 Wyckoff Avenue.

What kind of life was in store for Victoria Zielinski? Would she have moved away from Bergen County across the Hudson River to Manhattan, that tiny isle bursting with outsize dreams, ready to spit out those who couldn't hack it? Or would she have fled the East Coast altogether for somewhere more far-flung?

The tragedy of early, violent death is that it strips away the person and leaves only the act, the making of the dead girl, rather than the celebration of the lived life. The killer has the power. The one who dies loses it all. Victoria Zielinski not only lost her future, her power, and her promise on the night of March 4,

1957: she lost her existence, overridden by the needs and wants and desires of the man who murdered her.

AT 7:30 THAT EVENING, Vickie and her younger sister, Myrna, walked down Wyckoff Avenue to where Ramsey ended and Mahwah began, small towns linked by the same street. Vickie was heading for Barbara Nixon's house, where she and her best friend were going to do their bookkeeping homework together and then study for a test the following morning. She and Barbara couldn't have been more different. Vickie was short, dark, fun loving. Barbara was taller, blonder, less inclined toward humorous hijinks. But once their friendship took hold at the beginning of their freshman year, it stuck.

Since the streets were poorly lit and sidewalks were scarce, the Zielinski girls often kept each other company at least partway on any evening walk. When cars zoomed past on the two-lane road, pedestrians barely had time to jump out of the way. The girls felt unsafe walking alone, but what they were afraid of was being hit by a car, a far more common event in Bergen County than being murdered. As on other nights, once Vickie got close to the Nixons' place, Myrna turned around and walked back home. She arrived before 8:00 p.m., giving her a half hour of homework time before she was due to go back out to meet her older sister.

Vickie wore blue jeans, a coral cardigan sweater, her navy blue Ramsey High jacket, and red gloves, her customary silver heart chain adorning her neck. She arrived at Barbara's house on the corner of Fardale Road and Chapel Street at around a quarter to eight. The girls did their homework and then listened to the radio and talked for a little while.

At about 8:30, Vickie left the Nixons' for home. Myrna, still deep in her own homework, needed a nudge from her mother to remember that it was time to go. She left the house ten minutes late, at twenty to nine. She figured she would run into her older sister along the way.

She did not. Myrna kept walking but saw no sign of Vickie. She made it all the way to the Nixons' by ten of nine, thinking that Vickie might still be there. She was not. Barbara's family told Myrna that Vickie had left, on schedule, twenty minutes earlier.

Myrna walked back home, confusion and worry mounting. There was still no sign of Vickie or anyone else walking along Wyckoff Avenue. A two-tone green Ford, going well over fifty miles an hour, zoomed past her where Wyckoff met Crescent Avenue, and Myrna recognized the driver: an older boy named Donald Hommell.

Myrna had met Hommell the previous year after he and his family moved to Ramsey from Vero Beach, Florida; Don, nineteen at the time, had just been honorably discharged from the navy and now worked at a local drugstore. Good boyfriend material for her sister, but Myrna was sure that they had never dated, because Vickie's dates had to come inside the house and meet at least one of her parents. Don hadn't done that. Even Myrna knew he cared less about girls than playing baseball; he dreamed of a tryout with his favorite baseball team, the St. Louis Cardinals.

"Where is Vickie?" her mother asked when Myrna walked in the door.

Myrna had no answer. They waited an hour, and then another. Her mother didn't want to wake her husband up quite yet. He'd gone to sleep not long after Vickie had left the house, exhausted from his work as a truck driver for the borough of Ramsey, and had to be up early in the morning.

At midnight, when Vickie was an hour late for her curfew, Mary went upstairs and woke up Anthony.

"She's not home? Maybe she's down at the ice cream parlor," he said. But Mary, Myrna, and eldest daughter Mary Faye, who was staying at the house that night, insisted otherwise. "Daddy, Vickie is missing," Mary Faye insisted.

Anthony took Mary Faye's car, parked closest to the road on the driveway. He drove down Wyckoff Avenue and bumped into a couple of police officers he knew, alerting them that his daughter was missing. From there he drove into downtown Ramsey, in case Vickie was out and about somewhere. When he didn't see her, he drove to the Nixons'. Anthony decided not to knock on their door "because there was no light." (Later, Barbara would tell the Passaic *Herald-News* that she had heard a car horn not long after Vickie left and later heard the sound of a car slowing down near her house.)

When Anthony returned home on the chance that Vickie might have shown up, he was gravely disappointed. Neither he nor Mary could bring themselves to go to sleep. They stayed up all night, worrying, fearing the worst, hoping for the best.

The next morning, just after daybreak, the Zielinskis went out again to find their daughter. Anthony drove his own car this time, his wife beside him in the front seat. They searched in circles, starting small, then making progressively larger circuits of the neighborhood. At the point where Ramsey ended and Mahwah began, they noticed a scarf lying in the mud at the intersection of Fardale Avenue and Chapel Road, near the home of S. C. Kromka, whom Anthony and Mary knew slightly.

Anthony wanted to keep searching, since the scarf wasn't far from a sand pit, a swath of excavated earth fashioned into a seven-foot quarry. It had become a lovers' lane because it was just far enough off the road to afford privacy for the amorous. He told Mary to call the police at the Kromkas' house and stopped the car to let her out. Mary knocked on the Kromkas' door and asked to use the phone. She also asked if Mrs. Kromka had seen any sign of Vickie, but the woman had not.

When Mary made the call at 9:12 a.m., the responder told her to wait by the car for an officer to arrive. But Anthony had already driven across Chapel Road to the sand pit. He stopped the car when he saw something on the ground. Here was a black loafer. There was one of the red gloves Vickie had been wearing. Then her father found her necklace, the silver chain that should have been around her neck but now lay in a sand pit off Fardale Avenue. Knowing that the police would be on their way to the Kromkas', Anthony decided to walk back to his wife. He arrived just as Mahwah Police Department captain Edmund Wickham pulled into the driveway at 9:20 a.m.

The police captain told Mary to stand by the Zielinskis' car and "not to let any traffic go by" lest the crime scene be corrupted. He and Anthony headed back to the sand pit to continue searching. Wickham started walking slowly toward the lane, where he noticed a trail of tire tracks leading to the pit. They followed the tracks toward the pit, which was about 250 feet from the road. Anthony noticed blood and footprints on the ground and then spotted the other black loafer.

They found Vickie's body at the bottom of the embankment. She was facedown in a jackknifed position, "as if she had been rolled down from one of the stony mounds," a reporter would later write. Her sweater still covered her arms but had been pulled up to reveal her torso. Her bra was pushed up, the straps broken. There were bite marks on her exposed right breast, but her dungarees were still in place. An autopsy would later confirm that she had not been raped and that her hymen was intact.

It was the damage to her head that revealed the brutality of Vickie's murder. Her nose and jaw were severely fractured, with several teeth broken, and her skull had been crushed. Two blood-drenched rocks, one of them weighing as much as twenty-five pounds, sat nearby, pieces of brain spattered around them. Raphael Gilady, the Bergen County medical examiner, later characterized what happened to Vickie in a single, awful word: *decerebrated*.

Her father could hardly comprehend what he was seeing. Fourteen hours earlier, the Zielinskis had been eating dinner and Vickie had been talking about going to her best friend's house to study. To her father, Vickie had been the "jolliest, nicest, smilingest kid in the world." Now someone had destroyed her.

When he saw Vickie's body, he called for Mary. "She came over," Anthony told the *Bergen Evening Record*, "and I tried not to cry but I couldn't help myself." The paper didn't report what Vickie's mother had said—or felt.

It was obvious from the evidence on the ground that Vickie had struggled mightily with her killer. Her dad had taught her judo so she could protect herself if necessary, and it was clear that she had tried. It looked as though she had managed to escape from a car and run to the top of the embankment, where her killer had caught her. Only a couple of heavy rocks had stopped her struggle.

"I'll find the guy," Anthony later told reporters. "I found her and I'll find him and I'll tear him limb to limb." Neither he nor the police believed they'd have to look far. Guy W. Calissi, the Bergen County prosecutor, told reporters, "I would say at this point that this vicious slaying was done by someone she knew." Someone sadistic enough to murder a fifteen-year-old in such a manner. Someone in the grip of incomparable rage.

Less than twenty-four hours later, police would have a suspect.

2

The Mercury

JOE GILROY picked up the phone at 3:30 p.m. on Monday, March 4. Eddie Smith was on the line, asking for a ride. His request was typical of their friendship, which began after Eddie was discharged from the marines three or four years earlier. If Eddie needed help, Joe was there to provide it. Never mind that he might have other plans—or that he might want to take it easy, seeing as how he had worked the third shift at Continental Can until eight that morning and was barely out of bed, feeling the effects of a cold.

Eddie had quit or been fired from all kinds of jobs—truck driver, salesman, mechanic—so many that Joe had lost track. Now he was out of work again, let go earlier that day from a gig installing equipment for a Mahwah-based muffler business after skipping work the prior Friday and Saturday. Eddie was supposed to be a smart guy with a high IQ, but somehow he could never stay put at school or at work.

Eddie was twenty-three, a year older than Joe. He'd grown up all around Bergen County: born in Hasbrouck Heights, then moved seventeen miles north to Ramsey in his early teens for reasons he didn't like to talk about. Joe knew that Eddie's parents had divorced when he was seven, that his mother, Ann, had re-married a man named Alex Chupak, someone she worked with at the Bendix Aeronautical Corporation, and that she could be extremely protective about her son. Eddie's older brother, Richard, was also married and lived not far away.

Eddie had lived with his mother and stepfather after leaving the marines. He told people it was because he'd lost hearing in his left ear, but there were whispers of his having gone AWOL or having some kind of nervous breakdown that put him in the hospital for a while. Whispers, too, that in his youth, he'd gotten in the kind of serious trouble that lands you a spot in juvie. (Eddie didn't talk about any of those things). Then last June, he'd married and moved out. Eddie now lived in a trailer park on Pulis Avenue in Ramsey with his wife, Patricia, and their baby girl named Patti Ann, born two days before Christmas. (Doing the math suggests why Eddie and Patricia married in the first place.)

Joe sometimes wondered why Eddie still ran around Bergen County as if he were a bachelor, but he figured it was better not to pry. Eddie had a temper that flared at expected and unexpected times. He didn't like it when people told him what to do. One reason why Joe was so obliging was that he'd learned that if he didn't do what Eddie wanted—and this time, he wanted Gilroy to pick up him up at Paramus Bowling Alleys—he'd be the target of an intense chewing-out that would last for days. Eddie tended to make up his mind quickly about people and didn't change his attitude much. He liked Joe, and for Joe that was better than the alternative.

Joe got to the bowling alley an hour after Eddie phoned and found his friend spending his last paycheck—all $44.76 of it—by himself. Eddie was drinking beer and watching people bowl, waiting for his pal Charles "Rocky" Rockefeller, one of the alley employees, to get off his shift and bowl with him. Joe bowled four or five games with Eddie and Rocky. At 6:30, all three climbed into Gilroy's light blue 1950 Mercury convertible and drove down Route 17 back to Ramsey.

Joe stopped at the drugstore to pick up some cold medicine. When he got back into the car, Eddie had another favor to ask: Could he borrow the blue Mercury? He said he needed to go get some kerosene for the heater at the trailer. Joe said sure, so long as Eddie had the car back in time for him to head out later to meet some friends. Eddie said that wouldn't be a problem and suggested that he'd bring the car back early enough they could go out and get another beer or two before Joe had to meet his friends. Joe agreed.

Eddie and Rocky dropped Joe back at his house around seven. Joe ate his supper, then watched the new episode of *I Love Lucy* to pass the time. His phone rang sometime around 9:15. It was Eddie, saying he wasn't feeling well and didn't feel like going out for beers. He couldn't get the kerosene heater working, so he and his wife and baby would have to go to his mother-in-law's house in Ridgewood for the night. Could Joe drop them all off there before taking his car back? Once again, Joe said yes.

Eddie arrived in the blue Mercury around 9:45. He didn't seem so sick to Joe. He also volunteered that he'd returned to the trailer and changed into a different pair of pants. "I threw up on them and had to toss them away," Eddie explained. Joe found the whole thing odd. He was concentrating on the task at hand, which was to hop into the car so they could head to the Bogert Trailer Court to pick up Eddie's wife, a young woman a couple of months shy of twenty, and their baby, then ride with them to Ridgewood to the house of Geraldine Horton Johnson, Eddie's mother-in-law.

After he dropped off Eddie and his family, Joe got out of the front passenger seat and switched to the driver's side. Before he sat down, he glanced at the mess of things in the back seat—baseball gloves, cleats, bats—which had been adjusted a little so Eddie's wife and daughter could fit in. Only later did Joe wonder why one of the bats was so scuffed up. And there was a dark spot on the seat cover that hadn't been there before and another spot on the floor mat.

———

JOE GILROY'S PHONE rang again at 11:30 the next morning. He was still in bed, lazing around after staying out until 1:30 a.m. drinking beer and watching television at a friend's house. He picked up, and again it was Eddie Smith, yakking into his ear, asking if Joe would come get him and his family from his mother-in-law's house.

Joe agreed but said it would take him a little while to get there. He ate a quick breakfast and afterward dozed off. At 1:00 p.m., Eddie rang, wondering when Joe was coming to get him. Joe shook off his sleepiness and got in the car. He stopped off at the Amoco gas station, a local hangout in Ramsey, where he ran into Don Hommell, another friend of his and Eddie's. They spent a few minutes hanging out. Hommell wanted to know if Gilroy wanted to play basketball later that day.

Joe said, "No, I have to go down to Ridgewood and pick up Eddie."

"I'll drive you to Ridgewood," Don offered, which wasn't as odd as it seemed. Hommell drove a 1954 Ford that ran better than Gilroy's Mercury. The two men climbed into Don's car and set off.

It turned out Hommell had another reason for offering to chauffeur Joe; he'd heard about Victoria Zielinski's murder on the radio earlier that morning and wanted to talk about it with Joe, who had also learned the news. "Eddie had your car last night, didn't he?"

"Yes," said Joe.

"He had your car, and maybe he had something to do with this."

Joe reacted right away. "No, he couldn't." He didn't get how Don could be so suspicious of their friend.

"Well, when we get to Ridgewood, I am going to tell him that they know it is a Mercury and they found tire tracks and they are going to check all of the Mercurys in Bergen County."

When they pulled up to the house, Eddie came out to them, holding some blankets. If he was surprised to see Joe in Don Hommell's car, he didn't comment.

Eddie got into the back seat. Hommell turned around. "Did you hear about the murder?"

Eddie said he had.

"Well, they know it was a Mercury." Hommell turned to wink at Joe. He then told Eddie about the tire tracks and about the cops checking all the Mercurys in the county. Smith looked startled by that news. He got back out of the car and went into the house to get his wife and baby.

Once they were all settled in the back seat, Eddie asked Joe, "Where's your car?"

At the gas station in Ramsey, said Joe. It wasn't working so good.

A few beats passed before Don said, "Guess what? When I was coming home from work, I seen Vickie's sister walking up the road, and I blew the horn at her." Joe could not recall how Smith had responded, but he did remember either Eddie or Patricia picking up a lipstick from the back seat and handing it to Hommell.

"Maybe this is Vickie's lipstick," someone joked. Later, Joe realized it had been Hommell, who then said, "No, it's not," and threw the tube out of the driver's side window.

After that, the conversation veered away from murder. When they got to the trailer park, Eddie decided he needed another favor from his friends. He walked Patricia and the baby inside, then came back with an old pair of sneakers he wore to play basketball at Don Bosco Preparatory High School courts, which he put into the back of Hommell's car. He said he wanted to go downtown to get a cup of coffee.

Yet again, Gilroy and Hommell acquiesced. But Don deliberately drove past the scene of the murder on Chapel Road. As they passed the sand pit, Hommell said, "When they get this guy, they are going to hang him."

"No," said Eddie. "He will probably plead insanity."

Downtown, they parked the car and split up. Eddie went to the coffee shop, and the other two went to Mepeck's department store so Don could buy a new pair of sneakers.

When they left the store, they saw Eddie walking up the street. "Come on, Ed, let's go play basketball," Gilroy called.

"No, I want to go get a haircut."

So Don and Joe left Eddie downtown. Around 3:30, Hommell dropped Gilroy off at the gas station so Joe could get his car. They found Eddie there, sitting in a car belonging to another of their buddies, Dave Villarosa. Joe left them there. He had some thinking to do.

As he drove home, Joe remembered that once he and Eddie had driven past Vickie and her friend Barbara, walking down a street. They'd pulled over to chat, and Eddie had said something to Vickie that Joe hadn't heard. All he knew was that it had upset her enough for her to threaten to tell Eddie's wife if he didn't leave her alone. He also remembered now how frightened

Vickie had looked. Maybe his friend did have something to do with the murder after all.

An hour later, Joe went back to the gas station. He had to know if the dark spots on the seat cover and floor mat of his car were, in fact, blood. He showed the spots to Don Hommell, who was still at the station, and Rocky Rockefeller, along with two other acquaintances, Willie Anderson and Tony Saveriano. The consensus was that the spots were blood.

A little over twenty-four hours after Vickie's murder, Joe Gilroy gave a statement at the police station in Mahwah.[*] He told the police the whole story as he knew it. He also showed them the baseball bats in the back of his car. The cops paid closest attention to a Ted Williams bat, the one that Joe had noticed, which was dirtier than it should have been. The markings were not light, the kind that would result from hitting a baseball, but dark.

After the police finished questioning Joe on Tuesday, March 5, and said he was free to go, he saw Eddie one more time. It was near midnight, at the police station.

---

[*]   Gilroy told that to the *Bergen Evening Record* but denied having said so to the *Paterson Evening News*. I'm inclined to trust the *Record*'s reporting more.

3

"If You're Looking for a Fall Guy . . ."

KILLINGS DID happen every now and again in Bergen County. The day after Victoria Zielinski's murder, the local papers reported on the latest developments in the case of a fifteen-year-old boy accused of bludgeoning a Paterson woman to death the prior November, the culmination of a violent robbery. Two months after Zielinski's death, another fifteen-year-old girl, Ruth Starr Zeitler of Fair Lawn, would be strangled to death by a classmate. But the savagery with which Vickie had been killed was something unique—or at least it seemed that way to the cadre of law enforcement officials charged with finding her murderer.

The police spent all of Tuesday afternoon and evening questioning anyone who might be a possible witness or suspect—nearly two dozen Mahwah and Ramsey residents, many of them teenage boys who went to school with or knew Vickie. Almost all of them were immediately ruled out as suspects.

Vickie's murderer, likely blinded by rage, had left physical evidence behind. The tire tracks leading to the embankment of the pit were consistent with Firestone tires, and other marks at the scene suggested the presence of a light-colored car, such as the 1950 Ford Mercury convertible that belonged to Joe Gilroy. The police had found dark hair clutched in one of the girl's gloves dropped near the road. Bloody footprints suggested that the man wore a size 9 shoe. And the bite marks on Vickie's breast showed that her assailant had buckteeth or at least a significant overbite.

When police picked up Edgar Smith for questioning at 11:30 p.m. Tuesday night, the first thing they noticed was his freshly shorn hair. They had quizzed nearly two dozen men and boys about Vickie, and that guy was the only one to have gotten a haircut. Why today, of all days? Eddie didn't give a reason. At first, he didn't say much at all, remaining calm through the barrage of questions. He knew Vickie, sure, everyone in town did. He'd given her rides home in his car if he saw her on the street and she'd asked. But he denied killing her.

Smith was questioned at Mahwah police headquarters by Fred Galda, the Bergen County assistant prosecutor, while detectives Gordon Graber and Vahe Garabedian, as well as Captain Carl De Marco, observed. The interrogation continued through the night, in the presence of several newspaper reporters—something that would never be allowed today. One of them, the *Paterson Evening News'* Pierce I. Rosenthal, reported that when Galda showed Eddie the two bloody rocks, the murder weapons, Eddie shuddered. "Let me think, let me think," he said. Then after a beat: "No, I never saw them."

As the questioning dragged on, Eddie began to tire. He complained he was so cold he was shivering. Eventually he began to tell them things. Like he'd thrown away his shoes in a garbage can on Mechanic Street. Like he'd thrown away his pants because they were covered with vomit. Like he'd worn a jacket on the night Vickie died, "which will not do you much good because I washed it."

A little later on in the morning, Galda and his detectives took Eddie by the sand pit where Vickie's crumpled, crushed body had been found. Eddie cringed as they drove past. He refused to even look. He complained again that he was cold. Galda, the assistant prosecutor, lent him an overcoat, which Eddie wore for about forty-five minutes. Several times Eddie asked for coffee with milk and sugar. The police gave it to him each time. They were trying to be cordial so they would not be accused of mistreating their suspect. A different detective, named Sinatra, took Eddie out for breakfast, letting him sit in the front seat of the car to be closer to the heater.

Officers Ulric Fairbanks and Addison Waldeck had found Eddie's discarded pants at 6:20 in the morning, two and a half miles from the sand pit, closer to the trailer park. There was no sign of vomit on the pants, but there was a single bloodstain present. Later in the day, when the patrol officer brought the pants into the interrogation room, Eddie admitted they were his but couldn't explain how the blood got there. And later, he couldn't explain why the blood was type O—Vickie's blood type—not A, which was his.

"If you're looking for a fall guy," Eddie blurted at one point, "why don't you grab Don Hommell?" Bergen County law enforcement made a note of this. (It would later become a point that haunted the case.)

The police took Eddie to the medical examiner's office. As officers watched, Smith stripped naked so that Raphael Gilady, the county's medical examiner for the past twenty-seven years, could conduct a physical examination. Gilady reported finding four lentil-sized dark blue bruises on Eddie's left knee and kneecap, a bigger bruise with reddish borders and a reddish yellow center on Eddie's right knee, and still another bruise on his index finger. All the bruises were recent. Smith said he didn't know how he got them. Gilady also determined that Eddie walked without difficulty, which seemed to contradict his complaint of having hurt his ankle while bowling with Joe Gilroy and Rocky Rocke-feller on Monday afternoon.

An officer took pictures of Eddie and got him out of the clothes he was wearing and into coveralls. There was a blood spot on the neckline of his T-shirt. Eddie said he had cut himself shaving. But there were no marks on his face or neck to support that.

By 10:00 a.m. on Wednesday morning, March 6, Eddie was ready to talk. Before he agreed to make a recorded statement, though, he asked to speak with a priest. The prosecutor's office called in Father Albert Sokol of the Don Bosco Preparatory High School in Ramsey. Eddie had gone to high school there in the late 1940s, and Sokol was someone he trusted. Eddie spent half an hour alone with the priest. After Sokol left, Eddie signaled that he was ready.

At ten minutes before one, Eddie sat in a room with a group of Bergen County men who, by their very jobs, would intimidate most people. They were Assistant Prosecutor Fred Galda; the office's lead investigator, Walter Spahr; the police chiefs of the Mahwah and Ramsey police departments, Charles Smith and Henry Voss; and Louis Kalstad, a sitting member of the grand jury. (Chief Prosecutor Guy Calissi would show up just before 2:15.) Arthur Ehrenbeck took the notes. Smith asked for another cup of coffee with sugar and cream, and they brought him one. Under oath, over the next three hours, he told them the first version of what had happened to Vickie Zielinski.

It wasn't a confession, not exactly. Eddie said Vickie got into his car around 8:40 p.m. He said they had a conversation about her cutting school, but "I wasn't listening too close to what she had to say." He remembered her saying something about her father—that she would go home and "tell him you are like the rest of the guys." He said he grabbed Vickie's arm as she tried to get out of the car, then swung at her with his right hand. He "had a feeling of running somewhere" on soft ground. "I don't know where I ran or how far or anything." He remembered his right foot was cold and that after he got back home, he realized he had only one shoe left and that his khaki pants "had blood all over them." He said he never thought a thing about it. He just took them off "like I had grease on them."

After Joe Gilroy had shown up with Don Hommell and they'd talked about hearing about a girl murdered on the radio, Eddie said he had asked Don, "Was that Vickie that got killed?" and "I guess I was actually asking as if I didn't know myself." When Hommell told him that the police were checking the registration of every Mercury in Bergen County, "that's when it hit me really hard I must have been the one who really did it."

When the group took him out to the crime scene again to reenact what he'd just told them, Galda asked Eddie whether he had been mistreated while in the custody of the Mahwah police. It's as if Galda recognized that the police treatment of Eddie would be scrutinized in later appeals.

"No, sir," Smith replied.

"Everybody treat you all right?"

"Better than I expected."

"Very well. It's nice to hear."

The prosecutors, Smith, and the police went back to the sand pit one last time after Eddie finished giving his statement that afternoon. Eddie pointed to the spot "where I imagine I struck her with my fist," another spot where he picked up and threw Vickie's brown leather pocketbook. Then, later, he showed them the garbage can near the trailer park where he threw out his shoes.

A little over an hour later, the group went to the Mahwah police station so that Edgar Smith could sign his sworn statement and be formally charged. He was charged, but he didn't sign the statement, which became a point of contention during the trial and beyond. Nevertheless, Guy Calissi went out to the lobby, where scores of reporters and photographers waited. He announced that Edgar Smith had been arrested for the murder of Victoria Zielinski, though "I can't say he admitted anything."

———

THE ANNOUNCEMENT OF the arrest came early enough for the evening newspapers to get the news onto their front pages. A number of stories fixed upon one detail: that Edgar Smith had once lived on Elm Street with his mother and stepfather, a mere three blocks away from the Zielinski home on Wyckoff Avenue. The *Bergen Evening Record* proved to be the fastest and most comprehensive with its coverage. One of its reporters tracked down Joe Gilroy (inexplicably called "Patrick" in the story), who spoke of Eddie, his friend-turned-murder-suspect, in contemptuous tones: "I'd tell you the number of jobs he's had but I don't have that many fingers to count them."

Townspeople were quick to note Smith's penchant for flirting, as well as his "handsome" appearance—a broad-shouldered, slim-waisted, curly-haired blond young man of medium build who played halfback in high school. "He had beautiful eyes," one woman (presumably among those he'd flirted with) said, "but would never look at you." At the Bogert Trailer Court one of Eddie's neighbors noted that Patricia wasn't seen around much, but then trailer parks were a place where "each family tends to mind their own business." Another neighboring couple was more critical. They said Eddie "acted like a teen-ager," was never home, and "did as he pleased" without any reproaches from his wife.

Adding further intrigue to the arrest was the discovery of a car registered to Eddie at a body shop in Fair Lawn, unclaimed for at least a week. There was a surprise in the trunk: a submachine gun with Soviet branding and "Oriental" writing on the breech. The authorities quickly surmised that Eddie had acquired the weapon in Korea during his stint in the marines and that it had not been fired recently. But why would he keep such a gun in the trunk of his car? The question was never answered. Maybe it had something to do with what he'd once told marine psychiatrists: "I've always been able to do as I please. No one can tell me what to do and they never will be able to."

One former employer told the Paterson *Morning Call* that Eddie was "very irresponsible. He lost many jobs because he would just stand around with his hands in his pockets. When asked why he wouldn't work, he'd say: 'I just don't give a damn.'" And Charles Schanz, the same Ramsey High School principal who spoke so glowingly of Vickie, did not mince words about Eddie, who'd once been a pupil for a mere eight months at Ramsey High, one of three different high schools he'd attended. Schanz described him as "irresponsible" and said that his grades had been poor.[*]

But another account from Eddie's high school days painted a more positive picture, even if it stretched the truth. Robert Curley, the PR director of and onetime sportswriter for the Passaic *Herald-News*, had been Eddie's high school football coach at St. Luke's in Ho-Ho-Kus. Eddie had attended that school for only two months before enlisting in the marines, but his love of playing football and fixing cars had made a lasting impression upon Curley—as did something else.

"I'd like to be a sports writer when I'm through with school," Curley remembered Eddie telling him. Eddie had, apparently, been a weekly correspondent for a local paper while at Ramsey

---

[*] Schanz later denied making those comments to the Passaic *Herald-News*.

High, allowing him to obtain a press card. He told his coach, "There is magic in a press card. You get to see games and don't have to pay."

Smith had visited Curley at the paper's office in Passaic just a week before the murder. He told Curley that he had a good job, claiming to work for an "automatic pin-spotting company"—making machines that set bowling pins in lanes—that planned to send him out to Ohio, "and what's more they're paying me $2 an hour plus expenses." He said he was going back to school. He professed awe at being married and having a daughter. Curley thought he seemed content.

He didn't know that Smith was not, in fact, employed by that company. That he wasn't going to go back to school. And that he was, in fact, perennially unemployed.

———

PATRICIA SMITH WAS thunderstruck by Eddie's arrest. She couldn't believe that the father of her daughter had been accused of making advances to a teenage girl and killing her when she refused to submit. Patricia did know their marriage was not one for the storybooks, despite telling reporters "it seemed as if we'd never been so happy." She wished Eddie would stay at home more. She wished he could keep a job. She wished he wouldn't be so angry all the time, though he never took it out on her and acted only with kindness toward the baby. But murder? Impossible. She simply refused to believe it, and when reporters found her at her mother's house, she told them so. (Her mother, Geraldine Horton Johnson, refused to speak with reporters, but Patricia felt compelled to.)

Only the month before, Patricia had given Eddie a card for his twenty-third birthday that conveyed how she felt about him:

"This brings a birthday wish and a lot of love, you bet/To the wonderful guy I fell for the first time we met./And the longer we are married, the more in love I get."

Patricia went to visit her husband as soon as she was allowed to. She got to see him for ten minutes on the afternoon of Thursday, March 7. She brought Patti Ann with her, along with her mother. Patricia was taken into an inner room at the County Prosecutor's Office in Hackensack, which was in the same building as the courthouse and the jail, where Eddie was waiting for them. Geraldine took the baby, leaving the couple alone together.

Eddie kissed his wife. Patricia wept in his arms. She later refused to tell reporters what they had spoken about. "Leave me alone . . . he didn't know what he was doing." But it wasn't difficult to infer that he'd assured Patricia of his innocence. The swagger he displayed in photographs published by the *Record* and the *Herald-News*—not to mention all over the country—was bravado, covering up his abject terror at what would happen next. The prosecutor wanted to move to trial quickly. If Eddie was convicted, he'd be sent to the gallows.

Patricia and her mother walked out of the prosecutor's office to a throng of reporters yelling questions and flashbulbs popping. Patricia held up baby Patti Ann as a shield from the prying cameras, but the reporters persisted. Frantic, Patricia slipped and nearly fell on the floor. Detectives rushed to make sure she was all right and then escorted the trio to a waiting car.

———

A COLUMN BY *New York Daily Mirror* crime reporter Claire Curran captured the mood of so many in Ramsey and Mahwah upon learning of Victoria Zielinski's death: "After murder, what? The shock. The numbness. The appalling disbelief it happened at all."

Losing Vickie meant losing the sense of communal trust small towns like those prided themselves on.

Girls and women stopped walking down the streets at night and going to the Corral to dance. After the sand pit became the scene of a murder, it lost its appeal as a lovers' lane, and cars ceased to park along the side of the road on Fardale Avenue. The mask of security had been ripped off to reveal the muck underneath, making people more afraid, more wary, more withdrawn.

For the Zielinskis, the arrest and arraignment of Edgar Smith were a relief, but the "appalling disbelief" Curran called attention to in her column proved excruciatingly accurate for them. Their daughter was gone. No arrest, no arraignment, no trial could ever bring back her back. She was buried on the morning of March 8, four days after her murder. That the culprit was Edgar Smith was a shock, but it wasn't a total surprise, at least not to Mary Faye, the eldest sister, who, being closer to him in age, had been acquainted with him longer. "Smith was always pestering me to get him dates with Vickie," she told authorities, according to the *Scranton Times-Tribune.* "Finally I told him to go home and pay some attention to his wife." Knowing that the man police believed had killed their daughter was in jail was at least some comfort to the family, grieving their inexplicable, vicious loss.

More than a hundred people attended the midmorning requiem high Mass at St. John the Evangelist Roman Catholic church in Honesdale, the town where Vickie had been born. She lay in a sealed white casket, the color matching the snow blanketing the winding path leading to the church. Flowers sent by Ramsey High and by coworkers of Vickie's father adorned the coffin.

The casket was carried up the center aisle to the front of the church by Vickie's uncles Henry and Joseph Zielinski and her cousins John and James Bonham. Anthony held tight to his wife, who could barely stay upright. Their remaining children, Mary Faye, Myrna, and Anthony Jr., walked behind them, also weeping. A much younger cousin whom Vickie had adored, twenty-two-month-old Jolie Zielinski, wailed, "Bickie . . . Bickie . . . Bickie."

The service was conducted by the Reverend Peter S. Kane, who had baptized Vickie and married her parents. He noted that a eulogy after a Catholic funeral Mass was unusual but in this case, under these circumstances, necessary. "Victoria was a girl who had everything to live for," he said. "She was beloved by her parents and was a credit to her school. She can be compared to the great women of the church who died rather than give up their honor."

This was, perhaps, a rather overwrought thing to say about an adolescent girl. But Father Kane's words were likely an attempt to quiet the town gossips ready to besmirch the dead girl's reputation. The dead are beyond the reach of slander. But the remaining Zielinskis would have to live with what people thought about Vickie for the rest of their lives. Violent death can bring families closer. Vickie's death split her family apart.

———

EDDIE'S MOTHER, Ann Chupak, believed in his innocence immediately and did not waver. She also knew exactly whom she wanted to handle her son's defense. Joseph Gaudielle had a reputation for successfully defending more murder suspects than any other lawyer in Bergen County. He agreed to take Eddie on as a client and to put forward a plea of insanity. He brought in expert psychiatrists to examine Smith, and the Prosecutor's Office hired at least three more to conduct their own separate evaluations. All of them found him fit to stand trial.

Edgar Smith was indicted by a grand jury on Friday, March 8, on the testimony of just two witnesses: chief of county detectives, James Stewart, and Guy Calissi, the prosecutor. He appeared in court again a week later for the formal arraignment, which took all of five minutes. He wore glasses and was dressed in a white shirt, light-colored sports trousers, leather shoes, and a light yellow tie. He stared straight ahead and never moved as Gaudielle entered a not guilty plea. Judge Arthur J. O'Dea eventually set the trial date for April 22, just over six weeks after Victoria Zielinski's murder. Patricia sat stoically next to Ann, who cried throughout the proceedings.

Both sides objected to the date. Joseph Gaudielle explained that he had "a dozen other matters to handle," stressing that defending Smith was "a tremendous responsibility." Judge O'Dea was firm in rejecting that clear attempt at stalling: "This case is more important than your other matters, Mr. Calissi." But he did allow for an extra week on top of the four weeks already allotted, saying "With your skill and capability as an attorney you should be ready in that time."

The time crunch became more pressing for the defense when Gaudielle's associate had to be hospitalized with (and later died from) an unexpected illness. Gaudielle quit representing Eddie on March 22. At Gaudielle's request, Judge O'Dea appointed John E. Selser, a former Bergen County assistant prosecutor—and onetime colleague of Guy Calissi—who had recently switched to being a criminal defense attorney. Selser, though a veteran lawyer, was less experienced at murder trials than Gaudielle was and would have far less time to prepare. He asked the court to postpone the trial for a month. He got a three-week extension, to May 13—a tight timeline for a death penalty case.

Selser retained a private investigator, Andrew Nicol, to dig through Smith's statement and past and find something, anything, that could help. Nicol delivered a fifty-page report that was a collection of statements, rumors, and hearsay gleaned from interviews with all sorts of people around town. Selser went so far as to announce in a May 2 hearing that the "wrong man is before the court today on a murder charge."

Selser told Judge O'Dea that a mental health evaluation would show Smith suffered from "a schizophrenic personality," which gave him amnesia about the night Vickie Zielinski had died; allowing a psychiatrist to administer the drug sodium amytal— also known as "truth scrum"—to counteract the amnesia would reveal both what had really happened and the actual culprit. Edgar, said his lawyer, did not just approve of the sodium amytal proposal, he was "anxious" to take it, along with a lie detector test. Judge O'Dea signed off on both the truth serum and the lie detector, which Smith took the following morning. The results were not revealed for years, but neither helped Smith.

As defense strategies go, it was a gamble. When one has the option simply to poke holes in the police interrogation strategy or a prosecutor's case, to blame someone else for murder is a high-risk strategy. But Selser decided to go for it. During jury selection, he asked, repeatedly, whether any of the prospective jurors had heard of a man from Ramsey named Donald Hommell. He would, Selser said, explain the question more fully during trial.

Guy Calissi was ready. So, too, were Anthony and Mary Zielinski. They and their children wouldn't be allowed to watch the first two days of the trial because they would be called as witnesses. But they had put their faith in the Bergen County prosecutor to do what was right and deliver some kind of justice for Vickie.

4

Openings

RON CALISSI took his seat in the first row of the courtroom balcony on Wednesday morning, May 15. Leaning on the railing, he could peer down and see Judge Arthur O'Dea banging his gavel when the courtroom was out of order. He could study every member of the jury, who would be sequestered in a nearby hotel when not listening to testimony. He could watch Edgar Smith, in his gray sports jacket, dark slacks, white shirt, and dark tie, displaying little emotion as the proceedings got under way, as well as his defense lawyer, John Selser. And he could see the more than two hundred spectators keen to witness the spectacle of the murder trial—already one of the most media-covered cases in Bergen County history.

But Ron paid closest attention to the two men sitting at the table designated for the prosecutors. There was Fred Galda, the assistant prosecutor, whom he'd met many times. And there was his own father, preparing to try the highest-profile case of his life—the one that had him so distracted and preoccupied for the last two months. Ron knew that his father thought seeking the death penalty was just in this case, but he could tell how much it weighed on him.

Ron had known something unusual was happening on the morning of March 6 because his dad had called a cab to take him and his older sisters to school. Guy kept to a daily morning routine: he was up early, had breakfast with his wife and children, and then, at 7:30 sharp, bundled his kids into the car for the school dropoff. First he took Carolou, sixteen, to the Ridgewood station so she could catch her train to the Academy of Mount Saint Vincent in Tuxedo Park, New York. Then he dropped off Ron, ten years old and in the fifth grade; Elaine, twelve; and Beverly, nine, at Our Lady of Mount Carmel School, a short distance from the train station. Finally, he ferried Guy Jr., the oldest at seventeen, to Morristown Prep, the private school he attended. And then he drove to work at the Bergen County Courthouse in Hackensack.

Despite his long hours and the complex cases he tried, Guy Calissi rarely missed the school run. And he usually got home in time for dinner at six, after which he and his youngest son would feed the wild ducks in the pond behind their house. But that Tuesday night, Guy didn't make it home in time for dinner. Ron's mother told the kids he was late because he was investigating the murder of a teenage girl in Mahwah. Ron had to feed the ducks on his own and asked his best friend, who was more interested in trapping muskrats in the Saddle River right by the pond, to tag along instead.

On Thursday night, Guy again arrived home later than usual. "His face was taut," Ron wrote fifteen years later, in his book, *Counterpoint: The Edgar Smith Case*. "He was not his usual witty self. I could observe that he wasn't much in the mood for an arm wrestling contest; our nightly ritual at which I lost every time even when I used both hands and pressed my feet against the chair for extra leverage."

Guy wasn't in the mood to talk about the murder, either. But

Ron, ever curious at age ten, kept asking his father questions, coaxing out details such as how old Victoria had been, how she'd been killed, and who had been charged.

Most kids would have had trouble taking in the brutal details, the stuff of nightmares even for the fully grown. Ron was furious that anyone could be so violent to a girl, but he was already keenly interested in the law, in justice, and in politics—all the worlds his father circulated in and made his living from. His father took him to lunch on occasion with some of the police detectives, usually during summer vacation. Ron also insisted on tagging along whenever Guy gave a speech on a Sunday morning.

For Ron, it was less a chance to eat all the ham and eggs he desired—though that was certainly a perk—than it was to hear his father speak and be well received. People loved Guy's sense of humor and his ability to speak off the cuff. They paid attention when Guy explained the two types of people who choose politics as a career: one group wants to do good, and the other wants to do well. And Ron cheered when his father was interviewed by a major television network, during which he criticized the media for being "responsible for making this the era of the exaltation of the jerk" and commenting that vigilante groups were "as useful as udders on a bull" in helping out law enforcement.

When it came time for the trial of Edgar Smith, Ron knew that his school principal, Sister Josepha, would grant him permission to go to the courthouse to see his father at work. To his surprise, she allowed him to attend every day.

The Guy Calissi on display in Judge O'Dea's courtroom was not the man Ron knew as his father. As Ron later recalled, he was a man in a "completely different setting than I had ever seen him before." He was quiet. He was thoughtful. He was working from notes. He had come to terms with the "awesome responsibility" of trying a death penalty case and had decided to accept it.

Even Ron sensed how tense everyone seemed as opening statements were about to begin, as if electricity coursed through the air. Then Judge O' Dea looked toward the counsel table and nodded. "You may open, gentlemen."

Guy Calissi stood and walked toward the jury.

———

SLOWLY AND METHODICALLY, Calissi laid out the state of New Jersey's case against Edgar Smith. He brought up the bloody pants and his belief that Victoria Zielinski's death was willful and premeditated, the result of thwarted sexual advances and the culmination of a chase along Fardale Avenue to the sand pit. "We will show you that on the night in question, March 4, 1957, that the defendant and Victoria Zielinski were alone in the sandpit, alone, no one else was present, and that this murder was committed by Edgar Smith . . . and Edgar Smith alone."

This was no casual pickup, said Calissi. Edgar and Victoria had known each other. He'd driven her home from school several times. They'd hung out sometimes at the Corral. "He intended to kill her, to silence this girl. We will show you that this was a brutal, a savage, a sadistic killing."

John Selser was next. He described Edgar Smith's day on Monday, March 4, from the job loss to the outing at the Paramus bowling alley to borrowing Joe Gilroy's car to stopping off at his mother-in-law's house to driving down Wyckoff Avenue, where he spotted Vickie walking down the street by herself. So far, that was largely as the prosecutor had outlined, but then Selser's statement veered sharply away.

He claimed that when Edgar stopped beside Vickie, she said, "I want to talk to you." That she got into the car but didn't want Myrna, her younger sister, to see her riding with him and suggested Edgar turn onto Crescent Avenue. She described skipping school and intercepting a note that had been sent from school to her parents before they could see it.

Selser said he felt awkward about relaying to the jury why Vickie had said she wanted to talk to Eddie "because Smith doesn't like the fact told, but it has got to be told because the girl said to Smith, 'your wife is running around, she is having an affair with the oil man.'" Never mind that Patricia was the mother of a two-month-old baby and hardly left the trailer except to go to her mother's house. Upon hearing that so-called news, Selser said, Edgar slapped Victoria, insisting "It's not true."

Selser then told the jury that as Vickie and Edgar sat in the car, a second vehicle came along Chapel Road and stopped behind them with the lights off. Vickie got out and went over to the other car, and got into an altercation with the other driver. Smith thought the other man was Anthony Zielinski, Vickie's father, who he knew to be very protective of his daughter.

Edgar, thinking he might need to defend himself, grabbed a baseball bat from the back seat of Gilroy's car. Vickie and the other figure moved closer to him. He could now see that the man in question was not Vickie's father but Donald Hommell and that "the girl was bleeding from the side of her head in the hair line and bleeding badly."

Hommell, in Selser's telling, said that Vickie had fallen and struck her head. Smith claimed he got Vickie into the car and was ready to take her to the doctor but that Hommell "yanked her out of the car." The blood gushing from her head wound was what had drenched Edgar's pants. Hommell assured Smith he would "take care of it, I'll take care of her, you go on."

Edgar drove home to the trailer camp, where he realized he'd lost his shoe and had to go back to the crime scene to retrieve it.

Selser told the jury that a female witness had placed Hommell, not Smith, near the crime scene the next morning and said she had asked him what he was looking for, to which Hommell had answered, "Mind your own business." Smith himself encountered Don Hommell one more time that evening, around 9:30 p.m. or so, after he'd found his shoe, and asked about Vickie's whereabouts. "Don't worry about it," Selser quoted Hommell as saying. "It's all right. We are all in trouble, and if you mention my name, I will kill your baby."

Hommell's throwing away Vickie's lipstick the following morning was further sign of his being the actual culprit. "I know he is capable of the thing charged by me against him," Selser cried, "and I believe that Smith is as innocent of the killing as I am."

Guy Calissi interjected, "If the Court please, I wish counsel would stick to what he is going to prove and not what he particularly thinks."

Selser apologized—up to a point. "I guess I should not have said that. That's for summation. But that is the case. I deny absolutely that Smith is the man who caused the injuries that resulted in the girl's death and I think we shall establish this to be the truth."

———

IT WAS A sensational beginning to a sensational trial. By not only pointing the finger at another suspect but naming him, Selser sent a jolt through the courtroom and into the wider world. Newspaper headlines that evening and the following morning made the most of it: WITNESS IS ACCUSED IN N.J. GIRL'S MURDER (New York *Daily News*, May 16, 1957), DEFENSE CONTENDS MURDERED GIRL SEEN WITH ANOTHER MAN (*Asbury Park Press*, May 16, 1957), POINTS TO ANOTHER IN MAHWAH MURDER (Paterson *Morning*

Call, May 16, 1957), and SECOND MAN PUT AT MURDER SCENE (Passaic *Herald-News*, May 16, 1957).

But the trial had only just begun. Myrna Zielinski was the state's first witness. In a halting voice that required the judge to ask her to speak up on multiple occasions, she described what happened the night Vickie died. She mentioned seeing Don Hommell's car zoom past her on Wyckoff Avenue. She began to cry after describing her older sister's pocketbook and again after seeing Vickie's jacket in evidence, requiring short court recesses.

Selser began his cross-examination by attempting to poke holes in the timeline and undermine Myrna's credibility, to little avail. Then he turned his attention to Don Hommell. Did Myrna know him?

"Yes."

"You knew that Don was friendly with your sister Vickie, didn't you?"

"She knew him."

"Had he come to the house for Vickie at any time?"

"No."

"You say you never saw him do it?"

"He never came—he never took her out."

"How do you know?"

"Because all her dates come in. All my sister's dates come inside."

Selser then asked who all the other dates were, leading Calissi to object. The objection was sustained.

Next Calissi called Barbara Nixon, who testified to Vickie being at her place that night, doing homework, and what time she left. Many years later, she remembered being scared and upset on the stand, but she kept her cool, did not cry, and answered both lawyers' questions directly.

Vickie's mother, Mary, did not fare as well. She broke down when Calissi asked her about seeing Vickie's body: "Having seen your daughter at the sandpit, what did you do?"

"What would any mother do?"

Once again she broke down while describing exactly what she saw. "It was horrible—I saw her brains scattered on the ground."

Selser didn't cross-examine Vickie's mother and had very few questions for her father. There was not much to be gained by exacerbating her parents' sorrow in front of the jury.

Over the next two days, a procession of law enforcement officials, including Captain Edmund Wickham, investigator Russell Ridgway, and detectives James Stewart and Gordon Graber, took the stand. Their testimony allowed Calissi to show Vickie's bloody clothing to the jury and to the public, as well as the rocks believed to be the murder weapons. "The whole situation was just saturated with blood," Stewart testified about the crime scene.

When Calissi brought out the smaller rock for Stewart to identify, he seemed anxious not to hold it for any longer than he had to. When he put the rock onto the railing in front of Stewart, it very nearly fell into the detective's lap. As Calissi reached out to steady it, he grimaced. (Stewart, who did steady the rock, cracked a smile.)

Mary Zielinski, listening to policemen talk about the murder of her daughter, could not hold back her tears. Two female jurors gasped at the sight of photos of Vickie's body entered into evidence. And when the photos were shown to the court, Edgar Smith, who was usually able to maintain his equilibrium, put his hands over his eyes, his face going pale. When Calissi placed Vickie's watch on the table in front of him, Edgar flinched.

But he had himself under control again when Joseph Gilroy took the stand on Friday morning, May 17, even when his friend implicated Edgar again and again—describing Edgar's borrowing his car, his discovery of blood on the seat cover and the floor mat, and the strange ways Edgar had acted on the Monday night and Tuesday afternoon. Gilroy, a strong witness, stood up well to Selser's cross-examination.

At 3:30 that Friday afternoon, Guy Calissi had a surprise for the court. "The State calls Donald Hommell," he announced.

Only that morning, he had told reporters that he would not call Hommell. Calissi had dismissed the idea of Hommell as an alternate suspect and felt confident his testimony would not be necessary until the rebuttal stage. Calissi had clearly changed his mind. Reporters later speculated that it had to be when Joe Gilroy, under cross-examination, admitted it was Don Hommell, not Edgar Smith, who had said that the lipstick that Hommell had tossed out of his car had belonged to Vickie.

As Hommell walked toward the stand, a visibly flustered John Selser stood up to ask for an immediate recess. He was keen to cross-examine Hommell but felt that late on a Friday afternoon, after a long week of testimony and with the weekend looming, was not the time to start. "I would rather that his examination be not broken into parts and very honestly, sir, I am tired," Selser explained. "I am exhausted and I should so much be grateful to the Court were we at this time to recess."

When Judge O'Dea reminded Selser that there were still about twenty minutes left in the day, Selser doubled down. Calissi did not object to Selser's request to adjourn until Monday morning; having the entire weekend to prepare for this witness would be helpful to the state, too. O'Dea granted the adjournment.

5

"I Just Threw It Out the Window"

IT RAINED hard on the morning of Monday, May 20, 1957, but that did not deter people from lining up to get into the main courtroom in Hackensack as early as 7:45, even though the trial wouldn't start until 9:30. One of the lucky ones who found a spot in the gallery was Mary Higgins Clark, who lived in nearby Ridgewood with her husband, Warren, and their four young children. They'd moved to Bergen County from New York City in search of a less crime-ridden place to raise their family. Clark had been writing short stories and had finally sold her first, "Last Flight to Denubia," to the Catholic magazine *Extension*.* After six years of magazine rejections, the $100 paycheck was welcome, but the validation of her writing was even sweeter.

Success and riches as "the Queen of Suspense" were far in her future. Personal tragedy arrived sooner with the sudden death of Warren in 1964, which meant that she had to find an immediate way to support her children. But on that spring day in 1957, Edgar Smith's trial was the most exciting thing to happen in Bergen County in years, and Clark wanted to witness the spectacle for

---

* The story was published under the title "Stowaway" in 1958.

herself. Two decades later, she reflected that watching the trial had catalyzed her career as a crime writer; she also mentioned it in her breakout 1975 suspense novel, *Where Are the Children?*

When Donald Hommell took the stand that morning, he faced an extracapacity crowd. People had been let in to stand behind the seats on the upper balcony, and chairs had been added to the main floor. All of them were there to hear from the man Edgar Smith's lawyer had identified as the real killer.

Guy Calissi's direct examination didn't take long. He established Hommell's whereabouts on the night Vickie died, then concentrated on the conversation in the car the next day among Don, Joe Gilroy, and Eddie Smith. Calissi asked Hommell about the lipstick. "Well," Don replied, "when Eddie Smith and his wife had got in the car I guess one of them handed it over the front seat to either Joe or I first. Kiddingly it was said that it could be Vickie's."

"Who said that?"

"I don't know, sir."

"Was it you who said that?"

"I can't remember, sir."

"What happened to the lipstick?"

"I just threw it out the window."

What is perplexing about this exchange is that Calissi did not ask Hommell *why* he had thrown the lipstick out of the window. His failing to do so was a gift to Selser, whose cross-examination proved to be relentless.

The defense lawyer pressed Hommell: he'd known that the lipstick was Vickie's, hadn't he?

"No, sir."

"Whose lipstick did you recognize it to be?"

"That I couldn't say, sir."

"Why did you throw it out?"

"It meant nothing to me."

Then Selser asked Hommell if he had gone out with Vickie. Calissi immediately objected to the question, but O'Dea let it go. Selser repeated the question, asking if Don had known Vickie pretty well.

"Casually, that is all," Don said, though he admitted that Vickie had been in his car a month earlier.

"Well, as a matter of fact, Vickie was your girlfriend, wasn't she?" Selser asked.

"No, sir. Definitely not."

Selser asked how many times Vickie had gone out with Don. Calissi again objected, but the judge allowed the question.

Hommell answered that he'd been out with Vickie "very few times." When Selser pressed him to be more specific, Don said, "approximately ten times at the most."

The adversarial relationship between Calissi and Selser boiled over when the defense lawyer, in the heat of the moment, called Hommell a "psychopathic liar."

Calissi took umbrage at Selser's declaration. "Well, I have a 16-year-old boy and I wouldn't want my boy to be called a psychopath."

"Your boy I wouldn't call such," said Selser.

"I don't know about that."

Then Hommell's father, sitting in the audience, cried, "I don't want him to call mine one either."

The lawyers sparred more in a sidebar out of the hearing of the jury, and the judge directed Selser to cut short his cross-examination. On redirect, Calissi asked some more clarifying questions about Hommell's movements on that Monday night. Hommell testified that he'd left his job at the drugstore and headed for Pelzer's Tavern in Mahwah in the company of Charles "Rocky" Rockefeller. He confirmed that on the way there, he passed Myrna Zielinski walking down Wyckoff Avenue toward her home. And, Calissi asked, did he see Edgar Smith during the evening of March 4, 1957? "Definitely not, sir."

Selser returned to cross-examine Hommell a second time. Once more, he grilled the young man on every move he made and every action he took on the night of March 4. Hommell was steadfast in denying everything that might link him to the crime. He said he had never spoken to a neighbor named Mrs. Wood, who was the witness who had told police she had seen him searching for something in the area of Pulis Avenue. He certainly denied telling her to "mind her own business."

Selser pressed on: "Do you remember saying to Smith on the drive from Ridgewood to the trailer court, 'Don't forget, you have a baby?'"

Hommell's answer was emphatic. "Definitely not, sir."

"Do you remember saying to him, 'It would be unwise to mention my name?'"

"Definitely not, sir."

Selser then tried to ask obliquely about the bite mark on Vickie's breast. "Your teeth, your front teeth protrude out beyond your lowers, don't they?"

"No, they don't," said Hommell. Selser asked him to open his mouth to show to the jury. Hommell complied.

"Nice teeth," Calissi commented. "He has good teeth."

"Yes, they are," said Selser. The defense lawyer continued his barrage, challenging Hommell on when he had seen Myrna walking and on statements he had made to the defense's investigator, Andrew Nicol. Hommell held his ground. He denied all of Selser's insinuations that he killed Victoria Zielinski. He said he hadn't seen her for weeks before her murder. He also denied that he had been arrested in connection with Vickie's death. "I was just questioned, sir."

Calissi had one last question for Hommell: "Did you, Rocky, Gilroy, and Smith play baseball together during the warm days and during the baseball season?"

"Yes," said Hommell. "Occasionally we would be playing and Ed Smith would drive up and he would want to play with us."

Selser had nothing further to ask, and Hommell was able to leave the stand.

Before the day ended, medical examiner Raphael Gilady testified about his examination of Edgar Smith on March 6 and finding the new bruises, as well as to his autopsy of Victoria Zielinski's body. He described the crushing of her skull and the "total loss of [her] brain." His examination had also revealed that the fifteen-year-old was still a virgin.*

Things got more interesting when Calissi asked Gilady to indicate a time of death. The medical examiner wanted to be cautious and not commit to an absolute time frame because of the cold weather on the night of March 4, but under the prosecutor's insistent questioning he settled on a time closer to midnight. That ended up muddying the waters enough to open the door for Selser to try to alibi Smith, who had placed himself at the scene no later than 9:00 p.m. Could Gilady explain the discrepancy if he approximated the time of Vickie's death closer to midnight? "It could have been earlier than 11 o'clock because the prevailing weather was so cold and the body might have stiffened up, according to standard data."†

---

* We now know that the lack of an intact hymen does not indicate that a woman has engaged in sexual activity and that the presence of an intact hymen cannot prove virginity. But that was the medical standard during the 1950s.

† Colder weather and falling temperatures cause rigor mortis to set in earlier and last longer, sometimes for days. Gilady's time of death estimate for Vickie's murder was even more of an approximation and did not rule out an earlier time of death in the slightest. What medical examiners know

It was not clear to Calissi what effect the medical examiner's inconsistent testimony might have on the case or if it would negate Don Hommell's strong performance on the stand. He also called more law enforcement agents and investigators to the stand in quick succession, including Charles Smith, Henry Voss, Charles deLisle, and Walter Spahr, all of whom bolstered the prosecution's case against Edgar.

Calissi and Selser's sparring turned even more contentious on the morning of May 21. When Calissi wanted to enter Smith's statement into the record as part of his direct examination of the court stenographer, Selser objected and moved to call Edgar to the stand to testify to whether he was under duress when he gave the statement. On the stand, under oath, Edgar insisted that he'd been cold and shivery the whole time and that he'd had only a couple of cups of coffee and two eggs for sustenance after police had taken him into custody near midnight on March 5 until the end of the interrogation at noon the next day.

"At one time during the statement they provided to you a glass of milk, did they not?" asked Selser.

"I never got the glass of milk," Edgar replied.

"He is leading this witness something terrible," cut in Calissi. O'Dea asked Selser to knock off the leading questions.

As a rebuttal witness, Calissi called Louis Kalstad, the grand jury member who had witnessed the police interrogation. What was the defendant's condition? "He seemed all right to me in every way," answered Kalstad. "He was smoking cigarettes one after the other, drinking coffee up in the Prosecutor's Office."

"Did he register at any time any complaint?"

"No," Kalstad replied.

---

now, with far more confidence than did Gilady and his peers, is that time of death is difficult to pin down.

After more back-and-forth between prosecutor and defense attorney, Judge O'Dea made his ruling: Edgar's statement could be entered in the record and stand as evidence, because he had admitted to his guilt and said, "That's when it hit me really hard I must have been the one who really did it." The jury was called back, and Calissi then read the entire sixty-page statement in court.

Calissi wrapped up his prosecution a few minutes after eleven the following morning. Selser immediately moved for an acquittal, arguing that there was very little evidence tying Edgar to Victoria Zielinski's murder, including but not limited to the medical examiner's testimony—that "there is nothing to go to the jury on which [they] could find the defendant guilty." O'Dea icily shut Selser down and swatted the motion aside, saying that Dr. Gilady's testimony under cross-examination made it very clear "it would be very difficult to fix the exact time of death."

The court recessed, and at two that afternoon, John Selser called his first defense witness: Edgar Smith.

6

"Eddie and Don Aren't Friends Anymore"

MAY 22–28, 1957

THIS WAS the moment the crowd was waiting for. To see and hear Edgar Smith, the accused murderer of Victoria Zielinski, explain what happened in his own words—and to decide whether he was guilty of killing the fifteen-year-old girl. Don Hommell sat in the rear of the courtroom. He was keenly interested in whether his former friend would maintain that Don was the killer but didn't want to draw the attention of the press by sitting anywhere conspicuous.

Edgar's wife and mother sat close to the front. Neither woman had displayed much emotion during the prosecution's presentation of the case. Now, with the man they both loved set to tell his story, their feigned calm evaporated, revealing the naked anxiety both women felt. How would Edgar hold up on the stand? Would he be a good witness or a terrible one? The answer turned out to be both.

Selser first questioned Smith about his whereabouts from the morning of March 4 into the early evening, then through the time period immediately before and after Vickie's death and what he did later that night. Edgar rattled off a rapid-fire account of the events, pretty much as he'd described them in his recorded statement. He admitted to only a few memory gaps and paid great attention—perhaps too much—to the smallest possible details, from road routes to estimated distance and times to the small talk between himself and another customer when he was trying to purchase kerosene at the service station. He testified that he had taken Vickie to the sand pit and parked there because she told him she "wanted to tell [him] something, it was important." When she accused Patricia of having an affair, he said, he grew so angry he slapped Vickie and ordered her out of the car, telling her she would have to walk home.

Selser then asked what happened next. Edgar responded that at that point, he noticed another car come up behind him. "I was afraid to see who it was. I thought it might be Vickie's father. I turned back to the car, twisted my ankle and fell. I reached into the car for a bat."

Selser pressed him to continue. Edgar described how he saw "two figures walking toward me." He closed the car door and stood next to the passenger side. "The two people continued walking, and when they reached a few feet from me I saw who it was."

"Who did you recognize [them] to be?" Selser asked.

Edgar paused. "It was Victoria Zielinski and Don Hommell."

Hommell got up abruptly and walked down the aisle all the way to the second row, normally reserved for the press. Smith and the jury looked up. Edgar, who had kept his confidence throughout his direct testimony, faltered at the sight of his former friend. He lowered his head. His cheeks flamed. But he composed himself within seconds and soon resumed his testimony in a loud, clear voice. Hommell stayed put.

Reporters seemed to be somewhat impressed by Edgar's testimony, with one from the Rockland, New York, *Journal-News* commenting that "someone is lying coldly and deliberately. The state says it's Smith and has indicted him for murder. Selser and Smith say it's Hommell. The jury will decide. The cross-examination of Smith could help. Only one thing is crystal clear: Eddie and Don aren't friends anymore."

The next day, it was Guy Calissi's turn to go after Edgar. Over his four-hour cross-examination, Calissi revealed contradiction after contradiction, discrepancy after discrepancy in Smith's testimony, to the point that Edgar finally admitted that the entire statement he had made on March 6 was a lie: "I developed that story out of my imagination."

In his statement, Edgar had said that he'd tried to prevent Vickie from leaving his car by restraining her wrist but that she had wrestled free of his grip and gotten out of her own volition. On the stand, he testified that he had ordered her to "get out and walk." Edgar insisted that the second version was the truth; when he'd made the original statement, he'd been frightened to tell the truth because of Don Hommell's threats.

What about his assertion during his interrogation that if the police needed a fall guy, they should look at Hommell? "You weren't afraid [of him] then?" asked Calissi.

Edgar slipped and said he wasn't but later clarified that no, he actually *was* afraid when he told the police they should nab Hommell instead.

"Even though these were incriminating answers, you made them up?" Calissi asked, understandably incredulous.

"That's right," replied Edgar.

Edgar mostly stayed composed under cross-examination but for a slight tugging on his chin. But when Calissi asked if he had been "trying to love this girl up"—if he had tried to molest or assault Vickie in any way—he flushed. He leaned forward in the box and shouted, "I did not, sir!"

"Didn't you grab your jacket off and pull off her sweater and bite her—"

Edgar said he hadn't done any of those things. He also vehemently denied Calissi's next questions, which laid out the gory details of the murder for the jury, including Vickie's pulled-up sweater and the fact that her right breast had been bitten.

"And she said she was going to tell her father?"

"No, she did not," said Edgar, though he clarified that he had said that in his statement.

"This is a lie, too?" Calissi demanded.

Smith said yes. "As I told you before, I was afraid because of threats toward my wife and child."

Calissi asked if Edgar had grabbed the baseball bat, chased Vickie down Fardale Road, and struck her—and that was the cut he said he saw after she ran from the car? The prosecutor waved the bloodied baseball bat at the defendant.

"I did not."

"And after you hit this girl, isn't it a fact with the baseball bat, you threw [it] away and you dragged her back to the sand pit, took her up on the knoll and crushed her head with the rock?"

"I did not."

Selser finally objected, calling Calissi's waving of the bat and his raised voice "belligerent." But it was too late: the prosecutor had damaged Edgar's credibility, if it ever existed at all.

———

NEXT SELSER CALLED Rosella Wood, a widow of about sixty living in the Franklin Lakes section of Mahwah, who had told his investigator that she'd seen two young men, one of whom she identified as Hommell, searching for something near her home on the morning of March 5. She testified that she'd noticed them when her two dogs began to bark. She'd gone out to ask what they were looking for, and that's when the man she identified as Hommell said, "Mind your own business." But under cross-examination, Wood's credibility crumbled as Calissi brought up the fact that the boys she saw would have been about twenty-five to thirty feet away, too far for her to make a definitive identification of anyone.

Patricia Smith took the stand the next day, May 24. She had turned twenty earlier in the week and celebrated her birthday by visiting her husband in jail. Now, in a quiet voice that betrayed a trace of annoyance at having to answer questions, she testified to Smith's state on March 4 and 5. She said her husband had not been feeling well for two or three days and carried the smell of vomit when he had arrived home. She said it wasn't unusual for Eddie to throw away clothes he'd dirtied; he had done so before. Patricia couldn't provide an alibi, but she certainly tried to do so. Calissi's cross-examination of her was fairly benign.

When Selser called Frank Gilg, a druggist at the pharmacy where Don Hommell worked, the testimony did not go as the defense attorney planned. Rather than casting doubt on Hommell's whereabouts on the night of Vickie's murder, Gilg bolstered his alibi. He said that Hommell left the Wyckoff Pharmacy between 8:35 and 8:40 p.m. in the company's green-and-white station wagon to go to Ridgewood, where he picked up a prescription at another drugstore. Hommell returned shortly before 9:00 p.m. He set down the car keys, prescription, and change and left the store again. Vickie would already have been dead by the time he got back onto the road.

It was clear to the audience in the courtroom how damaging Gilg's testimony was to the idea that Hommell could have killed the girl. The timeline simply didn't work. As a dumbfounded *Rockland Journal-News* reporter commented, "The question will be asked in legal circles for years: Why did Selser ever put Gilg on the stand, or did he know he might as well because Calissi was holding him back for rebuttal?"

When Selser's final two witnesses, tavern owner Herbert Pelzer and one of the bar's regulars, failed to show up to testify, the *Journal-News* wrote, because Selser's investigator, Andrew Nicol, had told the two to go home. The defense rested rather abruptly at 2:35 p.m. on Friday, May 24.

Edgar Smith's trial had many dramatic moments: shouting witnesses, glaring spectators, another suspect named; thirty-seven witnesses for the prosecution and a dozen for the defense. And as John Selser and Guy Calissi prepared for their closing statements on Monday, May 27, Bergen County reeled from another calamity: a second murder of a teenage girl.

———

RUTH STARR ZEITLER—Starr to her friends—was, like Victoria Zielinski, fifteen, dark haired, and dark eyed. She lived in Fair Lawn, sixteen miles southwest of Mahwah, and attended Fair Lawn High School. She'd last been seen on the morning of May 17, and her family and friends feared the worst. Their fears became reality less than a week later when Starr's body was found by two children in a heavily wooded area near Paramus. She'd been strangled, and wads of tissue had been stuffed into her mouth. Schoolbooks and clothes surrounded her half-naked body. There were clear signs of sexual assault.

Bergen County police and prosecutors Fred Galda and Guy Calissi easily ruled out any connection to Vickie's murder. The deaths of two teenage girls two months apart was simply an awful coincidence. Right away the police zeroed on the last person to see Starr Zeitler alive: eighteen-year-old Ronald Marrone.

He was a star of the Fair Lawn High track team, nicknamed "Marrone the Miler." He was apparently so religious that he attended church three times a week, sang in the choir, carried a Bible wherever he went, and had gone to see Billy Graham at Madison Square Garden on the night Starr went missing. Marrone had admitted to driving Starr to Radburn Center, allegedly at her request. Soon police learned that he had been apprehended for molesting a little girl, who'd had tissue stuffed into her mouth during the assault. Even though Marrone had been acquitted on that earlier charge, the police found that eliciting a confession from him proved to be easy.

"I'm making this statement to God," said Marrone, clutching his Bible tightly to his chest during his final interrogation by police. Marrone's father professed bewilderment to the press after the boy's arrest. "It seems impossible. He must have had a split personality. . . . He couldn't bring himself to kill a bird or a small animal. He loved children. He used to mind the neighbor's kids." Then he added, "If he is guilty I want the kid put away so nobody else can get hurt."

Ronald Marrone went on to plead *non vult* (no defense) to murdering Starr Zeitler and was sentenced to life in prison. He served fourteen years before being paroled in 1971 and lived the rest of his life in obscurity, first in New Jersey's Ocean County and later in Alabama.

The swift arrest and charging of Ronald Marrone as the Edgar Smith trial was ending took its toll upon local law enforcement officials, already plenty overworked. Guy Calissi, in the press conference announcing Marrone's arrest on Monday, May 27, had nothing but praise for his investigators, quite a number of them having previously worked to apprehend Edgar Smith. But he could not conceal his lack of sleep, worrisome in that he would need energy for his summation in the Smith trial later that day.

John Selser went first. He told the jury and the court, "I want you all to understand that I hold no brief for any person who would destroy the life of a person, whatever the sex and whatever the age. . . . But I believe also that those who are near and dear to Vickie have the right of knowing the truth." Selser laid out his case that Edgar wasn't the murderer and Don Hommell was a more likely culprit. Yet Selser himself admitted that Edgar's story about throwing away the bloody trousers because he was sick was "ridiculous." He also stressed for the jury that he didn't know how Vickie was murdered: "And you don't know how that girl was killed. Yet you are supposed to find Eddie Smith guilty of having done it." In the end he leaned hard on reasonable doubt: "I don't have to prove the guilt of someone else. The State has to prove the guilt of Eddie Smith."

Calissi began his summation by thanking the jury for their patience and for putting up with the inconvenience to their lives over the past few weeks. Then he addressed the issue of how hard it was to fix the time of Vickie's death; he said it was now up to the jury to decide how best to deal with the doubts about that. Next, he attacked Selser's defense strategy of naming and blaming Donald Hommell for the murder: "What a disgraceful thing to have to cope with—a friend pointing his finger at you and saying to you, 'You committed this crime.'" It was, he said, "an attempt by a malicious, vicious mind to throw into this case that little confusion, that little bit of doubt which it is hoped by the defense will create the reasonable doubt that is necessary in a case of this kind." All the defense was hanging on, Calissi continued, was "straws."

One final time, the prosecutor went through the evidence against Edgar Smith: the bloody pants, the bloody rock, his incriminating statements to police, his testimony on the witness stand. "We are dealing, I say again, with a very cunning man who sits here before this jury and this Court for over two weeks, doesn't bat an eyelash, shows absolutely no sign of sympathy or remorse and believes that this is just one of those things. My stomach and my heart, well, it feels the way I know it feels and I know there are others in this courtroom that feel the same. The only person that seemed unconcerned in this court was Smith himself."

The following morning, Judge O'Dea delivered his instructions to the jury: they could find Edgar Smith guilty of first-degree murder, as charged, with a sentence of death; guilty with a life sentence; guilty of second degree murder; or not guilty. "It is the eyes of your own conscience that you make a proper judgment," the judge warned.

Judge O'Dea's instructions to the jury lasted ninety minutes. The jury began deliberations just after 11:30. One hour and fifty-one minutes later, just before 2:00 p.m., they had a verdict.

7

"It Can't Be"

MAY 28–JUNE 4, 1957

GUY CALISSI was taken aback by how quickly the jury had reached their decision. They hadn't even requested sandwiches and coffee. He was nervous as to what it meant. Would it be a finding of guilt or an acquittal?

After the group of ten men and two women filed in, Judge O'Dea asked the foreman, Adolph Schaefer, to deliver the verdict. Guilty of murder in the first degree, Schaefer announced— one of the fastest verdicts of death in New Jersey history.

Edgar took it in without any visible reaction, though both his mother and his wife began to weep. Patricia buried her head in her white-gloved hands, and Ann, dark glasses covering her eyes, put an arm around her daughter-in-law. "It can't be. It can't be. It can't be. He didn't. He didn't," Patricia repeated in heaving gasps.

Victoria's mother, Mary, also burst into tears when the verdict was announced and put her head on her husband's shoulder.

Judge O'Dea told the jurors that if he had been in the jury box, he, too, would have made the same decision about Edgar Smith's fate. He told them they shouldn't take on the weight of responsibility for sentencing a man to death. It was the law, after all. He set sentencing for the morning of June 4 at 9:30 a.m.—three months to the day that Victoria Zielinski died.

Later, Anthony Zielinski told reporters, "I feel better than I did. This has been a terrible ordeal for my family. But even though I feel better now, what happened today doesn't bring back my daughter." He and his wife found Guy Calissi near the rotunda of the courthouse. Mary shook hands with the prosecutor and offered profuse thanks for his efforts on behalf of their daughter and their family. "Justice has been done," Calissi told her in earshot of the reporters. "I had a duty to do, and I'm tired. You don't feel any glory or praise. It's just a job you have to do."

Calissi was beyond tired—"If I told you the amount of sleep I've had in the last two weeks, you wouldn't believe it, so I won't tell you"—but before he went home to catch up on his rest, he had one last thing to say to the media: how livid he was at the defense strategy. Even his own wife, Ethel, had quizzed him about the possibility that Don Hommell might have been at the sand pit. "This made me particularly mad. My wife is an intelligent woman, yet the talk about Hommell raised a question in her mind." That was why, in his closing statement, he had carried a double burden: "I not only had to prove Smith guilty, I also had to show that Hommell was innocent."

When a reporter for the *Bergen Evening Record* found him at his home in Mahwah, Don Hommell couldn't contain his bitterness. "I hope he gets what's coming to him," he said about Edgar. "I always said he'd fry in July." He added that no one really liked Edgar, because he was a man who was always using people. "I was never his friend. Who could be his friend?"

Selser was appalled at how quickly the jury rendered its verdict. "It was too fast. They couldn't even have read Smith's statement, much less read through 98 exhibits in the case. They must have made up their minds before." With his client continuing to insist on his innocence, Selser argued as much to Judge O'Dea on the morning of Edgar's sentencing and was already talking about appealing.

Just before he passed sentence, the judge asked the convicted man if he had anything to say. He did not. Judge O'Dea ruled that Edgar Smith would die in the electric chair at Trenton State Prison as soon as July 15, 1957.

PART II

THE DEATH HOUSE

(1958–1962)

8

Patricia

JUNE 1957–AUGUST 1958

THE LAST time Patricia Smith held her husband's hand was on June 4, 1957, the day he was sentenced to die for the murder of Victoria Zielinski. Edgar Smith did not, in fact, fry in July; the date was postponed by his lawyer's immediate petition to the state appeals court. Edgar's mother had also hired two additional attorneys, William Richter of New York and Robert Hicks of Washington, DC, to argue his case in the federal system, including the US Supreme Court if need be. There would be motions to stay execution dates and motions to overturn his conviction entirely and get a new trial on the basis of existing and new evidence. All those legal moves led to more delays for Edgar and more anxiety for Patricia.

She and Patti Ann fled the trailer park not long after the trial, moving in with Geraldine in Ridgewood. Mother and daughter also spent a considerable amount of time with Edgar's mother, Ann, and his stepfather, Alex, who still lived on Elm Street in Ramsey.

Patricia was grateful to have a solid roof over her head and extra child care for her baby. The Chupaks' new pet kitten, Goombah, added joy to lives in dire need of good cheer. Patti Ann, dark and green eyed like her mother, was Patricia's main reason to get up in the morning. "No matter how little I feel like smiling or laughing, I can't help it around her," she told the *Paterson Evening News* in the summer of 1958.

Patricia was, by the standards of the day and of Bergen County, a dutiful, devoted wife. She visited Edgar every month, sometimes twice, at the Death House, seventy-seven miles southwest of Ridgewood. Trenton State Prison's main structure housed many hundreds of inmates, but the Death House was smaller and gloomier, with room for eighteen cells lined along one wall in two tiers and painted light green. At the far end were the execution chamber and a tiny morgue. The only windows were located on the opposite wall to the cells, opening on an air shaft. A skylight allowed the sun to filter in during the day, and the lights were never turned off at night.

Edgar's cell was on the upper tier, within thirty feet of the execution chamber. It was outfitted with a bed, a sink, a toilet, and an electric light. He had no table or chair, because prison officials believed they could be refashioned as weapons, so he wrote letters, legal and personal, sitting on the bed and stored them in the cardboard boxes he was allowed. He could eat a hot breakfast at 7:00 a.m., served through a slot in the cell door from a food cart, but he could skip it if he was still asleep or didn't feel like it. The same went for lunch, at 11:30 a.m., and dinner, at 4:30 p.m. Each of the meals was served with a prison-approved spoon and dish, which the prisoner had to return immediately after he finished eating.

The Death House kept the inmates in near-total solitary confinement. Edgar wasn't allowed out of his eight-by-eight-foot cell, save for an hour a day for exercise, a weekly shower and shave lasting fifteen minutes at most, and supervised half-hour visits with his wife. The guards let Patricia sit on a chair in the corridor close enough to see Edgar in his cell but dropped a wire mesh screen between them so that they couldn't touch each other. Edgar, like the other incarcerated men, had tremendous difficulty adjusting to the deprivation, loneliness, and isolation. His change in circumstances was even more unfathomable to his wife.

For the Smiths' second wedding anniversary, on June 8, 1958, the prison wardens gifted the married couple with an extra fifteen minutes of visiting time. This was a big deal for the Death House. As Edgar's mother, Ann Chupak, later said, "You wouldn't coop up a dog that way or the ASPCA might get you."

Patricia dressed primly, per state regulations. Separated by the mesh screen, she sat in the chair and Edgar stood in his cell. She told him about their daughter, Patti Ann, now a fully walking, talking eighteen-month-old, and of the hope she had that his attorney might reverse his fate.

The forty-five minutes slipped by quickly. At the end, Patricia whispered, "Until next month." She left the prison and ducked into an idling car, where a friend was caring for Patti Ann, who wasn't allowed to see her father. Patricia's wedding ring was inscribed FOR BETTER OR FOR WORSE, and a locket she wore carried the words TILL DEATH DO US PART. But this was a level of worse beyond reasonable imagining. Death should come decades in the future, of natural causes—not imminently and at the hands of an executioner. Ann Chupak, on more than one occasion, called her daughter-in-law brave for not breaking down.

———

ON JUNE 25, 1958, the judges of the New Jersey Supreme Court voted unanimously to uphold Edgar's murder conviction. "The record leaves no room to disturb the jury's finding," wrote the author of the opinion, William A. Wachenfeld. Guy Calissi, the prosecutor, took no joy in the ruling. "This is one of the most unpleasant tasks that a prosecutor has to do," he told a UPI reporter the following morning. "There is no glory or pleasure to it." Judge O'Dea set a new execution date for the week of August 17.

John Selser swiftly announced his plan to appeal the sentence to the governor of New Jersey, Robert W. Meyner. "I don't want that boy to die on the week of the seventeenth for anything," Selser told the papers, knowing the governor would read it. But after a clemency hearing on July 30, Meyner refused to commute Smith's death sentence, announcing his decision a mere five hours after the hearing ended, saying "I have weighed the entire matter with the utmost gravity, having in mind both the seriousness of the sentence imposed upon Edgar Smith and the nature of his crime."

With that avenue closed, Richter and Hicks filed for an execution stay to the US Supreme Court. Selser, meanwhile, dropped a bombshell: a notarized statement, dated July 3, from bar owner Herbert Pelzer, who swore that despite Donald Hommell's testimony, Hommell had not been in his bar when Victoria Zielinski was murdered. Not only did Pelzer swear to that, he named three patrons who could back him up.

In his affidavit, submitted as part of Edgar's last-ditch appeal to the US Supreme Court, Pelzer stated that Hommell had pressured him to say that he was at the bar on the night of March 4, 1957. "I wish to make this last and final statement because I want to tell the whole truth," said Pelzer. "I thought the truth would come out, but now I see Edgar Smith is going to die and I cannot withhold God's honest truth." Bergen County prosecutor Guy Calissi, who had gone to Washington to reply to the defense's motion, not only was skeptical about the content of the Pelzer affidavit but thought it would be more pertinent as part of a request for a new trial, not a stay of execution.

The next few days saw a flurry of whiplash-inducing news reports. Supreme Court Justice William J. Brennan, Jr., denied Edgar's bid for a stay of execution without further comment, but the state scheduled one more hearing on the matter of whether Smith could or would be granted a new trial—set for August 13 and presided over by Judge O'Dea, the man who'd sentenced Edgar to death.

The fourteen-witness, two-day hearing provided more surprises. Two women, Marie Brewer and Catherine Ferber, claimed that while they were out shopping, they overheard the wife of one of the jurors, Theodor Hundemann, telling someone else that her husband said, "The Smith family was lying to save Smith." That conversation, if true, was potential grounds for a new trial. Hundemann strenuously denied the charge in court, as did a juror guard, testifying that the only time Hundemann made a telephone call was to request new shirts from his wife.

A US Army private named George Self also testified. He claimed that he had seen Donald Hommell out and about in Ramsey's shopping district on the night of March 4, 1957. Hommell, of course, denied that. Self's statement landed with added surprise because he was married to the Zielinskis' eldest daughter, Mary Faye, who was pregnant with their first child. She also took the stand to say that she had seen a car that evening that Hommell was known to drive but hadn't noticed him as the driver. Self admitted that he didn't know Hommell well enough to say for sure that he was the man Self saw that night.

Pelzer, the bar owner, also didn't acquit himself well during the hearing. Slumped in the witness chair, plucking at his bow tie, he admitted during questioning by Guy Calissi that he had made past statements to police that contradicted his affidavit.

One point in particular, on whether Rocky Rockefeller had asked Pelzer to provide Hommell with an alibi for the night of the murder, "just isn't so," said Pelzer. Then the prosecutor asked Pelzer whether he'd been convicted of a crime. Pelzer said no. Calissi brought up his no-contest plea on a bookmaking charge, which had resulted in a suspended sentence of one year to eighteen months in prison. "And you say you were never convicted of a crime?" the incredulous Calissi asked.

"I thought if you get a suspended sentence it means you are not convicted," replied Pelzer.

Judge O'Dea wasn't swayed by the new witnesses. He denounced Pelzer's testimony in the strongest possible terms, calling the bar owner a "thoroughly unreliable, incredible witness, careless with the truth." He denied Smith's bid for a new trial and set the execution date for August 19, 1958.

Selser was so distraught over the decision that he vowed to quit practicing law after more than forty years, he told the *Bergen Evening Record* on August 15. "I can't take it anymore. It's too emotional."

———

PATRICIA SMITH RARELY commented to reporters, leaving the press seeking and public statements to her mother-in-law. But the imminent execution of her husband spurred her to speak up after Judge O'Dea's ruling. "I feel that if the people who are withholding evidence in this case would come forward now my daughter would not go through life with the stain of her father dying in the electric chair," she said in an interview with Eddie's old football coach, Robert Curley, now the Passaic *Herald-News*' PR director and columnist. "If they come forward now his life can be spared." She began to sob. "I pray to God that someone will come forward and tell the truth."

"We'll do everything in our power . . . run, drive, or walk anywhere to prove my boy's innocence," Ann Chupak told Curley when he came to the house to interview her and Patricia. "Even if my son dies in the electric chair Tuesday night, I'll not stop until I've tracked down the real murderer." Insisting that she wasn't "just an hysterical mother," Chupak said she wouldn't ever wish such a wrongful execution on "another mother's son."

Both Ann and Patricia planned to visit Edgar over the weekend, knowing it could be for the last time. Before the visit, Patricia received a letter from her husband. She hadn't wanted to read it aloud to a reporter because she thought Eddie wouldn't like it. She gave the letter to her mother-in-law to read. Ann read a few sentences before breaking down, after which she fled the living room. Patricia continued where Ann left off. Then she, too, began crying.

> *Darling Tricia, my loving wife, this week is going to be a real test of your love and courage if things go badly for us. Above all else, for the sake of our daughter, don't let anything happen that may happen break you down, don't give up on your own life. Without you to guide and protect her, she will be lost. For her and for the love of me, don't be afraid of anything in the future.*
>
> *Face what you must knowing that my love and heart will always be with you. My greatest and only desire is to be home with you both. But if I can't be, I know you are a good mother and will devote your love and life to [our] daughter. These are the things I want you to do, things I trust you to do.*
>
> *Thursday is still two days off and I may be wrong for a*

*change but the feeling of everything being over is too strong for
me to ignore.*

*Honey, this is going to be an awful hard letter to write since
we still don't have any idea what is going to happen. By the
time you get it, you will know where we stand.*

If Patricia didn't know then, she certainly did during the family visit on Sunday afternoon. Edgar's aunt and uncle were allowed forty-five minutes, while his mother made the most of her thirty-minute slot. Patricia was allowed to stay for three hours. As she recollected later, "Even though we haven't seen much of each other it [was] hard to hold a sustained conversation."

The Death House was a spooky place, but that particular Sunday, Patricia felt an added chill. Eddie had told her that a patient in the prison infirmary "went out of his mind . . . or something." And as husband and wife spoke, "the patient would let out with screams and shrieks. It was like an old *Dracula* movie. We'd sort of smile at each other each time we heard the howl." Both she and Edgar were trying to be brave, but neither of them was kidding themselves or each other.

Edgar made three requests. He asked his mother, "Please write to Mrs. Zielinski and tell her that although I'm going to die for the crime the real murderer has yet to be caught." Mrs. Chupak promised she would. "The poor woman probably will tear up the letter," said Ann, "but I'm going to write it."

To his wife, he said, "I'm granted one final wish by the state. Please bring my wedding ring down for me to wear Tuesday night." She promised she would bring the ring, a simple gold band, during the Monday visit.

He implored prison officials to bequeath his eyes to the local eye bank. "Since I can't live, someone should have the benefit of my eyes." Ann was nonplussed by that wish. "Let the blind stay blind and not see the filth of the world," she told Curley. Then her resistance ebbed a little. "It's Eddie's wish and I guess he's right. Let some poor soul be granted the right to see." She paused, and her voice cracked. "He has such lovely blue eyes."

Patricia's visit ended at ten minutes before 5:00 p.m. As she prepared to leave, a guard rushed up to her. Perhaps he believed in Edgar's innocence, but it was more likely he felt bad for Edgar's wife. "Here's a little something for you. My son found it in our garden. Maybe it will bring you some luck."

To Patricia's amazement, the "little something" was a four-leaf clover.

———

THE HOURS TICKED by on Monday, August 18, ever closer to the death of Patricia Smith's husband by the decree of the state of New Jersey. The day began with the foulest of luck, at total odds with what the four-leaf clover had promised. A last-minute attempt at an execution stay was turned down by the appellate court. Governor Meyner announced in a television broadcast that he had no plans to grant clemency to Edgar Smith—just as he'd decided the prior month—but was happy to consider any new evidence, should it emerge. John Selser, Edgar's lawyer, immediately sought to appeal to the New Jersey Supreme Court.

A member of the New Jersey Legislature, C. William Haines, also implored Meyner to reconsider. Haines had spent the summer speaking out against the death penalty and pushing forward a bill to replace it with a minimum thirty-year prison term. But the legislature wouldn't schedule a debate on the bill until mid-November. That would be too late for Edgar Smith.

Patricia was only dimly aware of the morning's bad news when she went with Smith's family to the Death House for their final goodbyes. His mother, Ann, went in first, around 11:00 a.m. "I won't say goodbye, so I'll say so long. . . . I'm going to try to see Governor Meyner," she told her son. But Meyner refused to see her.

Edgar's older brother, Richard, and his wife, Anita, were next. Richard looked his brother in the eye. He'd asked the question before, but this time it felt more urgent. "Did you kill her?"

"No, I didn't" was Smith's calm, immediate reply.

Finally, it was Patricia's turn. Edgar sat in his cell, the heavy mesh screen separating them. The only contact they were allowed was to touch fingers, and that would have to suffice. "It was the last half hour to be together," Patricia later recalled. "We were trying to make small talk and laugh a little." Two clergymen also visited, attempting to keep the Smiths' spirits steady.

At around 3:00 p.m., just before their visit was to end, a prison guard rushed toward the couple, saying, "I have good news for you kids." Edgar's execution was postponed indefinitely, a stay granted by New Jersey federal court judge Mendon Morrill.

"I don't know how high I jumped from my seat," said Patricia. "Then we looked at each other and we both had tears in our eyes but we just smiled." Patricia began to dance around the hall of the Death House, as two other prisoners, Fred Sturdivant and Ralph Hudson, cheered. The guards, too, had grins on their faces. One cracked, "If you kids don't stop carrying on, we'll have to turn you loose in the yard!"

Patricia ran out to the waiting room to tell Richard and Anita. Ann already knew. Patricia kissed her mother-in-law.

Judge Morrill had issued the stay after William Richter, Edgar's New York–based lawyer, had rushed a last-minute motion to the federal court on the grounds that the convict's constitutional rights had been violated. It was the identical motion that US Supreme Court justice William Brennan had turned down because the case was still pending in state court at the time, before it upheld Edgar's conviction.* "I don't know if this boy is innocent or guilty," said Richter. "I entered the case too late for that. But I do know that there is too much doubt in this case to execute this boy."

Reporters pounced on the car carrying Edgar's family away from the prison. Patricia stared out the passenger's side window, her brown hair swept up, her eyes bright and wide, reflecting her shock at the sudden turn of events. "I'm happy," she told them. "I haven't had a chance to think about what it means." But as the news spread around Bergen County, she felt the partial lifting of a burden. It seemed to her that she was no longer a pariah but an object of sympathy. That she would stand by her husband now meant she was loyal, not deluded—a heroine of sorts or at least someone to root for. When she took Patti Ann to the barbershop for the little girl's very first haircut shortly after the stay was announced, she didn't feel judged by the other people in the shop. She could breathe a little.

Patricia's hope was that justice would prevail and that those she believed had lied at the trial "will tell the truth this time." Edgar wasn't as optimistic. "I really can't say how he feels," she told *Bergen Evening Record* reporter Robert Comstock on Tuesday night when he interviewed her at her mother's house. "We try to kid each other along. But I don't think he's quite as confident as I am. How could he be, in such surroundings?" With Edgar's life still at stake, Patricia mused, "your life revolves around four words that are bigger than they look—why, if, maybe, and someday."

---

* It emerged later that day that the state attorney general's office had issued its own separate stay of execution, served to the prison warden at 2:00 p.m., but Smith's lawyers had not learned of that until after the fact, to considerable anger and frustration.

The stay helped Patricia tamp down her doubts. Because she did have doubts. How could she not? But having them and telling other people she had them were quite different things. Her doubts were no one else's business—just like what had really gone on in her marriage to Edgar.

———

IN THE FALL OF 1955, Patricia Ann Horton was eighteen but looked several years younger. With a slender neck, an open face, and eyes that yearned for love, she was perfect pickings for a young man like Eddie Smith when they met at a party that September. Recently out of the US Marine Corps (honorably discharged for medical reasons, he explained), Eddie presented well to her parents, and Patricia took a shine to his mother and stepfather, too.

He was her first, her only, and she loved him so much that it seemed the most natural thing in the world to go to bed with him. Why would she have refused, even if Eddie pressured her a little more than she was totally comfortable with? She knew how sweet he could be, how charming. And when she discovered she was pregnant, he did the right thing and married her. It was what he said he wanted. It was certainly what *she* wanted.

Patricia wasn't stupid. She knew people in town would count the months between a June wedding and a December baby. But she didn't brood about it, with so much else to preoccupy her, such as keeping house while heavily pregnant for a new husband prone to coming home too late for dinner. She mostly didn't pester him about it. He got so upset if she did that Patricia felt squashed and meek. She knew she would always lose an argument with him, so she tried to avoid fighting.

She also never refused him in bed. "If he wanted sex, he always got his way," Patricia recalled in an interview with detectives more than four decades later, in 2000. "Saying 'no' didn't do much good. . . . I learned it was easier to submit to him than to resist. . . . When he wanted sex, he had to have it right then and there, no two ways about it. . . . It was going to happen whether I wanted it or didn't want it."

But one night when Eddie arrived home late, Patricia snapped. Dinner was long cold. She'd been worried and asked him why he couldn't have called to let her know he was delayed. He blew up and grabbed a kitchen knife—she would never forget that it was serrated—and came for her until he loomed over her with the knife close to her face. Terror snaked through her then, though she tried hard to bury it as deep as she would later bury her doubts about his innocence.

She also tried hard not to think about the time Eddie joked about his idea of "the perfect murder." He'd gone on about stabbing someone to death with a sharp icicle, which, when used, would then melt and disappear. She'd heard him out, figuring it had to be a joke. What a ridiculous idea. That violent death was on Eddie's mind before the murder of Vickie Zielinski— well, thinking about murder wasn't the same as actually doing it, right?

Her husband had flaws. Many of them, some too reprehensible to defend. But being a lousy, controlling, aggressive, sex-demanding husband didn't make you a murderer. Did it?

9

Divorces

AUGUST 1959–SEPTEMBER 1962

WITH THE swift conviction of Edgar Smith, Victoria Zielinski's case was supposed to be closed—no matter the attempts to stay his execution. But her murder remained an open wound for her family. Vickie, had she lived, would have graduated from Ramsey High in 1959. Her classmates dedicated that year's edition of the yearbook to her, featuring her photo and a memorial inscription, a somber tribute in stark contrast to the increasing attention to the man convicted of killing her.

The media coverage made things worse for the Zielinskis. When Smith avoided the electric chair on August 18, 1958, thanks to the federal court's last-minute granting of a stay, the Zielinski family did not know how to react. "It's been hard on us," Mary told a *Paterson Evening News* reporter. "I'd rather not comment right now." When the reporter filled her in on the precise details of the stay, which she hadn't known, Mary hid her reaction. "It's in the hands of the state and I don't want to judge him either way," she said. But she must have been bewildered to witness the collective shock of the town over the brutal murder of her daughter slowly transforming into sympathy for the convicted killer.

The Zielinskis had moved away from their Wyckoff Avenue

home, painted bright yellow, to a house on Darlington Avenue, no longer within walking distance of the sand pit at the corner of Fardale and Chapel Roads. The sand pit looked different, too, now overgrown with brush.

Vickie's father, Anthony, was still filled with rage and grief, which he took out ever more aggressively and violently on his wife and surviving children. On Sunday, December 8, 1957, Mary called the police on her husband after a family quarrel. They arrested Anthony, charging him with disorderly conduct. He appeared in magistrate's court on Tuesday, December 17, after being freed on $500 bail. There is no record as to what happened with the charges.

Mary finally filed for divorce in August 1959, accusing Anthony of "extreme cruelty." The charges set out in the divorce petition were so incendiary that later articles about Vickie's murder excluded the details out of respect for the family. Mary said that Anthony had "repeatedly and freely abused [her] and called her many foul and obscene names, degraded, belittled, berated, threatened, and defamed [her] many times in the presence and in front of her family and children."

His alcohol use had intensified in the years leading up to the divorce, as had his philandering. His wife claimed, "When I would question him about his whereabouts, he would flaunt the fact that he was going out with women and became particularly violent about this." He also accused his wife of infidelity during many a drunken rage. Their life, Mary said, "became a state of almost open warfare." One particularly appalling incident allegedly took place in 1954, three years before Vickie was murdered, when Anthony, according to his wife, "committed sodomy with our family dog, Penny. Because of this, we absolutely did not speak for 3 weeks."

Matters grew even more upsetting after Vickie's murder. One

of Anthony's foul-mouthed tirades on the night of November 8, 1957, spurred Mary to move into their dead daughter's room. In her petition, Mary said that the "utter wretchedness and misery" of her situation could only worsen if she had to stay married. The divorce was granted in October 1959.

After the decree, Mary moved to Paterson, taking Myrna and Anthony Jr. with her. She got a job operating a punch press (a machine press that cut holes in material) at the Cleveland Container Corporation. But on June 29, 1960, Mary mangled her right hand in the press, resulting in the amputation of three fingers. Sometime after the accident, Mary and the younger children moved to Northern California. They were eventually joined by Mary Faye, the three children from her six-year marriage to George Self, which would end in divorce in 1964, and Mary Faye's second husband.

Anthony, meanwhile, remarried in 1960 and moved to Hasbrouck Heights with his second wife and stepson. "We were all pretty blue for a while," Anthony told the Bergen *Record* in 1977 about the dissolution of his first marriage. "And that's what broke us up." New Jersey, like many states, does not make divorce records public,* which may explain why Anthony's bland version of the breakup was printed uncontested.

———

IN PUBLIC PATRICIA Smith remained the picture of a loving, attentive wife as the 1950s ended and the 1960s began. If there was a local court hearing, she attended it, almost always with her mother-in-law. When the state supreme court turned down an-

---

* A copy of the divorce petition was included with the case material in William F. Buckley's archives.

other bid for a new trial, and when federal judge Mendon Morrill stepped in around Thanksgiving 1959 with another stay of execution, she kept the faith.

"He didn't kill her. He didn't kill [Vickie]. So why should I give up hope? He's innocent. I don't need to know anything more than that," she told the *Paterson Evening News* in early May 1959. Yet in that same interview, Patricia brought up the strangeness of being the wife of someone on death row. She said it was "as if this were all happening to someone else. As if I were reading about someone else in the papers or living another person's life. Crucially I find it difficult to believe." After Judge Morrill died in March 1961 and the assignment of the case to a new judge led to yet more delays, she kept up the mask of unwavering support.

She visited her husband once a month, as was permitted. She received his letters, which ranged from gushing to petulant, and accepted gestures such as the coded classified ad he posted in the *Record* for their fourth wedding anniversary: "DEAREST SMITTY—Love and gratitude for four happy years. EDDIE." Patti Ann turned two, then three and four and five. Patricia's dark-haired, green-eyed baby was a proper person now, who had questions about her daddy. Patricia wished she could answer them, but she found it impossible to explain to a small child that her father could be executed at any moment, tomorrow or years from now.

Those were especially difficult questions for Patricia because she existed in a state of limbo. She wasn't a widow, but she wasn't a wife. On top of that, her doubts about Eddie's innocence weren't going away. Divorce was an option, but it would take time and effort in early 1960s New Jersey. Still, she needed a proper father for her daughter, one who, after their marriage, could adopt Patti Ann and give her his name so that she wouldn't grow up known as the child of a convicted murderer on death row.

Eventually Patricia got involved with Gene Hafford, a businessman living in the nearby suburb of Midland Park. As to why Gene took up with Patricia, hindsight provides a simple answer: she was young and attractive. Given what he had done to his own life—busting up his own marriage in the spring of 1961 and leaving behind a baby daughter—he might also have genuinely loved Patricia. Loved her enough to spirit her away from Bergen County, from New Jersey, from the East Coast, and marry her in Reno, Nevada, on New Year's Day 1963, about half a year after Patricia's Reno divorce from Edgar was final.

Love, however, couldn't quite make up for the fact that Hafford was still married to his first wife, Arlene, when he married Patricia, which Patricia may have discovered only when Arlene finally sued for divorce in June 1963 on grounds of desertion. What Patricia thought about this is lost to time. She concentrated on the marriage, the two children she would have with Gene in their new home in Colorado, and raising Patti Ann away from the spotlight.

Patricia was determined never to speak about her daughter's birth father again to anyone. Especially not to an investigator living in the neighborhood who kept asking uncomfortable questions and tried to get her to sign some papers swearing that Edgar had been home on the night of Vickie Zielinski's murder. To him, she denied being the wife of Edgar Smith. Patricia wanted to shut the door on her past for good.

———

IN THE SUMMER OF 1962, Edgar witnessed the final goodbyes of two men who had been incarcerated at the Death House almost as long as he had. Fred Sturdivant was executed on July 3 for the murder of his four-year-old stepdaughter, while Joseph Ernst was sent to the electric chair on July 31 for the murder of his ex-girlfriend, Joan Connor. Edgar had been on death row longer than those two men, as well as the seven others who had joined him in the Death House since his conviction.

As was then the custom, inmates about to be executed were allowed to walk from cell to cell to say their goodbyes. When one of the condemned men stopped by Edgar's cell, he asked, "Is there anyone you want me to say hello to when I get down there?" The question stunned Edgar. How do you answer a question like that?

Edgar was in legal limbo. Robert Hicks and William Richter, the lawyers who'd represented him in federal court, no longer represented him because the money had run out. He had a new court-appointed lawyer, Stephen F. Lichtenstein, and the case had a new judge, which meant more delays. He also had to contend with the end of his marriage, which hadn't come as a huge surprise to him. He knew Patricia was seeing someone else, someone who could be there, in flesh and in spirit, for his daughter. But he wanted to have some say in the narrative. On September 6, he sent a statement to the Bergen *Record*, which the paper printed in full:

> I wish to announce that my wife and I were divorced in the State of Nevada on June 27, 1962, by mutual consent. The grounds for divorce were 3 years separation without cohabitation. Both Mrs. Smith and I believed a divorce at this time to be in the best interest of our daughter. Mrs. Smith assures me she still believes in my innocence and has every hope for my eventual vindication.
>
> For my part, I wish her all the luck in the world. I sincerely hope and pray that she and my daughter will find the happiness and security I failed to provide them. She was a fine wife and I have the deepest respect for the cour-

age she has shown these past 5 ½ years. I know she will continue to be a good mother to my daughter.

The new year brought more convicted men to the Death House, as well as the welcome distraction of television sets, three lined up in the corridor tuned to stations controlled by the guards. Most of the time the inmates wanted to watch shows such as *The Beverly Hillbillies* and *Gunsmoke*. Edgar liked sports, especially football. But after the football season ended, he requested that he be moved to a cell far away from the TVs. He had realized that he'd spent his years in the Death House existing, when he could have been living.

It looked like he wouldn't know whether he would live or die until well into 1964. In the fall of 1962, Edgar had decided it was time to get a college education. He wanted to turn his back on his old, shiftless self and strive for something greater. After "scoring brilliantly," per a prison official, on his high school equivalency exam, he began a correspondence course in accounting and business organization from Penn State.

He also obtained books and magazines through the prison library to slake his newfound thirst for reading. A certain prison chaplain was a devotee of a seven-year-old magazine that catered to those identifying as conservatives and passed on his copies to Edgar. When that chaplain was transferred from the Death House to Trenton State Prison proper, Edgar lost his access to *National Review*—a loss he felt keenly.[*]

Edgar's fondness for *NR* got back to the magazine's founder and editor, William F. Buckley—an affinity that would alter both men's lives in immeasurable ways.

---

[*] This is the version, more or less, that William F. Buckley repeated in various articles beginning in 1965. I was not able to confirm it fully.

PART III

THE CONSERVATIVE

(1962–1966)

10

A "Lifetime" Subscription

1962–1963

WHEN WILLIAM F. BUCKLEY, JR., became interested in the plight of
Edgar Smith in the fall of 1962, he wasn't yet the man synony-
mous throughout the world with the word *conservative*. Still in
the future were his campaign for mayor of New York City, his
television show *Firing Line*, his public (and legal) spats with Gore
Vidal, a level of celebrity that landed him regular appearances
on late-night television talk shows, impressions of his distinctive
mid-Atlantic accent by comedians, and his likeness on the cover
of *Time* magazine, and his relationships, some advisory, some adversarial, with presidents Richard Nixon, Gerald Ford, Ronald
Reagan, and both of the Bushes.

Also forthcoming was this 1980 assessment by the columnist
George Will: "All great Biblical stories begin with Genesis. And
before there was Ronald Reagan, there was Barry Goldwater,
and before there was Barry Goldwater there was *National Review*, and before there was *National Review* there was Bill Buckley with a spark in his mind, and the spark . . . has become a
conflagration."

Buckley, at thirty-six, was the present and future of the American conservative movement, and he knew it. *National Review*,

the magazine he had founded in 1955, was read avidly by those who were deeply discomfited by communism, liberalism, progressivism, and any other threat to what they believed made America great. Buckley had started the magazine on a wave of optimism several years after the surprise success of his debut book, *God and Man at Yale*, which excoriated his alma mater for its entrenched liberal ideas, and from the intervening time he spent as a CIA agent in Mexico and writing (with his friend, Yale debating partner, and brother-in-law L. Brent Bozell, Jr.) a boosterish book for disgraced senator Joseph McCarthy, *McCarthy and His Enemies: The Record and Its Meaning.*

Buckley was the right man at the right time to launch a movement. Other men—and it was almost exclusively men—had advocated for a distinctly American-flavored conservatism to counter the social programs created during the four-term Franklin Delano Roosevelt presidency: the New Deal and Social Security. But Buckley's relative youth, his erudite bearing, his idiosyncratic mannerisms, and his smile, deployed to win over the most skeptical of people, made his ideas—some of them downright repellent—seem palatable. His brilliance at debate, evident during his college days at Yale, perhaps indicated that he was more skilled at countering than advocating, at attacking rather than building a consistent argument, and at surface understanding rather than deeper thought. But he was the right man for the time.

That Buckley shone most when he could rebut someone else was no accident. He grew up learning how to do just that from his father, William F. Buckley, Sr. (always known as Will), a Texas oilman who had spent a number of years in Mexico. Will Buckley had helped fund and support the military dictatorship of José Victoriano Huerta Márquez, only to be kicked out of the country in 1921 after a new regime took over. Will taught all ten of his children—WFB Jr. was number six—that it was their duty to act as counterrevolutionaries to prevailing thought and that their best allies would always be one another. The Buckley children had one another's backs and almost never questioned their father's ideology. Rather, they upheld his ideology throughout his life—he died in 1958—and for many decades afterward.

The positive parts of the Will Buckley ideology were loyalty, duty, devotion to family, and an attitude of unhesitating kindness and generosity to their chosen ones. The negative parts were legion. Will passionately believed in laissez-faire capitalism, especially the idea that anyone intelligent and clever enough could rise to the top and free enterprise would take care of the rest. It was a faith he'd learned from his upbringing among southern Democrats in the late nineteenth century, but his faith in meritocracy excluded a wide swath of people.

Will Buckley was openly anti-Semitic and would rant about Jews being "interlopers within a Christian nation." The younger William held his father's vicious prejudice until he served in the Second World War, where it likely disappeared after his hearing accounts about the Nazi genocide of Jews and the US military's effort to liberate the death camps. In an interview with his first biographer, John Judis, Buckley compared himself to a "well-known figure" who had "once told me he would leave the room if ever someone in it said something about the Jews which he had heard routinely at his own dinner table. That exactly expresses the situation in my home."

Will also railed against Blacks, teaching his children that they, being White, were the superior race and that Blacks, being inferior, did not deserve the same rights and privileges. Will didn't care much for Indigenous people, or for Latin Americans of any country, though he was happy to do business in countries such as Mexico and Venezuela so long as they promoted US interests and money. The son took far, far longer to repudiate his father's racism than his anti-Semitism.

Less than two years into its existence, *National Review* stoked controversy with an unsigned—though Buckley-authored—August 1957 opinion piece titled "Why the South Must Prevail," which argued that Blacks were, in fact, an inferior race who should be denied the right to vote or at least prevented from doing so until they could "cast an enlightened and responsible vote." Though the magazine published rebuttals, even by its own staffers, Buckley defended his original column, shifting his point of view only slightly to argue that "uneducated" Blacks *and* Whites should not be able to vote.

William F. Buckley believed in his ideology with the fervor of a Catholic, which he also was. That Catholicism had marked him as an outsider growing up in the Buckley manse in Sharon, Connecticut, a status that tightened the web of loyalty among himself and his siblings. That web excluded nearly everyone else because, the Buckleys felt, they themselves had already been judged and excluded by the larger community. Will, fervent in his belief that his children would develop into superior beings, essentially homeschooled them, hiring Spanish and French teachers, music instructors, and experts in all manner of activities to tutor them, further setting them apart from their peers. William Jr.'s Catholicism propelled him to choose his Yale mentors with care, to attack authority figures he felt were anti-Catholic, and to worry that the United States would lose the Cold War against the Soviet Union, causing atheistic Communist ideas to propagate in the United States.

There were giant paradoxes at Buckley's core, though. His brilliance, even brutality, in debate covered up what his sister Patricia Bozell once described as a wall he had built "to protect himself" from cutting criticism. "Bill was always so sensitive as a child. . . . He would never show it on the outside and he would come out fighting, but he would be raw, and at night he'd say something. He'd show you that he'd been cut to the quick."

In his teens, Buckley had a reputation for being haughty, arrogant, and competitive, described by one of his childhood friends as a "Little Lord Fauntleroy type" who, because of his ability to put others down with a cutting remark, was feared and disliked by his classmates. Yet at the same time, adolescence was when he first developed a capacity for deep and abiding friendships. There was one consistent point about those friendships: ideology was *never* their basis. Buckley, in fact, actively disdained the idea that friends had to share the same views. If they did, that was wonderful, but if they did not, there were plenty of other reasons for affection and warmth between people.

"I don't think I had one single friendship that I could count an affectionate relationship until I met Bill," said the British historian Alistair Horne, who first encountered Buckley at Millbrook School, a boarding school across the state line in New York, which both attended in the early 1940s, when they were in their teens. Horne and Buckley began their relationship "outrightly hostile to each other," in part because Bill, parroting his father, did not believe that the United States should get involved in fighting the Nazis; Will Buckley was a committed America Firster, as were several of his children. Horne thought otherwise.

When the December 7, 1941, attack on Pearl Harbor made it clear that the United States would have to join the war effort, sixteen-year-old Buckley changed his tune and found that he and Horne had more in common than they had realized. "The outstanding thing about Bill, as I remember him at age sixteen or seventeen," said Horne, "was an unashamed ability to show affection and to *care* about his friends."

That ability, more than a decade after he died in 2008, was

what Buckley's friends and associates kept bringing up in interviews. He was kind to them. He was generous. He helped them out of dire financial straits, without hesitation and often without his name attached. Whereas almost all of the biographies and critical studies of Buckley have focused, correctly, on how his peculiar brew of counterrevolutionary ideology influenced American conservative thought from the mid-twentieth century onward, they have spent less time on Buckley the human and how his private actions influenced people on a personal level.

William F. Buckley, the ideologue, has to figure in the telling of his growing acquaintanceship with and advocacy for Edgar Smith. But it is Buckley, the person, who was most directly affected. He thought that Edgar was acting in the best possible faith, with the greatest of intentions, only to realize, too late, that he was doing no such thing at all.

———

IT BEGAN WITH a newspaper column by Edgar's former high school coach (and longtime pen pal) Robert Curley, published in the Ridgewood *Herald-News* on July 19, 1962. Curley described a day in the life of the Death House prisoner, the single hour in a given week when he was allowed out of the cell, and the reading material he had access to. Edgar enjoyed reading nonfiction and had just finished reading William L. Shirer's *The Rise and Fall of the Third Reich* over the course of five days. Edgar, who professed to be "an ardent Barry Goldwater fan," also, for a time, read *National Review*. A staffer at the magazine read Curley's article and flagged it for his boss's attention—which was how William F. Buckley learned of Edgar's existence.

Buckley wrote Edgar a letter in September 1962 expressing his thanks and offering to give the inmate a complimentary (or "lifetime") subscription to *National Review*. The letter was rejected by prison officials, who said that Buckley was not an "authorized correspondent." Edgar learned of the rejected letter from officials and asked his mother to tell Buckley to contact Edgar's attorney, Steve Lichtenstein. Buckley sent a telegram to the Death House—which would be read by officials first—on September 26 to let Edgar know he was in touch with both his mother and his lawyer. As a result, Buckley was finally allowed to correspond with Edgar on October 9.

Buckley sensed that Edgar's plight—and possible innocence—would be a good story, but felt that he didn't have the legal acumen to tell it himself. But the *National Review* staffer who had flagged the *Ridgewood Herald-News* article for Buckley to read did. Donald Coxe, then twenty-seven—a year younger than Edgar—had come to the magazine by way of Toronto, Canada, where he had attended law school.

Though Coxe did not give up his law license, he wanted to pursue a career as a writer. He had written freelance pieces for *National Review* while still living in Canada, and the magazine had offered him a staff job, for which Coxe and his wife ended up moving to New York. But even Coxe, with his legal bona fides, ran into difficulty arranging to visit Edgar.

Coxe's application to the New Jersey Superior Court to see Edgar in person at the Death House was denied by Judge O'Dea, who reportedly said he wouldn't permit "the Edgar Smith case to become another Caryl Chessman case." Chessman's plight was not only infamous at the time but fairly fresh in the mind of American state courts. A career criminal, the twenty-six-year-old Chessman had been convicted in California in 1948 on multiple counts of robbery, kidnapping, and rape and sentenced to death for those crimes.* His protestations of innocence found a large audience after he wrote and published a memoir, *Cell 2455, Death Row: A Condemned Man's Own Story*, in 1954, with the encouragement of the San Quentin prison warden, who told him he should do something with his life.

Cell 2455, Death Row became a best seller, inspired a film released the following year, and turned Chessman into a cause célèbre for those advocating for the abolition of the death penalty. Chessman published three more books—smuggled out of prison after the warden who'd encouraged him had a change of heart and banned him from writing, let alone publishing—but he did not evade the gas chamber. He was executed on May 2, 1960. At the time of his execution, he was the longest-serving inmate on death row and believed by many to be innocent.

There was no evidence yet that Edgar had any aptitude for writing, though he certainly protested his innocence in every available legal forum. Thoughts of Edgar's writing a book were far from anyone's mind, including his own.

———

EDGAR SMITH AND WILLIAM F. BUCKLEY corresponded with each other for the remainder of 1962. By this point Buckley had learned more of the particulars of the case and found himself in agreement with the doubts about the timeline established at the

---

* Capital cases for kidnapping and rape that did not lead to murder were unusual but not uncommon in the late 1940s thanks to loose interpretation of the 1932 Federal Kidnapping Act, colloquially known as the "Little Lindbergh Law," named for Charles Lindbergh, Jr., infamously kidnapped and murdered in 1932. In *United States v. Jackson* (1968), the Supreme Court ruled that kidnapping alone was not a capital offense, effectively repealing the Little Lindbergh Law, though too late for Chessman.

original 1957 trial and that had become grounds for subsequent appeals. But the story remained with Donald Coxe, who was writing to Smith separately and growing more convinced that, at minimum, Edgar deserved a new trial and that, perhaps, he was innocent of the murder of Victoria Zielinski. "These things move slowly," Buckley wrote Edgar on December 20, "but I hope the delays do not wear down your spirit, and that during this season especially you will be comforted by a close relationship with God."

Buckley wrote again on January 18, 1963. He told Smith that Coxe was still having trouble arranging an in-person interview as a reporter, but perhaps the prison warden might allow Coxe to visit as a legal professional:

> We will continue to bear down through the ACLU (with respect to any civil rights violations in possibly denying access to a lawyer.[sic.]) But legal maneuvers take a great deal of time, and it might be possible to cut through if only we can appeal to the sense of fairness of the Warden. He ought to know that National Review would not sensationalize the case, but rather advance the cause of justice to which he is, after all, presumably himself allied.

It worked. Coxe got his approval and journeyed down to Trenton State Prison to meet with Smith, under the usual conditions: Edgar in his eight-by-eight-foot cell, Coxe sitting in a chair in the Death House corridor, the two separated from each other by a mesh screen. The interview was brief. "He answered the questions quickly, and without any sort of doubt or hesitation," Coxe recalled. "I was waiting for him to think, 'Okay, now what is he looking for? Let me try to stay ahead'—because I'd seen that before." The interview confirmed Coxe's belief from his correspondence that Smith was "either a really brilliant fraud or he's innocent."

But Coxe couldn't finish the article because Edgar's case was, once more, in limbo. The Third Circuit Court of Appeals was supposed to decide whether Edgar had been coerced into giving his initial statement to police and should therefore receive a new trial, and the long delay meant that neither federal nor state courts could do much. That frustrated both Buckley, who was keen to publish, and Edgar, who was coming up on the sixth anniversary of his arrival at the Death House.

Six months earlier, on January 22, another man had been executed. Ralph Hudson had been convicted for the December 27, 1960, murder of his estranged wife, Myrtle, in an Atlantic City restaurant. He was supposed to be serving a six-month sentence for assaulting her and for making threats to the friends who were sheltering her. But he'd been let out early for Christmas, and at the earliest opportunity, he killed Myrtle. He hardly bothered with appeals. He ate a last meal of roast beef, smoked one final cigar, and kept his silence right up to the moment of his death.

Edgar's latest appeal to the federal courts was denied on July 24. He told Buckley that the 2–1 vote had actually given him some measure of hope since, Edgar wrote, "for the first time, a Judge saw things my way." Buckley agreed, as did Coxe. That lone dissent allowed for a small chance that the next appeal, to the US Supreme Court, could produce an outcome more favorable to Edgar. After studying the newest legal documents, Coxe finished a draft of his article and sent it to Buckley at the end of August.

Buckley, who was already leaning toward reasonable doubt, was even more persuaded by Coxe's solid, if plodding, journalism. The piece detailed the gruesome particulars of Victoria Zielinski's murder, Edgar Smith's trial and conviction, and the perceived holes in the case, zeroing in on the uncertainty about the time of death and Don Hommell's seemingly inconsistent behavior. Coxe raised enough questions that Buckley was pleased to print it in the October issue of *National Review*, and Edgar was even more pleased to read it when Buckley sent him the very first copy of the issue, hot off the press.

Coxe's piece* did not garner much national attention. Buckley continued to correspond with Smith, trying to puzzle out how he could remain apparently serene about his innocence, knowing that "someone else is guilty." Buckley expected that Edgar would rail at the injustice of his possible execution; by refusing to adhere to that well-worn narrative, though, Edgar became more interesting to him.

Edgar soon had another favor to ask of Buckley. He had learned that his ex-wife, Patricia, and their daughter, Patti Ann, had moved to Colorado and hoped that Patricia might be persuaded to sign a prepared affidavit attesting to his whereabouts on the night of March 4, 1957—a document he felt certain would help with his case. Could Buckley recommend a lawyer out there? Buckley passed on a name, which, to Edgar's amazement, was of someone "in the same town in which my former wife lives. . . . As a matter of fact, you only missed by a couple of streets."

Buckley began to be drawn in by Edgar's increasingly chatty letters. This long paragraph, written on October 21, was one of the first times Edgar spoke of anything other than his legal situation, and provides the first real glimpse of the writing ability that later captivated Buckley:

---

* The piece was one of Coxe's last as a staff writer at *National Review*. He and his wife soon returned to Canada, where they felt they could have a better, and more affordable, quality of life for themselves and their children.

Perhaps some Sunday afternoon the Hayden Planetarium [at the Museum of Natural History] could devote a special show to attempting to depict the various seasonal positions of the stars in the Liberal Galaxy. It would be, quite literally, a "moving" show. Of course, with the Hayden's Zeiss projector capable of showing some 9,000 stars, including those as dim as the sixth magnitude, it would be necessary to carefully check with the Sunday Morning Times for last minute adjustments. One can never be too sure in which part of the sky "Alpha Soapy" will appear at a given moment.

Edgar then piled on some more flattery in a November 18 missive: "I am very much thankful for the fact that since I have been in contact with *National Review* I have been quite fortunate to become acquainted with some very nice people. I wonder if *New Republic* would have been as good to, or for, me." The sweet-talking worked, and then some.

11

"My God, I Wish I Could Be Absolutely Certain"

1964

BY 1964, William F. Buckley was fully committed to the cause of freeing Edgar Smith from death row. Edgar's descriptions of his life in the Death House and the constant confinement of the prisoners in their cells astonished him. "I am staggered by the inhumanity of the arrangements which prevent you from taking exercise," Buckley wrote on March 25. Smith downplayed the disadvantages in his reply the next day: "It isn't all bad, I walk a lot . . . like the 'pussy-cats' in the zoo."

Buckley's outrage at the treatment of death row prisoners spurred him to offer Edgar a chance to write about capital punishment for *National Review*, at the "regular fee" of $50 per printed page. Edgar was, naturally, surprised and pleased by the idea. "While I do have definite views on the subject of Capital Punishment, I wonder if I could express them as well as I would like to be able to do," he wrote on June 24. "Any statement I might choose to prepare would be a statement based on my personal convictions, it would make no difference if money were involved."

Buckley had become more invested in the case, including setting up the basis of a legal defense fund, as Edgar's appeals kept going nowhere. Edgar's second attempt to sway the Supreme Court in his favor was denied on February 17, 1964. The expense of this new round of appeals, and the new angles of argument that would be necessary to begin again in Judge O'Dea's Bergen County courtroom, meant that Steve Lichtenstein could no longer afford to work the case. Lichtenstein's replacement would continue to focus on Edgar's lengthy police interrogation and whether his rights had been violated.

In March, the court appointed Stephen Toth to represent Edgar. Their first meeting, Edgar confided to Buckley, "left me with a bad taste in my mouth." Toth seemed confident he could prepare for a habeas corpus hearing on April 17, despite having a mere two or three weeks to "familiarize himself with the case, research the appeal, and plan his argument. To top it all off he isn't even asking for more time. I smell a rodent!! His long association with the State leaves me wondering if maybe that association hasn't become a habit." Edgar tried to have Toth removed as counsel more than once, to no avail.

The habeas hearing took place as planned on April 17. As expected, Judge O'Dea denied Edgar the right to a new trial and affirmed the execution date he'd set in March. Even after the motion was denied, Toth resisted being removed as Edgar's lawyer. "Can you imagine a lawyer saying he would not be dismissed?" Edgar wrote Buckley on May 10. "It all adds to the 'aroma' I detected when he was appointed."

Edgar was even more upset with his new lawyer because the case at the center of a recent US Supreme Court hearing bore striking parallels to his own. *Escobedo v. Illinois* was being argued as to whether criminal suspects did, in fact, have a right to counsel during police interrogations as a Sixth Amendment right. That case had grown out of a 1960 murder after which the victim's brother-in-law, Danny Escobedo, had been interrogated for more than fourteen hours without an attorney present—despite repeated requests—and implicated himself in the murder. The Court would ultimately rule in Escobedo's favor.

Since Edgar hadn't been allowed access to a lawyer during his own interrogation, he saw a chance, however small, that the highest court might hear his own case, too. Toth clung on until July, when the New Jersey Supreme Court upheld Edgar's conviction again, after which there was no more use for Toth. Edgar would go forward on his own until the legal defense fund raised enough money to rehire Steve Lichtenstein.

News that Buckley called the "first really important break" had emerged the month before. Donald Hommell, who'd had his tryout but never ended up playing professional baseball and was now married with two small children, had worked as a guard in a juvenile reformatory in Delaware between July and September of 1963. After several inmates complained of physical abuse and the ACLU took up the story as a civil rights violation, a warrant was issued for Hommell's arrest. Hommell left the state for his onetime hometown of Vero Beach, Florida, and fought extradition for months but eventually turned himself in.

"Being entirely realistic about things, I would suppose that the only real value to me of Hommell's difficulties would be if a new trial were granted," Edgar wrote to Buckley on June 14, "then I could very well raise hell on the question of [his] credibility as a witness for the prosecution." Buckley also admitted that at that point Hommell's troubles were more interesting than useful.

Edgar's newest appeal to the New Jersey Supreme Court was denied over the summer, which left the door open to his being executed. "It is even more abrupt than I had expected it to be," he wrote Buckley on July 13. "I have, in the past, been willing to accept the various Court decisions with a reasonable degree of equanimity; this time I find I am rather unhappy. However what is done is done." Buckley was impressed with Edgar's imperturbability about the state of things; Edgar, in response, kidded Buckley about using such a specific word as "imperturbability": "Only a guy with a secretary to do all the work would use a word like THAT!"

In August, though, another stay of execution came through, entirely as a result of Edgar's own legal maneuvering. Buckley was thrilled with the news and also complimented Edgar as a "superb auto-dactic [sic]." But his praise was tempered by feelings he expressed in the close of his August 18 letter: "My God, I wish I could be absolutely certain you hadn't [written as "haven't" in the letter, then struck through] killed that girl."

Edgar replied two days later, with two paragraphs addressing Buckley's anguished question:

> *My God, I wish you* could *be absolutely certain I didn't kill that girl, but you know what they say about "death and taxes." I think, for now, that I am satisfied that you* aren't *certain that I* did *kill her. Besides, do you really think it would do any good for me to tell you I didn't? Would that convince you? Disclaimers of guilt are a dime a dozen around this place.*
>
> *From an idealistic point of view, if you are uncertain about my innocence, it follows that you must be uncertain about my guilt, as well, and I am entitled to the full benefit of your doubt. Where is your conservative belief in established judicial principles?*

Edgar responded more sharply to Buckley's continued expressions of admiration for his apparent "serenity" in his seventh year on death row. "I am, quite frankly, somewhat disturbed by your very apparent misapprehensions as to my state of mind," he wrote on September 12. "Your references to my serenity, imperturbability, etc.; impute that I am some Buddha-like anachronism, fast approaching Nirvana. Tell me—does the fact that I am in the Death House mean to you that I should be perpetually atop a soap-box, shouting my protestations to a cold, cruel, unhearing world."

Then Edgar, for the first time, addressed William F. Buckley as a "friend" (even though he did not switch from addressing him as "Mr. Buckley" to "Bill" for quite some time):

> *I assure you, my friend, if I thought soap-box oratory would serve me any good purpose, I would climb onto the closest box handy, and put George Wallace to shame. The fact is that what you mistake for serenity, or an air of detachment, is nothing more or less than the realization on my part of the fact that my situation is not going to be improved by breast-beating and lamentations, however loud or sustained—it can only be changed by and in a court of law.*

Perhaps, Edgar mused, his letters "should be appropriately tear-stained when they arrive at your office, giving them a more pathetically desperate quality. . . . Take my word for it—I feel quite deeply about my plight, but getting emotional isn't going to solve anything. Such are the facts of life!"

In his response, Buckley clarified his meaning:

> *I admire your facing up to the facts of life. Obviously you are under incomparable emotional strain. You apparently have reflected on the fact that many people who are under such stress are incompetent to handle reality, and under the circumstances cannot observe anything going on in life other than themselves*

and their own hurt. This is what you have managed, and this is something you have every right to be proud of.

Communication slowed between the two men over the fall of 1964. Edgar was preparing his latest petition to the US Supreme Court. Buckley was traveling at his usual frenetic clip, including to Chicago, where he debated the lawyer Melvin Belli on capital punishment—Belli against, Buckley in favor. ("Inconclusive," he wrote Edgar on October 21.) Barry Goldwater's presidential bid failed in November, and Lyndon Johnson was elected president, a blow for Buckley, who had used *National Review* as a platform to mobilize and support the Goldwater campaign.

Yet their friendship had become established enough that Edgar finally felt comfortable addressing Buckley by his first name. "I hadn't intended to," Edgar wrote on October 22, "but I'm in a hurry to make tonight's mail, and I'll be damned if I'll start this letter again." He also sent Buckley the petition he'd prepared. Buckley, after reading it, sent words of praise on November 3: "When you are retried and exonerated, you will no doubt make a handsome living as a lawyer." In his reply, Edgar laughed off the suggestion of the law: "If the opportunity presented itself, I'd prefer to get a commercial-instrument ticket, and do some corporate flying."

Edgar filed his Supreme Court brief around Thanksgiving. There was nothing to do but wait and keep writing Buckley. The New Jersey prosecutor, Guy Calissi, had thirty days to reply but faced a setback: his appeals expert—as Edgar admitted, "the only person who ever worked on my appeals—he was acknowledged as one of the best in the country"—died suddenly, and his replacement needed extra time, ultimately granted by the Court, to study the details of Edgar's case. Buckley took the news with dark humor, writing on November 30, "Since people have to die,

I guess it's not profane to be glad that in this case it had to be the gentleman who was so successful at persuading the courts that you should predecease him."

Buckley was later touched by a gift Edgar sent him for the holidays, a Metropolitan Museum of Art calendar. "I would have liked to have done more," wrote Edgar in response on December 18, "but circumstances made it impossible. Perhaps I'll remember you in my will, and leave you my collection of *National Geographic* maps." Buckley took the kidding response and raised it on December 22: "Thank you for promising to remember me in your will. Since I am ten years older than you [actually eight] and engage in activities far more perilous than yours, with perhaps a single exception, I should think it highly unlikely that I shall reap any such harvest."

The more serious matter was whether Buckley would, finally, be allowed to visit. Edgar had told the court that he needed to see Buckley because the other man would be hiring lawyers to help his case. Even though the Trenton State Prison warden emphatically opposed the request, Judge O'Dea granted it on January 29, 1965. Seven weeks later, Buckley was in a Trenton-bound car, preparing to meet his longtime correspondent—and now friend—for the very first time. The dungeons would be thrown open for his inspection. But who would be inspecting whom?

12

Meeting in Trenton

MARCH–OCTOBER 1965

WILLIAM F. BUCKLEY arrived at the Death House on March 19, 1965, with much on his mind. He had returned home after a more fraught edition of his annual trip to Switzerland, where he'd thrown out the prior year's work, thirty thousand words' worth, on a book that was supposed to be his magnum opus on conservative thought. Then his wife, Pat, had broken her leg, requiring them to cut the trip short so she could recuperate in New York. He had canceled all but one of his public speaking engagements, a February 18 debate with the writer James Baldwin at Cambridge University on whether the American Dream was at the expense of Black Americans, a debate that he—and the audience—felt he'd lost but that would become an instant classic, remembered decades after the fact.

What occupied Buckley's mind during the trip to Trenton was what he and Edgar Smith would be allowed to discuss during the visit. He'd received a letter from Edgar saying that the New Jersey deputy attorney general had interpreted the court order to mean that the two men would be forbidden to discuss whether or not Edgar had killed Vickie. Considering that a new execution date of April 27 had been set just three days before the visit, not being able to discuss the murder would be a problem for both men. Edgar suggested taking it up with Judge O'Dea in court, but Buckley decided to go to Trenton anyway.

When he got there at 1:00 p.m., his driver circled the "squat red-stone" prison in his borrowed Cadillac—Buckley's usual vehicle, a Triumph, had just broken down—looking for what Buckley later described as "the tiny doorway through which prisoners are unwelcome." He had to have been struck by the incongruity of his situation. He, William F. Buckley, Jr., the leader of American conservative thought, son of the elite, recently returned from Switzerland, about to visit the self-educated Edgar Smith, convicted murderer, man of the working class.[*]

Granted entrance through the tiny doorway, Buckley was taken to see the assistant warden, Arthur Edmonds, who asked Buckley if he knew of the restrictions imposed by the deputy attorney general.

"I do," replied Buckley.

"Would you please wait a few moments to meet Warden Yeager first before going in to see Mr. Smith?"

Buckley agreed, and while they waited on the warden, he engaged Edmonds in conversation. He asked when the last execution had taken place. Edmonds replied that it had been in January 1963—which was when Edgar's Heath House cellmate Ralph Hudson had gone to the electric chair.

"When was the first?"

"At the turn of the century."

"How many men had died in that chair?"

---

[*] "Man of the working class" reflected Buckley's perspective; it is far more plausible that Edgar Smith belonged to the middle class, since his family could afford to send him (however briefly) to private school and to pay several lawyers.

"One hundred sixty." Fourteen men presently waited for execution in the Death House.

Buckley's final question for the assistant warden was to ask where Bruno Hauptmann, the convicted kidnapper and killer of Charles Lindbergh's son, had stayed.

"The cell directly above Smith's."

Then Howard Yeager, the warden, stepped into the office. Buckley described him as "a big man, tough, duty-minded, but nonetheless friendly." After they exchanged formalities, another official took Buckley to a private room to be frisked.

"Empty your pockets," said the official.

Buckley did so. But when the official moved a metal-detecting wand from his head to his chest, an "angry and sustained beep" sounded. He asked Buckley to examine his breast pocket. "Out came a Scripto pencil, with the little offending aluminum catch. The search went on. Twice more the Frisker (pat. pend., I noticed) caught me *in flagrante*, but finally it reached my shoes, and finding there not a file nor even a razor."

Buckley next met with Captain Malkin, the prison official entrusted to take him to Edgar Smith's cell. Here's how Buckley described what transpired:

> We moved to a great partition, and a turnkey opened the door. We stepped into a circular, silo-like structure, from which two corridors went out, where the regular prisoners were quartered. It is completely enclosed and high above it, surrounded by bulletproof glass, is the central communications center of the prison. From there an official will confirm, or deny, an escort's instructions to the turnkeys, who communicate with the center by walkie-talkie. The central command had to be consulted before we were let

out of the silo, at the opposite end from which we had entered it, out onto the open compound, to walk a hundred fifty yards to the small, isolated, windowless fort-within-a-fort, where the condemned go before stepping conveniently into the far end of the same building, to sit down in the electric chair.

Again, radio control confirmed Captain Malkin's instructions to open the door, and it creaked open, admitting a ray of daylight for the briefest moment, visible to the first three or four of the doubledecker cells. Naked light bulbs hung overhead, and three television sets were blaring in the corridor, one for three prisoners, programs by majority vote, stations tuned in by the guards. I was led to the very end of the corridor, to within a few feet of the electric chair, from which I was separated by a metal door.

There in his cell, on Buckley's right, was Edgar Smith.

Buckley couldn't see the other man very well through the steel mesh screen. "I found myself wondering why it was necessary to exercise the Frisker on me. It was all I could do to see Smith. I could not have passed him a needle, even assuming Captain Malkin had nodded."

He could, however, hear Edgar speak. For the next hour, that's what the convict did. It was the voice, Buckley wrote, of someone who "betrayed a background of football lockers and poolrooms and beer taverns, faintly coarse, utterly inconsistent with his writing style, which is Victorian to the point of prudery. ('*Damn!*' he wrote on hearing my wife had broken her leg a few weeks earlier. '*What bad luck!*')" What he didn't realize was that Edgar put on the "prudery" for Buckley's sake and that it did not reflect his actual personality.

For the first half hour Edgar barraged Buckley with "an almost forbiddingly technical analysis of his legal situation" that Buckley struggled to comprehend. Suddenly, Buckley got it: Edgar was doing everything in his legal power to stay alive and to get his conviction overturned so that he could get a fair trial. He was impressed with Edgar's grasp of the law, describing him as "resourceful and ingenious."

As Captain Malkin started to lead Buckley down the corridor at the end of the hour-long visit, he stopped to talk with a guard, leaving Buckley standing next to the cell of another death row inmate, one far older than Edgar Smith.

"Hello, Mr. Buckley."

Buckley was surprised at being addressed by name, but he later learned that all the prisoners knew the names of every visitor to the Death House, since so few people visited.

"Hello," Buckley replied, but had no idea where to go from there. He could not ask the other man whom he killed. That would be deeply inappropriate. But the idea of discussing the weather, current events, or any other topic seemed absurd. He and the inmate managed only to exchange nervous smiles before Captain Malkin rejoined Buckley and led him away.

When Buckley stopped to say goodbye to Warden Yeager, he found himself making one last chatty observation. "Smith seems quite confident he'll leave here one of these days."

"Well, that's a safe prediction," the warden said, chuckling. "He'll leave here one way or another."

———

EDGAR WROTE BUCKLEY later that afternoon, "Before anything else, please let me apologize for failing to thank you for taking the time to visit me. It seems that this environment has wreaked as much havoc with my manners as with my diction." He worried that Buckley had been confused by the visit, given the supposed limitations of their discussion, but "at least you know now that there really is an Edgar Smith."

The levity in Edgar's letter belied his concern about the looming execution date of April 28, the timing seeming to coincide with the newest notice of appeal. The pressure began to mount again. "I do wish our visit could have been longer. . . . Perhaps someday we will be able to sit down and have a long talk, without worrying about any regulations. How about adopting me? You could then be on my regular family visiting list. . . . THAT would go over big with Judge O'Dea!"

Judge O'Dea, however, denied Edgar's latest bid for a new trial. Then the New Jersey Supreme Court turned away Edgar's already pending request for a stay and his leave for appeal on April 13. With both state and federal appeal avenues closing off again, his next option, repeating the same sequence as in 1958, was to go back to the US Supreme Court and ask Justice Brennan to issue another stay, which he did on April 17. Edgar learned the news from his mother. "It was my pleasure to tell him," Ann Chupak told Buckley afterward. "He did not believe it was true until it came on the noon news."

Granting the stay on Good Friday, Edgar wrote Buckley, "is in itself singularly appropriate. I will now sit back and bide my time until the end of the term, the 21st of June." Edgar described further filings and decisions that would have to happen that would extend his life and keep him on death row, opting for dissonant bonhomie: "all of which means you can leap aboard your boat, head for Nassau and the Out Islands and forget about 'young' Smith for the next six months."

Then part of his habitual mask dissolved. "Frankly, my friend, things were a bit close for a while; I had the suspicion I was lacking a sticky wicket. You can bet your best ski boots that the State isn't going to throw any parties for Justice Brennan this month. [I've] gotten to be a burr under the judicial saddle."

Buckley was preparing for another weeklong speaking trip and took a few days to respond."I am . . . of course, infinitely relieved that you got the postponement," he wrote on April 27. "You handled that very well, I should say. And you must let me know now what you plan to do in October, given the various alternative reactions of the Supreme Court at that time. Which of them do you believe most likely?" Edgar wasn't sure what to expect, he wrote back: "Earl Warren has formed the habit of saving the real controversial decisions until last. Maybe so they can skip town . . . leaving everyone in a daze."

By May 13, Buckley had returned to the *National Review* offices, and he wrote to Edgar the following week. He closed that letter with a surprising statement: "Keep writing. Strangely, your letters cheer me up."

The pace of his own correspondence to Edgar slowed, though, because Buckley had decided to run for mayor of New York as the Conservative Party candidate. Though the campaign was a lark—Buckley famously quipped during a press conference that if he won, he would demand a recount—he had more serious opinions about the criminal justice system, namely that he opposed the establishment of civilian review boards to investigate allegations of police brutality. Buckley believed that New Yorkers were under more threat from rising crime than from the police. He won just 13.4 percent of the vote, but his campaign made him a national figure in a way that nothing had before.

But he hadn't forgotten Edgar. In fact, he had decided to write an article for *Esquire* about Edgar's case, and their epistolary friendship, for the magazine's November issue—and use the fee to further the already existing legal defense fund. He was also in more regular touch with Stephen Lichtenstein, whom he had recently hired to represent Edgar again. Ironically, Buckley was too busy working on Edgar's case to write the man at any great length.

"I was totally flabbergasted when he told me that you had made arrangements for him to represent me," Edgar wrote Buckley on July 21, after Lichtenstein visited the Death House to give Edgar the news.

> *I had hoped that you might find some way to help me out, but you have really caught me unprepared and at a loss for words—a rare event, indeed. Of course, I am extremely grateful, as I am certain my family will be when they learn of it. But now, with the worrisome question of legal representation out of the way, I am faced with the even greater problem of how I am ever going to repay you. If I should get out of this pest-hole—and I have high hopes that I will—I may spend the remainder of my days sweeping the floors at* National Review.

Edgar wrote again on August 1, expounding at length about the way police brutality undermines law and order—a rare instance when he didn't impress his friend. "For the very first time, I must own I found your comments a wee bit platitudinous," Buckley responded four days later. "Because what you have to say is on everyone's tongue. What you don't have anything to say about is the dilemma of our time, namely, what to do about the evanescing rights of people *not* to get killed, *not* to get raped, *not* to get robbed."

Much to the annoyance of Buckley and Edgar, Judge O'Dea

denied a request for a second visit to the Death House, since the discussion of legal funding could now be handled through Lichtenstein, Edgar's rehired lawyer. Both men were aware that the judge would become even less accommodating in the coming months, once Buckley's *Esquire* article was published.

13

Waiting for Death

NOVEMBER 1965–DECEMBER 1966

THE *ESQUIRE* ISSUE containing Buckley's article, "The Approaching End of Edgar H. Smith, Jr.," appeared on newsstands on October 19, 1965. The advance publicity, the seeming incongruity of law-and-order William F. Buckley advocating for the innocence of a man on death row, and the extensive quotations from Edgar Smith's letters made the piece an immediate sensation.

Reactions to Buckley's piece ranged from praise to scorn. What did not seem to garner much notice, let alone criticism, was his description of Victoria Zielinski, referring to her in the article as "flirtatious" without any supporting evidence—suggesting that he took Edgar Smith at his word. (A decade and a half later, Buckley would write of Vickie as a "nubile teenager.") He also referred to another matter that had not been made public during the original trial in 1957: nine years earlier, a young girl had gone to the police after a violent encounter with Edgar. Buckley characterized her as having "a querulous record," again without citing anything to back up the assertion.

The most specific and pointed critique of Buckley's article actually came from the subject himself, in an at times rambling letter dated October 22, 1965, three days after the issue hit newsstands. Edgar wanted to convey, "as they pop into my head, some of my impressions." He warned Buckley not to take every- thing he wrote at face value: "My idea of humor is a bit strange and some of the quotations you used did not mean exactly what they seemed to mean."

He took issue with Buckley's characterizing his prose as "Vic- torian" or "prudish": "*That* is something I've never been accused of before." And he joked about being defamed: "I've spent less time in poolrooms than you have, and more time in expensive cocktail lounges I couldn't really afford than in beer parlors I could afford. Matter of fact, I thoroughly dislike beer. Your basic premise is, however, quite correct: I do speak *terribly*, but this is very much the result of the past eight years. I concede I'm not a Bill Buckley."

Edgar also chided Buckley for falling "into the same trap so many others have when you quoted 'midnight, give or take an hour'" with respect to Victoria Zielinski's approximate time of death. Edgar's lawyer, John Selser, was the one who had fixed on midnight as the time of the murder. The doctor, Raphael Gilady, had testified to saying "about twelve hours . . . give or take an hour." Since Vickie's autopsy took place at 1:00 p.m. on the fifth, Edgar argued that the girl had to have been killed even later than what was supposed, because of one other matter that the coroner had testified to: that rigor mortis sets in more quickly in freezing weather.

Edgar also argued with Buckley about the blood saturation of Vickie's bra. In his mind, this saturation meant "it could not have been around her waist before she was seriously injured, be- cause the tops of her dungarees and her panties were spotless." He offered his own theory as to what had happened: "I think she was killed and dragged feet first up the dirt mound, causing her sweater to slide up ('feet first' because there was no sand or dirt under the waistband of her pants. [*sic*]) At the top of the mound, the killer grabbed her bra to pull her over the top, and the bra tore loose. This accounts for the bloodstain between the cups, right where he would grab. Sound more reasonable?" If Buckley responded to that theory, which seemed to incriminate Edgar as much as anything else, it is lost to history.

Buckley did wonder why, at this point, Edgar was not pressing harder to win further reprieves from execution and, ideally, earn a new trial. Edgar, replying on November 4, explained that in New Jersey, the burden of proof on the defendant is so high that any new evidence he and his lawyers want to introduce has to lead to a *probable*, not a possible, likelihood of a different outcome. He wrote, "I've had my chance to argue my point of view; the courts aren't going to allow me to keep on arguing and re-arguing until I find the right combination. The fact is, Bill, I believe I could reargue my case in such a way as to get a different verdict, but the courts are not about to give me a new trial just to find out if I'm right."

Edgar did seem to understand that his nitpicking of the legal issues might put off the friend who had just argued his innocence in a prominent magazine. "Sometimes you give me the impression that you think I'm trying to avoid a discussion of the facts," he wrote, "which isn't true. I just don't want people running hither and yon, spending money and getting their hopes up over nothing more than someone's pet theory, which up till now hasn't an iota of evidence to support it." That was why he never professed enthusiasm for one of private detective Andy Nicol's more out-there theories: that Vickie's father, Anthony, might have had some involvement in an older unsolved murder near Honesdale, Pennsylvania:

> *Even if there was a murder over there, and Nicol's suspect is the one who committed it, so what? It doesn't prove that a) the*

same person is guilty here, or b) that Smith isn't guilty. The
best it would do is prove that Nicol's suspect is a bad character
who can't be believed, but his testimony isn't an important
part of the State's case—it could be thrown out in its entirety
and not be missed. Comprende?

Buckley responded to Edgar's long missives with more kindness than they deserved. "I have always been interested in the
sort of ennui you seem to have respecting the facts of the murder, in contrast with your vivid and contagious interest in matters of law," he wrote on October 27. He also made a prediction
that would prove astonishingly prescient: "You will get out of the
death house as the result of your knowledge of the law, not as the
result of your knowledge of the murderer."

Buckley could nitpick as well as the death row inmate. "You
are oversensitive, my friend. In the first place, I didn't say you
spoke 'terribly,' though I'd have said exactly that if indeed it were
true you did speak that way. I was making a purely sociological
observation." The same went for whether Buckley had called
Edgar "Victorian" and "prudish"—only the writing, not the man,
he insisted, and said that this was a good thing: "Don't, for heav-
en's sake, work to change it."

Buckley ended his letter on a note that betrayed his deep worries over Edgar's plight: "I hope the appearance of the article
has not hurt you in the penitentiary. I don't mean to be cynical,
since I suppose there is nothing that can make life worse for you
in the penitentiary. But sometimes the inflections of the guards,
or the personnel in charge there, can mean a great deal, I'm sure.
And it is in this respect I hope you have not been hurt."

Edgar assured Bill he was fine, he appreciated the concern,
and he hoped he wasn't taking their relationship too much for
granted. He also wished Buckley luck in the mayoral election: "I

have a feeling you will top 400,000 [votes]—which should fur-
row some brows." Buckley's attention, however, had shifted away
from the election, which he knew he would lose, to the sudden
death of his father-in-law, which necessitated a trip to Vancouver,
British Columbia, for the man's funeral. Upon his return, he had
a letter from Edgar, dated November 9, which included a cat-
egorical assertion: "Now, since everyone seems to attach a great
deal of importance to it, I will state here and now that I, Edgar
Smith, did *not* kill Victoria Zielinski. And if anyone wants that
statement under oath, it can be found in the transcript of my trial
testimony."

Buckley did not need that assurance. He now believed in Edgar's innocence to the fullest extent. So, too, did many who
read the *Esquire* article. Contributions to the Edgar Smith Fund,
at the address listed at the close of Buckley's piece, had poured
in. By year's end, more than six thousand dollars had come in:
$1,500 from the *Esquire* fee, the rest from outside donations.

———

BUCKLEY HAD ALSO devoted one of his On the Right columns to
Smith. "A Lonely Man Waits for Death," which appeared in
newspapers on November 9, 1965, reiterated most of the points
of the *Esquire* piece—which Buckley urged people to read—but
in a way that feels more stark and emotionally resonant than the
longer magazine article:

> Edgar Smith went to the Death House not far removed from
> the wasteful class of humanity, a young man clearly derac-
> inated; bored and boring. He emerges as a profoundly in-
> teresting human being, brilliantly self-educated, balanced,
> witty, cool beyond the point a battery of psychoanalysts

could have achieved working on the most plastic personality. The Death House is commonly thought of as a dehumanizing institution and it mostly is that. But it brought out in Edgar Smith a most extraordinary man who may not succeed in triumphing over the chair, but has clearly triumphed over himself.

Buckley also mentioned the case in television appearances and at *National Review*'s annual dinner on November 11, where two special guests were in attendance: Edgar's mother, Ann, and his brother, Richard. "She is happy to have finally met the man behind the voice on the telephone," Edgar wrote Bill three days later. Ann also met Barry Goldwater prior to the dinner, and "she made sure he didn't get away without a brief conversation."

Two weeks after the column ran, Buckley received an unexpected gift: Judge O'Dea had decided to approve a second visit to see Edgar after all, so long as they limited discussion to financial arrangements for legal assistance. The Death House would set the terms and conditions of the visit, including the exact date and level of supervision.

Buckley was confused by the news, because he heard it secondhand from people who had heard it on the radio. He hadn't known that Judge O'Dea held a hearing to approve the visit for which he was supposed to be present. But once his confusion dissipated, he was thrilled. "It seems at this point to be a clear victory for your ingenious brief," he wrote Edgar on November 23. The next visit was scheduled for December 30, after Buckley's ten-day lecture tour and the Christmas holidays.

Their second visit together was more relaxed and more effusive, going far better than the first, which had left Buckley off balance. That visit, which capped a rather eventful year for both men, also cemented their bond. Or at least that was what Buckley believed—and what Edgar took great pains to make sure that Buckley believed.

———

"GUESS WHAT? I believe I have finally convinced myself that I am capable of writing a book," Edgar wrote to Buckley on April 2, 1966. Waiting a day to write the letter meant it was no April Fool's joke. The year to date had been mostly quiet. All of death row seemed to be waiting for the US Supreme Court to rule on *Miranda v. Arizona*, which would decide whether statements given by suspects who were never informed of their constitutional rights prior to being interrogated can be admissible in court.[*]

Edgar had also heard rumors that he and his fellow prisoners would be moved out of the old Death House into a different unit within Trenton State Prison. "There is only one empty cell left in this place, so one of the wings in the prison is supposed to be converted for us since it has many more cells," he explained to Buckley. "It's just off to the left as you come through the inside, double doors. Remember? With inmates doing the conversion work, capital punishment might be ancient history by the time the job is done. I don't know what they will do about having the Death House in one place and the 'chair' in another. Maybe they will buy a helluva long extension cord! Whatever the method, I'm sure the State will work out some tidy 'Final Solution.'"

While waiting on a big move and a potentially monumental Supreme Court decision, why not take his self-taught skills as a legal writer further and fashion something more creative?

———

[*] *Miranda v. Arizona*, decided on June 13, 1966, ruled that suspects were protected by the Fifth Amendment specifically against self-recrimination. It would profoundly change policing in the United States.

"I know that might NOT sound like a big deal to you, but I've never before thought I could get past the first page, or even the first line. Now, however, after much examination, I've got a pretty good mental picture of two books, and eventually I am going to take a crack at one or both," he wrote. One would be about his case. The other on why capital punishment was no deterrent and prison reform was a must. Both would be in longhand, because death row prisoners were refused access to typewriters.

"Eventually" was the key term here. First and foremost, Edgar lacked an ending, which only time could supply. Then there was the lack of research facilities inside the Death House. Books were severely restricted. Edgar wasn't able to contact librarians or archivists since they weren't on his approved correspondents list. Waiting made him most impatient. When news came in, even when it wasn't in his favor, he tried to find some sliver of hope. But it became more difficult.

"I could probably get away with using this beastly weather as an excuse, but the fact is that I've been sitting here feeling sorry for myself—a luxury in which I don't often indulge," he admitted in a letter to Buckley on July 7, explaining a weeks-long silence. "I only wanted to let you know that I'm still here, and that I haven't been secretly assassinated—or worse?"

Buckley, who had just returned from a "blissful" summer cruise aboard his sailboat, the *Suzy Wong*, had himself been busy with the launch of *Firing Line*, his new weekly television interview show. He was pained by Edgar's pathos and felt compelled to ask what he characterized as an odd question: "Do I know you well enough to ask whether it has occurred to you to pray for your deliverance?"

He had hoped to cheer Edgar up, but it had the opposite effect. "The years are beginning to catch up to me, and *that* I can't shrug off as just one of those things," wrote Edgar. "Then too,

I am apparently going to have to waste a year, at least, asking the Third Circuit for the right to be heard on the merits of my appeal—a right already mine. That is what really burns me up; I'd rather have a judge give me a completely prejudiced and erroneous refusal on the merits than to have my appeal dismissed without hearing by a chicken-hearted clod who hasn't the guts to make his own decisions."

Buckley also updated Edgar on the defense fund coffers— $6,500 went to the lawyers, which left very little—and wondered if Edgar might write Judge O'Dea again to allow more in-person visits, "in company with Steve [Lichtenstein], with the understanding that I may have to see you from time to time without Steve. The benefit of this arrangement is that if I should need to see you instantly, the visit could be effected without time-consuming folderol. If I need to see you in private, we'll have to go through the motions. Is this feasible?"

Edgar said he would try. But he had ventured further into the maw of the depressive state that had gripped him all summer long. "I am becoming resigned to the fact that I have about as much of a chance as a snowball in hell" of being freed from prison, he wrote. And even if he *was* freed from the Death House, what would he do with himself?

Buckley had never seen such a despondent letter from his friend. "You depress me," he wrote back on September 8. "It is hard to urge you from the outside, to continue to hope. But you must do so, and regain confidence that one day, and perhaps not too far distant, you will be free and vindicated." Buckley said he had put in a word with his congressman in Connecticut, Donald J. Irwin. He wanted to call Lichtenstein again. Edgar gave a noncommittal answer, instead suggesting that Buckley nudge the lawyer about future visits: "I depress you? You may be certain that I don't depress *you* half as much as I depress *myself*. Like most people, I'm my own worst enemy. I'm a born pessimist and a cynic."

The bulk of their correspondence was cordial, even affection-ate in parts. But every now and then the two men would argue, as they did that summer, over a pro-police column of Buckley.* "I see where you have decided to support your local police," Edgar wrote on July 10, 1966. "Can't say I blame you—they have cer-tainly supported you. Can't say I agree with you, either." What followed was an exegesis of how police brutalize minorities, spe-cifically referring to the case of George Whitmore, Jr., wrong-fully convicted of the "Career Girls Murders" of Janice Wylie and Emily Hoffert in 1963.

The letter is worth considering in full for the incongruity of a death row inmate schooling a public intellectual on the crimi-nal justice system:

> *It might be different if you know something about how the police actually handle members of minority groups, but I suggest that you know about as much about that as a Mississippi cottonpicker knows about yacht racing. I further suggest you won't learn about the problem by reading PBA†press handouts. I'll give you a clue, my friend—when the "fuzz" grabs a kid off a Harlem street corner for "questioning," they just don't quite go about it the same way they do when they want to question the heir of Mr. "Moneybags" in Darien. I could cite a million variations in the way the police handle different classes of people, but perhaps this question sums it*

---

* The column in question, "New York at the Police Squad," was not pub-lished until July 19, 1966; it is conceivable that Buckley sent Smith an advance copy of the column to read. The first sentence of Edgar's response refers to a popular John Birch Society slogan and bumper sticker.
† Police Benevolent Association, i.e., the New York City police union.

up: Do you really believe the New York cops would handle your son the way they handled George Whitmore? If you think they would, then you are a lost cause. If you agree that they would handle your son differently, then you must agree that an "outside" review system is needed.* To have police officers judging other police officers, as is presently the case, is something akin to having the Young Americans for Freedom sit in judgment when some future Goldwater is accused of actions detrimental to republicanism. You know what I mean? It's like the Bobby Baker investigation all over again. Tell me—what action did the police take against the cops who got the confession out of Whitmore?

Frankly, Bill, I can't understand what it is that makes people like you think the police are some sacred group whose actions are above supervision by the poor folks who have to foot the bill. So what if a lot of the charges made against the police are untrue? If you look at the statistics you'll find that a lot of the charges made by the police are thrown out of court—if they ever get that far.

Buckley shrugged disagreements like this one off because Edgar was his friend, and he was loyal to his friends. Edgar also still needed his help, so there was no point in taking such criticism to heart.

On December 29, almost a year since he'd last seen Edgar in the flesh, Buckley traveled to Trenton for the third time. This visit was different. It took place in the Death House's new location, to which the prisoners had been moved only the day before.

---

* Edgar's comment about needing an "outside" review system references the PBA's referendum to end the police civilian review board, set up by Mayor John Lindsay (see Rick Perlstein, *Nixonland* [New York: Scribner, 2008]).

A prison official took him to Edgar's new cell, and this time there was no mesh screen between them. "For the first time, I had a real look at the man I had twice visited," Buckley later wrote, "and with whom I have exchanged several hundred letters." His natural impulse was to reach his hand through the bars and shake Edgar's hand.

He hesitated. "Would it be all right?" he asked his escort.

The prison official shook his head. "Better not."

Even with no screen, Buckley felt that the encounter had been stilted and awkward, and he was as "disconsolate" after leaving the prison as he had been on the prior two occasions. "I simply haven't got used to that kind of colloquy and I feel wooden and fear that I bore you," he wrote a few days later.

Edgar couldn't have cared less about being bored. He cared more about being able to speak candidly with Buckley during his visits to the Death House. He also reported having made progress on the book he'd first mentioned in April: "If I can discipline myself to regular daily work I should have a rough draft prepared in about six months. What I have in mind is an historical account of events, interlaced with my personal impressions and observations. . . . More about my project later. Want to be my agent?"

The answer, as would become evident in 1967, was yes. William F. Buckley put Edgar Smith in touch with an editor at Alfred A. Knopf named Sophie Wilkins. That decision would create a life-changing, soul-altering connection for all three people.

PART IV

MAKING THE BRIEF

(1967–1968)

14

Lunch at Paone's

NOVEMBER 1967

SOPHIE WILKINS was anxious. She was about to meet William F. Buckley for lunch at Nicola Paone, an Italian eatery near the *National Review* offices that was one of his favorite restaurants. She knew she could hold her own and that she could be witty and sparkling at business lunches when she needed to be, especially when the mission was to woo authors into signing with her at Knopf. But this meeting, on the afternoon of November 14, 1967, was different.

She wasn't at Paone's to sign Buckley up as an author; he was already spoken for, and besides, she felt, she couldn't possibly work on projects akin to *God and Man at Yale*, a "silly title for an indubitably silly book." This meeting was about Edgar Smith, their shared interest, the one whom, decades later, she would speak of as the center of an intellectual triangle so fraught as to have been taken out of the pages of a Russian novel.

Sophie had first written to Buckley after his *Esquire* piece had been published in October 1965. She had sent a donation to Edgar's defense fund and inquired as to whether he might be able to receive books and letters in the mail. Buckley had told her yes to the books, so long as they were sent directly from a publisher, but no to letters, since only people approved by the state of New Jersey could write to him.

She'd been struck by the literary quality of Edgar's correspondence that Buckley quoted in the article. She wondered if there might be a book in his story, and if so, she wrote Buckley, she wanted to edit it.

Sophie had joined Alfred A. Knopf in 1959 as assistant to the editor in chief, Harold Strauss. She had started acquiring books of her own a few years into the job, but the pickings weren't as plentiful as she'd liked, and she'd had some difficulty getting her acquisitions approved by the higher-ups.

Knopf was one of the most prestigious publishing houses in the United States, still nominally run by its founder and namesake, Alfred A. Knopf. But the company would go through major changes during Sophie's first years there. Random House had acquired Knopf in 1960, and then both companies had been bought by the electronics corporation RCA. A new publicity director, twenty-five-year-old William Loverd, had joined the company in 1965, and Ashbel Green, in his midthirties, had joined as editor the year before. Strauss would retire as editor in chief in 1966 to concentrate on select projects. The house was in transition, but the key to the transition was the pursuit of profit, never Sophie's primary goal as an editor.

Sophie wasn't sure if she was part of the old guard or the new guard. She had started at Knopf at the age of forty-four, making her significantly older than the other editorial assistants (as well as some of the editors). She had lived a far more unconventional life than the other female assistants, who cycled through the company on their way to eventual marriage and children. Their lives more resembled the ones described in Rona Jaffe's hit 1958 novel *The Best of Everything*; Sophie, however, was a different sort.

She had emigrated from Vienna in 1927, at the age of twelve, along with her mother, Deborah Prombaum, her older sister, Anna, and her younger brother, Ephraim, reuniting with her father, Hyman, who'd arrived in the United States a few years earlier. Sophie hadn't known a word of English upon landing at Ellis Island but had picked it up fast enough to graduate from Thomas Jefferson High School in Brooklyn four years later and to pursue bachelor's and master's degrees in comparative literature at Brooklyn College. She later became a doctoral student at Columbia University, studying and sparring with the literary critic Lionel Trilling, supporting herself by working as a secretary in the English Department office and teaching freshman composition.

Sophie was on her third marriage, to the author and literature professor Thurman Wilkins, and had two sons, Adam and Daniel, by her second husband, the psychiatrist Alvin Meyer. (Sophie's first marriage at the age of nineteen, to Meyer Klein, was so brief she hardly ever discussed it.) "Those years of marriage to Prince Charming, when Cinderella should have been so happy, seem in memory the most agonizing of my life," she once wrote of her time with Alvin. "I felt completely off base, didn't really know what was expected of me, how long this magic could last." Two abortions, eleven years apart, bookended the marriage.

By 1967, her decade-long union with Thurman was also running into trouble. When she'd met him, Thurman seemed stoic and placid, and the boys took to him right away, which persuaded Sophie that he would be an excellent stepfather. But Thurman's calm began to evaporate within a few years of their marriage, as he struggled with his mental health. There would be hospitalizations and breakdowns in his future, and Sophie, despite being devoted to him as a caregiver, despaired of the encroaching loneliness, worsened when both Adam and Daniel moved hundreds of miles away for college.

Sophie's personality and demeanor, too, marked her as alien to those she worked with at Knopf. Whereas others' general bearing was quiet and reserved, Sophie was loud and passionate. When measured rationality was the norm, Sophie's gregarious outbursts stood out. Still living coworkers recalled Sophie as brilliant and entertaining but also exhausting. ("She drove everybody crazy, and yet everyone was fond of her," recalled Robert Gottlieb, the longtime editor in chief who joined the company in 1968.) She did not abide by professional norms and operated at a higher temperature than was usual at Knopf. That made getting her desired book projects through to publication all the more frustrating of an experience because the editorial board said no far more often than they said yes to her ideas.

Sophie sensed commercial opportunity and professional salvation in the letters from Edgar Smith that Buckley quoted in his *Esquire* piece. Usually, she gravitated toward translated literature, a means of putting her native and still fluent German to use, as well as her decent French (and in small but lethal doses Yiddish). She had a few favorite crime writers, such as Dashiell Hammett—a cornerstone Knopf author—but the crime genre, in fiction and in nonfiction, tended to bore her.

What spurred Sophie to push herself out of her comfort zone to write William F. Buckley was her belief in Edgar Smith's innocence, and whether Edgar might be interested in writing a book. If he was, she wanted to be the conduit for that belief to reach an even larger audience. "I daresay this question has been asked and answered many times over by now," she wrote Buckley in the fall of 1965. "But I would like to go on record, at least, that this house is interested, if there is such a possibility."

Sometime after Edgar mentioned writing a book in his letters to Buckley, his mother, Ann Chupak, got in touch with Sophie. In her May 23, 1967, letter, she wondered if the Knopf editor would be interested in seeing the manuscript-in-progress. Sophie certainly was and wrote Chupak to that effect two days later, on May 25. Once the formalities with Trenton State Prison were worked out, Sophie wrote her first letter to Edgar in July 1967.

By November, their strictly professional correspondence had become far more than that, but only Sophie and Edgar knew the full extent of the change. This was not something she planned to impart to Buckley at their first lunch meeting. It was enough to compare notes on the death row convict.

At Paone's, she expected to be terrified by his "haughty look" and the "twenty-dollar vocabules [*sic*]" she knew from his wildly successful weekly television show, *Firing Line*, his twice-a-week syndicated columns, and his unsuccessful New York City mayoral campaign. He stalked into the restaurant "like a heron" and sat down beside Sophie at their appointed table. His smile was brilliant, his manner genial. At one point, Sophie quipped, "Ah well, let's not be juvenile." To which Buckley replied, "Ah, let's!" All her reservations about him dissipated immediately.

Right away, Sophie told Buckley what strange bedfellows they were: "me, an immigrant, [born] in Vienna just before the imperial double eagle was plucked to death but still Kafka-Musil-Hasek country . . . and the two of us about to spring, if we could, a possible killer who was nevertheless a gifted nonchalant man who couldn't conceivably be allowed to be fried alive by the ridiculous state of New Jersey."

By the end of the lunch, Sophie Wilkins and William F. Buckley were firm friends, a friendship that would persist long after the story of the Edgar Smith case ended. But Edgar was their original purpose, and even after everything went spectacularly wrong, Edgar was their shared experience, one that, like survivors of a war, only the two of them could fully share.

"For me, it was a once in a lifetime opportunity," Sophie wrote Buckley in 1979. "And because of it, I was able to forget all scruples about whom I might be having to do with, about the monster who had brained Vicki [*sic*] Zielinski and my natural revulsion from such an incomprehensible creature as that. I 'couldn't believe' this man had actually done it, not the man who had written such letters to you and to me; it had to be untrue."

Two decades later, she was still writing to Buckley about Edgar. In a letter dated July 4, 1998, she wrote, "There is certainly a book in the weird coming together of three people as different as the three of us, for a psychologist at least, but it will never be written." Sophie's declaration echoed one of Edgar's earliest letters to her, in the fall of 1967, pooh-poohing Sophie's concern that her missives to him would get into the wrong hands: "Forget it. You, your letters, everything you place in my hands will be well cared for. I'm good that way." Sophie, naturally, took him at his word.

On both of those fronts, she was wrong.

15

"They Must Think I Am Houdini"

MAY–NOVEMBER 1967

SOPHIE WILKINS'S correspondence with Edgar Smith was, at first, entirely professional. She'd learned from Ann Chupak that as of May 1967, he was fifty thousand words into a book, roughly half-way through the manuscript, according to his own calculations, and expected to be done by mid-July. Normally, Sophie preferred to see complete manuscripts, but she made an exception for Edgar. She told his mother, "The only reason it would be desirable for me to see a part of the manuscript while the author is still at work on the rest is that I might be able to save him time and labor by editorial advice, in view of the fact that this is his first book."

Sophie was also glad "to hear that your son is as well as can be, in the circumstances, still fighting his good fight; that he is writing a book, the second-best thing he can do." She wished not only to correspond with Edgar, she said, but to send him books of his preference. Ann wrote again on May 28 with news that Edgar had declined the last offer: "At this time he is so busy with his writing that he cannot take time to read a book, and he really loves to read!"

Chupak then told Sophie in a June 11 letter that it would be tricky for the editor to correspond with her son overtly about business purposes, lest the prison authorities become suspicious about their death row inmate having an income. She suggested a workaround: Sophie could be put onto his list as a "friend" and write personally rather than on Knopf stationery. Sophie understood, but she hoped that the required personal designation of "friend" wouldn't prohibit discussions of a book in progress between the professional editor and the would-be writer.

There was one more unexpected complication to sort out: when the Death House officials learned Sophie was married, they insisted she obtain signed approval to correspond with Edgar from her husband, Thurman. "It is their way of being certain that no extramarital hanky-panky is going on," Edgar explained in his first letter to Sophie on July 24, 1967. "How about that? They must think I am Houdini."

That first letter, front and back of a single page as mandated by Trenton State Prison, also got to the heart of the matter: the state of his book. "I had planned to be finished this month," Edgar explained, "but the more often I read the rough draft the more convinced I become that with more time and effort put into it, I can produce something much better than I dared hope. . . . I expect to keep at it through the summer."

Edgar was also considering Buckley's advice to get a literary agent for the project. "Bill thinks I may have a money-maker. I hope so." Since Buckley, through the defense fund he had set up, had been paying Edgar's legal bills ever since the *Esquire* piece had been published twenty-one months earlier, Edgar said, "I'd like to be able to repay some of that." He even knew what his next project would be: "fiction." And when he signed off— imploring Sophie to wait for a second letter explaining the book project in more detail before she replied—he noted the lateness of the hour: "It is 5:30 A.M., I am night people: up all night, sleep all day. The fellow in the cell next to mine thinks I am part vampire because I dive into bed just before sunrise."

As promised, Edgar's subsequent letter delivered more detail about the book, which he had provisionally titled *Murder in Mahwah*. He'd aimed for a sixty-thousand-word manuscript, but that "did not begin to tell the story." It also read like "a very long, very dull, legal brief—and one full of holes." To get around the gaps, Smith decided to "discard documentation in favor of interest and continuity." If that meant re-creating scenes based on speculation and inference, rather than what he himself had witnessed or had other knowledge of, then so be it. "In that sense, then, it is part fiction. But nothing *material* is fictionalized." He had already worked on chapters about Vickie Zielinski's murder, the police interrogation, his arrest, and his trial. What remained to be written were sections about what happened after his conviction and death sentence, and his posttrial appeals. The final manuscript, he expected, would run close to 125,000 words.

Edgar's letters met with Sophie's enthusiastic approval, as she conveyed in her July 28 reply: "You are right about wanting to polish your work. If you see where you can improve it, it will be worth the time it takes." She then reiterated her wish to read sample pages, citing her bona fides (Columbia University as department secretary, freshman comp instructor, and graduate student; translation work for other publishing houses; and her own writing) as to why she was qualified to judge whether his material would be publishable.

She also thought that getting an agent was a good idea but was confused as to why Edgar was asking her for advice. He explained on August 5 that "inmates of this pestiferous establishment" were not allowed to deal directly with a publisher; instead, "we must do so through family, friend, or attorney. It is an institutional rule, not a statutory prohibition."

Sophie also made one early editorial suggestion that Edgar start with his arrest and not the background. "The drama of such a start hooks the reader, and afterward he will be much more patient with background fill-ins than he will if asked to start with background he hasn't as yet a strong reason to be interested in reading about." Suggesting Franz Kafka's *The Trial* as a model, she offered to send him a copy, which he accepted.

In other early letters, Edgar listed the fiction writers he had read and liked, in an attempt to establish his literary interests and bolster his intellectual bona fides: "I've read most of C. S. Forester, all of Kenneth Roberts (terrific), Frank Yerby (ditto), Thomas Costain (ditto), Hemingway (ho hum), and Paul J. Wellman. Also, all of Leslie Charteris, all of Harold Robbins, most of Agatha Christie—who doesn't love 'Mrs. [*sic*] Marple'?" Whatever he read came from the prison library (which he had access to after the move to the new wing in 1966), which also meant that he had read some duds: "Some months ago, I tried *Valley of the Dolls* (nothing) and *Tai-Pan* (even less, if possible. [sic.]) Gave them up . . . repetition gets dull very quickly." As for *Naked Lunch* by William Burroughs, "I thought it was magnificent, *if* one happened to have a table with one short leg. It might even be handy on camping trips, to get the fire started on damp mornings."

The frequency of their exchanges grew, with Sophie writing multiple-page letters several times a week and Edgar stacking two-pagers together whenever possible. Their correspondence abated later in the summer of 1967 while Sophie was traveling throughout Europe, but it did not stop; rather, it changed tone. The "strictly professional" barrier began to relax, with Edgar doing most of the boundary breaking.

———

"HELLO, MY WIDE-EYED, liberal friend," Edgar began his August 5 letter. He told Sophie that Vienna, after Barcelona, was "the city I should most like to visit." Having seen cities "from Philadelphia to Hanoi" thanks to his youthful travels, he half joked, "Paris you can have. I should much rather visit West Nyack." So if Sophie ever desired "a guided tour of the back alleys of the Orient, the playground of my misspent youth, I shall be happy to trade you same for a tour of Vienna—preferably at Christmas."

Sophie had, in one of her early letters, complained about "getting old and cranky." Edgar protested this: "You can't be *that* much older than I am—at least from what my mother tells me, and I can assure you that *I* don't feel old. Would you prefer to be young and giggley [*sic*]? That would be a fate worse than life, or whatever. Besides, the Smith Theory of Gerontology is that a woman is not old until the last rites have been said over her."

Edgar walked the comments back a little in a later letter: "Was I being too forward, or whatever, when I commented on your comment about 'getting old and cranky'? It is my way, much to the dismay of my mother. I am, I suppose, a bit brash, but I try to be nice about it!" He also took issue with Sophie's assertion that power is a masculine interest. He doubted that political workers, which Edgar asserted without evidence were largely women, "are all motivated by a pure sense of duty, rather than by the excitement of being close to the action. It may be true that many women *have* been disillusioned by their traditional view of power—what did they expect?—but when women *do* aspire to power, and when they *do* get on top, ho boy, are dey sometink!"

After Sophie described a brief dalliance with a Greek man while on her European vacation in self-deprecating fashion, as was her way, Edgar countered with a personal anecdote of his own:

*Why shouldn't the Greek find you interesting? I do. While still
a fuzzy-cheeked nineteen, in Hawaii, I lived for six months
with a woman forty-three, a Mrs. Rich-Bitch from Palm
Beach, also an ex-Russki—her folks skipped in October, 1917.
'Twas the best, most instructive, six months of my life. After
her, young chicks were like Dullsville. I was astonished to
discover that women can* talk. *Until then, I thought girls only
blushed and giggled—before and after.*

That was a prelude to expressing more overt interest, which
Edgar did in the beginning of September:

*Why should it be so wonderful that El Greco did not let you
feel the difference in your ages? What sort of ill-mannered
clods are you accustomed to? If a woman is interesting, I can't
see what the hell difference it makes* how *old she is. You, for
instance. I couldn't care less if you were 20, 90, or 190—I dig
you, and I don't know what else counts. Age, good looks, etc.,
only count with a woman with an empty head. [I] discovered
11 years ago that young, beautiful, oversexed, empty
headed women make marvelous house pets, but lousy wives.
(Something tells me that I could prove to be quite a surprise for
S. C. Wilkins.)*

Over the course of the fall, their correspondence became
more frank and intimate. Sophie would later claim that it had
been a ruse on her part, a way of providing a degree of thrill to a
condemned man in dire need of it. But the thrill was hers to feel
as well, a diversion from loneliness and depression and a chance
at fulfilling some greater mission—that the end, a publishable
book, could truly justify the means.

"Why are you so special?" Edgar wrote on September 25.

It's difficult to express. You are, if it makes sense to you, just the sort of bright, witty, sophisticated, almost too intelligent woman I need to break me out of the dull mold I've been in for much too long. When I first began thinking about this a couple of weeks ago, I thought of how great it would have been if we had met, say, 12 years ago; but then I realized that 12 years ago I was a total, unprincipled, and unambitious bum you would not have wanted to meet. We would have had nothing in common, not a thing to talk about. It is, therefore, in that way at least, good that it has taken us so long to become acquainted, though I must admit I am still a bit wary of "brainy" women. . . . Intellectually, you are to me as champagne to a guy who never has had anything stronger than coke.

Whatever wariness Edgar expressed then and whatever similar reservations Sophie had about the increasingly personal tone of their correspondence soon fell away entirely. On October 5, Sophie wrote of "love talk" and spending a week together in a state of sexual frenzy—or, as she termed it, "nightriding." Edgar, meanwhile, fantasized about "some catty old broad" approaching Sophie in the ladies' room at El Morocco and asking "Dahling, where *did* you find that divine young man? To which you reply: Dahling, eat your heart out!"

Three days later, on October 8, Edgar was even more direct about their developing relationship: "Sophie baby, you and I have been astray all our lives; we're just recognizing the fact." The next day, Sophie parried, "Sure, I love flattery, but it's like drink, I can't hold it like a lady; just don't say you haven't been warned of the dire consequences, is all." Still, she sent him photos of herself as she was then—a woman in her early fifties—and obliged when he asked for more.

She knew the score, or so she thought: "One of our troubles is that we know each other only through words on paper. This creates illusions. If I had thought for a moment that there was the slightest chance of being allowed to see you, and be seen, I'd not have bothered about all those photos, which don't really give you realities either."

Edgar was having none of her self-putdowns. "Let's just dig each other and forget the whys and wherefores," he wrote on October 11. "So far we've been good for each other, and nothing else *really* counts when two people get together. No?" Ten days later, he still wrote as if they had not fallen off a precipice:

> *I am* not *deluding myself into thinking I have fallen in love with you, nor do I harbor the illusion that you have fallen in love with me, however slightly. I recognize our sweet talk for what it is: the freedom of expression permitted between friends. I* am *aware, more than you perhaps, how easily a fellow cut off from women, as I am, can mistake friendship for love, and overreact to statements he would, under different circumstances, accept in the context they were intended.*

Sophie, meanwhile, repeated her own philosophies about sexual mores. "I don't believe in mono-anything: monotheism, monogamy, monotony," she wrote him on November 5. "A man like you should have more than one woman in his life . . . by a man like you I mean a born lover, gifted that way; a talent has to be exercised, encouraged; it is a source of joy and we have too few of these to throw away what we have. I mean it."

The correspondence got hotter and heavier further into November. By that point, Edgar had let slip that he didn't much care for his first name. His older brother, Richard, had nicknamed him "Igor" as a child, and his fellow Death House dwellers picked up on it to tease him about being Frankenstein's assistant. Sophie, because of her auburn locks, transformed into "Red," a nickname that would persist between them through the next two years. The next threshold author and editor needed to cross, having broken so many boundaries already, was to meet in person. Edgar joked that when they met at last, they would be "like two virgins on their wedding [night]."

The meeting took some time to organize. The restrictions were looser than when Buckley had arranged his first visit in 1965, but Sophie still had to receive formal permission from the prison, which took some doing.

When they did meet, on November 11, 1967, it didn't go quite as planned.

16

Blood, Nerves, Vibrations

SEPTEMBER–DECEMBER 1967

EDGAR SMITH, while wooing Sophie Wilkins by letter and drawing her deeper into his psychological web, hadn't completely set aside the business aspects of their correspondence. He was frustrated with his progress on the book. "God only knows when the book will be done, and He isn't talking, at least not to me," he wrote Sophie on September 7. "More rewrite required. What the hell! If you females can take 9 months to have a baby, I can take half that to create a monster-piece—no [F]reudian slip."

By October 3, Sophie's enthusiasm was tempered by impatience: "Oh, Edgar, Edgar you can write! I really and truly can't wait to see that ms. How much longer, please?" Three weeks later, on the twenty-eighth, he conveyed advice from his lawyer, Steve Lichtenstein, who had recommended "only 6 or 7 minor changes in the ms—an hour's work." He told Sophie that otherwise the lawyer thought he did "a good job . . . continually interesting . . . some parts outstanding. What do lawyers know?"

He instructed his mother, Ann, to send Sophie six draft chapters, "ranging from complete to nearly complete (about 100 pp.)" and also slipped in William F. Buckley's phone number so that they could be in further and better communication about preparing the manuscript for publication. After Sophie read through the pages, and after meeting Buckley for the first time at Paone's, she wrote herself a memo in mid-November (though she would not present the book for acquisition to the editorial board until the following March). The first two chapters, she felt, "go swimmingly, arouse & sustain interest." Things went wrong in the third chapter, which, she felt, relied too heavily on biography yet did not contain enough about his family members. She also wondered how Edgar had become "the brash, rebellious, playful character that contributed to his 'accident.'"

She felt the structure of the book, at that point, "resembled a doughnut: circles around a large hole in the middle where the murder story should be. But this is not a murder story, but rather a demonstration of the incredible shoddiness, viciousness, brutality, savagery, stupidity of the machinery of so-called justice." A few days later, Sophie expressed additional reservations to Edgar about his seeming reticence to speak about himself: "You simply must learn to open up more, to allow room for the non-factual, the emotional, the blood and nerves and vibrations, the guts and what's inside them, not necessarily pleasant but an inalienable part of life as it is lived, the sweat, the tears, but also the heroism."

There was, in other words, much more work for Edgar to do to get the manuscript into publishable shape. This Sophie told herself, was the ultimate, and only, reason she was all in.

———

SOPHIE WAS AT last about to meet Edgar in person. On the morning of November 11, 1967, she traveled by train and hired car to Trenton State Prison. She dressed primly, per prison regulations, and tried to tamp down her sky-high expectations. She passed through security and was led into a room with a glass partition through which she would be able to see Smith and talk to him through the headset on the table in front of her.

Then he appeared. *This* was the man she'd been corresponding with for all these months? *This* was the man whose book she was eager to midwife into existence, who had, through his letters, blasted through emotional and sexual barriers? He still had his youthful looks but had put on weight over a decade in the Death House. He kept his mouth closed most of the time so as not to display the prominent gap created by the recent extraction of two infected front teeth, even though she had reassured him, "What's a couple of teeth between friends?" He was taciturn and uncommunicative, and when he did speak, his pronounced northern New Jersey accent seemed at odds with the tone of his letters.

Sophie felt awkward, talking too much to fill in the gaping silences, what she said clanging off key. The meeting ended before she knew it, and it was time to trek back to New York City. She was disappointed, yes, but mostly with herself.

Edgar, however, had an altogether different opinion of the visit. "What a complete joy to see you!!" he wrote her later that night. "You are charming, delightful, and not just a bit intoxicating; there are going to be some long days and nights 'twixt now and the next visit, at which time I shall do my best to be a *talker* rather than an eye-gazer." It was the first letter—but hardly the last—that he would sign "Love, Eddie."

Sophie felt compelled to explain the disconnect she had felt during the visit. "I was too impatient to see you," she wrote on November 12.

> *The main point at issue, the thing that I guess was making you most unhappy, the missing front teeth, would still have been the same. It will do no good to tell you how childish your feeling about that is; to tell you that, on the contrary,*

all I really saw in the brief glimpse you allowed was that
they hadn't been able, even by doing something so drastic
as removing 2 front teeth, to change or affect adversely the
extraordinary shapeliness of your lips.

She wanted Edgar to know that she herself knew she wasn't
nearly as entertaining in person as in writing: "Had it occurred
to you that my letters might be the *best* thing about me, everything else being inevitably a letdown?" But she determined to
visit him on a monthly basis, as they both desired. Her next visit
to Trenton State Prison was scheduled for December 2. By then,
Edgar was finishing another round of revisions, which met with
her approval. "He did a superlative job on the 'brief' you know!"
she wrote Ann Chupak. "Incredible, for a first try or for anyone.
The fact is, he has *style*."

The mask behind which Sophie hid her depressive bouts also
slipped during the intervening weeks, when she fretted about a
period of time when she didn't receive any letters from Edgar.
He called her out about this: "Your letter of the 24th read like a
Prologue to a suicide note. You act as if you are in love, or something. But it's good; it shows that you are the one needing the
education, about *me*."

The dark cloud apparently lifted by the time they met again
in person. "Sweet Red, I am still walking around in a bit of cloud
after seeing you today," wrote Edgar.

I don't know that I'll ever be able to tell you how exhilarating
it is to be so near to you. Igor wasn't just flattering when
he said you are a terribly exciting woman, far more so than
anticipated. Perhaps the secret is your aliveness, the way you
seem to have your batteries fully charged every instant. Judas

priest! What are you like when uninhibited by telephones, glass
windows, time limits, etc.?

The correspondence deepened into ever more dangerous emotional territory. "Love is a delicate perishable thing, like the human soul . . . and it has to be treated like a rare orchid if you want to keep it alive," Sophie wrote on December 8.

At Christmas, Edgar sent her some reflections on their relationship: "Into my life came this little slice of paradise. At first it was just another something to contend with, nothing important, to be ignored as much as possible." But then, or so he wrote, something had changed: "What the hell is this . . . you boob . . . you're falling in love. Open your eyes, stupid. . . . You've had it. Face it boy, Cupid has shot you right in your fat butt. You're a goner."

He personified the change in his emotional status by inventing a split personality—the emotion-laden "Igor" versus the rational "Smith"—but it didn't change the declaration: he was "in love, head over heels in love with that delightful, exciting little chunk of heaven dropped into his life by a couple of playful angels, and that he needed and wanted—Boy! does he want—her very much."

He professed shock about his feelings:

A lot of women have come and gone in my life, but never
one I've so much wanted to love, nor have I been so happy to
love, as you. You've put meaning back into my life, and that
alone would be reason enough for me to love you. I want you,
obviously, but even more—is that possible?—I want to be
with you, here in the visiting room, walking through the city,
dining out, dancing, in some quiet place where it is just you
and me and our imaginations, anywhere, everywhere.

Sophie was flattered and thrilled but still skeptical of his feelings. As 1967 turned into 1968, the skepticism would disappear entirely. The author-editor relationship between Edgar Smith and Sophie Wilkins entered much more emotionally treacherous territory.

17

Hatkic

1968

SOPHIE WILKINS began the New Year by writing to Edgar Smith about another one of his artistic pursuits, one he had hardly mentioned to William F. Buckley in their years of correspondence. In addition to working on his book, he was also producing artwork, ranging from oil portraits of himself or other prisoners to landscapes and cityscapes to miniature renderings of flowers, which he often referred to as "flahrs." (Photos of his artwork still exist among Sophie's papers.) "Your colors remind me of a favorite, Paul Delvaux," she wrote, referring to the surrealist Belgian painter. "All you need, for instance, in the one with the tall trees, is a tall nude right smack in the center, staring at you with big black eyes, and you've got a Delvaux."

Sophie continued to be vexed by the disconnect between the frankness of her writing compared to her inhibition when she saw Edgar in person. "I just can't feel that we are communicating, as the current jargon goes. My mind goes blank—I don't know what to say—I wonder what we would find to say to each other if at liberty?"

Edgar was pressing her to come more often. Sophie didn't

think it wise to increase the number of visits since "it takes almost all day, for just half an hour of staring. . . . I can't feel at my best, so I feel diminished by it, as though bound to leave you with a worse impression of myself than you'd have had, had I kept away." That particular letter was rich in insight into her inner life and struggle. She'd given up on going out or inviting people over, partly because of her own social anxiety but mostly because of the emotional cost of caring for her husband and her own encroaching depressive moods.

Sophie also noted something Edgar had told her before, that she was "smart but not bright," and agreed: "You noticed how slow I am on the uptake, in conversation, haven't you? But part of that is owing to my sense of constraint with the damned telephone in my hand, talking through a pane of glass."

Sophie preferred to write at a clip so hypergraphic that Edgar couldn't possibly keep up with it in his replies. She also confessed that she continued to reread his Christmas letters, those declarations of love, "between 7 and 11 times, one right after the other and then starting with 1 again, if you had seen it you'd have phoned Bellevue, but nobody sees it because I shut the door to be alone with you." Every time he wrote her or told her what she most wanted to hear, Sophie disclosed on January 6, "I am glad but I also feel like a thief—and obligated to fight it off, not to allow myself to simply accept or enjoy it."

Sophie, perhaps as a means of compensating for her cravings for love and attention from sources that couldn't provide them, tried to differentiate between love and friendship: "A friend can say all kinds of things to the other without hurting the friendship; on the contrary, lovers *have* to be diplomats. Actually, friendship would be by far the most comfortable and comforting relationship between us. But it's not a matter of choice, I fear."

Sophie visited Edgar again on January 20. He called it "one

of the best, happiest, most fun-filled days of my life." That night, he wrote:

> *I woke up this morning in love with you, and tonight I'll go to bed utterly, completely insane for you. Did you notice it? Somewhere during the visit there was one quiet moment when we just looked at each other and that said all there was to say. If there ever was a chance for us to put on the brakes, even if only to slow down, we both know now that it's much much too late. We is goners!*

Writing three days later, Sophie concurred: "Isn't it funny that the more you know declarations are not necessary—you're right we said *everything* with one long look; I'll never forget it, wouldn't want to; your eyes looked greener than ever."

More nicknames proliferated. He dubbed her "Sarah" and sometimes "Dolly" or "Doll," but the one he seemed to prefer most was "Owl," presumably for her watchfulness (though he still often called her "Red" or "Little Red"). He was "Igor" or "Eddie" and on occasion "Fou" (French for "mad"), clearly a nod to how intense and crazy their epistolary relationship had become.

The nickname he preferred began appearing in letters as of February 26: "Ilya," a Russified nickname for "Igor" that Sophie had alighted on (as an acronym for "I Love Ya") and Edgar embraced. Many, many passionate and racy letters signed with that nickname followed over the course of the next year or so. And Edgar increasingly included elaborate postscripts, such as this one from May 5:

1. Soitanly!

2. Of course!

3. Absotively!

4. Posolutely!

5. I duz!

6. Love ya!

Bubbling under the professions of love on both sides was a more carnal aspect, which found expression in what Edgar referred to as "hatkic epics" ("hatkic" was an acronym Sophie devised for "have to keep it clean"). Those long letters, exceeding twenty single-spaced pages, weren't sent through the Trenton State Prison system, lest snooping censors create problems and revoke the privileges of its increasingly famous Death House inmate.

But there was no page limit on communication between Smith and his lawyers; Edgar could send them anything, at any length. So, as long as his and Sophie's "epics" were enclosed in sealed envelopes tucked into his legal correspondence, falling under the rubric of attorney-client privilege, the censors would be none the wiser. Beginning sometime after that January 20 visit when they had exchanged their long and wordless look, Edgar and Sophie got to work spinning "sagas" that were ferried through Smith's lawyer, Steve Lichtenstein, as "personal and confidential."

Though the first such "epic" has never surfaced, Edgar referenced it in a letter to Sophie on February 8: "It should . . . cure you of the notion that thy prince is cool, reserved, unemotional, etc. Whatever the *words* used, the thought behind the epic, from start to spinish [*sic*], is that I am gone over you . . . I may be hatkic, but hatkic with talent."

It isn't clear when William F. Buckley learned of the true nature of the relationship between author and editor, but both

Edgar and Sophie suspected he caught on early. Sophie even referenced the changing relationship ("[Edgar] has been locked up so long, clearly a gifted lover") to Buckley in a November 7, 1967, letter, a week before they met in person for the first time. And recalling one visit in late January 1968, Edgar relayed that Buckley had told him that he thought Sophie "marvelous" and "the greatest" and that "he has also, methinks, added EHS + SCW and come up with SOS . . . and is getting a secret kick out of the whole thing. Shall we have him for our best man?"

Edgar had made a point of telling Buckley how deeply he felt about Sophie in a letter immediately after her visit to the Death House on January 20: "To put it discreetly, she and I have become exceedingly good friends (Boy, there's some 'beating around the bush' for you.) I am utterly *fou* about her. . . . She is a perfect doll, terribly good to me. While it seems like a hell of a time in my life to say it, life has never been more fun." Many years later, Sophie would write Buckley about the "'hot' sexual involvement with the Prisoner of Trenton," further confirming that Buckley knew of the "more-than" element.

So how "hot" was Sophie's epistolary relationship with Edgar? One characteristic example was from an "epic" sent to Sophie in late April. In it, Edgar detailed how he had written a more tame letter to her, flopped onto his prison bed, and begun to daydream, "and it didn't take much of that to get Houdini standing up looking around for a [certain] owlet. Well, at this point I got curious, grabbed a ruler, and began jotting down some specifications. I lied to you! But it was a white lie because I didn't mean for you to take those 7" literally."

Then, Edgar wrote, he had run into a vexing issue: "How does one measure a prick? Along the top, side, or bottom? Decided on the top. How about circumference? Where? It got complicated, but what finally emerged is as follows:

What a crazy hatkic thing to do. If anyone had seen me sitting here with a ruler, measuring my cock, I would have been certified right then and there. But it was funny. Everytime [sic] I put the cold, plastic ruler against it, the fuckin' thing began to go down. What I do this for is beyond me. The best way is to slip it in you just as deeply as it will go, to the root, then you will know exactly how it fits.

He also professed to be a big fan of cunnilingus:

If there's going to be any prolonged kissing of that sort, you leave it to me at the start. You just sit on the edge of the bed, lie back, make me a necklace with those beautiful legs of yours, and enjoy yourself. That or get up on top as in my dream! . . . Honey, as strange as it may seem after all these epics, I've never before felt this way about a woman's cunt, and I don't know why I have this great urge to kiss and lick yours, unless maybe it's because I want so much to convince you that I do love you. Brat [referring to Patricia, his first wife] was just as clean and sweet as sugar candy, and I did enjoy eating her, but I never felt strongly about it. If she hadn't been so much in favor of it, I'd hardly have bothered. With you, however, it's something I feel I have to do; I really want, perhaps even need.

And on Edgar went in a similar vein, acknowledging "what a couple of nuts we are. Two supposedly grown-up people. Just goes to prove that love is simply a pleasant form of insanity. You do know that I love you, don't you? That's what all this is about. Two kookie [sic] exhibitionists just mad about each other." Perhaps the best way to sum up the way he described his feelings for Sophie was this line: "I wanna mess around in *all* your orifices!!!"

Sophie did not keep copies of her own "epics."* She likely destroyed them out of a growing sense of embarrassment and shame, as well as fear that someone else might read them. Based on Edgar's descriptions, as well as her own allusions in letters sent directly to him, she didn't resort to the sort of crude and graphic sexual descriptions that marked Edgar's contraband correspondence. She was no prude, but profane language was not her style. And she seemed to be as sexually gung ho about Edgar as he was about her. Was it real? Was it mutual manipulation in the form of epistolary masturbation? Was Edgar conning Sophie or vice versa or both?

Sophie, in later years, claimed that her dealings with Edgar had always been in bad faith: that she had simply longed for a book she could consider her own and had coaxed it out of him "by whatever means were available." After all, so long as he remained in prison, their face-to-face meetings would always be supervised, separated by glass windows and telephone receivers. And Sophie was still married to Thurman Wilkins and had no intention of severing that tie. For a supremely lonely woman, as Sophie was, a torrid affair of the mind had to be as much comfort, even pleasure, for her as for the imprisoned convict.

Their erotically charged letters often mentioned what could happen if Edgar was released from the Death House. The possibility, however fantasy-laden, did exist. Both clearly knew that

---

* As for why Sophie kept Edgar's "epics" at all, she kept almost all incoming correspondence, filed away in boxes she did not touch for decades.

reality would pale in comparison to the elaborate scripts of imagination each had conjured up, separately and together. So long as reality remained out of reach and Edgar's release was in a permanent state of limbo, Sophie and Edgar could dream, by day or by night, about what might occur and how their relationship might deepen if they were granted pure freedom.

18

March to Publication

IN JANUARY 1968, Sophie wrote an editorial memo to her Knopf colleagues detailing why she was keen to publish the manuscript called *Murder in Mahwah*:

> That the author, a man of 34 now, has written this first book without previous experience or training, with only a rudimentary formal education, and under forbidding circumstances—the death house, he writes, is a babel of noise day and night . . . —even without considering these facts which make this manuscript an amazing achievement, I think it stands on its merits as a distinguished job of reporting on one of the cancer sores of our system of justice.

She compared Smith's book to Selwyn Raab's *Justice in the Back Room*, his 1967 account of the "Career Girls" murders and George Whitmore's wrongful targeting, with its "lurid instances of faked confessions extorted by the police."

Then she passed Edgar's manuscript on to a colleague, Angus Cameron, who was equally effusive: "This remarkable manuscript should with the kind of publicity breaks it ought to get for itself become at least a modest best-seller. It is certain to have a large paperback sale and it deserves whatever success it will have. . . . I am sure we will want to publish this and can do so with expectations, providing the publisher may be immune from action." Cameron added, with respect to the author's guilt or innocence, that if he'd been a juror and had had the data detailed in the book, "I would have voted 'not guilty'!"

In early February, Sophie spoke with Robert Lescher, a literary agent whom Edgar was considering signing with. William F. Buckley had expressed reservations some months earlier lest having an agent complicate financial matters already made complicated by Edgar's being on death row and having to funnel his earnings through Buckley. None of those reservations entered into Lescher's letter to Sophie on February 7. "It's a stunning work and I think I would regard it as being remarkable even if it hadn't been written under the circumstances that prevailed," he wrote. "But for Mr. Smith to have accomplished this task while alone, without access to even a typewriter or the usual aids authors have, seems to me a monumental task. I hope you'll tell him how moved I was."

Over the next nine pages of his letter to Sophie, Lescher wasn't shy about suggesting some areas of improvement. He took issue with Edgar's penchant for conjecture, since "the facts that [he] has mustered about this case are enormously impressive, but their credibility might be lessened." That was especially worrisome with respect to Edgar's reasons for not disclosing the full truth about the night of Victoria Zielinski's murder to the prosecutor, Guy Calissi, during his initial interrogation.

"[Edgar's reasoning] struck me as both confusing and evasive," wrote Lescher.

I suppose Smith himself was confused at the time, but that doesn't mean he ought to confuse the reader. What he ought to

do instead, I think, is to explain at much greater length here,
and perhaps later, his state of confusion and his fear. . . . Smith
is asking the reader to accept certain assumptions the reader is
likely to resist. If they were a part of Smith's thinking at the
time, he should do more to explain them.

Lescher also brought up a point that would become especially contentious for Smith over the next few weeks: his description of the role that Donald Hommell played in his version of this narrative and how his accusations that Hommell was the killer might set Edgar up for a libel suit. "Hommell is referred to time and again, and quite persuasively, as a psychopath, and I was left with the impression that Smith knew of this even before the crime. If he did, why did he leave Vickie with Hommell, particularly in the condition she was? If it was because he was afraid of being involved, afraid of what his wife would say if she found out, I think he ought to say so somehow."

Sophie visited Edgar on February 8, which also happened to be his thirty-fourth birthday, bringing Lescher's letter for him to review. The more she visited Edgar, the more she got used to the dissonance between the voice of his letters and the voice of his actual self. That dissonance never fully disappeared; she could never truly relax in his presence and never stop berating herself for her own perceived failings and slights.

Edgar took the agent's comments in reasonable stride, saying "It shouldn't be *too* hard to insert the clarifications." But he could also tell his insouciant attitude about the book bothered Sophie a great deal. He tried to explain: "[It] stems from my feeling that anything done so quickly and easily can't be all *that* good, certainly not in relationship to, say, a professional job like the Selwyn Rabb [*sic*]. Perhaps when I see that it is a success I will admit that it *is* good." He judged that he needed another six months of hard work to get the book into the shape he desired. And once it was in that shape, he could be paid and then pay off his growing legal expenses, too.

———

CHANGE WAS IN the air at the Knopf offices. On January 6, the *New York Times* published a bombshell story about the defection of three key book-publishing executives—editor in chief Robert Gottlieb, associate publisher Anthony Schulte, and Nina Bourne, vice president in charge of advertising—from Simon & Schuster to Knopf. For Gottlieb, who had been at S&S for twelve years, the change involved "new incentives" and "more opportunity"; it was an even greater change for Schulte, who had been at the company for more than fifteen years, and Bourne, who was closing in on twenty-nine years.

Gottlieb was the first of the trio to start at Knopf, which he did in February, along with his assistant, Toinette Lippe, who also moved with him from Simon & Schuster. Schulte and Bourne joined a month or two later. Sophie felt optimistic about the changes and felt there would be an opportunity for her to make more of a mark as a proper editor, not just Harold Strauss's former assistant.

She had allies among younger staffers, such as Kathy Hourigan, Knopf's chief of secretaries and the imprint's future managing editor (and now its longest-serving employee). Sophie memorialized her in a letter to Edgar as having "the lightest blue eyes I ever saw. . . . Irish sweetie, good as gold, quiet, shy, admirer of WFB before I knew he existed." Having a friend in Hourigan could only bolster the chances of Edgar's book to succeed inhouse, or so Sophie believed.

Before Sophie could formally present Edgar's book at Knopf's

editorial board meeting, there was a snag. The book had under-
gone a legal read by Arthur Abelman, a partner at Weil, Gotshal
& Manges, the law firm hired by the publishing house. Abelman
asked for a significant number of changes to reduce the probabil-
ity of a libel suit. Edgar pushed back on Abelman's recommen-
dations (whose firm he mocked as "Hedge, Fudge, Coolit, and B.
Bland" to Buckley) with considerable force.

"Every time I try to write or think about the [Abelman]
memo I get so goddamned angry I can't see straight," he wrote
Sophie in early March. "I tell you true, and best you believe it:
were it not for you . . . going out on a limb for me, I would have
called everything off and gone elsewhere as soon as I had read
the lawyer's memo. I've never been certain that [Knopf] is the
right type of firm to handle the brief, that will present and push it
in the forceful manner it requires, and the lawyer's namby-pamby
approach only reinforced that feeling."

Then he went in for the kill: "Bill knows how I feel about this,
and I have been assured, long ago, that others want the brief and
are not afraid to take it *as written*, and for one hell of a lot more
money." Edgar's attitude was even blunter in a letter to Buckley
on March 6: "Their reservations are legally dubious, over cautious, and incredibly illogical. . . . I will not be dealt with or regarded as a second class slob simply because of my situation, and
I feel I am being treated as such. I've given them two choices: 1)
either accept a full release from liability, or 2) accept the brief as
is. Barring either, I will take it elsewhere, where people are not
quite so afraid of controversy." Knopf's prestige was all well and
good, "but I can't eat it, or pay legal expenses with it."

Sophie attempted to soothe Edgar's wounded ego. "Your best
interest in this matter comes first and middle and last, and is subject only to your best judgment," she wrote on March 9. Sophie
was afraid of his "losing precious, irreplaceable time if this bogs

down into a stalemate. We must not let it do that! . . . And don't for a minute give my involvement a second thought." As she had explained in a previous letter, she was equally uncertain about which publisher was best for Edgar: "If my involvement made difficulties and hangups for you, I'd never forgive myself; much rather see you go elsewhere because all I want is the greatest possible results as fast as possible, wherever!"

Despite Edgar's laments, the bulk of the legal changes were made. What Sophie could not realize was how her comments about seeing him "go elsewhere" foreshadowed a breach so deep between her and Edgar that it threatened to sever their relationship for good.

———

THE SPRING PROVED to be vital both for the personal relationship of Sophie Wilkins and Edgar Smith, as well as for the book, whose title had now become *Brief Against Death*. Why the change? Because *Murder in Mahwah* had been deemed by the powers that be at Knopf to be too bland. Sophie had finally presented the book at an editorial meeting on March 19, where the manuscript was met with across-the-board enthusiasm, bolstered by thumbs-ups from Robert Gottlieb and Anthony Schulte. But everyone *also* agreed the title needed to go.

When Sophie floated the idea of calling the book *Brief Against Death* at the end of March, Edgar resisted. "When I say I don't like *Brief,* I'm being goddamned serious," he wrote on April 1. "You talk of educating readers. Surprise! You can't educate them till you've gotten them to buy and read, at which point the title is irrelevant. But I'm not going to argue. You'll hear from Steve in a day or two. *If he and Bill say "Brief" is okay, I'll go along.*"

He also joked that fellow Death House inmate Tommy

Trantino—who would later write a book of his own, *Lock the Lock*, which Knopf published in 1974—had suggested "Sex and the Single Inmate" as a title. (Sophie responded with equal joviality, "Sex and the Single Inmate is a loverly title, for the book you will write when you have a good comedy in mind, in a jailhouse setting, OK?")

Edgar made one more impassioned case for keeping *Murder in Mahwah* as the title in that same April 1 letter:

> *You know . . . I took several months and did a bit of research before picking the first title. I tried to tell you why, but you always said "later." You talk of 20,000 [copies] being hoped for. Baby, with the original title, I hoped for damn near 20,000 in Bergen County, alone. It was built around the fact that a couple of hundred thousand people up there know nothing about EHS, VZ, DH, or the crime; they didn't live there in 1957. But they have heard of Mahwah, and they damn sure would want to know what happened there. And it is one of the wealthiest, buyingest, book-eatingest sections in the country. Bookstores are popping up in every town.*

Whatever he thought Sophie and her Knopf colleagues believed, he wanted to make sure of one thing:

> *The people in Bergen County are far more important to me, can do more for me, than any others anywhere. If I swing them my way, I'm home free. Moreover, at a new trial, they will sit on my jury, not some reviewer from the New York Times; therefore they are the ones I must reach with evidence that will be inadmissible in court—truth serum notes, the arrest of Hommell, the Z. divorce, etc. And dammit! The original title will make them sit up and take*

notice. Instant recognition. There isn't another Mahwah in the world.

Perhaps that's why, when Sophie went to see him next on April 4, the visit didn't go terribly well, devolving into misunderstandings and arguments about the state of the manuscript. "It was *so* great to see you and be near you, as always, but we simply *must* get all this damned bizziness [*sic*] out of the way before it ruins more than just visits," Edgar wrote her immediately afterward. "Can't you understand, or won't you *try* to understand, that I really wasn't arguing with you today? I never once said I wouldn't accept the changes; all I tried to do is tell you why it was as it was to begin with, in case you might decide it's better left as is."

Sophie seemed taken aback in her reply two days later: "You talk as if there had been no sagas, no epics, no gettingthoroughly [*sic*] acquainted, no deep understanding, no nothing!" She claimed that Edgar had no reason to be upset ("arguing shows one's family; haven't had a good rousing family argument in so long, I'm positively starved for it!") and since they had spent the hour straightening out necessary changes, "and the time went like somebody was after it with a gun, so what's to complain?"

Soon Edgar sent Sophie another, even more racy "epic." Then he got nervous about having sent it, writing to Sophie by regular mail that he was worried that he might be giving her "the wrong impression about me and my prime interests, as well as giving you the idea that I somehow think such things are *your* prime interest. Do me a favor? When you do get this epic, before I see you again, take it with a grain of salt. Don't be misled by the emphasis on a specific area, okay? I'll do 'better' in the future."

But Sophie didn't seem to mind in the slightest. Uppermost in her mind was *Brief Against Death*'s march to publication. Once the manuscript was formally accepted by Knopf, Edgar was sent a contract to sign for a $10,000 advance (nearly $75,000 in today's dollars) against royalties. The contract had an unusual structure: Edgar was paid through a special account set up by William F. Buckley, who held his power of attorney so that he could conduct outside business on his behalf. That enabled Edgar to get around any violation of prison regulations that frowned upon his being directly compensated as an author.*

Sophie was also preoccupied with her upcoming presentation of Edgar's book at the combined Knopf and Random House sales conference, to be held on May 9 at the Waldorf-Astoria hotel. Only two weeks earlier, she had learned that *Brief Against Death* would be an alternate selection of the Literary Guild, and the meeting was her chance to further convince the publisher's sales team of the book's best-seller potential.

Edgar asked if his mother could attend. Ann Chupak was still supporting her son unrelentingly, visiting at every possibility. Sophie obliged her, though it was a highly unusual request; outside visitors were generally unheard of at internal publishing meetings. Sophie indulged Ann because the other woman was about to undergo surgery after months of suffering from health issues of varying sorts.

There was another surprise guest at the meeting, sitting up front with Sophie and Ann: William F. Buckley, who had already submitted his introduction to *Brief Against Death*, which he had adapted from his 1965 *Esquire* article. He had confessed to Edgar in a March 27 letter, written at the tail end of his annual Switzerland sojourn (this time with a stop-off in Madrid) that

---

* The unusual contract structure predated by more than a decade "Son of Sam" laws prohibiting prisoners from profiting off work directly connected to their crimes.

he was "rather stagestruck by this assignment," in part because he felt it "terribly important to keep myself out of this presentation so as not to cause any strategic damage," an exceedingly self-conscious evaluation of his own efforts.

Sophie's presentation—succinct about *Brief Against Death* and supplying the news that Buckley would be writing its introduction—was extremely well received by the Knopf sales force. Then she ceded the floor to Buckley, who gave a longer, effusive speech about Edgar and their friendship. Sophie received a note from Anthony Schulte afterward, saying "You were just right." Schulte also informed Buckley about his positive influence on the sales force: "Your talk greatly enhanced the impact on them of Edgar's book. I think there is no question that we'll have a very strong advance . . . we're off to a flying start."

Sophie, of course, expressed her own thanks to Buckley in a typically effusive letter:

Dear Bill:

(Words fail me!)
　　This is an authentic miracle only you could have achieved. This day you have made history: i.e., WORDS FAIL ME. I'm terrified. Will they ever come back??? It's like losing one's sight, man. (I was worried that the audience seemed to be missing some of your delightful witticisms, but no fear; I found out that they hadn't missed a word, not a nuance, but they were paralyzed with awe and helpless wonder.)

After the meeting, Sophie and Buckley and Ann repaired for lunch to a nearby Italian restaurant, the details of which Sophie relayed to Edgar later in the day: "Bill just quotes you and makes such a big hit every time. . . . I told him I was jealous because you write him better letters than me! You do, you palm me off with baby talk, anything is good enough for a woman as long as you cozen and flatter and make nice, right? WRONG! I want The Best of Edgar Smith, too!" It was dawning on Sophie that Edgar was skilled at being whatever the person he was engaged with wanted him to be.

Five days later, on May 14, Edgar seemed to oblige Sophie's complaints: "How long has it been since I told you that you're great? Too long, I guess. You are the greatest, and every time you think of *B.A.D.*, or whatever follows it, I want you to reach around, pat yourself on the back, and tell yourself; 'Sophie, baby, you're great!'"

She visited again eleven days later, after Edgar had implored her to come see him and help him sort through his writing struggles on his new project-in-progress: a crime novel then titled *New Utrecht*. He had started it earlier in the month and described it to Buckley as "a novel about a small town, New Utrecht, on the Hudson above Albany. . . . I have only a general idea of where the story is going. I've given some characters names, bodies, and a town to play in; now I'm just sitting here reporting what they have been up to, and mostly it's been no good." He hoped to enlist Sophie to help him through, even though she hadn't read any pages yet.

That proved to be a worse idea in person than by letter. Edgar had a hard enough time accepting criticism in writing, and in person it was worse. Their sniping grew so heated that during one visit, Sophie actually screamed at him. Both then realized that talking about business during visits was a terrible idea.

He wrote Sophie on May 29 to assert his own writing method over her editorial prowess: "I wasn't angry with you after our visit. It is just that I have my own system for writing, and while your way may be better, easier, cheaper, etc., my way is the one I like for me. That is if I go on. I haven't written a single word in a week. But all will work out, so don't fret."

She, in turn, apologized:

You shouldn't interrupt me when I am just trying to finish making a point. We can't have "just fun" visits—there is no such thing, even under ordinary circumstances, all sorts of considerations and things to hash over keep cropping up, so we must instead arrive at parliamentary procedure—each has his/her say, the other counts to 10 before starting to argue, how about that?

Apart from that, it was a fun visit, no?

Sophie kept herself abreast of Edgar's progress on the novel but disagreed with his approach to fiction. His biggest problem, she wrote on June 23, was that the novel was too bogged down in making a case rather than telling a story, which "doesn't really allow much interest in character, subtleties of behavior, motivation, destinies, apart from what you say it's all about."

The novel couldn't get interesting, she reasoned, "unless you are willing to see how complicated people are, and find the language for expressing these complications. Even a crime-and-sex story pure and simple, if there is such a thing, has got to have real people in it, in real places, in real times, and that is fully [*sic*] of detail, variety, complexity."

Buckley was delighted by the idea of Edgar's writing a novel. "All serious writers end up writing novels," he had written on May 23. "And you can see what that does to me!" But as Edgar's main confidant, he was privy to the inmate's barrage of complaints about Sophie, which Edgar finally summed up like this: "The trouble is that Sophie is an editor, and she has to edit everything she gets her hands on. You once warned me never to allow an editor to see anything but the finished product. I should have heeded your advice."

———

BUCKLEY FINALLY READ the complete manuscript of Edgar's non-fiction book at the end of May. "I have just read your 'megillah' (a word Sophie taught me)," he wrote Edgar on May 29, just before a planned trip to Greece. "I shall discuss the whole matter with you in person towards the end of June when I shall journey to Trenton. Meanwhile I am having your pages typed and directing that they should be sent to Steve [Lichtenstein]. . . . Don't misbehave!"

The note confused Edgar enough that he forwarded it to Sophie with an added scrawl: "Doesn't seem too enthusiastic about my 'megillah,' does he?" And a month later, as a catty aside: "Had you noticed that Bill is a lousy writer? He is! Sloppy, like me."

Sophie's next visit, on June 13, also didn't go well, which prompted another withering response from Edgar:

> *My! What a charming mood you were in. Reminds me of*
> *an old alligator I once met. . . . You've many times, in a*
> *charmingly helpless fashion, been grumpy and grouchy, but this*
> *was the first time I've ever found you tiresome. When horses*
> *get like that, they are shot and sent to the glue factory. I have*
> *a great many things on my mind lately, and although I could*
> *manage to find time to play guessing games with you . . . I'm*
> *not about to do it. So the next time you've got something on*
> *your mind, either say it or keep it to yourself.*

Sophie read that letter two days later, on June 18, and promptly set it aside. Then she changed her mind. "I'm hoping it will be easier to come out of my state of shock [over the angry letter] if I answer it," she wrote him. She felt responsible and explained that the extreme depression she'd been feeling lately had gotten the better of her and worsened when Edgar had asked for more photos of her. "If you could have reflected a bit, you might have understood what was wrong: those photographs of me. I tried to like them, but they confronted me with too much I can't really bear about myself."

They patched things up as the publication day of *Brief Against Death* loomed. In its fall preview, *Publishers Weekly* singled the book out as one to watch. Both Norman Mailer and Truman Capote received advance copies of the book around June 26. Sophie did not care much for Mailer: "There is an exquisitely vulgar little Yiddish saying, to the effect that you cannot dance simultaneously at two weddings with just the one ass you have, that someone should whisper into Normie Baby's ear." But, of course, she still hoped he would provide a blurb. (He didn't.)

Capote, however, did read *Brief Against Death* and "admired it!" Sophie wrote Edgar on July 10. Though he was willing to blurb the book, he was equally tempted to review it for a publication, with one large caveat:

> *Considers you guilty as charged! if he wrote, that's what*
> *he'd have to write. Gave Bill the option: choose, a blurb,*
> *no sweat; or an article, an attack! not on the book, on the*
> *author. Bill asked for a council of war. Tony, Bob, Nina.*
> *Goodhearted Nina said, not if it hurts* me *too much.*
> *Otherwise, everyone agreed that an article [was] highly*
> *desirable, regardless of which side it takes legally: big boost for*
> *book sales.*

Edgar replied right away, approving of Buckley's choice:

The more [Capote] says the better, good or bad, since the point
is that he did *take the time to say* something. *The thing now*
is to stir up a tsimmis, perhaps find an equal "name" to rebut
him. Norman Mailer, for instance, who doesn't hold much love
for Truman. As you well know, controversey [sic] is the stuff
that makes authors wealthy. Truman's words of woe could
be just the thing to cause those West Coast movie kings to say
"whoa! Maybe we're passing up a good thing." Like how often
does TC bother with other people's books. So, go!!

Years later, Buckley would write about Capote's reaction. When Buckley pressed him on why he felt Edgar was guilty, Capote replied, "I never met one yet who wasn't."

Otherwise, Edgar spent the summer months waiting, writing, and painting. The waiting was not only for *Brief Against Death*'s publication but for further word from Edgar's newly hired lawyer, Steven M. Umin of Williams & Connolly,[*] about the progress of the newest petition to the US Supreme Court. A decision earlier in the year, *Witherspoon v. Illinois*, which had held that anyone who did not believe in capital punishment could not be excluded from a jury pool in a death penalty case, could be interpreted as overturning death penalty convictions on constitutional grounds. Though it did not have an immediate impact on Edgar's case, it might affect a new ruling expected in the fall term of the Court.

---

[*]   Buckley had reached out to the firm's cofounder, Edward Bennett Williams, earlier in 1968. Williams, considered to be among the most prominent lawyers in the country, had agreed to represent Edgar in his appeals to the Supreme Court and had picked Umin, a Yale graduate, for the day-to-day duties—which also included visiting Edgar and reading through the book draft.

On August 2, Sophie received the first finished copies of *Brief Against Death*. Kathy Hourigan, now Knopf's assistant managing editor, delivered them to her, eyes shining: "Well, here's your baby!" The next day, Sophie took one of the hardcovers with her to Trenton State Prison and presented it to Edgar. Her doing so nearly proved fatal for the book's publication, as well as their relationship.

19

The Breach

AUGUST 1968

JULY 1968 was a good month for Sophie Wilkins and Edgar Smith. Their letters crackled; their visits, which had been so tense, became merry in anticipation of *Brief Against Death*'s impact on the world. The novel was progressing, but it was clear to both of them that the draft wasn't ready to be shown. "Everything you say about the writing . . . is so absolutely right!" Sophie wrote on July 25, clearly in a bid to encourage her author and amour. "You know everything, as if you were a real veteran pro of the game. You make me very very happy! Oh Ilya, you've got the biggest jewel of them all in your head. . . . All you have to do is stay like that; don't change. And keep at it."

Edgar also received a $2,250 check from the *Saturday Evening Post* for the excerpt of *Brief Against Death* that it was going to run, and Steve Umin, his lawyer, had sent a progress report on the latest appeal. Sophie's visit on August 3, to give him the freshly printed hardcover, was another bright spot. He wrote to Buckley that evening, saying he thought that Knopf had done a "beautiful job" with the finished version and he looked forward to reading it that night.

But the very next day, August 4, Edgar was in a state of rage.

He had read the first three chapters and flipped out over the most minor changes made by the copy editor. He wrote Sophie on August 4, "Darling, it is hot, damp, sticky, miserable, and I'm in a bad mood. . . . Why the bad mood? Brace yourself . . . BAD news! After three chapters, Ilya is ready to disown *BAD*. The jacket, format, etc., are great, but inside . . ." After listing some minor errors, he went for the jugular: "What makes me angry is the rewrite. There are sentences in there I wouldn't have written under the threat of torture. . . . Totally sickening, stupid sentence[s]."

Edgar told Sophie he intended to discuss the matter more with her on her next visit, but he made one thing clear: "If this is how it will be with everything I write, then I've written my last book." He then underlined the next sentence in red: "*In fact, as far as I'm concerned, I didn't write BAD. I wrote the manuscript, not the book*, and it may be a good thing I *am* in jail. If I went on the *Today* Show, I'd damn sure *tell* them I didn't write it. I'm not saying the book isn't good, it is, damn good, but it is *not mine*, not *what I wrote*, or *how I wrote it*."

He wasn't done: "If you want to give me hell for saying these things, go right ahead. You're entitled to blast me in return. I'm ungrateful, egotistical, insufferable, a nobody telling off the pros, etc., but I am, or *was*, also a writer who knows what he wants to say and how he wants to say it. Any publisher who doesn't like it can write his own book. I don't *have* to write for publication, nor do I have to *beg* anyone to publish me. It is strictly take it or leave it."

What's most astonishing is how quickly he then pivoted to declaring his love and adoration for Sophie, despite having disowned the book they'd spent the past year working on together: "Talk to me, loud and angry if ya want. I'll still love you."

Sophie, upon receiving the letter, immediately telephoned

Steve Lichtenstein, the lawyer Edgar still retained for state-related legal matters. She was, understandably, furious. The last thing she wanted to do was go through Edgar's complaints one by one with Lichtenstein. But it had to be done so his lawyer could know the full extent of his irrational behavior.

She followed up with Lichtenstein by letter on August 6, re-laying Edgar's complaints about the finished copy of *Brief Against Death*. A sentence that Edgar had judged "totally sickening, stupid" had been changed by the copy editor from "their knowledge" to "knowing"—a change, Sophie said, "I would certainly support against anyone. That this change makes his sentence totally sickening and stupid is hard to see. Of course we will have to go back to the manuscript to make sure, but I shouldn't think that Bill's typist could have taken it upon herself to change the sentence radically enough from the original to make such a comment rational."

Sophie then uttered a most prescient comment: "Frankly, is our friend psycho? This would not be the first indication I have had of *it*"—though if she had had such a prior indication, she had never expressed it to anyone in writing.

Then she set about answering Edgar's jeremiad, in a tone that was all business and controlled anger:

> *You are saying in effect that your publishers, that is, your editors, changed your manuscript beyond recognition, willfully, and ruthlessly for the worse? That is a very serious matter. I don't know if you can imagine how stricken I feel, thinking how you must be feeling, and also wondering what could have possessed your editors, who I gathered from you had been particularly devoted to you and done a great deal of hard work over and above the call of duty? Well, there is really only one thing to do: they will have to get the setting copy of the*

manuscript from their production people and see where those changes were made.

Sophie told Edgar that she believed that he had authorized Knopf to supervise copyediting without submitting the copyedited manuscript to him for review because it would be quite difficult to smuggle the manuscript back in, but the quickness of the production process was no excuse, she wrote. "All I can say at the moment is that I am terribly sorry to hear it; you are certainly within your rights [to]—indeed, you must—protest."

Until the matter was sorted out, she concluded, "I honestly can't at this moment continue writing about trivialities." She then asked Edgar for one favor:

I would so appreciate it if you could manage to return all photographs and letters, especially sagas, as quickly and as best possible? I shall live in a perpetual state of uneasiness until I receive them back—or at least until I have your assurance that you will do your best to get them back to me. I'm sure you'll understand. If you consider what the effect of your violent denunciation had to be, since I claim all responsibility for what happened.

A few days later, she wrote to him that she'd written her own racy sagas only "to make you feel you were not alone! To keep you company as best I could." Sophie was even more self-justifying in a note to Buckley: "I'd like you to understand that it was not for nothing, not purely biochemistry or whatever (biochemistry, like Nietzsche's syphilis, is the occasion, not the cause, in my view) but a form of gambling and adventuring deliberately engaged in, *pour le sport*, and let there be no weeping at the bar when I put out to see [*sic*]."

Sophie wrote to Steve Lichtenstein again on August 7. She wanted to impress upon him how serious Edgar's charges were and why she'd had to go into an all-business mode, but she also wanted the lawyer to be the conduit of communication between her and Edgar and to leave Buckley out of the controversy if possible.

> [Edgar] must understand that all friendship is suspended while this matter, which threatens my existence, is being cleared up. It is not the first time I have received a vicious slap from this strange man, to whom, and to whose cause, I may well have given myself somewhat too unreservedly. It always comes just when there is least reason to expect it: when one has just done something for him, or thinks one has, and is proud of it. I am determined that this shall be the last instance, however. Fortunately he no longer needs me; my job is essentially done.

If Edgar did go ahead with his threats to tell the public about the "bowdlerized" book, she warned, he should proceed with extreme care. "While his charges can be all too easily disproved, by the time they are, he may have succeeded too well in undermining public faith in the book, reducing to nil it's [sic] effectiveness in helping him bolster and possibly win his case, and making a shambles of everything once more."

That same Wednesday, in the early evening, Edgar proceeded to answer Sophie's letters:

> My poor redhead: your letters of the happy 4th and unhappy 6th are here, but I honestly wish the latter had gotten lost in transit. Must you take everything as a personal insult? Couldn't you have waited until I had finished reading and had prepared a detailed list for you? If for one moment I had

thought your reaction would be on a personal level, I'd just as soon burn the damn book, for you are more important to me than it is, far more. It is totally illogical for you to assume that any dislike for BAD must necessarily include dislike for you. You frustrate me, utterly, and leave me afraid ever to say anything to you but the most banal nothings.

The entire letter must have been nauseating for Sophie to read. It wheedled and cajoled, placed the blame squarely upon her for reacting to his anger as opposed to himself for his own irrational and damaging response, and descended further into irrationality: "True, one word was changed, but that is precisely the change I dislike. It has nothing to do with whether the sentence is correct, or whether anyone else would ever notice it, or even whether it improves the whole: all I am saying is that *I* don't like it. I *might* have written it exactly as it appears, but I wouldn't have done so in *that* context."

Later in the letter, even Edgar admitted that was "nitpicking," but he continued to argue points and then to flatter Sophie by calling her "the greatest, and you mean the world to me. I like you, and I love you."

The letter gained him no traction with Sophie. Before she could read his missive, she'd fired off another letter on Thursday insisting that all of her letters and photographs be returned at once. She told Edgar he needed to face the fact that he was "a trifle, shall we say insensitive, to other persons' feelings." She went through, step by step, the exact process from when the manuscript was typeset into a book to his outsize reactions and why she felt she must break off their personal relationship.

Sophie wondered if her reaction to what he had done to her— "Not for the first time, perhaps not even for the last, though I am trying to make it the last"—could "force you to see something that is deeply at the root of your life, the root of all your trouble, something in your personality and character it may be impossible to change but that it might be very helpful for you to at least *perceive*, as clearly as a human being may perceive his own nature; if you could gain an insight into what it is that causes you, inevitably I am afraid, to hurt yourself by means of hurting those who love you, and serve you, it might all be wonderfully worth while [*sic*]."

That paragraph is so perceptive and so knowing. Yet within two weeks, Sophie and Edgar had repaired their breach, patched up their profound differences, and resumed their more-than-friendship all over again—thanks, in no small part, to the interventions of William F. Buckley.

———

EDGAR AT LAST realized he had gone too far. "Clumsy Smith put his foot in it," he wrote Buckley on August 8, explaining that he had done a "terrible job" explaining "minor complaints" to Sophie. But contriteness immediately gave way to more complaining: "She reacted as if I had told her she has bad breath. Lord! She takes every single word as a personal affront. I have told Steve [Lichtenstein] that if you tell Sophie the weather is lousy, she thinks you are blaming her for it. It is a good thing she isn't coming to see me this weekend; she is angry enough to bring a gun and shoot me through the window." At least in the version he gave Buckley, Edgar had altered his tune: "All in all, my final verdict is that the book is fine, and that Sophie did a great job. If you think so, please tell her. She won't believe *me*."

A few days later, Buckley and Sophie met to discuss how things had fallen apart with her and Edgar. Buckley hadn't understood the full gist of the situation until then because he'd had other things on his mind. The Republican and Democratic national conventions were taking place over the summer, and he and Gore Vidal had been hired by ABC to provide commentary. Buckley had just returned from Miami, where he and Vidal had clashed so much over the course of the Republican National Convention that Buckley had suggested changing the debate format entirely. ABC, however, had refused. The conflict would boil over into unmitigated loathing on both sides. Vidal would call Buckley a "crypto-Nazi," and in response Buckley would utter a homophobic slur on air.

After his meeting with Sophie, Buckley wrote to Edgar on August 15, "It is quite true that her feelings were hurt. I know she is sensitive—so are a great many people. But it is also true that your letter—I mean the one in which you all but disowned the book—was cruel and unusual punishment for someone who all but broke her back in arranging for its production. I think the crisis is well over, and that now you have rediscovered your imperturbability she will herself soon be fully restored. I will keep my eye on her for you." That last declaration was mostly symbolic, what with the imminent start of the Democratic National Convention (and the subsequent infamy of his on-air exchanges with Vidal).

Edgar's mood also improved with the news that the Death House would allow the inmates to use the recreation yard for an hour a day, in groups of five or six, as soon as new sidewalks were put in. Several inmates had gone on a hunger strike, which had certainly influenced the decision. But Edgar didn't think it was the only reason. "The prison education director, who thinks the Death House restrictions are silly, has suggested that my book's criticisms of the prison authorities may be the actual cause," he wrote Buckley on August 19. "He says there is a feeling that I have—get this!—held the authorities up to 'public ridicule.' Interesting."

A week later, on August 26, Buckley reported receiving a "sweet note from Sophie and all is forgiven so I don't think you have to concern yourself." But Sophie had already written to Edgar two days before: "I was afraid and angry. What I chiefly feared was this: that you could be so 'cruel' to me even though your feelings hadn't changed and since this kind of thing had happened before, perhaps you were a man who was compulsively cruel to those (women) he loved and who loved him." It now seemed "a wild idea" to Sophie, but "the effort to take myself back almost gave me a schizophrenia; in fact, I couldn't." Neither Sophie nor Edgar, it seemed, could stop writing to the other, even as they both acknowledged the extreme pain and suffering caused by writing to each other.

Sophie, normally so preoccupied with her weight and appearance, had been astonished to step onto the scale the morning of August 10 and discover she had dropped seven pounds in five days and was down to 118 pounds, "something of a record, considering how hard I find it to lose even a lb a week, ordinarily." At the Knopf offices, people had come up to her saying that she looked awful. William Koshland, an editorial colleague, suggested that she take some time off, "go to a stupid movie, don't do anything."

A long letter written between August 9 and 10, sent via Lichtenstein, saw Edgar pouring his feelings onto the page ("What does one say when the world falls apart? Without you, without the sheer fun of knowing you, of looking forward to 'owl mail,' and to your visits, nothing else really seems worthwhile") and wondering if his initial recoiling from the finished book had been more about his own insecurity than the misdeeds of his publisher.

For Buckley had read the final version of *Brief Against Death* and sent him a telegram, telling him the book was a "triumph." Several others, including *Paterson Evening News* columnist Bob

Curley, also sang the book's praises to Edgar. "Is it possible that my initial dislike was in fact a reflection of my embarrassment at having done something damn well, which for me is unusual?" Edgar asked. "In other words, perhaps I was putting *myself* down, nitpicking because I didn't feel comfortable hearing so many compliments. . . . That's something to ponder." He told Sophie that he wouldn't write to her again unless she wrote to him.

Edgar also wrote to Robert Gottlieb, mostly to compliment the publishing house's and Wilkins's editorial work but also to kvetch about the copyediting changes. That incensed Sophie but did not deter her from visiting him on August 17, finding him in a euphoric mood. He had finally reconciled himself to the fact that, as she later relayed to Lichtenstein, "he is the author of a good book that will get a lot of favorable attention, despite having been failed by his publisher's minions."

Sophie couldn't help admitting the truth: her relationship with Edgar, in all of its "hatkic" glory, had been a great adventure, one she wouldn't have missed.

> But the time has also come for me to sober up and get back to doing my chores in a considerably less Romantic vein than I have this past year. It was exciting to be so closely acquainted with a type of person I would normally never have known at all. But in the end one realizes, a bit sadly perhaps, that it is after all necessary to stick to one's own kind. My kind? why, graduate students of literature, what else?

Edgar, however, would remain "her kind" for a while longer. *Brief Against Death* was about to be published, and its reception would exceed everyone's expectations.

20

Brief Against Death

SEPTEMBER–DECEMBER 1968

WITH THE MISUNDERSTANDING about the book's presentation now a thing of the past, the unlikely triumvirate of William F. Buckley, Edgar Smith, and Sophie Wilkins could prepare for the publication of *Brief Against Death*, where it would be transformed from a work read by few to a work read—and judged—by many.

It was a book that merited criticism but also made a convincing case for Edgar's innocence. Thanks to Sophie's extensive editorial efforts, *Brief Against Death* depicted Edgar as a wronged young man who happened to fall under police scrutiny for a crime he didn't commit—murder—even as he admitted knowing Vickie Zielinski, that she had been in his car the night she died, and that they had fought.

More odious, however, was the way Edgar painted Vickie as sexually voracious and manipulative (despite being fifteen), as if in order to save his own life he was determined to tar hers. *Brief Against Death* also depicted Don Hommell as the probable killer with sneering disdain (though he did cut all mention of Hommell being a "psychopath"). No wonder he had nearly run afoul of libel laws and needed to be pulled back from the brink. But

Vickie, being dead, had no such legal recourse to counter Edgar's descriptions.

Naturally, local newspapers reached out to Bergen County law enforcement officials for their reactions to the existence of *Brief Against Death*. Few obliged them with comments. County Prosecutor Guy Calissi declined on the basis that he hadn't read the book. "The case is still open. . . . After it is finally resolved I'll have comments to make. Right now, he is trying to sell a book." Chief of Detectives Walter Spahr was even less tactful: "All newspapers and books are rags."

Edgar was curious about the initial sales figures, and when Sophie asked if he would be upset if the book didn't sell well, he tried to reassure her. "Do you *really* suppose it would bother me so much if *BAD* flopped?" he wrote on September 3. "Besides, it *can't* disappoint me. I've already made . . . more than I expected, and that is just the beginning." Two days later, he changed his tune somewhat: "Let's sell a trillion copies; I want to see *BAD* on the best-seller list."

Edgar was pleased with the reviews, from Ruth Blum's "incredible" coverage in the Ridgewood *Sunday News* to the coverage in *Esquire*, *Time*, and *National Review*. Bergen *Record* staff writer Mark Howat deemed the book "amazing" and felt it raised a reasonable doubt about Smith's guilt in the reader's mind. Ross Macdonald's rave in the *New York Times Book Review* came to a similar conclusion: "If Eddie didn't kill Vickie Zielinski—and I find myself seriously doubting that he could have—he has been cruelly mistreated. . . . In view of the circumstances in which he produced it, Mr. Smith's book is rather a triumph." Macdonald's piece caused Buckley to crack, "For such a review as you got in the *New York Times, I* would go to the chair." (The paper's daily book critic, Christopher Lehmann-Haupt, however, was cutting in his review, concluding that Smith seemed "almost priggishly proud of his accomplishments" and came across "as an intellectual parvenu without the graces of insight.")

Edgar also looked forward to watching Buckley discuss the book on *The Tonight Show* with its host, Johnny Carson, on September 4, and on the *Today* show with Barbara Walters on the morning of September 10. "Gee, wouldn't it be fun for *me* to be out there plugging BAD, instead of imposing upon [WFB]? Taking your own book on radio and TV would, at least to me, be half the fun of writing one."

After Edgar watched his friend on *The Tonight Show*, he wrote Buckley in the wee hours of September 5:

> *I am not certain that I shall ever be the same. If I had a hat,*
> *I would very quickly try it on to be sure it still fit. Five more*
> *minutes of your compliments and I should have become totally*
> *insufferable. What can I say? I appreciate everything you have*
> *done, and are doing, but "thanks" seems an awfully weak way*
> *to say it. But I had better not get too effusive or I shall begin*
> *to embarrass you. Perhaps I shall buy you a Rolls-Royce—a*
> *Conservative black?—and let it go at that.*

Buckley also appeared—as did Edgar's lawyer, Steve Lichtenstein, and Knopf publisher Anthony Schulte—on television station WNEW's five-part special on *Brief Against Death* during its publication week. Reporter Lloyd Dobyns asked Buckley why the conservative had befriended the convict, "an unlikely combination, one that most people wouldn't imagine and some won't accept."

Buckley dismissed the judgment, saying "The notion that conservatives are less interested in justice . . . is highly self-serving and highly untrue. I know a lot of conservatives, including myself, who desire much more justice than in fact we have, because what we have now is something like 15 percent of malefactors actually ending up in prison. I'd like that figure to be 100 percent, but I'm certainly not disposed to put innocent men in jail, let alone execute them." He then repeated his assertion that Edgar Smith was innocent and that he was a person of "enormous gifts, great literary powers, and a great sense of human understanding."

Edgar's postpublication letters to Sophie oozed sentimentality. "My love, know what I'll be thinking watching [Buckley]? That if it had not been for a certain gypsy princess name of Sarai, there wouldn't *be* any *BAD*. Told you all that once before—first epic?—and it is true; Sarai really *is BAD*'s mother, and Boy! there were times when the labor pains were sompn [*sic*] else."

Sophie reacted to the book's publication in typical high Romantic fashion. "I should be finishing pressing chores but my heart is full of ilya and my throat is all swole up with emotions which will strangulate me if I don't ease up on the pressure by opening a valve, quick! emoigency," she dashed off late in the day on September 7. "DARLING ILYA! Can you imagine how I feel seeing your book in those store windows, with all the latest geniuses like Tom Wolfe, McNamara's which is likely to become a best seller too, I can't think of the rest except Vidal's [*Myra Breckenridge*] that Bill hates so much." In the grip of full publication fever, she allowed herself to admit to feelings she had tried to suppress: "I know you do [know] . . . how I love you, how very much I love loving you, how it nearly killed me when I thought, one desperate day recently, that I must stop, must tear it out root and branch."

The day before, Sophie had returned to the Death House to see Edgar one more time before she set off on her annual European trip, which would take her to Zurich for a week and then London for another week. The visit went so well that Edgar reflected in a letter to her afterward, "In some ways the tsimmis over BAD may have been the best thing for us; it shook us both up real good, knocked down some of our silly complacency, and now both of us are hooked more than ever. . . . You're always a sweet, very gentle magician's assistant, quite lovable, and who should know better'n he who duz?"

By October 10, two days after Sophie's return to New York, she had sales figures to share with Edgar: 1,594 orders of *Brief Against Death* over the prior two weeks, bringing the total to 14,025, with 18,500 copies in print. It was good news in that it made the book "6th-highest on [Knopf's internal] list of 30, led only by Childs, Updike, Richter, Spark, Bowen." But both Edgar and Sophie had hoped for better sales. Buckley, meanwhile, was floored by the avalanche of good reviews. "I swear I never saw such a universally favorable reaction to any book in my life. You must be awfully proud," he wrote Edgar.

A week later, Sophie and Buckley rejoiced that *Brief Against Death* had landed Edgar a special citation for the New Jersey Author Award, which would be given in Atlantic City on November 8. Smith, of course, could not attend the ceremony, so Buckley volunteered to go, over Edgar's protests that it was a waste of time, since he could also visit Edgar.

The good book news helped alleviate the trio's nervousness about what was in store in November: How would the Supreme Court rule on Edgar's most recent filing? Buckley couldn't stop himself from wondering if there might be a new trial at this time next year. "My Gods, that would be a trial for you!" he wrote Edgar in early October. "Biggest thing since the Scopes Trial." Edgar's lawyer Steve Umin wrote on October 29, "The mills of justice grind slowly, as you of all people need not be told. All I can hope is that your adrenalin is reasonably under control."

It turned out that the Supreme Court had punted on taking action until its return from recess in mid-November. Edgar learned of the "non-decision" on October 30 from Steve Lichten-stein, who had heard it from Steve Umin. As they waited for the next legal move, he returned to his novel, writing and rewriting pages. "Gee, is it fun to be writing again," he wrote Sophie on November 5. "Headaches, cramped hand, sore butt, and all. I have to make myself stop and go to bed, then I toss and turn all night juggling ideas for the next day."

Then came the big shock: on November 12, the Supreme Court granted the writ of certiorari—a decision to hear the case after reviewing lower-court decisions—and ordered the New Jersey District Court to consider whether or not Edgar was en-titled to a new evidentiary hearing on his bid for habeas corpus. (The lone dissenter was Justice Byron White, who preferred that the Supreme Court hold its own oral arguments after "granting cert.")

"Do you think the book helped? Or was it all Umin?" won-dered Sophie after Buckley had called her at work to deliver the news. "Oh my eagle, are you happy? Did you expect it? did you half expect it? Did you believe it when they told you? Don't you think it's the beginning of a new deal? I do. I do. I do."

Edgar was understandably ecstatic about the decision, but he tried to temper his feelings in his letters to Sophie and to Buckley:

> A whole lot of people, including WFB, Jr., wondered why I sat back, quietly cracking the books, imperturbably depending on the courts—instead of screaming like hell. Well, now you know. It may take a long time, and be very frustrating at times, but most of the time this slow, sometimes confusing, legal system of ours manages, usually in spite of itself, to work. The end is a long way off, perhaps years, but we're no longer at the bottom of the ladder.

Buckley saw no reason to temper his reaction. He sent a telegram to Edgar in the Death House right away: "This is a great day. The beginning of your vindication. Everyone wild with pleasure."

Umin went even further with his unbridled enthusiasm, as this very short letter to his client indicated:

Dear Edgar,

OooooooooooooEeeeeeeeeeeee!!!!!!!!!!!!!!!!

Yours, Steve

(Edgar duly forwarded the note to Sophie, who sent it on to Buckley, so he'd be "amused by this covering letter from an extremely dignified young Washington attorney, to accompany a certain Supreme Court decision.")

With the clock restarted and a fresh round of appeals set into motion, Edgar informed Sophie on November 13 that he would either stay put in the Death House "or if the judge wishes, I go out on bail like Sam Shepard [*sic*]." Buckley, meanwhile, was trying to figure out the best way forward for Edgar's legal defense, deciding that "the top full-time trial lawyer" at Williams & Connolly, Vincent Fuller, should handle the case, with Steve Umin on board in an advisory capacity.

He also implored Steve Lichtenstein, who had been Edgar's lawyer at the state level off and on since 1962, to stay on board, albeit in a more limited role. As he wrote him on December 16, "The conclusion is that we must go for broke this next time out. Even if we lose, we can I am sure count on Edgar's ultimate vindication. But the interval would then be harrowing. Even if we win, the gates to the prison will not thereupon open: but they will never look so obdurate again." If Edgar was to be released, Buckley believed, "the trail of gratitude will lead back to those dark days a few years ago when singlehandedly [*sic*] and for no compensation at all, you kept him alive." Lichtenstein agreed to stay on.

Edgar also wondered if the Supreme Court decision would help sales of *Brief Against Death*: "There is certain to be plenty of publicity, especially while the hearing is going on, what with me testifying and all. I'll bet Tony [Schulte] said: 'Whoopee!'" Knopf was looking for some good news, since the sales of the hardcover—though respectable, and into a third printing—weren't up to best-seller snuff, attracting a mere $8,000 advance (equivalent to almost $60,000 in today's dollars) from Avon for the paperback rights, which would include a new afterword by the author, covering the new developments.

As 1968 drew to a close, editor and author acknowledged how important each was to the other. Edgar wrote Sophie on December 8, "I've got so many fans—but only one owl, and it's she who counts." He backed it up with a Christmas gift of an expensive radio.

"I am reimpressed with what a *born* writer you are," Sophie wrote him on December 20. "Something so *refreshing* about the way you express things. No wonder people tell me when they finish *Brief* they just start all over again." Talk of love or not, Sophie knew her role was to midwife Edgar's writing. His first book was now out in the world. What would become of the next?

PART V

REASONABLE DOUBTS

(1969–1971)

21

Rogue's Wake

1969

FOR SOPHIE WILKINS, 1968 had been, as she wrote Edgar Smith on November 22, "the best most interesting most exciting year of my whole entire total life????" She also declared she had lived more in that one year than in any twenty others. But the new year brought a change in perspective: *Brief Against Death* was in the past, Edgar's novel wasn't going very well, and she found herself tiring of the high drama of her relationship with him, wishing for something quieter—and more professional.

Edgar, however, didn't share Sophie's sense that things needed to change between them. He'd also ended the year in the highest of spirits, what with the Supreme Court decision, more than three hundred pages written on the novel, and a flurry of romantic attention, old and new. He had rekindled a connection with an old high school flame, Jane Tremont,[*] the daughter of the owner of a popular restaurant in Ramsey, while simultaneously deepening a burgeoning romance with a former actress and legal secretary named Juliette Scheinman, who would go on to play a significant role in his life.

---

[*] Not her real name.

In 1957, Juliette had been living in Bergen County, more than a year into her marriage to the Wall Street broker William X. Scheinman and mother to their newborn son, Billy. The trial had been all over the local papers. After Edgar's death sentence, Juliette hadn't paid much more attention, eventually forgetting all about Edgar Smith and Victoria Zielinski, until she chanced upon a newspaper ad publicizing the publication of *Brief Against Death* in the fall of 1968.

Her life had changed a great deal in the intervening eleven years. Her marriage to Bill Scheinman ended when he took up with another woman, and she had long before left Bergen County for the Upper West Side, moving to an apartment on West End Avenue near Lincoln Center. A single mother of two—an older son, Douglas, was the result of a brief first marriage—Juliette went to work as a corporate secretary, work she would continue doing well into her seventies. She became politically active, serving on the board of directors of the Ansonia Independent Democrats, though her zeal would prove to have limits. In April 1970, when the group had decided to host a fund-raising party for the Black Panthers—akin to a comparable, infamous party hosted by Leonard Bernstein and his wife, Felicia, at their Upper East Side town house and brutally satirized by Tom Wolfe in *New York* magazine—Juliette had refused to pay the admission, did not buy any drinks, and did not contribute to the cause.

She also revived her interest in acting, going out on auditions with modest, though declining, success. Her features were striking, her hair the color of obsidian, cascading past her shoulders. She had a wide smile, a sense of style that made her look more expensively dressed than what she could actually afford, and deep blue eyes that promised laughter—but they belied childhood trauma (abuse by her older brothers) and adult strife. Fortunato was Juliette's maiden name, but fortunate she was not.

Most people, upon reading *Brief Against Death*, might have discussed it with their friends and left it at that. But a select few went further, donating money to Edgar's defense fund or writing a note of appreciation they hoped would reach Edgar himself. Juliette, however, tried to kindle a friendship with Sophie Wilkins. How they first connected is unclear; perhaps their reasonable proximity to one another on the Upper West Side—though "reasonable proximity" still involved a thirty-six-block separation.

The two women went out for drinks and discovered they liked each other enormously. Sophie encouraged Juliette to write to Edgar. She also encouraged Edgar to write to Juliette, in the hope that the other woman might offer added comfort and pleasure for the inmate, having already ventured too far, she felt, with her own emotions and sublimated desires. Let it be some other woman's turn. That woman could be Juliette Scheinman. Though when it *was* Juliette's turn—by the end of 1968, Juliette and Edgar had embarked on their own torrid epistolary affair—Sophie found she wasn't pleased by the news after all.

"Watch your step, smarty pants," she warned Edgar. "This female is plumb gone on you." Juliette was, indeed, entranced. She found she could write him with an open heart, and, at least in his letters, he appeared to respond in kind. Her first visit to Trenton State Prison on January 17—after they'd filled out the requisite forms describing Juliette as a "cousin"—made an indelible impression upon Edgar. Sophie had dressed smartly, and her letters to him had become heated, but Juliette was a whole other category.

Her love of Bloomingdale's and Bergdorf Goodman— affordability be damned—was borne out in what she wore and how she looked, what with the alligator shoes, the rust-colored Chanel dress, and the silver mink jacket. "One look at her and my first thought was, 'Oh, God, I couldn't keep a woman like that in stockings,'" Edgar admitted to Buckley in a letter two days after her first visit. She was out of his league but clearly wanted to play in it. Buckley was amused and delighted by the news of Juliette's entrance into Edgar's life.

The correspondence continued and grew more romantic and frank. Juliette confessed that she hoped to get married (in general, not specifically to Edgar) atop the Empire State Building. Edgar, sensing a Freudian symbol of the highest caliber, wrote back that *he* wanted to be married in the Grand Canyon.

As he wrote in late February, "I'm afraid, Bill, that your protegee—so sez the NY Daily Snooze—is way over his head with this chick. Wow! And of course Sophie and mother are ever alert to protect the last vestiges of my chasity [*sic*] from the onslaughts of said designing woman. I'm beginning to feel like a football that has been fumbled on the goal line with less than a minute to play in the game."

––––

EDGAR'S INCREASED ATTENTION from women old and new was a lot to juggle, and he didn't think much about the consequences of Sophie finding out the full extent of his epistolary flights of fantasy. In his mind, his relationship with Sophie was still humming along as it had in the past. "I am *very* happy, *very* much in love, and hope you are, too," he'd written her three days before Christmas. "It has been a good year for us. Next will be better."

Conditions on death row had improved for him, too. No longer was he confined to his cell but for a single hour. He had more time to go outside, to walk in the snow, and to interact with others if he chose. Book proceeds were plentiful enough that he was able (by tapping the bank account controlled by William F. Buckley) to buy a typewriter, a Sears portable.

But then his progress on the novel stalled, and that seemed to sour his attitude to everything else. "Have you ever thought that life is an endless series of stupidities, and that those who are happiest are only those who have been least stupid?" he wrote Sophie on January 5.

> I can't recall any time in my life when I've been less satisfied with the state of things than I have been lately. Don't ask me to explain; I'm not sure myself how I'd prefer things to be, or what it is I really want. Who said, "war is hell?" He was wrong. Life is hell, and I suppose for each of us it is a private hell of our own making. I think Bill and I will have to have a long talk one of these days.

Sophie also decided to pull back emotionally (and for good) in January. There wasn't a last straw, per se, but the problems at home were intensifying. Thurman's mental health continued to decline, resulting in a breakdown that hospitalized him later in the year. Hearing that Edgar had resumed a relationship with Jane Tremont also rankled. "This old woman is getting out of that shoe in which she was playing so many inappropriate games she didn't know what to do!" she joked to Edgar on January 7.

What Sophie didn't know then, though Edgar confessed some of it to Buckley on January 12, was that he hoped Jane "may someday be Mrs. Smith—a fact which is to be considered *the* secret of this or any other year." That hope was mostly unfounded, as his high school crush had no intention of leaving her marriage (and never did). She regarded Edgar as only a friend. Still, between Jane's visits and those of Juliette Scheinman, Edgar's romantic fantasy life had become far more complicated. He told Buckley, "Did you know that I so bedazzled the ladies? I guess I am just a big, bad wolf." Things were so complicated that he felt as if he were stuck in the pages of a novel titled *Rogue's Wake*.

Sophie's letters, meanwhile, grew increasingly self-lacerating, expressing her jealousy over Edgar's romantic foibles, casting aside her early attempts to play it cool. She compared her reaction to that of his mother in a missive dated January 16: "The only difference between Ann . . . and me when it comes to possessiveness toward our man is that I *try* to be conscious of it. I *try* to watch it, curb it, frustrate it, *because I despise it*. But I am afflicted with it just exactly like her or anybody."

A week later, on January 23, she wrote extensively of her feelings, though it's unclear if it was her final breakup letter or if she'd written back-to-back letters to Edgar ending things, as she'd done before. Nor is it clear how much the letter truly conveyed the depths of her anger at Edgar and at herself. "It dawned on me, suddenly, that the reason I had been behaving, not like a friend, certainly not like an editor, but like an hysterical wetnurse, was the fixed idea that there you were, all cooped up, and it depended on me to keep you in touch with life, love, self, soul, you name it!"

Sophie claimed that in her imagination, she was playing God and her "life-giving words" were keeping Edgar alive in the daily wretchedness that was the Death House. She looked back at "all the awful drivel I have written in over a year"—presumably the entirety of her correspondence, including the "epics"—and knew she would "never be able to look at it without dying of embarrassment! it will all be destroyed, sight unseen, as soon as I can catch my breath and ferret it all out." She implored, positively begged, Edgar to "drop all that . . . hatkic stuff, at once and forever" because "I only went along with it in order to keep things as lively and interesting as possible." Needless to say, however, Sophie didn't destroy most of the "awful drivel."

Edgar, too, had reached his limits of patience with Sophie's melancholy. "There is no refuting the curious logic by which you find that what you fear must be, is," he wrote on January 26.

> *You have been driven all your life by a lemming-like compulsion to give up that which you want most, to surrender so that you can convince yourself you didn't lose, to step aside to make room for your own shadow, and I know of no instant therapy to cure you at this late date. I've lost, and I've been beat—often—but quitting is something I know nothing about, except that, unlike a loser, a quitter can never become a winner. It takes guts to lose, but anyone big or small, bright or stupid, young or old, can quit—maybe that is why there are more quitters than losers.*

They did not keep the change in their personal relationship, from romantic to purposefully platonic, to themselves. Buckley knew all about it, corresponded about it, and expressed a mixture of amusement and bemusement about it. He assumed, contrary to Edgar's assertions, that Sophie was not, in fact, romantically jealous of Jane and Juliette and tried to reassure Sophie of her primacy in Edgar's world.

She begged to differ:

> *Of course I am jealous (I appreciate your intention, of course): I don't call it romantic, I think it's deplorable, but I am not a disembodied spirit, and after being cuddled, verbally, for a year, the only and enormously appreciated doll on the scene, it is positively nerve-wrenching to feel suddenly and totally displaced, superseded, upstaged, a spearbearer in the last*

invisible row, with two (2) new heroines out front prancing
about in their haloes and Bergdorf hairdos. Humiliating! and
so unnecessarily, too.

Edgar also saw the value in decreasing the frequency of his
letter writing to Sophie. While the two exchanged hundreds of
letters over that fevered year and a half between July 1967 and
December 1968, there are only a couple of dozen pieces of correspondence from January 1969 onward in Sophie's papers.

The timing also likely coincided with the cancellation of Edgar's permission to send and receive uncensored mail through
his lawyers in early April. Prison officials had flagged a missive
to Edgar from Jane, forwarded by Steve Lichtenstein. The fatal
blow to his ability to evade the censors was an erotic letter Edgar
wrote to Juliette Scheinman, though he tried to brush it off to
Buckley as "much too long a story to get into here, and the reasons aren't all that important."

After prison officials intercepted that one, they also put the ki-
bosh on the twice-a-month visits Juliette originally was granted
by Judge O'Dea. It would likely have made Juliette blush if she'd
ever seen it.[*] Its crude, hyperbolic eroticism—even more explicit
than the fantasies that Edgar had written for Sophie—was also a
promise of what might happen between Edgar and Juliette without the restriction of prison bars, walls, and rules.

The loss of uncensored mail transmission, coupled with the
climbing costs of both state and federal lawyers, further black-
ened Edgar's mood. "I am sorry that things have developed in
this manner because I know you will be concerned about me, but

---

[*]   The letter was included with the Bergen County Prosecutor's Office documents sent to the California Parole Board in 2000 as objection to Edgar's
possible release.

I cannot help it," he complained to Buckley on April 30. "I have had it—with the courts, with lawyers, with the day to day petty annoyances of this place. It is possible that I have finally discovered the half-life of imperturbability. I don't know. I do know that, one way or the other, something has to happen, and it has to happen soon."

What with the many months before the state court planned a hearing, even more months waiting for the decision, and then "2 or 3 years of appeals by the state," Edgar came to the conclusion "that I simply will not make it. Nor do I care to try." The next month, when he learned that habeas corpus hearings had been scheduled for two death row inmates—both, like Smith, from Bergen County but, unlike him, lacking in legal counsel—at a more rapid pace, Edgar's opinion was pure acid: "I should have been born black. I could then have called the judge a racist pig, at which point he would have apologized for being one and immediately granted the hearing."

After the confiscated letter fracas, Edgar's appropriately contrite *mea culpa* restored Juliette's visiting privileges in June 1969. Within two days of Judge O'Dea's ruling that she could once again visit twice a month, Edgar's cell was searched, and prison officials discovered contraband items, including half of a dull razor blade, half of a dollar bill, and his wedding ring. That resulted in ten days spent in "the hole" (full solitary confinement) and the revocation of the court order allowing Juliette to visit more frequently. Even though Edgar protested that he'd been allowed his wedding ring by the previous warden, "that apparently cuts no ice around here," he wrote Buckley on June 18. "Steve Lichtenstein told me that they are 'trying to tell me something.' I've got the message, loud and clear."

The following month, President Richard Nixon finally nominated two judges to fill vacancies in New Jersey's federal district courts: Leonard Garth for the Newark branch, and George Barlow, a Mercer County judge and former state assistant attorney general, for the seat in Trenton. The judges would not be confirmed by Congress until the end of the year, which put back the prospect of a hearing until the spring of 1970.

Once more in legal limbo, Edgar decided to focus on more pressing matters: finishing his novel and finding someone to publish it.

———

DESPITE THE REDUCTION in their personal correspondence in 1969, Sophie was still amenable to reading portions of Edgar's novel, now titled *A Reasonable Doubt*. In her estimation, its prospects of publication were not very good. The quality of the writing in *Brief Against Death*, and especially in their charged correspondence, simply wasn't present in the novel. The characters were stock, the language was turgid, and the plot seemed a fictional retread of Edgar's nonfiction book rather than a living, breathing chronicle of a town ripped apart by a murder. The only moderately interesting thing about the novel was the ending, in which the murder trial of the protagonist (and Edgar Smith stand-in), Ronald Kramer, ends in a hung jury.

William F. Buckley told Edgar he thought the novel "pretty good," though he'd mused to Sophie that "my own hunch is the same as yours—to wit, that Edgar is not a novelist." He also wondered why it was so sex oriented—was it because the style of the day called for it? Edgar expressed some degree of surprise at the reaction, in part because he could only rely on Sophie's version of what Buckley said, as Buckley's letter about it was lost in the mail. "[It] leaves me wondering whether I am a) a genius or b) surrounded by people with bad taste," he wrote Buckley in June.

"I find it wonderfully amusing that those who have read it think that it was shrewd of me to leave the ending up in the air. I wish I were that slick."

And was *A Reasonable Doubt*, in fact, as sex oriented as Buckley believed? "Wrong!" Edgar insisted.* "There is a lot of sex in the story because there is a lot of sex in the lives of the gas station types. Sex is the raison d'etre of all they do. Their cars are loud and gaudy for the same reason a peacock is loud and gaudy. They go where they go because they expect the girls to be there. If they steal it is to buy clothes and cars to attract the girls. If they work it is to get money for the same reason. When they fight it is almost always over a girl. It is a way of life one is not expected to understand. One has done it or one has not—it is that simple. . . . It is another world, my friend," he continued, "and the fellows who were in it were doing their thing long before the scraggly-faced hippies and their fat assed teeny-boppers ever discovered it."

Juliette Scheinman also read a revised version of *A Reasonable Doubt* in early September. She wrote Edgar to say how much she loved it. But Edgar himself was having second thoughts. "I wish I thought as highly of it," he wrote Buckley on September 10. "After looking at it for sixteen months, it got boring. I have higher hopes for the next."

What Edgar may have suspected was that no amount of revision could transform a book that didn't work into a book that worked. Sophie knew this but went through the motions nonetheless. She wrote an editorial letter outlining the book's strengths and (many) flaws to send further up the Knopf food chain, leaving it for her bosses to decide if *A Reasonable Doubt* was worth publishing. Robert Gottlieb, per his custom, read the manuscript quickly, possibly overnight. On October 24, 1969, he

---

* Edgar was, in fact, incorrect. The novel is quite sex oriented.

rendered his verdict: "A problem. As Sophie says, this just isn't a good novel—it's far too long, too flat, too uncharged, too un-novelistic."

But Gottlieb wasn't ready to let Smith go as a Knopf author. "I think all we can do is tell him that the book is potentially publishable (which it certainly is) if he does a lot of work; and that we would be glad to consider it more seriously if he does that work. I don't see how we can commit now to publishing a book we know isn't very good."

Since Knopf didn't want to commit and Edgar wanted to publish the novel as soon as possible to pay off his outstanding legal bills, he was free to shop his novel elsewhere. His agent, Robert Lescher, had already begun the process. On November 12, he received a letter from Jack Geoghegan, the president of the publishing firm Coward-McCann, expressing excitement about *A Reasonable Doubt*: "First, let me say again how very promising we feel Edgar Smith's novel is. *Anatomy of a Murder* does immediately come to mind, particularly in the expertise with which Smith delves into small-town life to reveal the cancer within and in the mastery of detail that goes into the trial itself."

The company was so enthusiastic about publishing *A Reasonable Doubt* that Geoghegan offered an advance of $15,000 (nearly $110,000 in today's dollars) and a 15 percent hardcover royalty, together with a promise to spend an additional $15,000 in advertising. Buckley thought the advance and advertising budget to be "sensational," while Sophie was pleased—and perhaps relieved—not to be publishing a novel she didn't believe in. Geoghegan did have one major reservation about the "full nature of the author's intent." Was the book's ending in a hung jury supposed to hint at a conspiracy against the wronged defendant? Or was it intentionally vague? Whatever the case, he didn't think Edgar would have to do too much revision to clarify the novel's significance.

Edgar was fine with that suggestion, telling Buckley, "For a deal like that, I would be willing to take the Bible through another draft, or as many more as will satisfy the McCann editors." He also clarified that he had kept the ending against his agent's advice, "and it would be the first thing I would have agreed to change for McCann." As of November 15, 1969, Coward-McCann became Edgar Smith's publisher.

It was a good way to close what had been a frustrating year for the Death House prisoner in which he waited for hearings that did not happen, wrote pages of novels that did not gel, went on a diet that didn't stick, and lamented that he was getting older. He characterized the year to Buckley as "too much work, too little food . . . and the usual—the total inability to understand women."

He had alienated Sophie romantically, and her regular visits were now more desultory than delightful; he had to juggle his attention from Jane to Juliette and back; better to focus on the steadfast friend, William F. Buckley, who did not demand much. In that spirit Edgar sent Buckley several gifts near the end of the year: first a tiny Sony radio and later some Cuban cigars. ("I am pleased to note your anti-Castroism does not go *that* far," cracked Edgar.) Such gestures of generosity spurred Buckley to write on December 1, "I shall carry [the radio] in my pocket, like the teenie-boppers, and when people in strange situations see the look of ecstasy on my face they will know that it comes to me via Japan from one of my very best friends."

Buckley's sentiment was heartfelt, and Edgar knew it. He would continue to use that sentiment to his best advantage, as Buckley wasn't fully aware—yet—of how much he was being used.

22

A Reasonable Doubt

1970

EDGAR SMITH felt frustrated. Weeks and months had passed, and the promise of a hearing in the early part of 1970 withered away. Even though his lawyer, Steve Umin, counseled him to be patient, he wrote to Judge George Barlow, the district court judge in Trenton assigned to his case, to complain about the delays and urge that a hearing finally be scheduled.

Barlow wrote back (by way of Umin) on March 3, "As you know, I regard the setting of such a date now as impractical and premature. Nevertheless, I recognize the legitimacy of Mr. Smith's demand for the earliest possible resolution of the matter and intend exactly that." Barlow viewed setting a date as "premature" because he had other pressing cases to attend to besides Smith's.

Umin successfully angled for a court appearance at the Bergen County Courthouse in Hackensack on April 17. It wasn't the full habeas corpus hearing the lawyers had wished for, but at least it was something. Two weeks earlier, Edgar was fitted for a new suit by the prison tailor and had photographs taken. "The basic question to be resolved at that time is: how well will Smith survive the sight of genuine, live, moving mini-skirts? I may have to carry a bottle of nitro pills to keep my pump pumping," he joked to Buckley.

Edgar ended up spending five hours sitting in the US marshal's office for what proved to be a two-minute appearance by his lawyers. They won a motion for oral arguments on a single issue—whether his constitutional rights had been violated—with a hearing slated for May 8. Still, it was Edgar's first time out of the Death House since his 1957 conviction. His mother and Juliette Scheinman, now officially his girlfriend, were allowed to visit for a few minutes, he received free coffee and lunch, and, as he wrote to Buckley immediately after the visit, the marshal was "begging for a free copy of my book."

But, he admitted to Buckley after the fact, Edgar felt barraged and confused by the exposure, at long last, to the outside world. "Filthy, the air stinks, the new buildings look like cheeseboxes, and the new cars look like toys Made In Japan. The dirt is what amazed me. I cannot remember the world being so dirty, and I wonder if I notice only because I was seeing it—almost— for the first time. I wonder if others, who are out there every day, realize how filthy the buildings and streets are, and how rotten the air smells." If that was how it was in Hackensack, population 36,000, he shuddered to think of what New York City, with more than two hundred times as many people, looked like. As for the miniskirted girls he had hoped to encounter, even they produced some surprise: "It is impossible to tell how old a girl is these days. They could be fifteen, twenty, or twenty-five; they all look alike, dress alike, walk alike, and when they smile, smile alike, one of those 'I'll smile but I don't want to' smiles."

Edgar, wearing his new suit and sunglasses, had been caught by news photographers on the way out of the building, and when Buckley wrote a week later to tell him he'd liked the photo that had appeared in the papers the next day, Edgar responded, "How could you say you liked that picture of me? It was terrible, made worse by the fact that the handcuffs were attached to a waist belt, thereby hunching me forward a bit and making me look even fatter, fatter than the fat I really am. . . . What I need is some of that new diet—I think they call it 'Freedom!'"

Edgar was back in court on May 8 for the habeas corpus hearing. Steve Umin brought his mother to the hearing; she gave Edgar the "V" sign and said "Peace and good luck" to him as he walked into court. Though Buckley was out of town and Sophie was likely stuck at work, Edgar's own mother and his brother, Richard, also attended, as did Juliette, accompanied by John Carley, a young lawyer Edgar had recently befriended. The press was out in full force, too, with reporters and photographers clamoring for space both inside and outside to get their glimpse of Edgar Smith.

Though Steve Umin argued valiantly that Edgar deserved to be granted a new trial and Edgar himself was impressed with Judge Barlow's grasp of the case, both lawyer and client would be disappointed at the outcome; the judge denied the habeas corpus motion on August 5.

Edgar's legendary imperturbability failed him. He grew so upset at Steve Umin for being slow to secure another date through the state court system that he wrote Buckley on September 26:

I have advised Steve that I do not want to hear what he hopes to accomplish, that he should visit me after he sees Barlow and tells me what he has accomplished. If there are no results, no specific date set for the hearing, no decision on reconsideration, or no papers prepared for an appeal, I do not want him to visit me. Instead, I want him to return to Washington and have his final bill sent to me. I am not paying for excuses, explanations, delays, promises, or bright expectations; I am

paying for results, and if there are no results, I do not intend to
go on paying.

Smith's screed understandably caused Buckley to worry that
Edgar might fire Umin and his colleagues at Williams & Connolly. Umin reassured him otherwise in an October 7 letter: "It
is very much a part of my function, as I conceive it, to serve as
the target for his periodic outrage. I am now and shall remain
his loyal ally under any circumstances, even if he should choose
to find new counsel." Buckley reacted with gratitude two weeks
later: "I can't begin to tell you how reassuring it is to know that
you are there to help Edgar—as I've said time and time again."

———

IN ADDITION TO the legal ups and downs, Edgar seemed determined
to foment displeasure among his intimates. Those intimates—
specifically, William F. Buckley and Sophie Wilkins—had become good friends themselves. Their mutual correspondence
became an exercise in triangulation among what Edgar was telling Buckley, what he was telling Sophie, and what Buckley and
Sophie understood to be the truth.

True, the friendship between Sophie and Buckley had its
roots in the making of Edgar Smith, author and now novelist.
But their bond was cemented, over a lunch in June and a dinner
in late October, for many other reasons, including the discovery
of another literary talent: a Yale undergraduate student named
David Quammen. Buckley had met Quammen in the middle
of 1969, and after a memorable dinner, Buckley offered to read
Quammen's novel-in-progress. So impressed was he by the prose
style and the examination of race relations by someone barely out
of his teens that he passed on the manuscript to Sophie, who also

loved it. (Knopf published Quammen's novel, *To Walk the Line*, in the fall of 1970.)

Sophie and Bill's championing of a debut author was an echo of how they had transformed Edgar Smith from prisoner to author and were continuing to augment Edgar's professional bona fides: Edgar had been elected to the US chapter of PEN as a result of Sophie's nomination, cosponsored by Buckley and Bob Lescher. The news made the *New York Times* because Smith was the first convicted murderer in the United States to be honored by the organization.

Perhaps Sophie's work on Quammen's novel had extra resonance because she was barely writing to Edgar and never visiting him anymore. Edgar told Buckley that his mother, who had recently spent a weekend with Sophie, felt the issue was that Sophie "feels she is no longer needed," what with her sons off at college, her husband still mentally unstable, and she herself mired in despair, which nothing—not even her annual trips to Europe or a summertime week on Martha's Vineyard—could assuage.

Sophie, however, felt as if Edgar was manipulating her and presenting the worst possible version of herself to Ann and Juliette. She allowed herself to vent to Buckley, "Our mutual friend lately reminds me of the little girl who had a curl etc? for when he is good he is very very good, but when he is bad he is awful."

———

EDGAR SMITH'S FIRST NOVEL, *A Reasonable Doubt*, was published by Coward-McCann in August, after several rounds of revision (and several discarded titles, including *Hostile Witness* and *The Sixth Trumpet*) that had occupied Edgar throughout the year. The book was supposed to have been dedicated to William F. Buckley, but a printer snafu omitted the dedication page.

Steve Umin's colleague at Williams & Connolly David Webster was an enthusiastic reader of the novel, singling out its astute depiction of lawyers who had tried many cases: "Sometimes I wish people would not write books and keep me up until 2:15 a.m. I read your 'novel' last night and as a result I am late for work this morning." Buckley, despite professing to enjoy the book, warned Smith to expect the worst, as "the sex bit in your book will inevitably annoy some readers and reviewers." At Edgar's request, Coward-McCann sent a complimentary copy of *A Reasonable Doubt* to Judge O'Dea, who returned it with a note saying that he wasn't allowed to accept gifts but "appreciates the thought."

The public reception of the novel proved to be surprisingly positive. Allen Hubin, who had taken over the Criminals at Large mysteries and thrillers column at the *New York Times Book Review*, featured the novel in his October 4 roundup. *Kirkus* judged it "a balanced, painstaking overview of the law as it responds to both the greatnesses and weaknesses of the people it serves." Edgar reacted with typical élan, as he joked to Agatha Schmidt, *National Review*'s research director, about a positive review in a Tennessee newspaper, "I *am* a genius! At least in places like Nashville!!"

The capper was a blurb by the legendary crime novelist James M. Cain, the author of *The Postman Always Rings Twice* and *Double Indemnity*:

From the time he slips his tiny hook into your lip and starts reeling you in on his gossamer three-ounce line, you are Edgar Smith's fish. He has the true novelist's gift for putting you under a spell, and his story, a case history in the manner of Capote, Mailer, Oates, Macdonald, Jack Webb on TV, and our other modernists, holds you from beginning to end, as he starts it cool, then warms it, then hots it, then brings it to a cherry red. *A Reasonable Doubt* is a shaking, memorable book.

With so much publicity surrounding the publication of the novel, several media organizations, including NBC, CBS, *Time*, the Associated Press, and *Newsweek*, sought to interview Edgar. The state of New Jersey was disinclined to allow their doing so, since the Department of Corrections had a long-standing policy of denying media access to inmates. Edgar tried to persuade it otherwise. "There is, to begin with, a very serious financial consideration, and in this I will be candid with you," he wrote the department's director, Albert C. Wagner, on August 3. "I need money, not only for my seemingly endless legal expenses, but to insure [*sic*] that when I leave this institution, I will not find myself just another ex-convict unable to find a job or support himself. You can well imagine, I am sure, what network and national magazine exposure would mean in terms of book sales and income. . . . I owe a great many people, including lawyers, a great deal of money, and I have a daughter whose future I wish to secure." Edgar had become the longest-serving death row inmate in the country, eclipsing Caryl Chessman's nearly twelve-year tenure in late 1969. His situation was unique and, it seemed at the time, unlikely to be replicated.* That made it a "golden opportunity for the State of New Jersey to show the rest of the country that rehabilitation *is* possible even under the worst of conditions."

The letter didn't work. Media access was denied. Edgar circumvented it in one clever way by submitting an "Interview with Myself" that became the basis of a *New York Times Book*

---

* The death penalty was repealed in 1972 by *Furman v. Georgia* and reinstated in 1976 by *Gregg v. Georgia*. Since then, those incarcerated on death row can expect to stay there for many decades, thanks to lengthening appeals times.

Review profile by Richard Lingeman in December 1970. The following year, he wrote a long piece for *Esquire* (for which he received $1,000). He also reviewed *Soledad Brothers: The Prison Letters of George Jackson* (also published by Coward-McCann) for the Philadelphia *Bulletin*, the Bergen *Record*, and *Playboy*. All of those publications subsequently commissioned additional book reviews, increasing his freelance income.

Edgar enjoyed the praise for *A Reasonable Doubt*, but he had other things on his mind, as he always did: working to secure his freedom and writing his next book. He finished the manuscript, a thriller centered around the assassination of the Soviet premier, a month before *A Reasonable Doubt* landed in bookstores. It was, as his agent Bob Lescher described it, "an entertainment, a suspense novel that isn't meant to be taken too seriously." But Lescher thought it worked very well—"Or will work well when certain minor problems are attended to."

Good legal news came unexpectedly in the last month of 1970: Judge George Barlow ruled that the November 1968 Supreme Court decision vacating Smith's conviction did require a full evidentiary hearing in the lower courts. Discovery would have to be completed by January 11 for the hearing, set for seven days after that. "All of which means we have everything we asked for and perhaps a bit more. Onward!" Edgar wrote Buckley on December 2. Because Barlow had moved on from the case, the hearing would be presided over by Judge John J. Gibbons of the Third Circuit Court of Appeals. Edgar thought him "something of a mystery judge" and girded himself for the legal fights ahead.

23

Bid for a New Trial

BEGINNING ON January 18, 1971, Edgar Smith spent the equivalent of a fortnight at the federal courtroom in Newark, with nights at the federal detention facility in New York City. He arrived in court each day in handcuffs, as was required. He wore the dark suit that had been custom made for him in the tailor shop of the prison. ("We like our people to look their best when they appear before the bar of justice," Chief Deputy Warden Arthur Edmonds told the Philadelphia *Bulletin*. "We think it's only right.") He'd let his sideburns grow, and the rest of his hair was far longer than his military-style crew cut of the late 1950s. Years of solitary confinement and lack of physical activity had fattened him until he was almost portly. Still, he looked good enough that a Bergen *Record* reporter overheard a female spectator remark, "He's still a very handsome man."

The Newark courtroom could comfortably seat just seventy-five people. Ann Chupak attended daily, as did Juliette Scheinman, who also visited Edgar at the New York detention center. Sophie Wilkins showed up in court several times. William F. Buckley wasn't present, as he was in Santiago, Chile; Frances Bronson, his secretary, and Agatha Schmidt, the research director at *National Review*, attended in his stead. One day, fifteen students from Matawan Regional High School showed up because they were studying capital punishment.

The press, not only from Bergen County and New Jersey but from all over the country, made up much of the daily audience. The longest-incarcerated inmate on death row—who had now published two books and was working on at least one more, who had the public support and private friendship of William F. Buckley, and whose professions of innocence were believed by more and more people—was guaranteed news.

The day before the hearing, the Philadelphia *Bulletin*'s Hans Knight published a long feature, which included interviews with William F. Buckley, Sophie Wilkins, and the private investigator Andy Nicol, all promoting their belief in his wrongful conviction, as well as a written back-and-forth with Edgar Smith. "I still have faith in the system of justice," Edgar proclaimed. "I certainly do not consider the years a total loss. If nothing else, the friends I have acquired over the past few years make up a great deal for what I have lost, maybe even more. . . . I really am an awfully lucky guy in some ways."

When Knight asked what he planned on doing when, or if, he got out, Edgar replied, "Well, now, I want a bath, a decent haircut, a good meal, and then I want to spend about three weeks lying in the sun on a beach in the Bahamas, soaking out the stink and the feel of prison. . . . Then I want to spend some time with my friends and family, meet some of the people I know only through letters, then find a quiet place where I can get back to my writing."

On the first day, the prosecutors, Edward Fitzpatrick and Harold Springstead, assured the crowd that Edgar was still guilty and that any "new evidence" presented at the hearing by Edgar's lawyers would be nonsense. He had murdered Victoria Zielinski and all of the legal machinations, all of the Supreme Court rulings, and all of the media hoopla couldn't change that. His statements to the police, Fitzpatrick said, "were given of his own free will. The investigation, rather than being the action of a vengeful prosecutor, as characterized in various journals and publications, was good police work without which the crime would not have been solved."

The prosecutors had made one significant admission in a press conference prior to the hearing: that Smith had not been apprised of his rights to remain silent and to have an attorney present during his interrogation and up to and after he had signed his statement. That was how things had been done in 1957, but almost fourteen years later, after the *Miranda* and *Massiah* Supreme Court rulings had established that incriminating statements made by a suspect cannot be admitted into evidence at trial if the suspect was not informed of his or her rights beforehand, it looked especially damning.

It was up to Judge Gibbons to sort through the muck of policing old and new, of confessions legitimate or coerced, of which rights had been violated, if any; to determine whether Edgar Smith should win a new trial and eventually, his freedom. The central question—did he, in fact, kill Victoria Zielinski?—was less important for the purposes of the law, even as it was most important to Vickie's family and to the towns of Ramsey and Mahwah.

Gibbons, a slender man with a shock of silvery, curly hair swept back from a high forehead, presided over the hearing with quiet authority; he spoke softly, sometimes inaudibly, choosing his words with care as he asked "brief, pointed questions" and made "short, sharp decisions," as the *Herald-News* later reported.

The hearing often seemed like a replay of the original trial. Joseph Gilroy, Edgar's former best friend, testified again about the borrowed car, the reddish spots in the front seats, and Smith's unusual behavior. Vahe Garabedian and Gordon Graber, career detectives in the Bergen County Prosecutor's Office, once again recalled the night they took Smith in for questioning, their recollections largely lining up with their original trial testimony.

Fred Galda, then an assistant prosecutor and now a judge, testified about Edgar's "cocky" demeanor while being questioned but also admitted that "Smith never asked me, nor was it brought to my attention that he ever asked to see a lawyer." He also revealed that Bergen County police had had enough to arrest Smith based on his wife's identification of the bloody pants, but they had never told her that she didn't have to say a word because of New Jersey's law guaranteeing the right of spouses to keep confidential communications between themselves.

Walter Spahr, flown in from Pompano Beach, Florida, where he now worked as a patrolman in an adjacent town, testified at great length. In *Brief Against Death*, Edgar had accused him of shoving him during the police interrogation. A cloud of scandal also enveloped Spahr when he was named by known mobsters, whose phones were wiretapped as part of an ongoing FBI investigation, as someone to protect, spurring him to resign from the Bergen County detective squad in 1970. Together, those allegations made Spahr a key target for the defense.

Spahr, sporting a blue sports jacket and a deep tan complementing his reddish hair, was asked about his interrogation methods. He'd questioned Edgar in a nine-by-twenty-one-foot room but had described being "closeted" with Edgar in a later report. "It makes the report sound nice," said Spahr about his word choice. "People say the police are stupid, so you make the report sound nice." He also explained that asking Edgar about whether Vickie had attacked him in any way was a spontaneous idea to try to "ascertain the truth." It worked, Spahr testified, as Edgar then revealed to him and another police officer that Vickie had struck him in the face and he began to cry.

Spahr also clarified his own physical conduct with Edgar. At one point, he said, the defendant rose up from the swivel chair and said, "I'm getting out." Spahr said he put out his hand—a "reflex action"—which caught Edgar off guard. He jerked away, falling over the chair and on to the floor. "I touched him with the tip of my finger on the shoulder," said Spahr. "I caught him off balance." Later, Spahr was asked whether violence had any place in police interrogations. "I don't think you have to—it puts you one step lower than the individual at hand. If a man is competent, he doesn't have to resort to violence at all." The police's job, said Spahr, "is to get the truth of the matter, not to box people in and frame them."

The next day, Judge Gibbons and the court spectators heard an audio recording of Edgar's original interrogation, which had been made by Guy Calissi without Edgar's knowledge and had not been presented at his trial. Fitzpatrick, the prosecutor, hadn't even known of its existence until a few weeks before the hearing, when he had been looking in the case files for something else and discovered the tape. Smith's lawyers protested, saying that no one could vouch for the tape's accuracy or even its chain of custody since the original 1957 trial. After the court stenographer, Arthur Ehrenbeck, testified that the tape and transcript were virtually identical, Judge Gibbons admitted the tape into evidence on the grounds that it could speak to Edgar's tone and demeanor at the time of his statement.

The tape was cued up and played. On it, Edgar told the police that he was giving a voluntary statement, though he had claimed many times over the years since that he'd been coerced into doing so, having not eaten or slept for long periods of time. Edgar hadn't known he was being recorded, of course, though the police had told him that the court stenographer was in the room.

Judge Gibbons had to adjourn the proceedings after five days because he had another case on his calendar. The writer of a Bergen *Record* editorial on January 25 was of the opinion that so much time had passed since the crime had been committed, a very different man was under the microscope:

> Let the record show that in 1957 a raw youth named Edgar H. Smith was in fact convicted of murder. Then why in the name of justice are we the people demanding the life of a middle-aged author named Edgar H. Smith? The assumption of modern penology is that jail is a place of rehabilitation as much as punishment.
>
> The career of Edgar H. Smith II is living proof that rehabilitation does in fact take place. The trial of Edgar H. Smith I, a man who no longer exists in fact, is evidence that society does not believe what it says about rehabilitation and redemption.

The hearing resumed on February 1 with the testimony of two psychiatrists who had examined Edgar soon after his arrest. (A third psychiatrist testified the following day.) They repeated their conclusions, which had not been introduced into the original trial and were thus being heard in open court for the first time, that Smith was a "sociopathic personality" who was prone to acting on impulse and expressed little remorse for his behavior. That did not make him insane or the victim of police coercion when it came to his statement. "It [the statement] was of his own free will," testified one of the psychiatrists, Joseph Zigarelli. "He had a rational intellectual choice to make those statements, and I feel that at the time he was able to do those things."

The following day, Guy Calissi testified. At sixty-one, he was suffering from a heart condition and took at least one nitroglycerin pill while on the stand. He described how Edgar had behaved like an "assistant special investigator" during the police investigation and interrogation. "Smith was very agreeable all night long. . . . The man was alert, willing, cooperative, anxious, and he readily went on the trips."

Calissi was then cross-examined by Umin's counsel, David Webster, about why no one asked Smith directly if he had killed Victoria. "The question was implicit," replied Calissi. "It's up to the individual in conducting the investigation whether he wants to ask it directly or indirectly." He protested the very idea of a coerced statement: "No one in that office would ever dare threaten anybody during my tenure . . . or they'd be out of there so fast they'd have burns in a certain place. There were no promises, no threats, no duress and no violence at any time in that office."

Webster did, however, succeed in tripping up the former Bergen County prosecutor on another matter. Calissi testified that he never asked Smith to take a lie detector test or to view Zielinski's body at the morgue. But Webster showed Calissi the trial transcript of his cross-examination of Smith: "You refused when I asked you to go down to the morgue and you said you didn't even want to look at dead cats." Calissi said he couldn't remember saying such a thing and he'd had no reason to take Edgar to view the body. But he admitted, "if that's what the record shows, I can't change it."

Calissi also inadvertently threw two former police detectives under the bus. Asked whether he had directed Walter Spahr and Charles deLisle in their interrogations of Smith, he said no. They also didn't generally conduct interrogations because, as Calissi revealed, "they were both not very good at it." After his testimony, the hearing adjourned once more. When it restarted on February 9, Edgar Smith took the stand.

———

EDGAR HAD SAID his piece about his arrest and conviction in thousands of pages of legal briefs, as well as in his book. But it was a different thing to see him testifying in the flesh, wearing a dark pin-striped suit with wide lapels and a yellow shirt with a black-and-yellow tie—to hear his voice, to see his mannerisms, as he described being interrogated for the murder of Victoria Zielinski.

Edgar, accompanied by two guards, walked down a stairway in the Newark courthouse to the holding room. He raised his hands as he passed a window overlooking the street outside the courthouse, as if he were already embracing the outside world he was battling to reenter. It was the day after his thirty-seventh birthday, and to celebrate, Juliette would be allowed to spend several hours with him that night, bringing along an apple-walnut cake for what would be an impromptu party for them and Edgar's lawyers. All told, he was in a good state of mind.

When asked about his statement on the stand, he said, "I gave in and gave them what they wanted. I didn't know what else to do." He spoke of feeling as though he were "in a cocoon, cut off from everything and doing what they want you to do." He claimed he never knew he had a legal right not to answer questions or accompany the police to the station. He said he became "so tied up in contradictory stories, I really didn't feel I had any choice but to give one more explanation. There were these pressures, asking me to take the lie detector test, wanting to take me to the morgue. . . . There was this overwhelming feeling of being in police custody. I felt I was in a box with no way out."

Fitzpatrick, on cross, pressed Edgar about his police coercion claims for more than five hours spread over two days. He quoted from the original 1957 trial testimony, when Edgar had been asked about being mistreated and had said that he hadn't been. Edgar, in the 1971 version, countered that coercion could amount to the "constant pressure" to make statements after twenty-four hours straight of questions, with little food or sleep, separated from his wife, lacking access to an attorney.

"Did you complain to anyone? Did you complain to your lawyer?" Fitzpatrick asked.

Judge Gibbons interjected, warning Fitzpatrick his line of questioning was a possible breach of attorney-client privilege.

Fitzpatrick pressed his finger onto a copy of *Brief Against Death* on the prosecution table. "Communications with his attorney were made public in this book."

Edgar was the last of twenty-six witnesses who had testified over ten days stretched out over four weeks. The transcript well exceeded a thousand pages. Judge Gibbons promised his ruling later in the spring, after considering further reply briefs due to him by March 22. Edgar went back to Trenton State Prison.

Webster and Umin were optimistic about their chances with Judge Gibbons. Umin, usually measured in his correspondence, was positively buoyant, which in turn gladdened Edgar as they waited for the decision. Also cheering Edgar up was *Esquire*'s publication of his self-interview in the June 1 issue, which appeared on newsstands on May 13.

On May 14, just a day after Edgar's self-interview was published, Judge Gibbons made his ruling: Edgar's conviction should be overturned on the grounds that his unsigned confession was coerced and was therefore unconstitutional. He ordered a new trial within sixty days or the state would have to release Edgar from the Death House.

24

Conviction Overturned

MAY–DECEMBER 1971

STEVE LICHTENSTEIN had the honor of telling Edgar Smith the news of the overturned conviction in person. Edgar was understandably elated, as was his mother, Ann, who happened to be visiting the prison. "I've got the three greatest lawyers in the world" was his only public comment on the matter. His private reaction is best summed up by the one-line note he sent to William F. Buckley's secretary, Frances Bronson:

Wheeeeeeeeeeeeeeeeeeeeeeeeeeeeeeeeeeeeeeeeeeeeeeeeeeeee!!!

To Buckley, he quipped, "*NOW* I understand what Vince Lombardi meant when he said that winning isn't the only thing—it's everything!" And to Frances Bronson, Edgar joked that his mother "set the world's record for the high jump from a seated position."

Ann declined to speak to the press. Edgar's brother, Richard, said he was happy that Edgar was getting another chance. "I haven't talked to the lawyers yet, so I don't know about his chances for getting a fair trial." Sophie Wilkins was elated by the news, which she learned from Frances.

Bergen County prosecutor Robert Dilts,* who had succeeded Guy Calissi in the office, had a markedly different reaction. "There are errors of fact and law in the judge's decision," he claimed as he announced that the state would appeal. He pointed out that "a retrial under any circumstances would be extremely difficult. . . . The state would be barred from using admissions made by Smith, which would make it even more difficult." Also, so many years had passed since Victoria Zielinski's murder that at least half a dozen people involved in the investigation and trial had died.

A Bergen *Record* reporter tracked down Vickie's father, Anthony Zielinski, who did not take the news of the reversed conviction well. He had spent years trying to avoid news about Edgar Smith, concentrating instead on his work, his remarriage, and his adopted son. Once a year, around Memorial Day weekend, he ventured to the cemetery in Honesdale, Pennsylvania, to place flowers upon Vickie's grave. "She was the sweetest daughter I had. She helped me mow the lawn and she was a 100 per cent athlete," he said.

He told the reporter that he knew people were amazed he had stayed in the vicinity of the murder, moving a mere ten miles from Ramsey to Hasbrouck Heights—coincidentally, Edgar's birthplace—after Vickie's mother, Mary, had divorced him and moved to California with some of their children. "What can I do? If I go to California, she'll still be dead." Anthony also reiterated to another reporter that "anybody kills my daughter, he should be punished—capital punishment—and I mean it. It will

---

* Days after his statement, Dilts was removed from office by the governor right after he gave a television interview on the Edgar Smith case. The reasons were murky, though it later emerged that in another case, Dilts had downgraded a hijacking charge after receiving a payoff from someone tied to organized crime. The state's assistant attorney general, Evan Jahos, assumed control of the Bergen County Prosecutor's Office.

deter the next one." When asked if he would personally "pull the switch" in the execution chamber, Zielinski said yes but that he would not take matters into his own hands if Edgar Smith did, in the end, get out of jail. "I'm not a guy to go out and get him. I'm not that hasty. Never in my life. God will punish him in some other manner."

Miami Herald reporter Anne Wilder also succeeded in finding and interviewing Donald Hommell, appearing at his workplace without prior warning. At first the man denied his identity and claimed to be Hommell's brother. When Wilder pressed him, he finally admitted who he was and began to speak, his halting words soon giving way to a torrent.

"He should have been electrocuted, as far as I'm concerned. I told what happened. I told the truth the first time, and I'll tell it again if I have to," Hommell, now thirty-four and a father of two living in Vero Beach, Florida, said. His life had not worked out very well, and his marriage was on the path to divorce. Then there was the whole business with the Delaware reformatory that resulted in his being charged with physically abusing several young men. The charges, nineteen in all, wended their way through Delaware family court as other boys accused Hommell of mistreating them, too.

But the judge, in a thirty-two-page opinion issued in February 1965, had deemed that Hommell's actions were those of a man inexperienced in and overwhelmed by the requirements of the job and the result of reasonable force. Hommell was acquitted of all charges. "The court is of the opinion that he did his best according to the limits of his experience handling boys, most of whom were obviously uncontrolled," said the judge. Hommell had left Delaware and moved to Fort Lauderdale before going back to Vero Beach five months earlier to work in his father's water-softening plant in Fort Pierce.

Hommell emphasized that Edgar's story of innocence was a fabrication: "He got Buckley and some of the big shots with him, and they're putting on the political pressure. . . . If it had been Buckley's daughter [who had been killed], he wouldn't have felt so kindly toward him. They should put Buckley in jail with him." He had thought it unlikely that Edgar would get a new trial but now professed not to care if the man was released as a result. "If he's smart enough to talk himself out of jail, I'm all for it. Smith must have made close to a million by now. He must be pretty wealthy."

Hommell's bitterness and preoccupation with money in Wilder's interview foreshadowed further troubles. By the end of the decade, Hommell, who by then had relocated to South Carolina, was reportedly convicted of mail fraud and failure to file his federal tax return, and would serve time in state prison.

———

AT A JUNE 8 hearing in Newark, Judge Gibbons granted Edgar bail on a $5,000 bond. He would be released into the custody of Buckley (who was back from his travels and attended the hearing) after a one-day stay in order to give the state time to appeal his bail. Edgar was planning to tape interviews for *CBS This Morning* and the *Today* show and begin his life as a free man. He spent what he thought was his last night at the detention center in New York City.

The following morning, his bail was revoked until the state of New Jersey's appeal against Judge Gibbons's ruling could be heard in mid-July. Edgar would not be leaving the Death House anytime soon. The champagne would remain on ice. He learned the news from US Marshal Anthony Greski. "Smith began to change color, just as you or I would," an unnamed official told the

Passaic *Herald-News*. He also began to weep. "But there was no cursing, no loud complaints. After the tears, he seemed resigned."

The Bergen *Record* ran a photo of Edgar in the car on the way back to Trenton State Prison, cigarette between his fingers as he waved to the cameras. His lawyers were dismayed, and so was Buckley, but Edgar insisted on seeing the bright side of the bail revocation: "The only bad thing that can happen to a writer is for nothing to happen. What happened this week is terrific material for the new book, and that will give me a tremendous opportunity to throw a few rocks back Fitzpatrick's way." As he waited for the appeal, he continued to work on this new manuscript, picking up where *Brief Against Death* left off.

He hoped the book could be published as soon as possible because, as he wrote Steve Umin on June 23, "I think the public is entitled to know everything about this case, everything that has taken place, in and out of court, to make it the sort of mess it is." But he told Bob Lescher that if he took his time, "it is going to be damn good, as good in a different way than *Brief Against Death*." He told his agent that he hadn't had that much fun writing since the first book—this was "the first things [*sic*] in ages I have *enjoyed* writing, and I think it will show in the final draft."

He was far more interested in the new project than in the assassination novel he had completed the previous year. Coward-McCann was willing to publish it, but only on condition that Edgar use a pseudonym and accept a significantly lower advance of $2,500. (He did. He chose the name Michael Mason, and the book, titled *71 Hours*, was released in the spring of 1972.) Edgar also recognized, with particular shrewdness, that the publicity was only getting started and that the public seemed to be siding more and more with his version of the story.

On August 2, the Third Circuit Court of Appeals upheld Gibbons's ruling, but did not make a decision on granting bail.

Having to stay put in the Death House did not sit well with Edgar, and he dashed off a fiery letter to Umin on August 5: "I think we *must* go for bail, that *we* must call the shots in this case, that *we* must control events, not simply sit back and react like pussycats to what the state wants to do." It was, in Edgar's mind, no longer a legal case but a political one. He felt it was necessary to "take the case to the people" by launching a media blitz. "If [the prosecutor] wants to waste several more months and a few hundred thousand of the state's money retrying me, I'm all for it; let's go to trial. But in the meantime I want it done in the open, not in the back room, or in [the prosecutor's] private office."

Edgar kept sending Umin demanding letters and griping to Buckley about legal strategy, so much so that Umin felt moved to respond to his client on August 26 with more force than was his custom, "I don't know whether you are compiling material for a new book, but your irate letters of late are getting out of hand. . . . When we go into discussions I will take 'my think-ing' into them, not yours, although every step I take is with your *wishes*, if not thinking, in mind. You are of course free to reject the outcome of any discussion or the lawyer who entered them."

Buckley, too, was taken aback by the tone of Edgar's letters to Umin, which he received as carbon copies from the prisoner. "He seems to forget that he is the object of the most extensive philan-thropy on your part," he wrote Umin on August 31, meaning that the lawyer was working the case for far less money than the firm customarily charged. "In a way I admire him for acting as though that weren't the case—because in the last analysis he is the prin-cipal, and oughtn't to be treated otherwise merely because he is the object of your charity. On the other hand, it is a bit much for him to stress the use of 'his money'"—unbeknownst to Edgar, Buckley had paid the lawyers himself that winter and spring, a fact he revealed to Edgar only a month or so earlier. "I do hope you won't become exasperated with him. You are on the way to achieving a legal victory which will lodge your name securely in legal history, and I hope his bad humor will not distract you from the satisfaction you are entitled to get from that fact."

Umin responded with gratitude on September 10, adding "I feel an obligation to respond to his salvos, partly just out of concern for him personally and partly to keep straight the 'record' he compiles for publication. . . . Incidentally, Mrs. Chupak has also written to me about Edgar's letters. She was lovely to do so and gave me carte blanche to spank him."

Edgar's ire against his lawyer dissipated before too long, which was a wise move: on October 12, the Supreme Court declined to hear further appeals of Gibbons's decision, meaning that the sixty-day clock for obtaining a new trial or his release had begun.

———

AS EDGAR'S LIFE took those whiplash turns, Sophie Wilkins was suffering her own dramatic reversals. Her husband, Thurman, was still struggling with mental illness. She continued to struggle with depression and bouts of mania. And then came the news, in mid-June, that Knopf editor in chief Robert Gottlieb had decided to let her go—though it would be spun as an amicable parting of the ways rather than a firing. Sophie would stay at Knopf through the end of the year.

Sophie was devastated but acted as if it wasn't a big deal. After all, she would have more energy to devote to translation work, which was, legitimately, occupying more of her time. Her health had worsened, and editing manuscripts had become more difficult. Plus, the projects that most stoked her passions were not being met with enthusiasm; even getting Knopf to reprint the hardcover of Edgar Smith's *Brief Against Death* to coincide with his hoped-for freedom met with considerable resistance. Sophie had also tried to get Knopf to publish William F. Buckley's *Cruising Speed*, an odd diary of a week in his life that would end up as a best seller when published by G. P. Putnam's Sons, but it was summarily rebuffed since her acquisitions usually didn't sell well. She wasn't good for Knopf's bottom line. "A person without a future has no real present, either," she wrote Edgar on July 18.

Her depression didn't lift for months. She tried to keep Buckley at bay, even calling one of their most recent lunches a "farewell appearance." But he would not be put off and insisted they carry on their friendship, both by letter and in person. "I have been a most egregious fool," she wrote Bill on November 2. "Add failure to that, and a person simply ceases to be socially presentable. And this is no mere matter of appearances; it goes to the root. . . . Still, but for Edgar, I would never have known you at all. So I must consider myself, on balance, to be a lucky fool, likely to go about the usual foolishness in the usual perky fashion."

Sophie once described to Buckley an encounter she once had with a friend of hers and her husband's. She had been telling the man all about Edgar "and his heroic struggle and your miraculous unwavering friendship or protectorship for him." Her friend had listened attentively. A long pause elapsed. Then he had uttered the following pronouncement: "I feel sorry for Buckley when that guy gets out."

———

THE MOOD IN Bergen County toward the end of 1971 could be best summed up by a Bergen *Record* editorial on October 15: "Let's call the whole thing off. Nothing will restore the life of the murdered girl, and nothing can restore the 14 years of life Edgar Smith has spent in prison." New Jersey had recently decided to

abolish the death penalty. Ronald Marrone, the teenager convicted of killing fifteen-year-old Starr Zeitler two months after
Victoria Zielinski's murder, was about to be paroled. Views on
criminal justice were becoming more reform minded, more about
rehabilitation.

And who better, at least to the public, represented that shift
than Edgar Smith?

Which was why Edgar pressed for a brand-new trial. His
lawyers, particularly Steve Umin, weren't as convinced; one stick-
ing point they brought up was that *Brief Against Death* could
be admitted into evidence at trial by a less sympathetic judge
than Judge Gibbons. *Brief*, of course, contained all the information, including his unsigned confession, that Judge Gibbons had
thrown out as inadmissible.

His lawyers believed that the best course was to attempt to ne-
gotiate a plea deal with the Bergen County prosecutors in which
Edgar would plead *non vult*—no contest—to murdering Vickie
and would then be sentenced to life in prison with the possibility
of parole, which practically speaking, amounted to about fifteen
years. And since he had already served more than fourteen, he
would be freed right away.

He grumbled and griped—to Umin, to Steve Lichtenstein, to
Buckley, to Sophie. But their consensus was that he should listen
to his earlier self: get totally free even if he wasn't actually legally innocent. "I just don't feel there is any alternative," he wrote
Sophie on October 28. The choice between "making a deal and
getting out, and not making a deal and staying in, ain't no kind
of choice, but it is the choice my lawyers have given me."

He was especially disgruntled that his lawyers and his friend
were of one mind. But eventually he remembered his daughter
and ex-wife, living in Colorado, and how their lives might be upended by a new trial. Then he got to wondering how long a trial

might take, how much money it would cost, with no guarantee of the outcome he desired. And he remembered how much Buckley had already done for him and how he could never fully repay the other man's kindness.

All of which led to an inescapable conclusion: take the deal, because it would allow him to be free.

PART VI

GETTING OUT

(1971–1976)

25

Non Vult

ON DECEMBER 6, 1971, Edgar Smith left the Death House and headed for the Bergen County courthouse in Hackensack. There he would face Judge Morris Pashman, ready to follow his lawyers' directive: plead *non vult*, and get out of prison.

The courtroom was packed long before the early-evening start time. Court had been delayed until 5:00 p.m. so that William F. Buckley, into whose custody Smith was being released, could fly back from Washington after a luncheon with Vice President Spiro Agnew. Frank Lombardi from the Bergen *Record* was there, as was Hans Knight from the Philadelphia *Bulletin*. The *New York Times*' man, Ronald Sullivan, was also present, as were reporters from news services with an international reach.

When Edgar, dressed in a dark suit with a patterned tie, his sideburns curling past his ears, at last stood to face Judge Pashman, he knew what he would say. Still, he felt a jolt uttering the words he had spent more than fourteen and a half years resisting.

"Mr. Smith, did you and you alone kill Victoria Zielinski?" Judge Pashman asked.

"I did," Edgar replied.

"Was anyone else there when you killed her?"

"No."

"Did you see anyone else in the area during the time you were in the sandpit with Victoria Zielinski?"

"No."

"After arriving at the sandpit, did you hit her?"

"I did."

Edgar's voice was nearly inaudible and remained so as Judge Pashman continued with his carefully orchestrated questions. But the result was seismic: Edgar had confessed to the crime. His admission was now a matter of public record.

"I am satisfied beyond any question and far beyond any doubt that Edgar H. Smith murdered Victoria Zielinski," Judge Pashman said. "I am satisfied beyond any doubt that he did it alone and that Donald Hommell, Jr. [the man whom Smith had accused], had absolutely nothing to do with the death of the victim. The defendant admits this to be the fact. The facts in this case firmly and convincingly establish that the defendant caused Victoria Zielinski's death. An impartial mind must conclude this."

Judge Pashman then handed down his decree: a prison sentence of no less than twenty-five and no more than thirty years. But he credited the fourteen and a half years Smith had already spent on death row as time served, lopped off yet more time for "good behavior," and suspended the rest of his sentence—four years, four months, and twenty days. That put Edgar on probation until April 26, 1976. He was allowed to travel outside New Jersey as long as he complied with the rules and conditions of probation: regular check-ins with a probation officer and not a whiff of criminal activity of any kind.

Edgar was free to go, except for one last hitch: he needed to be returned to Trenton State Prison for formal release from death row.

Two vehicles—a limousine driven by Buckley's regular driver,

Jerry Garvey, carrying Edgar's lawyers, friends, and family, and a smaller car for Buckley and Edgar so they could avoid the press onslaught—traveled from the Hackensack courtroom back to Trenton. The vehicles idled nearby, as none of Edgar's friends and loved ones—including Buckley—was allowed to enter the Death House to witness Edgar's release. The press waited outside the prison entrance. When Edgar walked out, the questions descended upon him:

"Mr. Smith, how does it feel to walk out of Death Row after fifteen years?"

"Could you tell us if you are happy to be free?"

Edgar answered some of the questions and ignored the rest, climbing into the rear of the limousine with Buckley to join the rest of the group. The glass partition between the front and back seats went up. Buckley handed Edgar a paper cup filled with rosé wine. He also pointed to a few brown paper bags stained with grease on the floor—"There's roast beef in those"—and pulled the cork from a fresh bottle of wine. "Welcome back to the free world."

As the limo wended its way from Trenton to New York City, the group toasted Edgar Smith's liberation and the next stage of his freedom: taping two episodes of *Firing Line*, set to air on consecutive Sundays.

Buckley took off his jacket and rolled up his sleeves. With the limo's telephone receiver cradled between his neck and shoulder and the typewriter he always kept in the vehicle on his lap, he began to write the introduction to the first show—featuring him and Edgar alone—as he spoke to his producer, Warren Steibel. During their conversation, they decided which reporters would appear with Buckley and Edgar on show number two, to be taped immediately after the one-on-one. Around 8:00 p.m., just before the car entered the Lincoln Tunnel, the interior lights went out thanks to a blown fuse. "The last few lines of the introduction were completed with me holding a match over the typewriter," Edgar later wrote.

Buckley and Edgar agreed that their interview, as well as the later interrogation by reporters, must communicate the message that Edgar was innocent of the murder of Victoria Zielinski and had pleaded guilty only as, Buckley would recall, "a necessary ritual for the sake of the judicial pride of the State of New Jersey." It was a tricky needle to thread, and venturing too far might send up a signal flare that would revoke Edgar's probation and send him back to prison.

The limousine arrived at the studio to a crowd of waiting photographers. Buckley rushed out first, and then Jack Carley and Edgar stepped out, followed by Jerry Garvey. But the photographers turned their attention to Carley. They assumed he was the newly freed convict, and he played unwitting decoy as Edgar and the chauffeur walked inside. Ten minutes later, Edgar was onstage, sitting across from Buckley, his right hand cupping his chin as he listened to the other man's introduction.

The audience was friendly. Juliette Scheinman, along with her son Billy, sat closer to the front, while Ann Chupak sat nearby. Sophie Wilkins was there, too;—she hadn't attended the hearing in Hackensack, as she was in her final month at Knopf and had many loose ends to tie up at work. During the intermission between episode tapings, Sophie went up to talk to Edgar. She couldn't stay for the second show but felt she had to at least shake hands and congratulate her former author. Edgar greeted her with a resounding hello and promised he would come to the Knopf offices the next day. She made it clear that it was the last possible week he could visit before her departure.

As planned, the direct Q and A between Buckley and Edgar was designed to show, without saying it directly, that Buckley did not believe Edgar's guilty plea. That set the stage for the second episode, when Ronald Sullivan of the *New York Times*, Hans Knight of the Philadelphia *Bulletin*, Geoffrey Norman, the articles editor of *Playboy*, and Jack Carley, acting as a legal analyst of sorts, joined the two men onstage. Buckley had apparently warned the men that Edgar would not answer questions that might undo his plea with the state of New Jersey. That didn't stop Sullivan from jumping right in: "I, for one, am confused. You told the court that you *did* do it; now you leave doubt here tonight that you did. Which way is it?"

Edgar swiveled his chair slightly before answering. "We still have this problem, that I'm on probation. I am still subject to the custody of the state of New Jersey. I still have an unexpired sentence, and I cannot undo what happened in court today."

Sullivan changed tack. "Let me ask Mr. Buckley: Why are you so convinced that he is innocent, after what you heard today in court?"

"Well," said Buckley, "what I heard today in court was a protracted yawn." He added that he hadn't spent nine years on the case to be "moved by a regurgitation of the principal points of the prosecution."

"You're convinced that he's innocent?" demanded Sullivan.

"I told you that."

"Then," Sullivan said, "he committed perjury today."

"Well, do you want to send him to jail for that?" Buckley replied.

"No, no," said Sullivan. "But you see the point I'm trying to make."

The discussion turned to whether the press should be allowed to cover all trials and Edgar's reaction to his newfound freedom, but then Sullivan had the microphone again. "I'm on this program, and every insinuation is being made by you and by Mr.

Buckley that you are innocent, that you really didn't do this at all," he said. "It's almost like Alice in Wonderland. I can't make the switch over from that courtroom to this program."

"We left Wonderland on the other side of the river," quipped Edgar.

When the taping ended, the adrenaline that had been fueling Edgar for the past nineteen hours started to evaporate. Taking pointed questions from newsmen in front of a studio audience, the heat, the glaring lights—never mind that freedom, after so many years, was here—added to his anxiety, which dissipated some when he, Buckley, and Carley went on a short ride to Buckley's Upper East Side maisonette, where there was to be a party in his honor.

His nearest and dearest were there that night, as were all manner of well-wishers from Buckley's circle. It was the first of many parties to come, including a memorable Christmas soiree at which Edgar was the guest of honor. He finally met Buckley's wife for the first time and was duly bowled over by the force of her personality ("Nothing, NOTHING anybody could have said could have prepared me for Pat Buckley,"* he told Sophie afterward), and he drank champagne well into the night.

At 2:30 a.m., Edgar borrowed the limousine and its driver, Jerry Garvey, to take his mother home to Ramsey. Edgar went along for the ride. As the car barreled down Main Street, he looked out the window for signs of change since he had last seen the small town. To his astonishment, the changes were few: different names for stores and a few new buildings. Otherwise, Ramsey was a 1957 time capsule.

---

* Pat Buckley, however, was not at all taken with Edgar Smith. According to a story passed around by those in attendance that night, when Edgar and Juliette Scheinman went upstairs for some private time, Pat apparently snapped, "Get that murderer out of my bedroom."

The limo dropped Ann off at her house, then took Edgar back to New York, to the St. Regis hotel. He went up to his suite, booked for him and paid for by Buckley, at 4:00 a.m., ready for sleep. It did not come. He tossed and turned until 6:00 a.m., wondering what was wrong. Then he realized the lights were out, something that never happened on death row. "I was utterly unable to sleep in the dark," he wrote in his 1973 book *Getting Out*. "I could have turned on a light, that would have been easy enough, but to have done so would have been to surrender, to return myself to prison, to put myself back in the Death House. No way. I was a free man, and I was going to sleep like a free man or I would not sleep."

Edgar finally drifted off when the sun rose. His first sleep of freedom.

26

Freedom's First Dawn

DECEMBER 1971

NO ONE should have been more thrilled about Edgar's freedom than his girlfriend, Juliette Scheinman. He seemed far less excited about this monumental change than anyone else did, which made sense since he'd been preparing and waiting for it during the fourteen years and nine months he spent in the Death House. But Juliette felt unmoored and more worried than she expected. Their relationship so far had been watched and censored, surveilled and sequestered, endlessly constrained by her being on the outside and his being in prison.

She had been a faithful correspondent and visitor. She had attended many of his legal proceedings: a court hearing in May 1970; another the following year; and, of course, the fateful one in December 1971, with the plea deal that had secured his release from the Death House. But now her presence as the "mystery woman" and "New York City divorcee," always at the inmate's side, attracted the notice of reporters.

"I love Edgar," she told the throng of newsmen just before the car ride to Manhattan. "I can't wait to get over the bridge [to New York City] with him." The reporters didn't need to know that she had tried to break off her relationship with Edgar twice during that tumultuous year of 1971. That was in the past. They both realized they enjoyed life together better than apart. Over the bridge, the future beckoned, one where they would have to learn how to be a couple, totally free with each other.

Late the next morning, Juliette met Edgar in the lobby of the St. Regis hotel. He'd finally woken up around 11:00 a.m. The Philadelphia *Bulletin* had assigned Hans Knight to follow him around on his first full day of freedom. First, Juliette took Edgar to Bloomingdale's to get him some new clothes. He rushed from counter to counter, Knight observed, clowning around with the staff, a cold long cigar or a lit cigarette stuck in his mouth, much to the horror of the security guards trying to enforce the store's no-smoking rule.

"I want one of everything," he roared. "I'm like a kid at Christmas. But those prices—20 bucks for a sweater? I used to pay 10 before I went to jail." He ended up buying a suede coat, a pair of brown pants, boots, several shirts, and a few pairs of socks. Just for fun, he tried on a fur hat. "Mister," said a sales clerk, seeing how ridiculous it looked, "you wear that outside, and you'll get arrested."

"Oh, boy," said Edgar, who began to laugh. "We wouldn't want that."

Juliette, who had told Knight she and Edgar were "good friends," tried to justify the spending spree. "Edgar needs everything. He only has one suit. But Edgar, do you have to use up all my charge account?"

"Well," teased Edgar, "I'm giving you a great Christmas present. Me."

Then Juliette dropped the humor. "He has been bottled up so long, gone through so much, he can't keep still. He is in high key, but he will run down after a while. It will be very hard for him to be just plain Edgar Smith." For now, Edgar was in the giddiest of spirits, and it gladdened Juliette's heart. "Look at him. My God, I'm so happy to see him like this."

The trio took a cab to the *National Review* offices. The driver, Louis Copperman, turned on the radio as he wended his way through Times Square traffic, catching an item about Edgar. "Take that fellow, I forget his name, that's supposed to have killed that girl 15 years ago. Sentenced him to the chair, know what I mean? But didn't kill him. All the time he says he didn't kill her, but they won't let him go. Now he says he killed her and out he goes, free as a bird. Maybe he killed her or maybe he didn't, but they kept him dangling like a monkey on a string. Right?"

"Right," said Smith from the back.

"Hell," said Copperman, "they should have killed him or let him go. You agree?"

"Well, I don't know," Edgar said.

"Yeah . . . but you don't know the whole story. The guy made one mistake. He should have pleaded guilty 15 years ago."

Juliette began to giggle at that point and could not stop. "Driver," she said, "turn around. You've got a celebrity here."

Copperman turned around. He looked at the trio but zeroed in on Edgar with his blue eyes and wide sideburns. "Yeah . . . you some kind of actor?"

"I'm the guy you were talking about," said Edgar.

Copperman took the news in stride. "You don't look like a guy who's been in the Death House. They must have fed you steak. You look great."

"It isn't the steaks," Edgar said. "It's the New York air."

"It'll kill you," said the driver. "You get out of the Death House, and this air will kill you. But say, how did you get mixed up in all this?"

Edgar brushed off the cabbie's question. "Read my book. You can pick it up in paperback for a buck and a quarter now."

At the *National Review* offices, Buckley greeted Smith with extra warmth.

"What a day," said Edgar, "what a day. I'm out of prison, and I still feel I'm inside it."

"It takes a while," said Bill.

"If it weren't for Bill, I'd be dead," said Edgar to the others. "He never lost faith. He was there when I needed him. What more can I say?"

Later in the evening, Edgar and Juliette went out to dinner, just the two of them and the reporter, to a Chinese restaurant Buckley had recommended. They dined on Peking duck. Edgar smoked cigarette after cigarette. After dinner, Juliet left the restaurant, while Edgar continued to talk to the *Bulletin* reporter. "You know why I'm here and not still in jail?" he asked. "Because I'm not black, poor or dumb. That's the secret. When you are accused of something, the prosecutor has all the cards. The jury sees a guy in handcuffs. Presumption of innocence? Baloney. They look at you and they think, 'You must have done something or you wouldn't be there.' I'm going to write about things like that. I would like to be a lawyer, but that's not possible when you're Edgar Smith. But I can write, and I will."

———

SOPHIE WILKINS WAITED all through Edgar's first full day of freedom for him to show up at Knopf. She'd alerted the secretaries to his impending arrival and otherwise spread the word that anyone could come and greet him. Bob Gottlieb went pale and begged off, saying that he was swamped with work to finish before the holidays. He and Nina Bourne, in Sophie's opinion, did not care for Edgar. His impending arrival at the office seemed to make some of her other about-to-be-former colleagues rather nervous, too.

To judge from the lack of correspondence between Sophie and Edgar over the prior two years, the two had grown farther apart. Edgar had vented to Buckley in a March 7, 1971, letter about Sophie and her apparent difficulty "to distinguish between manuscripts intended for publication and personal letters." He felt she was talking too much out of turn, especially to Juliette, with whom she continued to socialize and correspond. "There are many sins, but to me, the cardinal sin is failing to respect a confidence. I doubt Sophie and I will have much to say to each other in the future."

Buckley, naturally, didn't take kindly to Edgar's venting. "I cannot imagine any excuse sufficient for breaking off relations with somebody who has done for you what Sophie has done for you—none at all. I don't doubt that she has her shortcomings. But one of your strengths is loyalty, and I hope that by the time you receive this, the matter is patched up." But Edgar pressed on with his criticisms. "I know how you feel about her, and you know or should know, that your opinions and advice are not something I would lightly disregard," Edgar had written on March 7. "This once, however, you are very much mistaken."

Still, Sophie and Edgar had managed to recapture some degree of equilibrium prior to his release from prison, but now it was over. Edgar never showed at the Knopf offices. She gave the excuse to the staff that he "must have slept all day." But that evening, Edgar phoned to tell her that he had not been sleeping but out shopping, then visiting with Buckley, and the promised Knopf visit had totally slipped his mind. Next he canceled lunch without giving a reason.

"There is nothing more I can do for him, so he doesn't have

to bother to be polite," Sophie wrote Buckley. "Besides, I don't know how much I may have rubbed him the wrong way, with my impatience, peremptoriness, snobbery, and plain bad manners!" Buckley was appalled by Sophie's account of Edgar's behavior. "It is quite simply incredible, and I pray that there are explanations for it."

A week after Edgar's release from prison, Sophie wrote Bill an extraordinary letter. "I've solved it, I've solved it, I alone have solved it!" she wrote. "The Zielinski murder. You must be the first to know. The way it came to me in itself constitutes proof incontrovertible." Not in a court of law or of public opinion, but "among us, who alone matter, because we have given our hearts and minds to the case, it will constitute a landmark of detective work, which is why you must excuse my crowing a little."

The key, she wrote, lay with the women in Edgar's life.

> *There they are, mother, wife, Vicki [sic], et al. not excluding the undersigned though I played my part with limited liability, as it were, though intently enough to count. There we are, then, like so much litmus paper reacting at first as to a base and invariably, in time, as to an acid! turning first pink, then blue, or whichever way it goes. . . . And each, in turn, makes the simple, if occasionally shattering, discovery that Edgar is as phony as a $3.00 bill. This phoniness is of a splendid consistency, in that it applies to him not only as lover but as painter, writer, friend, man, you name it. THEREFORE, as they said in geometry, he is also a* phony killer. *Bill, Edgar did not wield that finalizing rock, he did not do it. His indignation at being penalized for that, his refusal to admit it, his anguish at having to say he had, in court, are as close to genuine as Edgar can ever get. . . . I'd say he beat her up, it was far more than a slap as he says in the book. He beat her*

*up enough to have really had reason to believe, when the news
dawned, "dat I did it."...*

*Well, I don't know about you, but this resolution of the
mystery makes me very happy, because it means he won't—
well, you know. Juliette, for instance, is perfectly safe,
physically. (I've always felt a little responsible about the
role I've played in glamorizing our hero, where someone as
vulnerable as this woman is concerned; she has my sympathy
because she is a child of poverty, was brutalized as an orphan
by her brothers, never really has found her inner balance ...
and still, at this stage in her life, still expects to find it in a
man, and has picked this of all men to find it in, mamma
mia!) I only hope that she is prepared (there's reason to believe
she is) and will make that $3.00 discovery in her own good
time without losing her cool too much.*

It is remarkable how astute, yet how deluded, Sophie was in
that letter. She would continue to pay the price of her delusion for
the rest of her life.

27

The Celebrity Convict

EDGAR SMITH, free at last, was a celebrity. The man, and what he had to say, attracted interest throughout the world. He had proclaimed his guilt in court and, for all intents and purposes, his innocence on camera. He had painted the guilty plea as a cynical, strategic response to the unfairness of the criminal justice system, a gambit that showed that any means necessary was the right choice for him. Those who believed in his innocence still believed. Those who believed in his guilt also still believed. Arguments persisted. Neither side prevailed.

John Selser, the lawyer who defended him at the original trial, spoke his mind to the Asbury Park *Sunday Press* in an article published on December 19, 1971: "I can't understand it at all that he finally admitted to the killing. But I approve of the end result because . . . I don't think he killed the girl." Selser also recalled meeting William F. Buckley for the first time when the man had come to his office to borrow the trial transcript in the early 1960s: "He kept the record about a month, and when he brought it back, he told me 'your man's guilty.' . . . Apparently he drew that conclusion just from reading the record." And then, clearly, he had changed his mind.

Selser reflected on why Edgar was originally convicted: "He acted as though he was on a picnic all through the trial. He showed no emotion. No concern at all." The publication of *Brief Against Death* also shook his faith in Smith. "In the book, he said I was very gentle and thoughtful and that I acted more like a father than his lawyer in addition to calling me incompetent. He pays me a tribute and then kicks me in the pants." Selser said he had kept the Christmas cards that Edgar had sent him from the Death House over the years. "I don't think I'll get one this year."

Steve Umin, whose legal work had helped free Edgar, might have received a holiday note from his client. But if he did, it wasn't something he wanted, and if he didn't, he might have felt some measure of relief. He would sever ties with Edgar within a year or two of his prison release and would, in private, make clear how little regard he had had for his former client all along.

———

EDGAR HAD MUCH to figure out now that he was no longer incarcerated. Where to go? What to do? How to live? Some answers came easily. He took refuge in Manhattan hotels as he looked for an apartment in New York City. He had to finish his next nonfiction book, which picked up where *Brief Against Death* ended. He was set on getting back his driver's license and buying a Volkswagen. He spent time with Juliette Scheinman, first at her apartment and later, after he found a place, at his.

He spent Christmas with his mother in Ramsey and before that attended holiday parties at the homes of Jack Carley and William F. Buckley. At one point in the evening at the latter fete, a guest caught Edgar staring at Buckley's youngest sister, Carol Learsy, who was, at thirty-three, extremely attractive—his gaze clearly lascivious in nature. But the stare also lacked charm, and there was something in Edgar's eyes the guest didn't like (as he confided to Buckley's son, Christopher, after the fact).

Two days before the end of 1971, the Bergen *Record*'s Frank Lombardi caught up with Edgar at the Heritage Diner in Hackensack. To the reporter's surprise, Edgar was able to walk around the same town where he'd been sentenced to death nearly unnoticed. The waitress served him a western omelet as if he were just another customer. He didn't look like a man who had spent all those years in prison, but then, how was such a man supposed to look?

Edgar said he experienced moments that caused him to flash back to the Death House. "I was packing my suitcase, and I reached up to turn off the light. I was looking for the drawstring from the ceiling light in my cell. Another time, I was writing, and it was about 11:30 [a.m.] and I looked around and wondered: 'Where's that guy with my lunch?' I realized I didn't have to wait around for a guard anymore, that I had to get my own lunch."

While he had been in prison, the outside world had felt unreal. Now the opposite was true. With the Death House ever farther behind in the rearview mirror, Edgar could concern himself with a different flight of fancy: whether his life merited adaptation into a film. "I don't think there's much drama there," he told Lombardi.

"Who would you like to play you?"

"Me," replied Edgar. He seemed serious. "I've always been a frustrated actor."

After lunch, Edgar and Lombardi strolled along Hackensack's Main Street. With time to kill before the bus to Port Authority arrived, Edgar stopped into a used-book store. He spotted some old stock certificates for sale. Lehigh Railroad; his uncle was set to retire from his job there after forty years. "How much?" Edgar asked the salesman.

A dollar, the other man replied.

"Sold." Edgar gave him a dollar.

"And five cents tax."

"Ahh, now I know I'm out in the real world."

A purchase of cigarettes later, Edgar climbed onto a bus—
"Just like other people in the real world," reported Lombardi.

———

THE DAY BEFORE Lombardi's article was published, Agatha Schmidt, *National Review*'s research director, married her fiancé. It would change her life's direction from working single woman—she had entered William F. Buckley's orbit in 1965 as a volunteer on his mayoral campaign—to the wife and mother Aggie Dowd. Her marriage helped her push aside an incident from earlier in December that disturbed her greatly.

Aggie had attended both of Edgar Smith's court hearings in 1971, the one that had reversed his conviction and the one that freed him. Witnessing Edgar admit in court to Vickie's killing was a shock. "I was so crestfallen and so disappointed," she recalled. Edgar had been Bill's cause, "and of course he became our cause, too." She was young and still believed that the courts aimed to provide justice and shouldn't be manipulated. Buckley's explanation that Edgar had to do whatever it took to be free didn't sit well with her.

She met Edgar properly shortly before the party at Buckley's place on his first night of freedom. A day or so later, she was working in her *National Review* office. No one else was around. She was typing something on the mainframe computer, situated such that her back was to the door. There was a sofa across from her desk. "All of a sudden, I heard this voice from my sofa. And it was Edgar Smith."

Aggie jumped. "My goodness, you scared me!" she cried. Edgar had arrived unannounced, unnoticed. "The feeling that I had when he came into my office was definitely a feeling of evil. I mean that sounds old-fashioned, but it really was. It was very uncomfortable and I'd never felt this before." It wasn't that he directed any malevolence toward her in particular, but she experienced a general feeling of being creeped out. She told her fiancé about it at dinner that night. She did not recall telling Buckley.

She resolved never to be alone with Edgar again.

———

WILLIAM F. BUCKLEY knew that Edgar Smith's freedom was a great victory. But he also recognized how hard it was going to be for the man to restart his life on the outside. "In a strange sort of a way, I fear that next year will be the hardest one for him," he wrote Ann Chupak near the end of 1972, a year after Edgar walked out of a New Jersey courtroom as a free man. "That will require the true adjustment. The first year is exhilaration, the second consolidation. I know he will benefit from your prayers, and mine."

Edgar had written to Buckley on January 26 of that exhilarating first year with an update from his new apartment at 235 West 70th Street, "I am slowly learning to survive in this city. First it was the phone company. They very suddenly found someone able to install my phone after I told them I was going to discuss my troubles on television. Now it is American Express. . . . As much as I hate to do things like that I find it's the only way to survive in this city; you simply have to threaten people to get anything done." He told his friend he planned to do "nothing but work" for the next few months, save for a brief trip to Chicago to meet with Geoffrey Norman, who edited his freelance work at *Playboy*.

After that, correspondence between the two men grew infrequent. Buckley heard from Edgar roughly once every two to three months, now that Edgar was free to travel outside the tri-state area, which he did in his newly acquired gold Cadillac. Buckley also received summertime postcards from Sioux Falls, South Dakota, and Reno, Nevada, as part of Edgar's cross-country road trip introducing himself to the interstate highway system, which he planned to write about for *Playboy* (the piece was never published).

Buckley wrote to Edgar in July, telling him of his desire for more written contact. "I have let you alone very much on purpose. But I am anxious that you should not think that I have lost my interest in you now that the guillotine has been rusticated. Take care, and let me hear from you." That desire went largely unfulfilled.

———

EDGAR'S UPPER WEST SIDE apartment was a three-minute walk from Juliette Scheinman's place at 205 West End Avenue. Juliette was wary, but after so many years of waiting, she was ready to see if her relationship with Edgar could blossom into something more permanent. She'd never truly gotten over her ex-husband and still loved him after a fashion, but that was no detriment, she believed, to pursuing a life with Edgar. But Billy still lived at home. How would Edgar get on with her sons? Was that even something she wished for?

Bill Scheinman did not remember if he ever spoke with his mother at length about Edgar, but he did recall Edgar visiting the apartment. The former death row inmate was pleasant to him and attentive to his mother. He made excellent dinners, including a Smith family recipe for Irish stew, as well as quiche Lorraine. Bill remembered the paintings on their own apartment walls, done by Edgar while in the Death House, and said that Juliette kept them until the end of her life.

He also remembered that suddenly, one day, Edgar Smith was no longer around.

Shortly after Edgar's release, Juliette had driven with him to Ramsey to visit with Ann Chupak. On the way there, he had had the notion to stop by the old sand pit, the scene of Vickie's murder. Why he wished to do so, Juliette did not ask. A local cop car drove past them. Juliette wasn't certain if the patrolman caught a glimpse of Edgar's face, but Edgar certainly noticed the cop. As he regarded the patrol car and the man inside, he said, "You'll never know."

Then came a second incident, in the winter of 1972. She and Edgar were taking a day trip, to upstate New York or perhaps New Jersey. On the way home, they got into an argument. Without warning, Edgar drove off the road into a heavily wooded area, no landmarks or signs of life nearby. He stopped the car. He didn't budge from his seat.

Juliette had the distinct sense that her life was in terrible danger, and that Edgar "was thinking about doing something to hurt her," as her son, Bill, later recalled.

Juliette tried to talk Edgar down and to get the car back on the road. Long minutes ticked by: five, fifteen, or perhaps hours. Finally, Edgar was calm again. He got back onto the highway and drove them home to the city.

Juliette broke off her relationship with Edgar the next time they spoke. He tried to contact her many times. She took none of his calls, answered none of his letters. She had felt the whisper of death walk up and down her spine, and she was not about to ignore such a warning.

When things turned from bad to worse for Edgar, Juliette was not the least bit surprised.

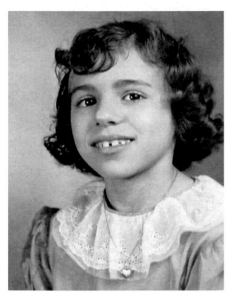

Victoria Zielinski, age 8

Liza Rassner

Victoria Zielinski, age 15

New York Daily News/
courtesy of the author

Dirt road leading to the sand pit; Edgar Smith's house trailer

Archives of Ronald Calissi

The Zielinski family at Vickie's funeral, March 8, 1957
From left: Anthony Jr., Mary, Anthony, Myrna, and Mary Faye

United Press/courtesy of the author

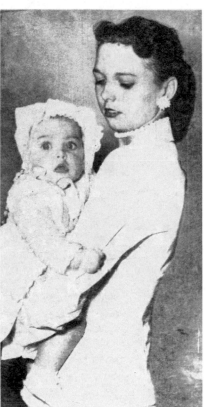

Patricia Smith with baby Patti Ann,
May 1957

Edgar Smith is escorted from the Bergen
County Jail, May 15, 1957.

Edgar Smith on the way to
the Death House, June 6, 1957
Associated Press

Patricia Hafford with daughter
Patti, early 1960s
Patti Hafford

William F. Buckley gives a final press conference
for his 1965 New York City mayoral campaign.

Getty Images

Headshot of Juliette Scheinman, early 1960s

William Scheinman

Sophie Wilkins at her office at Alfred A. Knopf, 1967

Adam Wilkins

Edgar Smith and William F. Buckley in conversation on *Firing Line*, December 7, 1971

Bettman/Getty Archives

Paige Hiemier, 1972, before she
met and married Edgar Smith
Al Paglione/The Bergen Record

Edgar Smith, January 1976; this
photo would be disseminated while
he was on the run for the attempted
murder of Lisa Ozbun.

Associated Press

Patti Hafford and her daughter Jennifer,
early 2000s

Patti Hafford

Lisa Ozbun, 1989

Stan Honda/Los Angeles Times

28

Counterpoint

1972–1974

EDGAR SMITH brushed off the breakup with Juliette Scheinman as just another casualty of his transformation from celebrated death row prisoner to celebrity ex-convict. Within weeks, he met someone new at a Greenwich Village bar. Eileen Conlon was in her late twenties, a flight attendant for United Airlines. She lived in Ridgefield Park, another Bergen County suburb, in an apartment down the street from one that Edgar eventually rented in November 1972.

He embraced his literary fame, appearing on talk shows hosted by David Frost, Mike Douglas, Merv Griffin, and Barbara Walters. He sat in on the corruption trial of former Bergen County prosecutor Robert Dilts. He gave keynote speeches about capital punishment and prison reform at local conferences for lawyers and at colleges, garnering up to $1,000 per appearance. He wrote for the *New York Times*, *Playboy*, and other magazines and newspapers. He was a star, and he basked in the attention.

Ronald Calissi watched the mounting adulation for Edgar Smith with a growing sense of outrage. The ten-year-old boy who had witnessed his father prosecute the man for Vickie Zielinski's murder was now twenty-five, about to be married, and an investigator in his own right, having worked in the Bergen County Prosecutor's Office and for a local insurance company. He channeled that anger into a project, a self-published book entitled *Counterpoint*, which he released half a year after Edgar walked free. The book, which ran over a thousand pages, included the full transcript of the 1957 trial, more than forty photos admitted as exhibits, the transcript of Smith's admission of guilt in court, and synopses of the court opinions on some of the appeals.

"My aim is to establish the facts of the case," he told the Bergen *Record* on May 8. "What I tried to do is present them in a fair way. I'm showing he's a liar, that the court never really made a mistake, that he was properly sentenced, and that the jury was right." *Brief Against Death*, on the other hand, he said, "arrogantly held law enforcement officials and the courts up to ridicule in an attempt to put doubt in the minds of the reading public."

Counterpoint had run so long, he said, because "[Smith] tried to chloroform the mind of the public by leaving out everything that would incriminate him." He said he would donate any proceeds of the book to charity, including St. Joseph's School for the Blind in Jersey City. "I didn't write the book to make money," he told the *Paterson Evening News*. "I just wanted to give people the truth." Buckley did not buy a copy of Calissi's book, and when Calissi sent him a complimentary copy, care of the *National Review* offices, he did not read it.

Edgar commented publicly just once about *Counterpoint*, telling the Bergen *Record* in December 1972, "Oh, I didn't think they allowed the kid to have that many crayons!" He also likely figured that he could rebut Calissi's book and buttress what he'd written in *Brief Against Death* with his own new book, *Getting Out*, published on January 29, 1973. But it was far more poorly received than his first. The courthouse reporter for the Bergen *Record* thought that "much of the information contained in the book should be relegated to footnotes or appendices." The *Washington Post*'s reviewer, Northwestern University law professor Jon Waltz, panned *Getting Out* as "unimportant, malodorous, and invincibly tedious" and "an effort to inflate one habeas corpus hearing and a cynical sequence of plea bargaining into a full-length book."

Waltz also suggested that the book had been ghostwritten, which prompted Jack Geoghegan, the president of Edgar's publisher (renamed Coward, McCann & Geoghegan in 1971), to send a letter to the editor: "I feel that to launch such an accusation with no substantive evidence, in a review that is apparently written in great anger, is literarily, journalistictically [*sic*], and ethically unsound." Waltz's reply was cheeky: "If Mr. Geoghegan prefers the term 'edited,' or if he really does insist that Edgar Smith was the unassisted originator of all that flatulence, it's all right with me. It is still a disreputable publishing effort."

William F. Buckley, to whom *Getting Out* was dedicated, was also dismayed. He found it to be "anemic stuff, larded with Spiro Agnew jokes" and was alarmed to discover in its pages "conspicuous . . . signs of ingratitude verging on coarseness." He was particularly upset with Edgar's "perfunctory credit" of Sophie Wilkins's hard work on his behalf. But the disappointment he felt over Edgar's new book would be the least of his worries when it came to his ex-convict friend.

———

EDGAR FOUND HIMSELF back in a courtroom in August 1973, this time as a defendant in a dispute with his landlord, Chrys Cross Company, which owned the luxury apartment building in Ridgefield Park where he lived. It claimed he owed $1,400 in back rent—roughly five months' worth. He countered that he was withholding the rent until the company did significant repairs. Beams were poking through the walls, and the light fixtures occasionally fell down. Edgar also claimed he had been promised that the building would have a sauna and a rec room by the spring. By July, both were still months away from completion. He said he had fled New York City to get away from the dogs. "I had to sterilize my shoes every night," he groused. But the seventy-unit building housed large dogs, in violation of renters' lease terms.

During the two-and-a-half-hour hearing, Edgar presented photographs of unpainted ceiling areas around a light fixture, studs in the ceilings, and a "muddy parking area" near Route 80, which he said he was forced to use when the building lot was full. "They call it Meadows West. . . . We call it Peyton Place South." He also called a witness, his girlfriend, Eileen Conlon, who lived around the corner. She testified to being present when the ceiling fixture dropped onto the floor.

Judge Paul R. Hout quite reasonably directed Edgar to deposit the back rent owed into a court-administered account until a settlement was reached. "I'm used to negotiating, I'm used to deals," Edgar quipped after agreeing to Judge Hout's terms. "I might write another book, *Brief Against the Landlord*."

But he returned to court once more in November, when the judge ordered him to pay two additional months of back rent or face eviction. Edgar complained some more about the inadequacies of the place. The judge was not moved: "If you're not satisfied, why don't you get out." Edgar's stubborn response was indicative of his attitude: he wanted to do as he pleased and to fight far beyond the time when he should stop.

Some months after his release from prison, Edgar had obtained a bank loan of several thousand dollars, guaranteed by Buckley. Then his celebrity started to wane and his writing opportunities began to dry up. By early 1974, Buckley learned that Edgar had defaulted on the loan. (Buckley had dissolved his power of attorney over Smith's assets after his release from prison, but he continued to act as a financial intermediary over any publishing-related income, as well as related investments.) Buckley had no choice but to pay off the outstanding debt. When Ann Chupak learned of her son's default and tried to send Buckley a check (through Frances Bronson) to cover the costs, he refused to accept it. Buckley also wrote to Edgar in dismay on February 20, 1974, to ask what he was up to. He did not receive a reply, and the friendship ruptured.

It would not resume for a year. By then, Edgar and Eileen had broken up and he had met the woman who would become his second wife, a relationship that would be critical—and damaging—in its own right.

29

Paige

1974–1976

PAIGE HIEMIER resembled Edgar Smith's first wife, Patricia Horton, not only in personality but in circumstances. She was nineteen when she encountered him at a bowling alley in the first part of 1974, close to the same age Patricia had been almost twenty years earlier, when she had met Edgar at a friend's party. Paige was short and slim, four foot ten and under one hundred pounds, with deep-set eyes and a strong nose; her size and her straight brown hair made her appear far younger than nineteen. Patricia, too, had looked younger than her years. Both were daughters of Bergen County; whereas Patricia hailed from Ridgewood, Paige had grown up twelve miles south in Ridgefield Park.

Paige was a prodigy. Her gift was music. She could play many instruments, though she gravitated most to piano. She could listen to a song just once and play it back note for note. She did the arrangements for the high school orchestra. One story went around that Paige had applied to and was accepted by Juilliard but decided not to go there. Instead she attended Bergen Community College, saving money until she could transfer somewhere better.

She was shy and introverted, preferring the company of animals to that of people. At fifteen, she'd advertised herself in the Bergen *Record* as "Girl who loves animals looking for work in a pet shop." Decades later, she would become a breeder of Savannah cats, a way for her to express love without getting hurt in return.

She met Edgar at Hackensack's Bowler City. She didn't know much about his background, though she had a vague sense that he might be important or famous or whatever. She was used to going out with boys around her age who had hardly any money. He was forty to her nineteen—an age difference that seemed even more marked when people in Ridgefield Park saw them driving around town in his gold Cadillac. "My dating her was almost as if the black knight had ridden into town and carried off the only authentic virgin around," he later wrote Buckley.

She claimed she had never talked to Edgar about the murder of Victoria Zielinski. But, in secret, she read *Brief Against Death*. "I didn't believe he did it," she said in 1988. "I thought I knew him. And he didn't bring the murder up. I honestly don't know why I didn't find out more."

Her choice of boyfriend was, to say the least, unpopular. Some attitudes about Edgar had not shifted since 1957. Paige's father got serious hell from his fellow volunteer firemen for allowing his daughter to date *that guy*. Her friends stopped talking to her. The manager of the bank where Paige worked called her in and fired her because he did not approve of her "choice of friends."

One time, when she and Edgar were out at a local bar, a stranger came up to Paige and delivered a warning: "You're going to end up like Vickie Zielinski." She thought the man was a jerk and got angry that Edgar just sat there instead of punching the guy out.

Finally, in December, her father told her that she had to stop going out with Edgar or she had no home with her family any-more. When Edgar brought Paige back after a date soon after that ultimatum, the door was locked.

Edgar said he was ready to marry her. Paige had no other options. She'd never been with any other man, but at the tender age of nineteen, she believed that Edgar completed her as no one else could. When he suggested that they blow town and go as far away as possible—San Diego sounded good—well, why not?

Just before Paige left with Edgar, Ron Calissi tracked her down. He asked her to lunch, where he urged her not to marry Edgar. He was a bad guy, Calissi said, and she would regret it. Paige heard him out. She understood what he was saying. But how could she turn her back on the man when he'd been so kind, so loving, so wonderful to her and everyone else had decided to shun her? She told Ron she couldn't take his advice.

Paige and Edgar moved to San Diego by the end of the year. They bounced around several apartments, including a stint at a friend's, before landing in a garden apartment complex in the suburb of Chula Vista along with three adopted cats. They married on the last day of 1974. Paige thought he had loads of money. Edgar had anything but. It was only a matter of time before her dreams curdled.

———

ANN CHUPAK HAD written to William F. Buckley in June 1974, nearly six months before Edgar and Paige's marriage, to alert him to Edgar's current financial state, which, after his default on the loan, remained bad. She hadn't heard from her son for five months, and bill collectors kept calling, asking her for money. When one had threatened to sue Edgar for nearly $600, she sent it to them and then decided to move so the creditors couldn't track her down. After all the money she spent on her son's case, she wrote, "I could no longer afford to pay his bills." She claimed that her son felt enough shame about the situation that he cried "many times." She also knew she shouldn't have paid his creditors. Sophie Wilkins, with whom she still corresponded, had advised her strongly against it, "but I guess mother's [*sic*] are not too bright."

Buckley wrote her back within days:

> *I have grieved, mostly for you. Edgar has acted very foolishly, and he is bound to suffer. I can hardly wish that he should suffer more, but I can certainly wish that you could suffer less. At least you have nothing to reproach yourself for—you did more than anybody I can imagine for her son, and it is by no means to be excluded that grace will touch him at last, and that before you finally end your life here, you will have cause to be proud of him. Meanwhile I am always at your service and bear no bitterness towards Edgar.*

Eileen had continued to call Ann after she and Edgar split, but Ann dreaded hearing Eileen's voice on the phone. She could not take the girl's litany of sad stories. She had warned the girl that Edgar would never marry her. When Ann moved to Florida, she did not send a forwarding address or telephone number to Eileen. And though Ann worried about the unsavory crowd Edgar had fallen in with in San Diego, who appeared to be dope dealers, she wrote Buckley that "if he becomes involved I would never raise a finger to help him, we only get out of this life what we put into it, so he is on his own, it is his life to make or break."

Buckley knew the score. "I hear nothing at all from Edgar, but I expect that one of these days I will," he wrote Ann in December 1974. "He is obviously unhappy. I hope that will change." Buckley also received a surprise foreign rights check for $500 later that month, which he immediately applied to Edgar's outstanding debts. Then one of Smith's friends wrote to say that "Edgar could use the money." Buckley replied that Edgar "knew perfectly well where to reach me and could speak on his own behalf."

Buckley finally heard from Edgar on December 19. He was in San Diego, along with Paige. He'd been in Mexico for the past few days and had learned, likely from Ann, that the $500 foreign rights check would be applied to the outstanding debts. Then he launched into why he'd been silent for so long:

> *I suppose my silence led you to believe that you had been ripped off. Not really, silence and anonymity equal survival in what I've been doing which you will read about in my new book . . . and at that time you will see the remainder of the money. Until then my best to you and your family during the holiday season and my regrets for what you must think.*

Buckley supposed that Edgar's sense of shame explained his lack of contact, as he explained to Ann in January 1975, adding:

> *But I don't think that that is any reason to make things too easy for him. If he wants in effect to borrow another $500, he should ask for it, don't you agree? I am sure that in his reserve somewhere is the strength of character he showed during those stunning few years in Trenton when he was resisting the death penalty. But he is going to have to climb out of it himself.*

Edgar wrote again in February and tried once more to repair the breach between himself and Buckley:

It is a bit more difficult to explain and apologize for Edgar
Smith. And it is a long story, so bear with me. Basically, the
story is that I screwed everything up, and I am in the process
now of trying to put it all back together again. I seem to have a
unique ability to mess things up so badly that, thereafter, they
can only get better. Hopefully, I have messed everything up
that badly now.

Edgar, in his telling, had gone to Buckley for help for the
bank loan he eventually defaulted on because he "was in debt so
deep to everyone from the IRS to Bankers Trust to B. Altman
that I couldn't have made enough money writing to pay them
off, not even if I wrote twenty-five hours a day and sold every
word." He'd had his hopes riding on a film deal for *A Reasonable
Doubt.* The deal went nowhere. Then he had met Paige, and the
relationship had met with violent disapproval from her father
and others. The two of them left Bergen County and moved to
San Diego "with roughly three hundred bucks between us."

From then on, Edgar recounted a sob story of the highest order. He told Buckley that Paige had found a job, then got laid off.
He wrote a nonfiction piece about drug smuggling that *Playboy*
rejected, then tried to write a novel based on his research, which
made him the "absolute reigning expert on the business of smuggling weed from Mexico and distributing it around the country."
(When that book idea was rejected by both agent and publisher,
he pitched a "popcorn novel" in which something called the
Israeli Defense League, headed by Rabbi Bernard Korstein—
stand-ins for the Jewish Defense League and its founder, Meir
Kahane—would attempt to assassinate Yassir Arafat at the United
Nations, with the FBI having to prevent it. That novel, too, went
nowhere.)

He claimed that under his pseudonym of Michael Mason he

had ridden the desert with the Border Patrol, the Customs Patrol, the DEA, "an assortment of shady friends of DEA I assume were CIA, with dope dealers, smugglers, transporters"—all for the purposes of the book, of course. "Wonderful story so far, isn't it? Especially since I'm the guy who had the world by the ass three years ago."

None of that adequately explained his lack of communication. Edgar continued:

> *I'm sure there was some way I could have contacted you, and some sort of understanding we could have reached regarding the loan, but I felt lousy about it, didn't know what the hell to say, or what to do, and so I just sort of shut off the world, split for California, and hoped that something miraculous was going to happen to enable me to square things with you. I should have known that miracles only happen to good people and dope dealers.*

The biggest of Edgar's many regrets, he wrote, was that he hadn't lived up to Buckley's expectations of him and "that I treated our friendship so badly, but I am what I am, and I just don't know what the hell to do about it except say 'good night' and go home to my wife."

Buckley took some time to digest Edgar's long letter. His response, on February 18, was a mix of wariness and worry: "One word of counsel: be very kind and thoughtful to your mother. You must not set up a situation in which you will be reproaching yourself for the rest of your life, so don't lose any time while you have it. End lecture." He congratulated Edgar on the marriage: "I know it will work out for you. The long decompression was inevitable."

After that exchange, their correspondence picked back up. In

March 1975—days after he had attended another trial where he believed the defendants were wrongfully convicted*—Buckley flew to California for a debate with former San Francisco mayor Joseph Alioto at the University of San Diego. Once the debate ended, he met Edgar and his new wife. Buckley was delighted to find Edgar in good humor and invited "Mr. and Mrs. Smith" along for drinks with Alioto at the bar in the hotel where Buckley was staying—not letting on to the former mayor who Edgar was.

When Paige went to visit the ladies' room and Edgar went out for a smoke, Buckley leaned over to whisper in Alioto's ear. This is the notorious Edgar Smith, he told the former mayor, who has spent more time on death row than anyone else in the United States and is a best-selling author. Buckley immediately felt ashamed of himself. Edgar dealt with such name-dropping wherever he went, and he'd finally fallen into the trap.

At the end of the night, Edgar insisted on paying. "You should not have seized the check," Buckley wrote him afterward. "And anyway, you promised me you were not going to use credit cards any more!" (Edgar had told Buckley that as he had struggled to dig himself out of the financial hole, he had destroyed all his credit cards—except, apparently, he hadn't.)

---

* Buckley, along with the folk singer Pete Seeger, the poet Allen Ginsberg, and others, had contributed to a defense fund for Gary McGivern and Charles Culhane, accused of felony murder in the 1968 death of a deputy sheriff as part of a thwarted prison escape in Ulster County, New York. McGivern and Culhane contended that a third man, Robert Bowerman, had acted alone in the escape attempt and the killing. The first trial ended in a hung jury; the men were sentenced to death after the second trial, but the verdict was overturned on appeal. The third trial, in March 1975, ended in convictions and prison sentences of twenty-five years to life. McGivern was ultimately pardoned by Governor Mario M. Cuomo in 1985, and he was released in 1989 but returned to prison on a parole violation six years later and died there in 2001. Culhane was paroled in 1992, but a drunk driving conviction sent him back to prison for eleven months in 1994.

Paige wrote to Buckley afterward to express her pleasure at meeting him: "Perhaps next time I meet you I will be able to tell you myself, assuming that Edgar lets me get a few words in! The only way to break into a conversation in which Edgar is involved is to invoke the anti-monopoly laws." Buckley wrote back contritely, "I was awfully anxious to talk to you about music, but I know how it is when two old friends get together and I apologize for my own garrulousness."

After their reunion, Edgar sent a letter (dated March 30) that included disturbing news: he claimed to be an informant for the DEA, supplying it with information he'd gleaned from his research for the drug story. There was a catch: "I haven't seen a penny of their money, and doubt if I ever will. What I am hoping, however, is that when this thing is done and over, DEA will provide me with a letter which I can take to the Governor of New Jersey and request a full pardon—something I had always intended to do eventually—in return for something like 'valuable services rendered to the United States Justice Department'—DEA's daddy." There was no way to verify the information, of course, but Buckley reacted in as distant a manner possible. "Suffice to say that I very much approve of your strategy and I congratulate you once again on your fine narrative," he replied on April 22.

Over the course of the year, Edgar continued to send his friend news of his revolving door of jobs: security guard and car valet in a La Jolla condominium, working the night shift; advertising man for the local newspaper; dishwasher and floor cleaner; PR rep for the San Diego Bicentennial Exposition until the company went bankrupt and could no longer pay him. "It seems to me that to start from the bottom in the way you were doing means a great deal psychologically, and will equip you to move faster and more happily in the direction you want," Buckley encouraged him. But there didn't seem to be much movement. Edgar's applications for writing, editing, and reporting jobs went nowhere. He passed various civil service exams but failed the background check.

Soon Edgar wasn't working at all. Paige kept them afloat, finding a job as a teller for a Bank of America branch while she took classes at Mesa College in anatomy and physiology in preparation for a full course load in the fall. But she was besieged by physical ailments: stomach pains, cramps, intestinal obstructions. She ended up in the hospital for more than a week for various surgeries, including a laparoscopy and the removal of an ovary and Fallopian tube.

Edgar described Paige's health issues as the result of female troubles. "That's awful about Paige," Buckley wrote back on November 3. "I don't know how to interpret it, knowing nothing about human insides, an ignorance I have cultivated with great effort over the years. I can only assume that it is awful but routine. Give her my best."

The truth, which Paige revealed to the Bergen County Prosecutor's Office decades later, was that her problems owed to injuries from repeated sexual assaults by Edgar. The disparity between his size and hers—Paige was four foot ten, Edgar closer to six feet—made those assaults even more wretched for Paige. She would go public in a 1989 *Los Angeles Times* interview with one incident: The couple had been play wrestling on the living room floor when Edgar grabbed her by the neck and began to choke her. She was stunned and began to lose consciousness. Two minutes or so later, his rage seemed to ebb, and he loosened his grip on her neck.

Buckley had no inkling of the true state of Edgar's marriage to Paige. He did receive a litany of Edgar's own grievances:

> *Twenty years after I left I am back sitting in a gas station on*
> *Main Street again, looking for a way out, if you know what*

I mean. It's all so familiar—just married, broke, no job, no prospects; just older, and hopefully, wiser. I've been to the mountaintop, as the man once said, and fell on my ass down the other side. But what the hell, if you can get up there once, why not twice? When you're all the way down, you have to go up or out, there's no other way, and I'm not ready to go out, not yet.

The last straws came on September 30, 1976, when Edgar went into the office of the *San Diego Union* to ask for a full-time job; the paper turned him down, saying there were no openings. He'd been assigned to write an essay for the op-ed page on the threat to First Amendment rights by judges' actions, including a controversial media gag order for a murder trial in Nebraska that had reached the Supreme Court. The paper's editor, Gerald Warren, rejected the piece, suggesting that Edgar needed to do additional research and revise it. This did not sit well with him.

Eighteen months after Edgar had written to William F. Buckley that he wasn't ready to "go out," out he would go. And just as he had been nearly two decades earlier, he was ready to take someone with him.

PART VII

BOILING OVER

(1976–1979)

30

Rage, Revived

TO THE CRIMINAL, a crime of opportunity isn't personal. When a man is determined to kill, rape, rob, maim, or all of the above, the target could be someone he loves or someone he's never met before. Someone he knows or someone he'd never dream of knowing. Someone he cares for or someone he despises. The impulse overrides everything.

For the victims, the crimes can only be personal. Attacks upon their bodies. Attacks upon their minds and souls. Obliteration of their very selves. Violent acts leading to years, if not decades, of aftermath for the victim, for those who love the victim, and for those the victim loves and cares for. One act with generations of ripple effects.

In 1976, nineteen years after she died, the family of Victoria Zielinski still lived in the shadow of her murder, their lives forever upended by the ending of her life. On October 1 of that year—thousands of miles away from them, in another state—the same shadow would be cast upon a different woman, a different family.

She, too, had the misfortune of being in the wrong place at the wrong time. She didn't know her would-be killer, but his rage was the same. And the act driven by that rage would come close to causing her death.

———

LEFTERIYA OZBUN FINISHED her shift at Ratners California Clothes, the clothing manufacturer where she had worked as a seamstress for seven years, at around 2:30 in the afternoon on October 1. She got off earlier than expected; her shift was supposed to end at 4:45, but there was no more work to be done that day, so her bosses decided to let everyone go home.

Lisa, as she was known, had no ride. She and her husband, Darwin, had only one car, and he wasn't due to pick her up until 5:00 p.m., after he'd finished his own day shift. Lisa, thirty-three, had come to America from Istanbul at age eighteen with her first husband. She'd married Darwin, also divorced, five years earlier, and they were raising a blended family of three kids. To kill some time while she waited, she decided to take the bus to a nearby shopping center. At about twenty minutes to five, she caught the bus back to L Street, getting off at the stop closest to the factory parking lot, running a little late. She expected that her husband would already be parked a few hundred feet away and picked up her pace, worried that he would be wondering where she was.

A car drove by Lisa, then made a sharp U-turn to block her path. A strange man in dark glasses jumped out. She thought he was going to ask her for something. Then she saw the knife.

Before Lisa could react, the man had the knife at her throat. He pushed her into the passenger seat of a 1966 brown Pontiac Tempest and taped her hands behind her back. "Don't say— Don't say nothing. Don't you try to scream. I'm going to cut your throat right now," he said. He put the car into reverse and drove with his left hand, keeping the knife at Lisa's side with his right hand.

"Keep your mouth shut," the man said. "I'm going to take your damn money, and I'm going to stick a knife in you."

"What do you want to stick the knife in me?" Lisa asked. "Why do you want to kill me? I have three kids in the house. If you want the money, take it and just let me go."

"Don't be stupid," said the man. He kept driving, the knife at Lisa's stomach.

Lisa knew with utter clarity that she would die if she didn't do something. "I could see it in his eyes," she told a *Los Angeles Times* reporter in 1989. "I'd never seen eyes like that. They were so cold and filled with hate. I knew if I didn't fight I'd never see my kids again."

She started to struggle, so hard that she kicked a hole in the windshield of the moving car. Screaming for help, she grabbed the wheel and hit the brake pedal, somehow evading the blade. He slapped her so hard she grew dizzy, then pushed her underneath him and used his weight to hold her down. Once more holding the knife on her, he pulled onto I-5 in rush-hour traffic, headed south. He was a full foot taller and almost a hundred pounds heavier than she was, and it felt as if all of that bulk was on her face.

"I can't—I can't breathe. Would you let me up, I can't breathe."

"You're talking to me, aren't you."

Lisa, still resisting, managed to get the tape off her wrists. She pulled herself out from under him and reached for the door on the passenger side with her feet.

"I'm going to give it to you," said the man. "You just keep your legs down."

That's when the knife plunged into her body, under her right breast, into her stomach, piercing her liver and diaphragm. It went in so deep that only the handle stuck out. She was so determined to keep fighting that she felt no pain.

Lisa managed to get her hands on the wheel. He tried to push her off and slapped her again. She found the horn and pressed it. The car began to swerve all over the place.

With both Lisa's and her captor's hands on the wheel, the car veered off the freeway at the next exit and stopped. The man was trying to keep her in the car when she pried open the passenger door. She struggled so hard that when he released his grip, she fell out the door, the knife still embedded in her stomach.

People rushed toward her, one of them a young man who'd been selling flowers by the exit roadside. Lisa could see her purse lying on the floor of the front passenger seat, visible through the still open door. "Please get my purse," she implored the flower seller, who had knelt beside her. With the driver sitting still, apparently stunned by the events, the flower seller managed to grab the purse.

Then the driver snapped out of his haze and sped away, but not before Frank Hobdy, a special agent with the Drug Enforcement Administration who happened to be nearby, took down the license plate number. Hobdy first followed the car on I-5 as it swerved erratically between lanes. He called in the license number of the Pontiac—527 COG—to the San Diego police. Once he got out of the car and saw that Lisa had been stabbed, he called for an ambulance. Darwin, who had witnessed his wife's abduction, had already called the police, frantic about her safety, but hadn't been able to make out the plates.

The ambulance ferried Lisa to Bay General Hospital for emergency surgery. The tip of the knife had missed her heart by a half an inch. As the surgeon, Morton Jorgensen, later testified, had the knife gone a few centimeters deeper, the resulting massive bleeding would likely have killed her.

Lisa was in intensive care for four days and stayed in the hospital for five more. On October 7, the press came calling. "I had never seen the guy before in my whole life, and I've never been more scared," she told a reporter from the New York *Daily News*. "I thought he was going to kill me for sure." Weeks later, recovering at home, she was still stunned by what had happened. "It [was] like something on *Bionic Woman*," she told reporters. "I would like to know why [he] did it."

When the police ran the license plate number, they found that it was registered to Paige Dana Smith. But Paige didn't drive the car. Her husband, Edgar, did.

31

On the Run

OCTOBER 1976

BETTY LOVELL'S telephone rang around six o'clock on the night of October 1. Edgar Smith was on the other end. He told her he was in trouble and that he and Paige needed a ride from the Bank of America branch in Imperial Beach where she worked.

Betty, a flight attendant for United Airlines, had known Edgar since 1973, when he had also become friendly with her husband, Jim. Whenever he asked a favor—such as if he and Paige could crash at the Lovells' house when money was tight—she said yes. She drove her Porsche to the bank and arrived at 7:15 p.m. to find Edgar and Paige waiting outside.

When they got into her car, Betty saw that Paige was crying. Edgar tried to explain the trouble he was in. He said it was payday and he was broke. He had offered a lady a ride in a parking lot and was going to steal her money. Betty didn't know what to make of the information. He then said he didn't have his car because he'd left it at a body shop. He didn't mention what his own plans were, but it was clear Paige needed a place to crash for the night.

The three of them got to Betty's around eight. Edgar stayed about an hour, then phoned another friend of his, Herbert

Sandler. "I have a problem. Can you meet me at Sheldon's?" he asked.

Sandler had known Edgar for about four years and had rarely heard him sound so agitated. He drove to the restaurant. When he arrived just before 9:30, he found Edgar sitting in a booth with Michael Pancer, a lawyer friend. Pancer was in the process of urging Edgar to surrender to the police.[*]

When Edgar spotted Sandler, he said, "You'll have to come into the middle of the story. It's already started."

Pancer interjected, telling Sandler, "Well, I don't think you ought to sit down here at this point."

Sandler took the hint and went to the counter to order some coffee.

After Pancer left, Edgar called Sandler over. He said he needed someone to drive him to Bill Durk's house on Pacifica Drive, across the road from the restaurant. Sandler said he would. After he dropped him off, he didn't see him again.

He did, however, get a phone call the next evening from Paige. Could Sandler come meet her the next day at Jalisco Auto Body Shop? She was dropping the car off, she said, and would need a ride home. She didn't tell Sandler that she would first be picking it up at the Alpha Beta body shop, where Edgar had left it, or that she was moving it so the police would have a harder time tracking it down.

Soon after Sandler arrived at Jalisco, Paige drove up in the brown Pontiac. The car had a cracked windshield.

The body shop owner didn't get around to examining the car until a few days later, when the police arrived to confiscate the car. At that point he saw blood on the carpet by the right-side door.

---

[*]   Pancer denied this exchange took place in a May 2020 interview.

———

SHORTLY AFTER MIDNIGHT on October 2, Barbara Fenity's phone rang. "I have a problem," said Edgar Smith. "Could I come over?"

Barbara and Edgar had begun to correspond in 1971, before he was released from Trenton State Prison. They continued to correspond after he got out and became better friends after he and Paige moved to San Diego.

"Stop joking around," she told him. She was certain he was out partying.

"No, I'm serious. I have a problem." Now he asked if she could come get him and gave her the address. She drove over to Pacifica Drive and found him waiting.

He refused to tell her what was going on, except that his car was out of commission after a run-in with a mail truck in Claire-mont. He stayed with Barbara through the weekend, and still he wouldn't tell her his problem. But he did ask to borrow some money, and she gave him $205 in cash.

On Monday morning, Edgar went into the bathroom and shaved off his mustache. After lunch, Barbara had to go to work. Edgar drove her there and asked if he could keep her car for the rest of the afternoon She said yes, so long as he picked her up at 5:30.

While Barbara was at work, Edgar went to the office of an-other friend, Stephen Jordan. He'd arranged to borrow another $100 but insisted the check be made out to his pseudonym, Mi-chael Mason. "I just need the money, I don't want to involve you." He'd told Stephen that he was on his way to visit a friend who lived in Mexico. Stephen wasn't at the office, but he'd made ar-rangements for the check to be ready for pickup.

Edgar picked up Barbara from her workplace as promised. Back at her place, he asked if she would drive him to Los Angeles

International Airport so that he could catch an overnight east-bound flight.

On the two-and-a-half-hour drive to LAX, Edgar gave Barbara some instructions. If he contacted her and said he was in Florida, he might actually be in New York. If he said he was in New York, he might really be in San Francisco. Like Betty Lovell, Barbara didn't know what to make of Edgar's directives, but she sensed it would not be a good idea to question him further.

At LAX, Edgar checked in, and then he and Barbara took the escalator to the airport bar and had a drink. He went to a pay phone and made one call, and then they walked together to the gate, where they said goodbye.

The next afternoon, Edgar called and said he was in New York seeing friends. Two nights later, Barbara saw on the news that Edgar was a fugitive, wanted for the brutal attack on Lisa Ozbun.

———

WILLIAM F. BUCKLEY heard that Edgar was on the run, accused of attempted murder, from Steve Umin, who'd heard the news from the Bergen County prosecutor. Buckley was dumbfounded but not surprised. "It did not cross my mind to say, 'It's got to be *another* Edgar Smith.' It's got to be a mistake," he later wrote. He immediately alerted Sophie Wilkins, who took it upon herself to call Edgar's mother.

Buckley also called the superintendent of his Manhattan apartment building on 73rd Street, where his son, Christopher, was staying. Buckley figured that Edgar would eventually come to him for help and wanted to be prepared for that possibility.

A few days later, in the evening, Christopher was home alone when the buzzer rang.

"He's here," said the doorman.

"What do you mean?"

"He's sitting in the lobby."

Good God, Christopher thought. "Well, call the police," he told the doorman. "I'll come and try to stall him."

He knew his father kept a .38-caliber Smith & Wesson Airweight revolver in the bedside drawer.

Christopher retrieved the gun and stuck it into his pocket. He ran down the stairs, took a deep breath, and opened the door that led directly from the apartment to the lobby, expecting to find himself "eyeball to eyeball" with Edgar.

It wasn't Edgar; it was one of Christopher's friends, whom the doorman had mistaken for the fugitive. Disaster was barely averted.

Edgar Smith was still on the loose.

———

MEANWHILE, EDGAR ACTUALLY *was* in New York City. He'd called his old *Playboy* editor, Geoffrey Norman, who was now working for *Esquire*. The editor allowed Edgar to use his apartment while he went out of town for a few days. While Norman was gone, Edgar kited some cheques under Norman's name and stole his Chevrolet Blazer, abandoning the car a fair distance from the apartment. "I felt betrayed," Norman reflected in 2021. "He had a certain kind of perverse celebrity, and that's what . . . unfortunately people in the media business look for."

By that time, Michael Pancer had contacted the San Diego police to tell them he was trying to get Edgar to turn himself in. He'd also fielded calls from Edgar, who was cagey about his whereabouts. Pancer continued to press his friend to surrender.

Edgar called Barbara Fenity on the evening of Friday, October 8, but Barbara told him she couldn't talk; Edgar's wife, Paige, and their mutual friend Betty Lovell were on their way over. Later that night, Edgar called back. He asked Barbara to call him from a pay phone and gave her a long-distance number.

When he picked up, Barbara screamed, "Jesus fucking Christ, Edgar, what did you do?" She yelled some more. He tried to cut in, but she was too busy venting.

"It was robbery," Edgar said. "It was only robbery."

"Edgar, you didn't know if she had a dollar eighty-two in her pocket or ten thousand dollars. You didn't know if she had deposited it in the bank, had lost the check, had cashed it—not cashed it, spent it. It doesn't make sense."

"It was pay day at Ratners," Edgar said.

A few days later, Barbara received a phone call from the police to ask whether any of her credit cards was missing. She hadn't thought to check before. When she did, she discovered that Edgar had stolen two of them. One was in her full name. The other was in the name of B. Fenity.

At some point during his first week on the run, Edgar took a train to Philadelphia. He later claimed to have gone to the cemetery in Honesdale where Victoria Zielinski was buried and said that was where he finally admitted to himself that he was responsible for her murder. He also claimed to have visited West Point, ninety minutes north of New York City, where he had an epiphany while sitting astride a British cannon overlooking the Hudson River. He also called his aunt, asking her to meet him near the World Trade Center and lend him $1,000. She did so but made him promise he would take the next flight to San Diego and give himself up to the authorities.

Then he was back in the air: Philadelphia to Chicago and, after a plane change, to Las Vegas. Not to San Diego.

———

THE PHONE AT the *National Review* offices rang on the morning of October 13. Frances Bronson, Buckley's executive secretary, always fielded his calls if she was in the office, even if he was physically present, so she was the one who picked up.

When she heard the voice on the other line, she took a beat to react.

"How are you, Frances?" said Edgar. "Where's Bill?"

Frances, too, had felt betrayed by the news of Edgar's new crime and his fugitive status. She'd believed in his innocence and had rooted for him. Somehow she managed to keep the emotion out of her voice.

"He's in Albuquerque," she replied.

"Can you tell me where to reach him?"

No, she said, then offered to track him down. "Where can he reach you?"

"I'm at a hotel in Las Vegas." He gave her the telephone number and the number of the room he was staying in.

Frances said her goodbyes and called Buckley as soon as she hung up. She gave him the details of the hotel location and number.

Buckley got off the line and called the FBI.

32

Arrested Again

FIVE FBI AGENTS arrived at the Fremont Hotel in Las Vegas just before 8:30 in the morning of October 13. They went with the security guard to the fourteenth floor. He used the key to open the door to room 1441. Guns drawn, the agents stormed into the room registered to Bob Fenity.

There they found Edgar Smith, his mustache shaved off and still dressed in a brown suit, sound asleep. The agents woke him up and asked him his name. He admitted that he was indeed the fugitive they were looking for.

He was unarmed. He was alone. He did not resist being handcuffed. He merely wanted to know how they found him.

The agents did not reveal that William F. Buckley had turned him in.

Edgar was arraigned in Nevada's Clark County District Court before Judge Joseph Ward, who set his bail at $500,000. After the hearing, he was bound over for extradition, the unlawful flight charges dropped so that the state of California could take over jurisdiction. On October 16, he arrived at the Metropolitan Correctional Center, San Diego, where he was held on attempted murder and kidnapping charges. At that arraignment, before Municipal Court judge Janet Kintner, he remained silent, except for one comment: "I won't waive anything."

After a preliminary hearing in San Diego Superior Court in which Lisa Ozbun identified Edgar as her assailant, he pleaded not guilty to all the charges. A trial date was set for early January but was later postponed to March. Bail had been set at $250,000, but Edgar's court-appointed lawyer, Thomas Ryan, argued that such a high bail was like having no bail at all and asked for it to be reduced.

The prosecutor was reluctant to reduce the bail, his mind made up after he learned that law enforcement officials had spoken with William F. Buckley, whom Edgar had listed as a character reference. When asked if he felt that Edgar was a reliable, responsible person, Buckley had replied, "No."

Once that news became public, Buckley declined to comment, telling the Bergen *Record*, "I don't talk to the press about what I say to probation department aides." In a November 29 letter to Ann Chupak, he wrote:

> *The newspapers keep calling about Edgar, but really what is there to say? When the probation officer from California called me to ask me the ritual questions, she arrived at the fifth: 'In your opinion, is the detainee reliable and trustworthy for purposes of bail?'—a strange question to ask under the circumstances. Of course I had to reply in the negative, but rather resented being asked it at all. Presumably with those charges pending against him, the state of California is better equipped than I or even you to pass judgment on the question of whether he should be set free.*

The judge finally decided to reduce Smith's bail to $100,000, which did not go over well with the prosecutor, Deputy District

Attorney Richard Neely, who called Smith the "greatest risk I've seen in 10 years I've been in this office." It also didn't go over well with Smith, who wanted it reduced further to $25,000.

At the bail hearing, Edgar had sworn that he hadn't been eluding capture. If he had been trying to hide, why had he used the name Michael Mason, the known pseudonym he'd used to publish the novel *71 Hours*? "Any reasonably competent police officer . . . would know I use that name," he said in a supreme feat of self-justification. He also claimed that after a New York newspaper published a piece about him while he was on the run, he decided to return to San Diego and surrender. "I can give you a list of a dozen people who would tell you I was on my way back here," he said. "If the court wishes I'll report daily anywhere you want me to."

The point was moot. Edgar couldn't afford to bail himself out, and none of his friends would help—especially Buckley, who broke his public silence about his fallen protégé in an On the Right column syndicated on November 20. "What are my 'comments'? Why, I believe now that he was guilty of the first crime," he wrote, referring to the murder of Victoria Zielinski. He then went on about how "this year and every year" guilty men are freed and innocent men are convicted. "Edgar Smith has done quite enough damage in his lifetime without underwriting the doctrine that the verdict of a court is infallible."

———

PAIGE WAS DETERMINED, at first, to stick by her husband. After the near-fatal attack on Lisa Ozbun she had flown back to New Jersey to stay with her parents, but she returned to San Diego after Edgar was arrested. She attended every hearing and every day of his trial, sometimes taking notes, and offering moral support when she could.

When her family told her about Buckley's column, she became distraught. She'd written to Buckley weeks earlier, thanking him for his help, "for being there and for being the person that you are." And now she learned that he'd been the one to turn Edgar in to the authorities—to betray them.

Paige telephoned Jack Carley, Edgar's onetime legal researcher and friend, to complain. Carley, who hadn't read the column yet, cautioned Paige not to jump to conclusions until she had read it herself. "I know I should understand Bill's feelings toward Edgar, but I'm afraid I can't," Paige wrote Carley after the phone call. "I am reserving judgement until I see the article and then I will contact him. I really hope it isn't true!" Once Carley read the column, he wrote Buckley, "I subscribe to your views entirely. As we both know, there is a good and bad Edgar, and the bad one is not a responsible member of society."

Paige paid a high price for believing in her husband. She was supposed to start classes at Mesa Junior College on Monday, January 31. Five days earlier, a grand jury handed down an indictment against her for being an accessory to Edgar Smith's crimes—helping him escape and trying to hide the busted brown Pontiac. Eileen Conlon, Edgar's old girlfriend, had been subpoenaed by the grand jury and flown to San Diego to testify before the charges were laid against Paige. "I really don't want to talk," she told a reporter after she finished her fifteen minutes of testimony.

Paige surrendered to the Superior Court and was released on her own recognizance. On May 23, she pleaded guilty to a lesser misdemeanor charge and was sentenced to probation. That summer, she volunteered as a research assistant in immunochemistry at the Scripps Clinic. Her supervisor, Sherry Ryan, who had met Paige because her husband, Thomas, had had the "dubious honor" of defending Edgar Smith, wrote a glowing reference letter to the judge, asking for him to resolve her legal problems as soon as possible.

"Before meeting Paige, I had automatically concluded that anyone as horrible as Edgar Smith must have a criminal for a wife," she wrote. "In this assumption I was very narrow, prejudiced, and very wrong. Unfortunately, others have also been narrow and prejudiced with Paige, as evidenced by employers who have fired her upon realizing to whom she is married (regardless of the quality of her work)."

Ryan had hosted Paige in her home on numerous occasions. She felt that Paige's compassion for Edgar's victims was genuine. "Paige is a proud person who has been crushed by the total collapse of her world. She has suffered from shock (actual clinical), confusion, disbelief, and devastating grief. I have made the analogy to her of the patient who has been informed that he has cancer. The various psychological processes that follow in the patient are not unlike those Paige has suffered."

Paige's criminal conviction was eventually dismissed. She now wished she could expunge Edgar from her life, but that was not to be.

33

"The Saga of a Bad Man"

EDGAR SMITH'S trial began on March 21, 1977, in San Diego County Superior Court. He had waived his right to be tried by a jury, pinning his hopes on the judge, Gilbert Harelson. Both the prosecutor, Richard Neely, and his defense lawyer, Thomas Ryan, declined to make opening statements. Lisa Ozbun took the stand just before 11:00 a.m. the next day.

In unflinching detail, she described what happened on the afternoon of October 1. She mentioned that the man wore glasses and a brown jacket. Neely asked her if she saw the person who abducted her in the courtroom. "Yes, I do," she said, pointing to Edgar, who was wearing the same clothes that Lisa had described. (She had also identified him earlier in a police lineup. When she saw him there, she became so anxious that she broke the pencil she was holding in half.)

Neely called several more witnesses, including Barbara Fenity, Betty Lovell, and Herbert Sandler; the surgeon who had operated on Lisa Ozbun; various police officers and detectives; and witnesses to Ozbun's struggle with Edgar in the car. Ryan called a handful of defense witnesses, but one of them was Edgar Smith.

His testimony proved to be astonishing. On the stand, he

freely admitted to being a sexual predator. It seemed as if Edgar was attempting to undermine the aggravated kidnapping charge; at the time, in California, kidnapping with rape as the motivation could garner a lesser prison sentence, with the possibility of parole, while kidnapping in order to rob did not. It was a risky line of defense, but Edgar felt, perversely, it was the only way to secure his potential freedom.

In a measured, deliberate manner, though he often seemed to be breathing unevenly, he admitted his festering anger and his desire to rape women, saying that he'd never seen the opportunity to act on those urges until Lisa Ozbun had become his target. He testified that he had lied to his wife, Betty Lovell, and Barbara Fenity in saying that his true aim was robbery. He admitted to the murder of Victoria Zielinski, as well as to the attempted molestation of a young girl while he was still a teen.

Edgar occasionally stopped to take off his glasses and wipe his eyes. On one of those occasions, his voice hardly audible, he claimed that he had gone to a cemetery in Honesdale to look for Victoria Zielinski's grave. Though he couldn't find it, "I stood in that cemetery in Pennsylvania and for the first time in my life I recognized that the devil I had been looking at for the last 43 years was me."

He said his life was a torment and he was tired of lying. "I could talk to no one. Everyone wanted the Edgar Smith who spent 14 years on Death Row for a crime he did not commit. I have lied to myself for years." It was while he was in West Point, he claimed, that he had realized he did not want to kill himself—that was the easy way out—but would eventually return to San Diego to turn himself in. He tried to sound contrite and remorseful, but the public at large, never mind the prosecutor, didn't see him that way.

"We feel he's using the rape motive to get the lesser penalty—

the hope of eventual freedom," a spokesperson for the San Diego County District Attorney's Office told the Bergen *Record*. "The confession to the first crime was meant to bolster his credibility. But let's face it. It's a recantation on top of a recantation."

On cross-examination, Richard Neely asked Edgar directly about the law statute: "Did you know . . . that kidnapping for the purpose of rape carries a lesser penalty than kidnap with intent to rob?"

Edgar answered that he did.

Neely pressed him further about how being out of work had made him feel less of a man; that Paige was the breadwinner while Edgar stayed at home, doing laundry, washing dishes, or watching soaps. Edgar kept his cool but only by the slimmest of margins.

The lawyers made their closing arguments. Neely urged the judge to deliver a guilty verdict and the maximum possible sentence. Ryan, without much to work with, could only insist that Edgar was a rapist, not a robber as the prosecution alleged.

The next morning, March 30, 1977, emotion rippled through the courtroom as Edgar walked in. A bandage covered his forehead. His nose appeared to be broken, his face was puffy and swollen, and both his hair and the blue prison shirt beneath his jacket were matted with blood. He looked as though he had been beaten up, though he'd insisted to the sheriff's deputies that he'd fallen out of his bunk bed. (The Bergen *Record* was predictably skeptical, also reporting that "thirty-eight prisoners who shared Smith's cellblock told the deputies they had seen and heard nothing.")

Paige began to sob loudly at the sight of her bruised and battered husband. "They did that to him," she cried, and vowed to get even with those responsible for assaulting him. (Others were overheard muttering that Edgar "had gotten what was coming to him.") Judge Harelson called for order and then announced that Edgar had been injured in jail and been taken to the hospital that morning.

Judge Harelson asked Edgar if he wanted to change his clothes.

"I don't know," he replied.

"Do you want to proceed to court in your present condition or do you want an opportunity to change into your clothes?"

"Makes no difference," Edgar said.

Thomas Ryan tried to interject, but Judge Harelson said, "I'd like to get an answer from him."

"I understand that, your Honor, but he's also told me that he wants to proceed with the sentencing at this time," Ryan insisted. "And it would be my request that sentencing be delayed. . . . Your Honor, I don't think he really knows what's going on."

"Well—"

"It's not anything he did himself, your Honor," Ryan stressed, then made a formal motion to delay the verdict. Judge Harelson agreed to postpone it a day.

On March 31, Edgar didn't arrive in court until noon. Judge Harelson asked how he was faring.

Ryan answered for his client, "Well, his physical condition is, he's still hurting. He's hurting badly but he understands where he is and what's going on." His client, he said, wanted to proceed.

Judge Harelson found Edgar guilty on all counts: attempted murder, kidnapping to commit robbery, assault with a deadly weapon, and attempted robbery. "After an entire comparison and consideration of all the evidence I am convinced beyond a reasonable doubt that the defendant did commit the crimes charged against him."

He then addressed the defendant: "Mr. Smith, I believe the verdict of a jury would have been the same as mine. I would also like to add, in my opinion, Mr. Ryan has done everything within his power, or anyone else's, to assure that all of the facts in your defense would be presented and that you would receive a fair trial. Whether you agree or disagree, I believe that you have."

The court finally reconvened for sentencing on April 25, 1977. Edgar tried to delay matters further with a convoluted legal argument about whether he should have been given a hearing on his sanity before the verdicts came in, since the judge had expressed "doubt" about his ability to continue trial proceedings and no one had examined him for his "lucidity or competence." Judge Harelson brushed that gambit aside. "Mr. Smith, I had no doubt on March 31, 1977, nor do I have any doubt now, as to your sanity on [that day] or your present sanity today. And your motion will be denied."

Then Edgar tried another tack, asking to be certified as a mentally disordered sex offender. "I had never heard of it until perhaps two or three months ago," he told the court. "Another attorney brought it to my attention. He discussed it with me. He explained to me what it was. I understand it is not an escape; that is not something in lieu of sentencing. I'm aware, as Mr. Ryan stated, that I am going to be sentenced to prison for a considerably long period of time. The question is whether I go there directly from this courtroom or whether I be given the opportunity to be treated."

He carried on with his declaration:

I am a Mentally Disordered Sex Offender, your Honor. I know it. I have probably known it all of my life. I didn't know what it was called, but I knew what it was. I've never in my life begged, I've never in my life pleaded, but today, your Honor, I am going to beg and I am going to plead and I am going to appeal to the Court's compassion. I don't know whether I deserve the Court's compassion.

I don't know whether I deserve anyone's; I certainly have very little for myself.

I have done a great many things in my life that were wrong, that I regret, that I cannot now change, but I do hope it would be that I never again do any of those things. . . . I don't know that it's possible. I don't know, your Honor, that I am amenable to treatment. I know that I want the treatment. I know that I want the chance. I want the chance not only to live with other people but I want the chance to live with myself, and that perhaps is the most difficult thing for someone in my position to do. I did it for forty-three years. I denied what I was. I didn't live with myself, I lived with a fantasy Edgar Smith that I created. I can't hide behind that fantasy anymore, your Honor.

It was an impassioned speech, replete with contrition. But the prosecutor wasn't buying it. He quoted one of the psychiatrists who had examined Smith before the trial: "The problem is that he is using all of this knowledge not for any real insightful change but rather for manipulative purposes. This is a man with extraordinary intelligence, sensitivity and perceptive capacity, and he uses all of this to get around people." Neely believed Edgar was trying to do so again. "And if there are three things that we know about Mr. Smith," he said, "he's antisocial, he's manipulative, and he's extremely dangerous."

Judge Harelson clearly agreed with the prosecutor. He sentenced Edgar Smith to life in prison without the possibility of parole. The former death row inmate and newly minted convict left the San Diego jail for San Quentin. But a new law, scheduled to go into effect on July 1, would allow for parole for those convicted of kidnapping with intent to rob. The new law was retroactive. Edgar would face his first parole hearing in just five years' time.

————

IN BERGEN COUNTY, some people celebrated Edgar Smith's return to prison. Most, though, felt shame mixed with anger that he had ever been let out at all. His first defense attorney, John Selser, completely changed course. "I'm sorry he wasn't executed," he told the Bergen *Record*. "How can I have any other thought than that he is as guilty as can be? Why should he so horribly mutilate that poor girl. . . . He made a damn fool out of me."

The original prosecutor, Guy Calissi, now a Superior Court judge, had never doubted Edgar's guilt. "I tried the case," he said. "I asked for the death penalty. I wouldn't ask for the death penalty if I thought he was innocent." But still, he said, he had found Edgar's admissions of guilt on direct testimony, not cross-examination, to be surprising.

Guy's son Ron, who took every chance to talk about his book, *Counterpoint*, as well as the apparent failings of the criminal justice system, to any group that would listen to him, was typically fiery: "He's a liar, a vicious, savage, remorseless killer who should have been executed 20 years ago when the jury found him guilty of first-degree murder." As for Edgar's so-called contrition, "It's a fake. He's trying to deceive the court, which is typical of Edgar Smith."

Edward Fitzpatrick, the prosecutor at the time Edgar had won his freedom in 1971, had since become mayor of the borough of Allendale. "This guy is a shrewd individual," he said. "He's now trying to use total honesty to aid his defense." But he saved his harshest criticism for William F. Buckley: "He questioned my ethics. Mr. Buckley made a mistake." He also wrote a letter, published by the Passaic *Herald-News*, urging Buckley to apologize to the "living victims" of Edgar Smith: namely, the Zielinski family, Donald Hommell, and Lisa Ozbun.

The *Paterson Evening News* tracked down Anthony Zielinski, who was still living in Hasbrouck Heights. "I hope he gets the same thing my daughter got . . . crushed her head to pieces and threw boulders on her body," said Anthony, now sixty-six. "I was always convinced that he was guilty. But he blindfolded the people here. I hope in San Diego he can't buffalo people like he did here." He was even more dramatic in an interview with the *Record*: "A rattler will give you a warning when it's going to strike again. But a copperhead snake will never warn you. It'll strike a second and third time if you let it." Edgar Smith, according to Vickie's father, was a human copperhead. The lifetime prison sentence was the answer to Anthony's prayers. "I just hope he doesn't let anybody change their minds."

The Bergen *Record*'s April 4 editorial made the most brutal, accurate judgment of all in its headline: the story of Edgar Smith was "the saga of a bad man."

34

"Used and Betrayed"

1978–1979

WILLIAM F. BUCKLEY had wanted to avoid further public comment on Edgar Smith after his November 1976 column. Privately, he was devastated. Jack Carley recalled a conversation in the aftermath of Edgar's arrest. "He thought he had made a terrible mistake, and he was blaming himself for what had happened," Carley said. He tried to convince Buckley that he had made no mistakes at all; that the system had, in fact, worked, because a faulty conviction had been overturned, and Bergen County had failed to convict Edgar properly of murdering Victoria Zielinski. "We had followed what the law required. We had gotten him out."

Buckley did not buy Carley's argument and felt that they did bear some responsibility for what Edgar had done after his release from death row. But he still felt moved to defend himself against Edward Fitzpatrick's public call for an apology in a column syndicated on April 19: "I questioned neither your ethics nor your integrity, but the excesses to which your zeal took you when you proposed reading Edgar Smith's love letters in open court to demonstrate something or other. . . . Your position was what one might call boilerplate hostility." Otherwise, he mostly rehashed his previous piece, commenting on the fallibility of courtroom verdicts.

The next month, Buckley was the featured speaker at the Morris County Bar Association in Morristown, New Jersey, honoring a police detective sergeant for his work. He stuck to his script for his speech, talking largely about human rights and issues of morality. Then, during the Q and A, someone asked him about the Edgar Smith case.

For once, Buckley was at a loss for an argument. He admitted he didn't know where Edgar had gone wrong. He hedged about his own pivotal role in helping Edgar gain his freedom. "If I had been a juror in that case," he insisted, ". . . I would have found Smith not guilty because it was not proven beyond a reasonable doubt."

He faced more pointed criticism at the Young Americans for Freedom convention in August 1977, where various conservative luminaries—including Henry Kissinger—gathered to roast Buckley at the Statler Hilton Hotel in Midtown Manhattan. When the topic of Edgar Smith came up, Kissinger cracked, "That's why Bill received letters this morning from David Berkowitz [the "Son of Sam" killer] and Marvin Mandel [the Maryland governor who had been convicted of fraud the week before]."

Buckley would be more eloquent in an article published in the February 1979 issue of *Life* in which he tried to explain how he had been "used and betrayed" by Edgar, fooled into advocating for his innocence. He walked the reader through his last interactions with Edgar, the attempted murder of Lisa Ozbun, the trial, Edgar's sentencing. He quoted numerous newspaper editorials inflamed by Edgar's return to crime and quick to blame—and mock—Buckley for propping up a murderer.

"Other than that I and Smith's other supporters were wrong, which is obvious—without its being obvious that we acted wrongly—what has come of it all? It is a pity that *nothing* that is generally useful has been written as a result of the Smith experience." He wrote that he still believed Edgar to be an extraordinary man, with "much social savvy and wit, qualities that won him friends and partisans among persons who had never dreamed of meeting, let alone befriending, a convicted murderer."

But it had become plain to Buckley, too late, that Edgar should never have been released from custody. "This is truly tragic, using that solemn word most solemnly. But it's like what his manager once said about Sonny Liston. 'You know, Liston has a lot of good qualities. It's his bad qualities that aren't so good."

Edgar learned of the *Life* article from Barbara Fenity, who had remained friends with him even after he had stolen her credit cards and ended up back in prison. She had apparently called him in tears, stung by Buckley's recounting of events and of her own role in them. Edgar reacted with predictable fury and vented his spleen in a vituperative missive to Buckley that teemed with irrational rage, mostly at Paige, whom he had decided to divorce. "Unless involving Barbara in the article was more of Paige's 'get even' game—she has always resented the fact that Barbara didn't also desert me, but has remained a friend—then I think you were very unfair to her," he wrote Bill on January 28. "She will probably lose her job because of the article, as well as the guy she was going to marry. The next time you and Paige sharpen your hatchets, leave the innocent folks alone. You have more class than that."

He sent his soon-to-be ex-wife an even more incendiary letter on February 1, detailing his many perceived grievances against her, threatening to "expose" her misdeeds and supply "special" photos to the press, and generally making her out to be the villain and himself the hero—an astonishing thing, considering that he had been convicted of murder and then attempted murder and was in prison: "You know, babe, you've often said we are very much alike, and that we have something very special between us. We are, however, quite different in one significant way: I have learned finally to stand on my own two feet and admit what *I* am, and admit that I need help, but you are still refusing to admit who and what you are." Paradoxically, he claimed that he didn't hate Paige, but perhaps that was because deep down he knew the grievous sins he was accusing her of were falsehoods.

He was particularly incensed that Buckley had quoted correspondence from her in his piece. "You still haven't learned, have you?" he wrote Buckley. "You are either the most trusting person I have ever known, or the biggest fool to come down the 'pike since Barnum's first customer. . . . One thing I can tell you right now, my once-good friend, is that if you don't get your head out of your ass and stop believing every sad story that comes your way, one of these days you'll find yourself up to your ears in your own shit."

And he wasn't done with the insults. "I hate to say this, Bill, but you're a turkey. I know you believe that I made a fool of you, and I suppose I did, though that was not my intention going in. Now, however, you are allowing yourself to be used again, and this time you have no one to blame but yourself. I am beginning to suspect that the reason you and I got along so well is that we were/are so damn much alike—we're both suckers for a sad story and neither of us learns from experience." He urged Buckley "not to be such a chump."

Bill responded on February 23. His letter to Edgar was extremely brief: "For your information, I have not paid Paige any money, nor has *Life*. I have not seen Paige since I saw her last with you." He signed it "Yours faithfully," a sign that he did not wish to prolong further correspondence with the ex- and now current convict.

Edgar sent Paige a copy of the vituperative letter he'd written to Buckley, which moved her to write Bill on February 7, "I want you to know that I never used you, intended to or ever will." She said she had no clue where Edgar got the idea she "collaborated" with Buckley for the *Life* article—perhaps the quotes from her letters?—but she didn't rule out a subconscious impulse for revenge on the part of her soon-to-be ex-husband. "I really would like to be able to tell someone everything I know, and to have it out into words—to tell everyone what kind of man Edgar Smith is."

She blamed herself for getting involved with him and regretted every day that she had done so. She had been angry at Buckley when Edgar had been arrested again, but then she had woken up to the facts. "I do consider you a friend and I do trust you. I only hope that you never have any doubts of my sincerity. I don't make it my practice to use people. Edgar seems to think he can get back at me for whatever his reasons, by trying to downgrade me in your eyes, and I don't want that."

Buckley responded to Paige's letter from Switzerland. "Of course I will be very happy to see you as soon as I return," he wrote on March 1. "Edgar sent me his incredibly intemperate, complicated, and neurotic letter to you. He suffers under the illusion that we have actively conspired against him, and that *Life* Magazine paid you a small fortune." Neither was true. "I will not encourage him if he attempts to strike up a regular correspondence."

———

NEARLY A YEAR after the attack, Lisa Ozbun and her husband, Darwin, filed lawsuits in state and federal courts against Edgar Smith. They asked for more than $1 million in damages for "assault, battery, intentional infliction of emotional distress, false imprisonment, and intentional loss of consortium." Darwin also asked for damages to account for "the loss of his wife's domestic services."

They also sued 150 unnamed defendants, 100 of whom were "authors, reporters, editors, photographers, newspapers, broadcast stations and others" whose reporting had contributed to Edgar Smith's eventual release from prison in 1971. The Ozbuns claimed that either the reporters had known they were disseminating false information or their actions had been reckless or negligent.

Edgar and the Ozbuns' lawyer were in sporadic touch about a settlement. At one point, Edgar claimed that he had taken out a $10,000 life insurance policy in the name of Lefteriya Ozbun, since he was otherwise indigent. The San Diego Superior Court ruled that the case should go to trial in 1982, but records indicate that neither party showed up in court and the judge dismissed the suit. (Decades later, Edgar would claim that he and the Ozbuns had settled for $50,000, which was to be paid upon his release from prison.)

But Ozbun kept fighting against paroling Edgar. In 1989, she gave her first (and only) interview since her near murder to the *Los Angeles Times*: "He can get out of prison in a few years, but I have to live with what he did to me forever. . . . He changed my life." Incidents in her daily life still summoned up bad memories of the attack. She would be out walking her dog, see a car pull over, and feel the need to get back inside her house. Men in white T-shirts paralyzed her with fear. She'd had to quit her job at Ratners because going through the parking lot, where she'd been abducted, had been too harrowing. "Maybe it's been so frightening because of how it happened. . . . It wasn't because I was careless, or out at 2 or 3 in the morning. I was just walking in the afternoon by the parking lot where I work every day. I was minding my own business—" She paused, shrugged, and stared out the window. Then she looked up at the reporter. "You know, everybody is still frightened for me. But lately, I haven't had the fear. . . . It just disappeared one day."

She felt grateful to be alive and to know that Edgar Smith hadn't expected her to be. (She would live another thirty years, dying in August 2019.) After Edgar was imprisoned, Lisa wanted to understand why he had picked her, of all people, and tried to kill her. She said she had read those of Edgar's books that she could find, hoping they might shed some additional light on what made him tick. "I just wanted to know why, after finally winning this freedom and getting that second chance he wanted so much, did he jeopardize it again? I never found the answer."

PART VIII

STAYING IN

(1980–2017)

35

A Strange Triangle

1979–2003

AS FAR AS William F. Buckley was concerned, there was no need to write or speak about Edgar Smith again after the publication of his *Life* magazine article in 1979. Perhaps he found the subject too painful. Those closest to him didn't bring Edgar up, and those who did got little back in return.

His son, Christopher, provided some insight into how his father had reacted during an interview in the *Boston Globe* three years later, upon the publication of his debut book, *Steaming to Bamboola: The World of a Tramp Freighter.* "He's a cheerful warrior," Christopher said. "Mind you, he also gets taken to the cleaners." Edgar Smith was the chief example. "If he were in this room now, I'd go after him with my bare hands. He betrayed my father. Yet I know that if my father were here, he'd treat Edgar Smith with kindness."

Though Buckley kept mum with many of his friends, it's possible he found prayer a means for expiation of any inner personal torment. He and Sophie Wilkins also exchanged many letters in which they discussed Edgar Smith. Surviving a relationship with the man seemed to bond people. Not only did Buckley and Sophie grow closer over the decades, so, too, did Buckley and Steve

Umin, who at one point, apparently, was in line to be executor of Buckley's estate.*

Sophie became Buckley's de facto first reader and unofficial editor of his novels, a series of spy entertainments featuring Blackford Oakes, a dashing, erudite, libertine Cold War–era hero who resembled his creator in many ways but not all. But Edgar's fate wafted through their correspondence like an unwelcome scent from the time Buckley came to the reluctant conclusion, as early as 1973, that Sophie's final evaluation of Edgar's character was correct. "There is a permanent coarseness there," he said, "that seemed to reassert itself almost within minutes of his liberation. A great pity."

The 1979 publication of *The Executioner's Song*, Norman Mailer's Pulitzer Prize–winning account of the crimes and execution of the murderer Gary Gilmore, caused Sophie to wonder what might have been said about Edgar in a thousand-page tome. "I keep brooding about how I of all people could have gotten so immersed in that punk's [Edgar's] situation and personality. Did the fact that Smith's mother appeared in my office, with the promise of a manuscript, just when my second son had gone off to Stanford and I was ripe for an ersatz 'son' in my life . . . have anything to do with it?" She thought there was another answer: that Edgar Smith was her writing alter ego, that getting a book out of a nonwriter satisfied some latent need to write a book of her own. It was a once-in-a-lifetime opportunity that allowed her to forget that he was the "monster who had brained Vicki[e] Zielinski." She couldn't fathom that Edgar had actually done it when he'd written such wonderful letters to herself and to Buck-

---

* Umin died in 2012 of frontal temporal degeneration, which he had developed several years earlier, making it unlikely that he was in fact the executor of Buckley's estate.

ley. But she couldn't let herself off the moral hook, either. "To this obsessive end I used him, I used Knopf, I used you."

Buckley and Sophie also commiserated when Jack Henry Abbott, the convicted murderer with literary talent who became Norman Mailer's protégé, went on the run after the stabbing death of Richard Adan, just weeks after a collection of his observations on prison life, *In the Belly of the Beast*, was published. "At least ours had the decency to wait a few years, and to botch the job," wrote Bill mordantly.

Neither heard directly from Edgar after his vitriolic jeremiad of early 1979. (Both did receive sporadic missives from his mother, Ann; when they eventually ceased, Bill and Sophie came to believe that she had died, which she did in 1993.) As the years passed, it seemed as if Buckley and Sophie would never hear from him again. Then, out of the blue, Edgar sent a letter to Buckley in May 1998 with some news: He had finally finished another manuscript. It was called *A Tale of Old San Francisco*, a project first suggested to him by Sophie back in 1969. He had begun working on the book while still incarcerated in Trenton but had lost track of his research materials after his release from the Death House in December 1971. When he learned that his old friend Barbara Fenity had kept the materials, he asked her to send them to him and resumed work on the book, which detailed the 1854 trial and possible wrongful execution of William B. Sheppard for the murder of his lover's father.

Edgar's literary agent, Bob Lescher, had long before severed ties with him, and there was no chance of submitting the project to a major publisher. Instead, Edgar arranged for a vanity press to print a limited number of copies of the short book—less than two hundred pages.

Buckley sent a copy of Edgar's letter to Sophie, Steve Umin, and Jack Carley. "Obviously you should feel no obligation on reading it," he told them in a joint memo. "I simply give it to you as objectively interesting. I intend to answer it." To Sophie, he added a blunter note: "As I say, you are free and indeed expected to toss it in the ash can." She responded, "That he managed to produce another book is after all gratifying because I did have something to do with introducing him to writing for publication as a way of life, so it wasn't all a bad thing."

After Edgar received Buckley's acknowledgment of his letter, he couldn't let Bill have the last word. "I was, to say the least, somewhat surprised (though not unhappy) to receive your brief note. I was distressed to hear that Sophie does not wish to read the Sheppard book, though I am pleased to note that she is well. I hope, too, that you and your family are well."

He wrote that he felt some urgency to apologize, but "it isn't that easy for me. Simply saying 'I'm sorry' is not difficult; it is whether that statement would have value to anyone other than myself that I doubt. I am acutely aware that with my track record any rational person would harbor grave doubts as to my sincerity." He said he had retreated to a self-imposed solitary confinement—refusing visits, limiting correspondence, waiving his right to parole hearings.

> *I do not like being in prison, and less so do I like the* reason *I am in prison, but I have adapted and found a sort of haven from any danger of rejection, except perhaps fatal self-rejection. . . .*
>
> *I will say, however, for what it is worth to you, that I deeply regret my betrayal of your extraordinary friendship. Perhaps Dante should have set aside a small corner of The Ninth Circle for people like me, those who so carelessly safeguard relationships of great value. You deserved better,*

as did so many others. You provided me with a greater opportunity in life than I could ever have hoped for and, being the schmuck *that I am, I let that opportunity slip through my fingers.*

Buckley did not respond to Edgar's letter, nor did he read his new book.

———

IN MAY 2003, nearly five years after the last interruption in their lives by Edgar Smith, Sophic Wilkins died. She was eighty-eight, and William F. Buckley—who would himself die almost five years later, in 2008—eulogized her in *National Review*. He wrote of their shared bond through believing in Edgar's innocence and their forging a deeper friendship even after their belief had been proven horribly wrong. "Sophie Wilkins unmistakably happened, and leaves indelibly in the memory her singular learning and sweetness."

Sophie had been far happier at the end of her life than during the Edgar Smith era. She and Thurman Wilkins had finally reached the endpoint of their marriage when he had decided to settle permanently in the Pacific Northwest. She had also found love with the poet Karl Shapiro, whom she had first met in the early 1940s and whom she married in 1985, as soon as her long-gestating divorce to Wilkins was finalized. She and Shapiro split their time between Davis, California, and Sophie's Morningside Heights apartment. Sophie had worked through years of emotional difficulties with her sons, Adam and Daniel, including periods when they had hardly spoken, and doted on her only grandson, Isaac. She had plunged into translating the entirety of Robert Musil's epic masterwork, *A Man Without Qualities*; her failing eyesight forced her to cede its completion to another translator, and the full two-volume work was published in 1995.

In the fall of 2002, Sophie had canceled lunch with Buckley only hours before they were scheduled to meet. "You can see how I can't take a chance on leaving you with such a last impression of me," she told Buckley. "Especially because to see me in terms of my physical degeneration is misleading. I am quite constantly cheerful and entertain myself by thinking everything through." Bill discovered that cheer when he visited Sophie twice in hospital, where she spent her final days. He found her to be "alive, unmistakably alive, in the way that only a very few people are alive, 110 percent alive." So she was, right up until her last breath.

They were a strange triangle, William F. Buckley, Edgar Smith, and Sophie Wilkins. As Sophie wrote Bill in July 1998, "There is certainly a book in the weird coming together of three people as different as the three of us, for a psychologist at least."

She died believing that book would never be written.

36

Vacaville

1980–2017

EDGAR SMITH thought he could fool people and beat the system. He thought, as he wrote in July 1977, that he could "litigate them to death." Certainly he tried. From prison, he sued Paige, his second ex-wife. He sued Ronald Calissi. He threatened legal action toward others, all of which went nowhere but sucked up his targets' time and energy, which was undoubtedly his aim.

But the last forty years of Edgar's life, spent in various California state prisons, showed he could neither fool people long term nor beat the system. His parole applications were denied. Forces in New Jersey and California rallied to write letters explaining how much of a societal menace he was and saying that he should never be let out of prison. His attempts at showing remorse came off as half-hearted, empty gestures. Psychiatric evaluations diagnosed him as a sociopath, a manipulator, someone who would always pin the blame on others, never himself, who might pretend remorse but lacked a conscience.

Interviews with the press, particularly in New Jersey, showed him as a prevaricating attention seeker. ("You know, 20 years between crimes ain't bad, when you compare it with the guys who come in here every few months after shooting this one, or stabbing that one," he boasted to the Bergen *Record* in 1978.) He also got married a third time, to Beverley Bevan, the mother of a former cellmate. Together they founded a travel company that chartered trips to horse races around the world. But within five years of the marriage, according to Edgar, Bevan had "dropped out of sight, closed up the business, and that was it, and I never saw her or heard from her again." (She died in 2003.)

"I don't think Edgar can handle life outside of prison," Paige Hiemier told the *Los Angeles Times* in 1989, when he was up for parole for the sixth time. "He'll be fine for periods of time, but when he's frustrated or rejected, he can't deal with it." She rued the day she ever got involved with him and worried he would be paroled. "People should realize that his last victim is very lucky to be alive today. The next woman he goes after may not be so lucky."

Paige sought to rebuild her life. She became a nurse and worked in New York City for a while, then gave it up when various physical ailments became too much. She exhibited signs of post-traumatic stress disorder and spent her time fly-fishing, breeding cats, and selling bicycle ornaments. She wrote a memoir of her time with Edgar that attracted the interest of several publishers, as well as television producers, but it was not published after he threatened legal action.

She could not outrun her ex-husband's campaign of vengeance. She received many harassing letters from him, usually arriving on her birthday, and they did not stop even when she moved and made sure that her new address in Bergen County wasn't listed anywhere. "Your move . . . surprised me," Edgar wrote in the early 2000s. "I know exactly where [your street] is. I learned your address from a friend who lives just up the hill from you. . . . Kind of a small world." She knew that he didn't have any friends in town. The details of her residence, hobbies, and activities could easily be gleaned from the Internet.

When Edgar was up for parole again in 2009, Paige gave an interview to Bergen *Record* columnist Mike Kelly. She was outraged and tired of hiding and wanted to fight back. "Why is Mr. Smith allowed to surf the Internet?" she asked in a letter to the California parole board. She wanted to know why he could stalk her via the Internet, which he was supposedly denied access to in prison. He had been moved to the High Desert State Prison near Susanville in 2008. Law enforcement officials speculated that he had someone on the outside, perhaps a private detective, tracking her whereabouts and other personal information. "For me, I just wish he would die," she told the Bergen *Record*'s Kelly in 2009. "That's the only way I'll be free of him."

———

PATRICIA HORTON HAD tried hard to break free of her first husband. After moving to Colorado, she had raised their daughter, Patti Ann, as if her second husband, Gene Hafford, were the girl's father. Patti didn't learn otherwise until she was sixteen years old, after Edgar got out of the Death House in Trenton.

He'd written Patricia multiple letters over the years, telling her he wanted to get to know their daughter. Patricia and Gene were firmly against the idea. Edgar was no innocent, upstanding citizen. This was yet another disruption from someone they did not want in their lives. Edgar's lawyers had interviewed Patricia on more than one occasion while he was in prison. She'd been contacted as a potential witness for his evidentiary hearing in January 1971 but had avoided having to testify, to her relief.

But Patti wasn't interested in a relationship with her biological father. "Once I found out what he did, I didn't want anything to do with the guy," she told me in September 2019. Her indifference persisted well into adulthood.

The Haffords, along with Patti and their other children, left Colorado for the Pacific Northwest soon after Patti graduated high school, in 1975. A few years later, in 1981, Patricia and Gene were divorced—not long after Patti's own brief first marriage, to the father of her daughter, Jennifer, ended.[*]

Patti had few complaints about her life. She loved her daughter and did whatever she could to support her. She became a bank teller and stayed in the business for a few years. She gave it up when she got married again and is now working at a McDonald's. At one point, Patti and Jennifer spent several years cleaning house for the true crime writer Ann Rule. (They never discussed Patti's connection to a notorious murderer with Rule, though Jennifer, in particular, was amused at the coincidence.)

Patricia suffered from several ailments—a dislocated shoulder, dementia, lung cancer—before she died in 2009. Patti was perfectly happy never hearing from her biological father—whom she referred to as her "sperm donor"—though she didn't hide his existence from her daughter. Jennifer was in tenth or eleventh grade when she was assigned to write about a murder. She chanced across a copy of *Brief Against Death*. "I literally stumbled across it, looking for a book," she said in 2021. At some point Patti admitted that the book had been written by Jennifer's biological grandfather, which was quite a way for a teenager to find out the truth. Jennifer later admitted how much it upset her that her mother hadn't been more forthright at an earlier age, and she vowed to be more open about Edgar's history with her own children.

After Patricia's death, Patti and Jennifer found a letter from Edgar addressed to his first wife. "So I wrote back," said Patti.

---

[*] Patti's and Jennifer's current last names are being withheld to protect their families' privacy.

"And then he wanted to meet me. He paid the airfare and everything down there." But there was no way she was traveling by herself. "I just didn't feel comfortable. I mean, this is Edgar Smith." She asked her daughter to go with her.

Jennifer, by then in her thirties, was all in on the visit to meet her grandfather. She'd long been fascinated with true crime stories, having read several of Ann Rule's books. The serial killer Ted Bundy was a particular object of curiosity, what with so many of his murders having occurred in the Pacific Northwest. But fascination with a genre was quite different from having a murderer in the family. "It made me feel weird, kind of like dirty . . . [that] I'm actually kind of related to this person," she said. Still, she hoped that meeting Edgar would fill in some gaps and answer some lingering questions.

Over the course of the weekend trip in Vacaville, Edgar professed to be thrilled to meet not only his grown daughter but his granddaughter. From the moment they met, Jennifer felt a powerful urge to be anywhere but in his presence. "There was no soul there . . . like you could just kind of see through him," she said. "He just didn't really care . . . like nothing you said would affect him." At one point, he told Jennifer that she should bring her two children on the next visit. "I shot him down real quick about that."

She asked him, point-blank, if he had killed Victoria Zielinski. "He said, 'no, I didn't do it.' And that was the end of the conversation." Jennifer was taken aback. To her, it was an open-and-shut case, as was the attempted murder of Lisa Ozbun. Edgar didn't provide the details of either crime, and neither Patti nor Jennifer pressed the issue.

Edgar did, however, admit to doing something that creeped his daughter and granddaughter out. A few years before her mother's death, Patti had received a copy of her high school transcripts in the mail. The letter did not include a return address. Patti and Jennifer both said they became so alarmed, they called the police. Edgar told them he was the one who had sent the transcripts through an intermediary because he wanted Patti to have the documents.

After the visit, Edgar wrote many letters to both Patti and Jennifer. He also called his daughter collect on a weekly basis. Sometimes Patti picked up the phone. More often she didn't. "Like, why does he keep calling me? I really don't want anything to do with him. He was just a random person in my life, basically." They were his blood family, but that didn't make them *immediate* family.

The only upside was that Edgar helped them out financially for years, providing money for Jennifer to take vacations with her kids or for Patti to go out for brunch with her daughter. The funds came from his monthly Veterans Administration checks (with extra checks on top of that from an investment account he'd squirreled away), but how did he have access to the VA when he was in prison for life? Patti wasn't sure. And why did he ask them to purchase things for him, such as stamps and coffee pots and typewriters, when he could have done so himself? Things didn't quite add up.

Though Patti stayed in sporadic touch with Edgar until a couple of months before he died, Jennifer eventually blocked all contact with him. She felt his letters were becoming more invasive, more full of information he shouldn't have had a way of knowing. "Once he found out I was having issues in my marriage, he got *really* weird." He started telling her what to do, writing snippily one week and effusively the next. Jennifer decided she could no longer put up with his changing moods: "I wrote him a three-page letter telling him to go fuck himself, more or less."

Neither Patti nor Jennifer ever attended a parole hearing for Edgar. "If they ever called me, the parole board, while he was alive," said Jennifer, "I would have said, 'Keep his ass there.'"

———

EDGAR SMITH'S FINAL parole hearing was on April 23, 2009. He knew that if he didn't convince the board that he was fully rehabilitated, that he should live the rest of his life as a free man, and that he had truly learned from his terrible mistakes, he would, for all intents and purposes, spend the rest of his life in prison. By that point, he'd had six heart bypass surgeries and several angioplasties. He suffered from diabetes and could barely walk, needing an ambulance to transport him to the parole hearing at High Desert State Prison, but his mind was sound.

He'd waived his parole hearings for a time, mostly because of despondency. Two years earlier, he had told the board, "I'm 73, I don't care anymore. I want to die, die, die." Now seventy-five, he was ready for his last shot. It did not go well.

He argued. He prevaricated. He showed no remorse. He needled his questioners. When the board delivered its verdict, it was emphatic and definitive: he would not get parole, and he wouldn't have another hearing until 2024. Board commissioner Sandra Bryson, who had just recently denied parole to Manson Family member Susan Atkins, who was dying of cancer, excoriated Smith for his lack of remorse, for his clear attempts to distort the facts and manipulate the truth, and for uttering things that shocked the parole board members outright.

If one could boil down the sociopathic mind to a single short back-and-forth, it would be the exchange Bryson had with Edgar referencing a long-ago accusation by Edgar's second wife, Paige:

PRESIDING COMMISSIONER BRYSON: And there was some indication that during sexual foreplay, you would choke [your second wife] out or come close to doing so, and she'd have to ask you to stop. Is that correct you did that, sir?

INMATE SMITH: Of course not. I probably should have, but I didn't.

BRYSON: You probably should have? Why is that?

SMITH: Because she probably would've liked it.

BRYSON: She probably would have liked it?

SMITH: She probably would have, she was not your average girl.

———

IN HIS FINAL parole hearing, Edgar made it clear he had no desire to speak with the press ever again. I learned this a week after sending a perfunctory request for an interview by letter, just before the 2014 Christmas holidays. I wrote that I wanted to ask Edgar about William F. Buckley. I noted in my letter that he might not respond because I knew his health was not good. To my surprise, he wrote back.

"Congratulations! This is the first letter I have ever written to anyone in Brooklyn," he wrote on December 19, 2014. What followed was a breathtaking document of self-aggrandizement, elliptical reasoning, and demands for information. He said that my letter was the second time he'd been asked for an interview about his relationship with Buckley. The other, apparently from an unnamed woman in New Jersey, he'd brushed off: "From her letter and envelope I doubted she could write her own name."

He claimed, "Generally speaking I do not grant interviews on any subject," but reiterated that Buckley "was my best friend, period." He described being "sandbagged too often, especially by people who do not know (or care) what 'off the record' means." He described a long-ago visit to him in San Quentin by Warren Steibel, Buckley's producer and director on *Firing Line*. He said that Steibel had come "with a script for a movie about [me and Buckley]. Until I said 'No' Warren had been a good friend." (Steibel, who died in 2002, told *New York* magazine twenty years earlier that Smith had originally given his blessing to the project.)

"I am not opposed to discussing this matter, but I would like to know more, particularly who or what sources you are relying on. There is a whole lot of crap out there." Edgar closed with a question: How had I heard his health was bad? "It is, but where did you hear that?"

He was baiting me. I knew he was baiting me, and I don't like being baited, and I did not respond all that well. I took his final question first, quoting him directly about his health problems from his 2007 parole hearing. I expressed surprise that he had written back, since I thought he no longer responded to journalists. ("And yet, you did not ignore my letter. How curious.") I asked when he'd last written to Buckley and vice versa.

Edgar's next letter was more subdued. He hadn't known of the deaths of various people in his life, Sophie Wilkins in particular, until I told him in my second letter. He quoted Latin. He didn't rule out further correspondence. But I sense an extended correspondence with him would lead me around in circles, ending up nowhere. He'd given so many versions of what had happened on the night of March 4, 1957, that I knew I wouldn't get a satisfactory answer. The voluminous written record, whether from Edgar's hand, Buckley's hand, court transcripts, or others, offered me more insight into why he was the way he was than anything he could have told me now. His response to the parole board, in 2009, when they asked him why he killed Vickie, seemed to make the most sense: "I was angry."

Instead, I sent a list of questions that he had not previously been asked, to the best of my knowledge. Such as whether he had any contact with his family, who was his designated beneficiary upon his death, and if he was working on any further books, be they fiction or nonfiction. I also mentioned offhand that Christopher Buckley was "not your biggest fan." Edgar responded to that letter, too.

The tone was blistering and blustery: "To begin with, I don't give a rat's furry ass what Christopher Buckley likes or dislikes. Mama's boys do not interest or impress me."* He wrote that it sounded as though I was preparing to write a book about him, and "paranoia or not, I doubt we have anything more to discuss." It was clear to me that he didn't like my questions. But then he did something curious: he answered most of my questions in detail and deflected the others with tidbits of his friendship with William F. Buckley—as if he couldn't help himself now that attention was upon him once more.

I did not write him back.

———

EDGAR SMITH DIED at the California Medical Facility in Vacaville on March 20, 2017. He was eighty-three, felled by diabetes, heart disease, and other health problems. The prison contacted

---

* I later learned that Edgar had written to Christopher, requesting permission to access Buckley's archives at Yale, and been denied: "It's the only time I've ever denied access on the grounds of, you know, fuck you," Christopher told me. I should also disclose that Christopher Buckley turned down my first attempt at archival access in 2015 but changed his mind in July 2019.

Edgar's daughter, Patti, who was his designated next of kin. She absorbed the news and discovered that she felt nothing. "I wasn't concerned about it. I didn't really care." The warden asked if she wanted any of Edgar's personal items. She said no. "I told them to do whatever they usually do with people's personal belongings." As for a funeral, Patti told them to cremate him and "keep the ashes."

Edgar's death went unnoticed by the press for months. I only learned of it two months after the fact, when my bimonthly search of his inmate number returned an error message—something that had never happened before. A spokesperson for the California Department of Corrections and Rehabilitation confirmed Smith's death in a terse phone call.

Edgar had outlived so many in his orbit. His mother, of course. His first wife, Patricia Horton. William F. Buckley, Jr. Sophie Wilkins. Steven Umin. Juliette Scheinman. Robert Lescher. Nearly every police officer and lawyer who'd been involved in his cases. Even Ron Calissi, who had spent so much of his life and energy ensuring that Edgar Smith remained in prison, had died of a sudden heart attack in 2016. Deborah Fredericks, Ron Calissi's widow, upon learning of Smith's death, said that Ron "would have been very pleased to know that Edgar was kept in jail to the end."

Paige Hiemier had been reluctant to cooperate with my project while Edgar was still alive. His years-long campaign of harassment had taken a toll on her, as had his ongoing threats of litigation. When I broke the news of his death to her, she told me she was glad to have that relief. She seemed more willing to cooperate. We spoke on the phone, off the record, almost a year later, in March 2018. After that conversation, Paige stopped answering my telephone calls, text messages, and emails. She's retreated into silence. I don't expect that to change.

———

PATTI, EDGAR'S DAUGHTER, called her own daughter after getting off the phone with prison officials. "Guess who died?" she asked. Jennifer guessed right away. Her reaction then was the same as what she told me nearly three years later: "I'm so glad he died in prison, where he belonged."

Coda

1948

KATHY BELL[*] began the walk home for dinner in good spirits. She'd spent the afternoon at a friend's house but wanted to leave by 5:00 p.m., because her parents had told her to be home before dark. She was excited about the next day, her tenth birthday. Her folks had planned a party. A few blocks away from her home in New Milford, New Jersey, she took a customary shortcut through a wooded lot, bounded by tall weeds and bushes on either side. Her mind was on the party, not on her surroundings.

Someone jumped out from behind the weeds. He was an older boy, about fourteen or fifteen, with a sailor-style hat atop his head. Kathy recognized the boy right away, and not only because the hat had the name "Smitty" sewn on one side. She'd seen him hanging around New Milford Grammar School and knew he lived near her. She didn't know why he'd be hanging around a school he wasn't enrolled in.

He blocked Kathy's way. Each time she moved, so did he. A step here, a step there, but still she could not get past him. His expression never changed. He just stared at her, saying nothing.

Kathy felt compelled to fill in the silence. "I have to go because it's my birthday and I'm going to have a big birthday party." A lie, but all she could come up with as fear engulfed her.

---

[*] Kathy's last name has been changed to protect her family's privacy.

When that didn't work, she begged, "Please, I have to go home, I can hear my father calling me."

The boy's eyes glazed over, as if he were in deep thought. Then he grabbed Kathy and threw her onto the ground, gripped her by the hair, and smashed her face into the dirt. She screamed for her father. She hollered for her mother. She begged him to let her go, fervently hoping that one or both of her parents might hear her.

He flipped her over and then straddled her. He tore open her coat, pulling down her pants and underwear to her knees. She continued to struggle to get free. He put his hand over her mouth and nose while pushing her head into the dirt. "Shut up," he yelled, again and again. Kathy found herself unable to scream any longer, not only because his hand was over her mouth but because the fear had engulfed her.

His pants were down, too, and his penis was out and in Kathy's face. "Suck this, suck this, you hear me, suck this." She knew what he wanted, and she was petrified that not doing it would endanger her, but she refused. "Let me go, please, let me go!" she continued to plead.

Then the boy reached for something; Kathy wasn't sure what it was, but it appeared to be a beer can "opened like a can of beans." As he reached for it, she managed to roll free and get away from him.

As she moved away from him, he warned her that if she told her parents, "no matter where you are, I'll find you and I will kill you. Do you hear me? I'll kill you."

She promised and began to run home. The journey seemed to stretch into eternity. As she ran, she yelled that she had changed her mind. She would tell her parents.

"Go ahead," said the boy. "I'll get away with it anyway."

She made it into the backyard and rapped hard on the back door, screaming and crying, holding up her pants. Dirt covered her clothes and face and streaked her hair.

Kathy's father opened the door and brought her inside. "What happened? What happened?" he asked over and over. She was unable to answer, even after he shook her more than once. Later, Kathy recognized her response as shock.

A policeman arrived at the house. He asked Kathy to tell him what happened and describe the boy who attacked her. When she did, mentioning the hat with "Smitty" written on it, the policeman said, "It's that kid Edgar Smith."

Sometime after that, Kathy went with her father and the policeman back to the scene of the crime. She went through the incident one more time there and then again at the police station in New Milford. At the station, she saw Edgar come in with his mother and stepfather. The three of them had been partway through dinner when police arrived at their home in New Milford to arrest Edgar.

At the station, together with his mother and stepfather, Edgar kept his hands jammed into his pockets. Dirt covered his shoes. He was chewing gum, and Kathy noticed that he looked rather unworried. Then he said something to her father. Kathy didn't hear what it was, but it caused another police officer to hang on to her father to prevent his getting at Edgar. The boy was subsequently arrested.

The Juvenile and Domestic Relations Court of Bergen County heard the case the week before Christmas in 1948. There, in the office of the presiding judge, Thomas L. Zimmerman, Edgar Smith confessed to attacking Kathy. He was put on administrative probation. He wouldn't have to report to a probation officer. He wouldn't have to account for his time and what he was up to.

Upon reaching the age of majority, his probation would be termi-
nated. Shortly thereafter, Edgar switched schools to Don Bosco
Preparatory High School, a private school in Ramsey.

EDGAR SMITH TOLD his version of what happened between him and
Kathy Bell in *Brief Against Death*. He painted Kathy as a liar, a
"screwball," a girl who had "accused other boys of the same offense, each time relating an essentially similar tale, which had
always proved to be untrue." He also told that version to William F. Buckley, who characterized Kathy, anonymously, in his
1965 *Esquire* article as untrustworthy.

Outraged, Kathy told her story to Ron Calissi, and he in-
cluded it in his 1972 book, *Counterpoint*. She wanted to combat
Edgar's "blatant lies," which were "besmirching my character."
She countered his version with particular force: "I never ac-
cused any other person of attempting to molest me; only Edgar
Smith."

She hoped that "people will understand, especially women,
what a traumatic experience like this can do to a 10-year-old girl
psychologically." She still could not get out of her head the idea
that if she had walked home from her friend's house ten minutes
earlier or later, Edgar might not have "been hiding behind the
weeds, waiting for me."

NEARLY THREE DECADES LATER, in 2000, Kathy told her story once
more to two detectives in the Bergen County Prosecutor's Office. They had tracked her down after hearing word that Edgar
was up for parole in California again. The office thought that the

more testimony from Edgar's victims that could be entered into the record, the more likely he would remain in prison for the rest of his life.

Kathy, by this point, was sixty-one years old. She had married and borne four children. She and her husband still lived in Bergen County, as did most of her children and grandchildren. She didn't like dredging up such awful childhood memories, but the alternative—Edgar paroled, possibly returning to Bergen County, but even being out in the world—was worse.

She described to detectives Steven Kearney and Leslie Endicott what had happened on the evening of December 6, 1948, in what they characterized in a report later sent to the California state parole board as "vivid detail" and "chilling precision." It was clear to them how much the molestation had altered Kathy's life. "She became a very rigid person, afraid to respond to harmless flirtations by boys. Although she married, she frequently found herself questioning her husband's normal sexual behavior"— which, though unstated, suggests the possibility that oral sex was a trigger for traumatic feelings later in life.

The most heartbreaking part of the detectives' report was what Kathy said about her daughter: "As a parent, she felt relieved that her own daughter became overweight because she felt it would protect her from predators like Edgar Smith."

That fear compounded her own terror at the thought that Edgar might be released from prison. "I feel absolutely horrified that a man that killed someone would be free to come out and kill me as he promised. I feel absolutely devastated that I would have to give any thought to this, that the justice system would not take care of the victims, a victim that had no idea that he would be let out after committing a murder and thought that he was locked up."

Kathy Bell died in 2008, the same year as William F. Buckley.

Edgar Smith outlived his first known victim, as well as his greatest mark, by nine years.

———

WHAT HAPPENED IN the car between Victoria Zielinski and Edgar Smith remains, more than sixty years after the fact, something of a mystery. Only she, the victim, and he, the killer, truly know, and both are dead. The truth likely lies closer to the prosecution's account than to Edgar's varying versions, though the mores and standards of society in 1957 precluded Guy Calissi—and by extension, the newspapers—from specifying the exact sexual acts Edgar wanted and how Vickie's resistance to his advances caused him to kill her.

Whatever the fifteen-year-old girl said and exactly how she spurned his advances clearly tipped Smith, a man already at maximum stress from losing his job, with a wife and newborn at home and the sense that responsibility he didn't want had been thrust upon him, over the edge. He had no self-control, so he took his frustrations out on the nearest object—for that, ultimately, was how Smith thought of Vickie; smashing her head in only confirmed she had no human meaning for him.

As an object, Edgar would dehumanize Vickie further in his writing. He introduced her in *Brief Against Death* as "a very pretty girl" and "an exceptionally well-developed fifteen-year-old, with a figure that belied her age—a fact she knew, was proud of, and made no effort to conceal. To the contrary, her favorite clothes were tight, form-revealing sweaters and blue jeans." He painted Vickie's fictional avatar in *A Reasonable Doubt*, Suzan Jeffers, with an even coarser, more lascivious brush: "If a fellow had a decent automobile and a couple of cans of beer, or a bottle of Thunderbird wine, Suzan was known, well-known, to be as easy a bit of sex as any girl in town." These passages are especially unsavory when one knows that they were written by Victoria Zielinski's murderer.

Edgar Smith spent most of his adult life trying to game the criminal justice system. He was determined, deliberate, canny, and manipulative. For several years, he got what he wanted and more: freedom, celebrity, a career as a best-selling author. He had the friendship of William F. Buckley, who went against his own conservative ideology to champion and advocate for Smith's innocence. But then he squandered it all.

His wrongful exoneration and the accompanying adulation obscured the damage inflicted upon so many women: his mother, who never stopped believing in him until she had no other choice; his former wives and girlfriends; his daughter and granddaughter; Lisa Ozbun, whom he nearly murdered; and of course, Victoria Zielinski, whose very existence was obliterated on the altar of his rage.

The legal maneuvering and obfuscation, as well as the support of the intellectual class, could not hide the truth: Edgar Smith hated women, and when he had the chance to hurt them, rape them, or kill them, he did.

Acknowledgments

SCOUNDREL, like my previous book, *The Real Lolita*, began life as a magazine piece. Unlike *The Real Lolita*, the piece was never published. I realized early on in the research and reporting process that the story was too big for a magazine piece, so I set it aside. Once I finished the first draft of *The Real Lolita* in September 2017, and the news of Edgar Smith's death became public, what had been back-burnered moved swiftly to the front as my next book project. Working on *Scoundrel* has been harrowing and joyous, excruciating and exhilarating, and not only because I completed various drafts during the height of a pandemic. It also depended even more on the input, advice, support, and sounding board of many people, in ways large and small.

Thanks first and foremost to my agents, David Patterson and Aemilia Phillips at the Stuart Krichevsky Literary Agency, who always have my back and shepherd projects—and authors—with such care and cheer. Thanks to everyone at SKLA, especially Hannah Schwartz, Ross Harris, and Stuart Krichevsky, and to my UK agent, Jane Finigan & Lutyens & Rubinstein.

Ecco has been my publishing home for three books and I remain humbled that I get to work with such a great team. On the editorial side, many thanks to Zack Wagman for acquiring the project ("This is so *you*, Sarah") and for input on early manuscript pages; to Denise Oswald for her smart and incisive editorial notes; and to Sara Birmingham for clutch work in the home stretch, and seeing *Scoundrel* transform from manuscript to book. I know how lucky I am to benefit from the work and brainpower of so many wonderful editors.

Thanks also to Miriam Parker, Helen Atsma, Martin Wilson, Sonya Cheuse, Meghan Deans, Caitlin Mulrooney-Lyski, Rachel Sargent, Ashlyn Edwards, Richard Ljoenes (for the truly outstanding cover), Allison Saltzman, Rebecca Holland, Lynn Anderson, Michelle Crowe, and especially to TJ Calhoun. Special thanks to Virginia Stanley, Chris Connolly, and Lainey Mays of the Harper Library Marketing team for their enthusiasm and support for my work.

This is also my second book with Anne Collins, who made special dispensation to keep *Scoundrel* on the Knopf Canada list even as she transitioned to a new role at sibling imprint Random House Canada. Anne's structural and line edits on the manuscript were wondrous, almost magical, in how they melded with my own brain and coaxed out a book from a computer document. *Scoundrel* would not exist without you. Additional thanks to Sarah Jackson, Rick Meier, Pamela Murray, Ashley Dunn, Matthew Sibiga, Martha Kanya Forstner, and Kristin Cochrane at Penguin Random House Canada.

Many thanks to booksellers in the United States and Canada, chiefly those who own and work at independent bookstores, for championing my work as an author and editor and for their boundless enthusiasm and excitement for crime stories.

Words cannot express how grateful I am to Rosemarie Ho, who fact-checked *Scoundrel* with a mixture of dogged investigation, scrupulous attention to detail, a keen eye for the truth (even when the legend would have been more fun to print), and good humor. She's also a fantastic writer of both fiction and nonfiction, and I can't wait to see what her future holds. Thank you, Rosemarie.

My residency at MacDowell, split between March and October–November 2020 because of the pandemic, afforded me the gift of time and space to finish the first draft of *Scoundrel* and then, in the fall, to complete the first round of book edits. Thanks also to Laura Miller, and to Juliet Grames and Paul Oliver, who kindly welcomed me into their homes, where I wrote portions of the first draft.

The last two years were an added reminder that friends, especially those in the same line of work, are invaluable and essential. Elon Green and Lyz Lenz read draft after draft, made me double over with laughter by text, Zoom, and in person, and are simply the best. Thank you to Pamela Colloff and to Terry Teachout for their enthusiasm and thoughtful comments on *Scoundrel*. Thanks to Megan Abbott, Jami Attenberg, Chris Bonanos, Taffy Brodesser-Akner, Alafair Burke, Isaac Butler, Steph Cha, Nicole Cliffe, Julia Dahl, Alison Gaylin, Lauren Goldenberg, Shira Hanau, Rob Hart, Nellie Hermann, Karen Ho, Elliott Holt, Rachel McCarthy James, Maureen Johnson, Tina Jordan, Mattie Kahn, Hillary Kelly, Kelly Link, Talia Lavin, Clair Lamb, Laura Lippman, Elizabeth Little, Lisa Lutz, Karen Olson, Pamela Paul, Ivy Pochoda, Bryon Quertermous, Abe Riesman, Jonathan Santlofer, Alex Segura, Sam Thielman, Dave White, Alina Wickham, and especially the Grotto.

Friends and family, chosen or biological, got me through global calamity, personal changes, and writing this book. First, thanks to my relatives: Sharon AvRutick, Joe Wallace, Jacob Wallace, Shana Wallace, David AvRutick, Kay Newman, Louis AvRutick, Alice AvRutick, and to the memory of my uncle,

Julian AvRutick. To my *khevre*: the Farber-Smigels, the Kaplan-Ejdelmans, the Helitzer-Temkins, Aline Linden, Anna Schnur-Fishman, Jordan Hirsch, and Rokhl Kafrissen. Heartfelt thanks to Jennifer Young, Dov Berger, and especially Miriam Berger Young.

The pandemic separated me from my immediate family for far too long. But when the world opened up and I was able to fly across the border and see them, the years melted away. Thanks to my brother, Jaime, to whom this book is dedicated, still and always the writer in the family. And to my mother, Judith, who still has so much to teach me, and who lives her life with such purpose and joy.

Notes

THIS BOOK is based on primary sources wherever available, including court documents and transcripts, prison and parole records, legislative records, testimony, and letters. I am grateful for the assistance of the following institutions: the Sterling Library at Yale University, which houses the William F. Buckley, Jr., Papers; the Rare Book & Manuscript Library at Columbia University, which houses the Sophie Wilkins Papers; the New Jersey State Archives in Trenton, New Jersey; the National Archives offices in Philadelphia, Pennsylvania, and New York City; and the Harry Ransom Center, University of Texas at Austin in Austin, Texas.

I also relied on local newspaper coverage of Victoria Zielinski's March 1957 murder; the May 1957 trial of Edgar Smith; the trial's aftermath, including the many stays of execution and denied appeals; coverage of his 1976 arrest and conviction; and that trial's aftermath. Key sources included the *Bergen Evening Record* (later the Bergen *Record*), the *Paterson Evening News* and *Morning Call*, the *Ridgewood Herald-News*, the New York *Daily News*, the *New York Times*, the *Scranton Times-Tribune*, the

Philadelphia *Bulletin*, and the *Los Angeles Times*. Access to these newspapers was primarily through Newspapers.com.

Biographical information about Victoria Zielinski and her family and Edgar Smith and his family was gleaned through census records (1920–1940), various indices for births, marriages, deaths, and obituaries, all obtained through Ancestry.com.

I conducted interviews for the book between 2015 and 2021. Rosemarie Ho conducted additional source interviews as part of the fact-checking process, and is cited accordingly. Sources included Myrna Zielinski, Barbara Nixon, Liza Rassner, Adam Wilkins, Daniel Wilkins, Isaac Wilkins, Caroline Hinkley, Stephen F. Lichtenstein, Jack Carley, Christopher Buckley, Michael Pancer, Geoffrey Norman, Paige Hiemier, Ronald Calissi, "Patti Hafford," "Jennifer Hafford," Ronald Sullivan, Kathy Hourigan, Robert Gottlieb, Nancy Nicholas, Toinette Lippe, Anne McCormick, David Quammen, Harry Camisa, and Tom Trantino.

Grateful acknowledgment for permission to access the William F. Buckley, Jr., Papers, as well as permission to reprint Buckley's correspondence, is given to Christopher Buckley, on behalf of the William F. Buckley, Jr., estate. Grateful acknowledgment for permission to reprint Sophie Wilkins's correspondence is given to Adam Wilkins, and to "Patti Hafford" to reprint Edgar Smith's correspondence.

On occasion, typographical errors have been corrected for clarity and are the only instances of altering quoted material.

ABBREVIATIONS USED

AAKR: Alfred A. Knopf, Inc. Records, Harry Ransom Humanities Research Center, University of Texas at Austin

EHS: Edgar Herbert Smith, Jr.

NJSA: New Jersey State Archives

SCW: Sophie C. Wilkins

SFL: Stephen F. Lichtenstein

SMU: Steven M. Umin

SWP: Sophie Wilkins Papers, Series I, Correspondence Files, 1934–2003, Columbia University

WFB: William F. Buckley, Jr.

WFBP: William F. Buckley, Jr., Papers, Yale University

INTRODUCTION

1 **Edgar Smith died:** David Stout, "Edgar Smith, Killer Who Duped William F. Buckley, Dies at 83," *New York Times*, September 25, 2017, B7; State of California, Board of Parole Hearings, High Desert State Prison, Susanville, California, April 23, 2009.

2 **Buckley at first took up:** Donald G. M. Coxe, email to the author, January 5, 2020.

2 **"Edgar Smith has done":** William F. Buckley, Jr., "Edgar Smith, Act III," On the Right, April 20, 1977.

8 **"would have made":** Adam Wilkins, email to the author, December 23, 2018.

1. "WHERE IS VICKIE?"

11 **She was the Zielinskis' second child:** *Bergen* [NJ] *Evening Record*, March 5, 1957, 1; and *Paterson Evening News*, March 6, 1957, 36, among other sources; Victoria's birth record obtained through the Social Security Death Index and Find a Grave, https://www.findagrave.com /memorial/7757106/victoria-zielinski.

11 **The Zielinskis met:** 1930 and 1940 census records list the Zielinskis as living in Honesdale; further information about their changes of address can be found in *Scranton* [PA] *Times-Tribune*, March 5, 1957, 1, and *Bergen* [NJ] *Evening Record*, March 5, 1957, 1.

11 **Anthony's and Mary's ancestors:** Mary Zielinski obituary, *Scranton Times-Tribune*, January 5, 2002, 26; Anthony Zielinski obituary, *Bergen* [NJ] *Evening Record*, January 20, 1983, 46; 1920 census records for Anthony's father, Joseph Zielinski, and Mary's mother, Mary Mozeliak.

11 **Vickie complained about her father:** Author's interview with Barbara Nixon, April 2, 2019.

12 **"Just a kid":** Ibid.

12 **Which, at age fifteen:** *Ridgewood* [NJ] *Herald-News*, March 7, 1957, 2.

12 **Vickie was an honor roll student:** *Bergen* [NJ] *Evening Record*, March 5, 1957, 1; *Paterson News*, March 6, 1957, 1; *Morning Call* (Paterson, NJ), March 6, 1957, 4.

12 **The summer before her sophomore year:** *Scranton* [PA] *Times-Tribune*, March 6, 1957, 1.

12 **In tenth grade, Vickie's marks:** *Paterson* [NJ] *Evening News*, March 5, 1957, 1.

12 **And Vickie did enjoy herself:** Author's interview with Barbara Nixon, April 2, 2019; *Bergen* [NJ] *Evening Record*, March 5, 1957, 1; *Paterson* [NJ] *Evening News*, March 5, 1957, 1.

12 **One unnamed girlfriend complicated:** *Bergen* [NJ] *Evening Record*, March 6, 1957, 2.

13 **One of the last photos:** Details gleaned from Ronald E. Calissi, *Counterpoint: The Edgar Smith Case* (Hackensack, NJ: Manor, 1972), 73 (203a); photo reprinted by the Associated Press, March 6, 1957.

14 **At 7:30 that evening:** The sequence of events leading to Victoria Zielinski's murder is drawn from the trial transcript, reprinted in full in Calissi, *Counterpoint*, and corroborated by newspaper coverage at the time.

14 **Since the streets were poorly lit:** Testimony of Myrna Zielinski, *State of New Jersey v. Edgar Smith*, reprinted in Calissi, *Counterpoint*, 65–87 (195a–216a); and testimony of Barbara Nixon, reprinted in Calissi, *Counterpoint*, 87–95 (217a–224a).

14 **Vickie wore blue jeans:** Ibid.

15 **At about 8:30:** Testimony of Barbara Nixon, *State of New Jersey v. Edgar Smith*, reprinted in Calissi, *Counterpoint*, 92 (222a).

15 **At midnight, when Vickie was:** Testimony of Mary Zielinski, *State of New Jersey v. Edgar Smith*, reprinted in Calissi, *Counterpoint*, 98 (228a).

16 **"Daddy, Vickie is missing":** Testimony of Anthony Zielinski, *State of New Jersey v. Edgar Smith*, reprinted in Calissi, *Counterpoint*, 107 (237a).

16 **Anthony took Mary Faye's car:** Testimony of Anthony Zielinski, *State of New Jersey v. Edgar Smith*, reprinted in Calissi, *Counterpoint*, 106 (236a).

16 **Later, Barbara would tell:** *Herald-News* (Passaic, NJ), March 6, 1957, 2.

16 **The next morning:** Testimony of Anthony Zielinski, *State of New Jersey v. Edgar Smith*, reprinted in Calissi, *Counterpoint*, 111–14 (241a–246a); testimony of Mary Zielinski, *State of New Jersey v. Edgar Smith*, reprinted in Calissi, *Counterpoint*, 100–4 (230a–234a).

17 **The police captain told Mary:** Testimony of Captain Edmund Wickham, *State of New Jersey v. Edgar Smith*, reprinted in Calissi, *Counterpoint*, 119–21 (249a–251a).

17 **They found Vickie's body:** Testimony of Anthony Zielinski, *State of New Jersey v. Edgar Smith*, reprinted in Calissi, *Counterpoint*, 105–18 (235a–248a); testimony of Captain Edmund Wickham, *State of New Jersey v. Edgar Smith*, reprinted in Calissi, *Counterpoint*, 119–21 (249a–251a); *Daily News* (New York), March 6, 1957, 4.

17 **It was the damage to her head:** Testimony of Raphael Gilady, *State of New Jersey v. Edgar Smith*, reprinted in Calissi, *Counterpoint*, 379–85 (509a–515a).

18 **Her father could hardly comprehend:** *Bergen* [NJ] *Evening Record*, March 6, 1957, 1.

18 **Her dad had taught her judo:** *Herald-News* (Passaic, NJ), March 6, 1957, 2; *Paterson* [NJ] *Evening News*, March 6, 1957, 36; *Daily News* (New York), March 6, 1957, 3.

18 **"I'll find the guy":** *Bergen* [NJ] *Evening Record*, March 6, 1957, 1.

18 **Less than twenty-four hours later:** Ibid.

2. THE MERCURY

19 **Joe Gilroy picked up the phone:** Testimony of Joseph Gilroy, *State of New Jersey v. Edgar Smith*, reprinted in Ronald E. Calissi, *Counterpoint: The Edgar Smith Case* (Hackensack, NJ: Manor, 1972), 229–56 (359a–386a).

19 **worked the third shift at Continental Can:** *Herald-News* (Passaic, NJ), May 18, 1957, 2.

19 **Eddie had quit or been fired:** *Morning Call* (Paterson, NJ), March 8, 1957, 1; testimony of Edgar Smith, *State of New Jersey v. Edgar Smith*, reprinted in Calissi, *Counterpoint*, 565–66 (687a–688a).

19 **Eddie was supposed to be:** His Mensa membership card, 1965, lists an IQ of 153, in the ninety-eighth percentile.

19 **He'd grown up all around:** 1940 census records for Joe Gilroy and Edgar Smith on Ancestry.com.

20 **his mother, Ann, had remarried:** Alexander Chupak obituary, *Orlando Sentinel*, August 3, 1994, 63; Social Security Death Index listing for Ann E. Chupak (1908–1993); Richard Smith (1927–1993), death announcement in the New Jersey Death Index, 1904–2000.

20 **Eddie had lived with:** Testimony of Edgar Smith, *State of New Jersey v. Edgar Smith*, reprinted in Calissi, *Counterpoint*, 512 (634a); Clinical record of Edgar H. Smith, Jr., CPL USMC, November 2, 1953, Tripler Army Hospital, APO 438; New Jersey Marriage Records, 1901–2017.

20 **Joe sometimes wondered:** Testimony of Joseph Gilroy, *State of New Jersey v. Edgar Smith*, reprinted in Calissi, *Counterpoint*, 229–31 (359a–361a); clinical record of Edgar H. Smith, Jr., CPL USMC, November 2, 1953, Tripler Army Hospital, APO 438; *Bergen Evening Record*, March 6, 1957, 1.

21 **Eddie arrived in the blue Mercury:** Testimony of Joseph Gilroy, *State of New Jersey v. Edgar Smith*, reprinted in Calissi, *Counterpoint*, 233 (363a); testimony of Patricia Smith, *State of New Jersey v. Edgar Smith*, reprinted in Calissi, *Counterpoint*, 707 (829a).

22 **After he dropped off Eddie:** Testimony of Joseph Gilroy, *State of New Jersey v. Edgar Smith*, reprinted in *Counterpoint*, 248–50 (378a–380a).

22 **Joe Gilroy's phone rang again:** Testimony of Joseph Gilroy, *State of New Jersey v. Edgar Smith*, reprinted in Calissi, *Counterpoint*, 243–64;

testimony of Edgar Smith, *State of New Jersey v. Edgar Smith*, reprinted in Calissi, *Counterpoint*, 543 (665a).

23 **When they pulled up to the house:** Testimony of Joseph Gilroy, *State of New Jersey v. Edgar Smith*, reprinted in Calissi, *Counterpoint*, 243 (373a); testimony of Donald Hommell, *State of New Jersey v. Edgar Smith*, reprinted in Calissi, *Counterpoint*, 310–11 (440a–441a).

24 **After that, the conversation veered:** Testimony of Joseph Gilroy, *State of New Jersey v. Edgar Smith*, reprinted in Calissi, *Counterpoint*, 245–47 (375a–377a); testimony of Edgar Smith, *State of New Jersey v. Edgar Smith*, reprinted in *Counterpoint*, 547 (669a).

24 **As he drove home:** *Bergen* [NJ] *Evening Record*, March 7, 1957, 1; *Paterson* [NJ] *Evening News*, March 6, 1957, 1.

3. "IF YOU'RE LOOKING FOR A FALL GUY . . ."

27 **Killings did happen:** See the front pages of *Bergen* [NJ] *Evening Record*, *Morning Call* (Paterson, NJ), and *Paterson* [NJ] *Evening News*, March 6, 1957; the *Herald-News* (Passaic, NJ), November 13, 1956, 1; and the front pages of the same papers on May 25, 1957.

27 **The police spent all of Tuesday afternoon:** *Bergen* [NJ] *Evening Record*, March 6, 1957, 1.

27 **The tire tracks leading:** Testimony of Joseph Gilroy, *State of New Jersey v. Edgar Smith*, reprinted in Ronald E. Calissi, *Counterpoint: The Edgar Smith Case* (Hackensack, NJ: Manor, 1972), 231 (361a); *Bergen* [NJ] *Evening Record*, March 6, 1957, 1.

28 **Smith was questioned:** *State of New Jersey v. Edgar Smith*, reprinted in Calissi, *Counterpoint*; testimony of Carl De Marco and Vahe Garabedian, *State of New Jersey v. Edgar Smith*, reprinted in Calissi, *Counterpoint*, 346–347 (476a–477a), 366 (496a).

28 **The interrogation continued:** *Paterson* [NJ] *Evening News*, March 7, 1957, 19.

29 **A little later on:** Testimony of Carl De Marco, *State of New Jersey v. Edgar Smith*, reprinted in Calissi, *Counterpoint*, 352 (482a); testimony of Edgar Smith, reprinted in Calissi, *Counterpoint*, 411 (541a); Edgar Smith, *Brief Against Death* (New York: Alfred A. Knopf, 1968), 82.

29 **Officers Ulric Fairbanks:** Testimony of Ulric Fairbanks, *State of New*

Jersey v. Edgar Smith, reprinted in Calissi, *Counterpoint*, 371–78 (501a–508a); testimony of Addison Waldeck, *State of New Jersey v. Edgar Smith*, reprinted in Calissi, *Counterpoint*, 487–92 (609a–614a); Smith, *Brief Against Death*, 92; testimony of Edgar Smith, *State of New Jersey v. Edgar Smith*, reprinted in Calissi, *Counterpoint*, 410 (540a).

29 **The police took Eddie:** Testimony of Raphael Gilady, *State of New Jersey v. Edgar Smith*, reprinted in Calissi, *Counterpoint*, 380 (510a).

30 **The prosecutor's office called in:** *Herald-News* (Passaic, NJ), March 7, 1957, 1; *Bergen Evening Record*, March 7, 1957, 9.

30 **At ten minutes before one:** Testimony of Edgar Smith, *State of New Jersey v. Edgar Smith*, reprinted in Calissi, *Counterpoint*, 456 (581a), 425 (552a–553a).

30 **It wasn't a confession:** Testimony of Edgar Smith, *State of New Jersey v. Edgar Smith*, reprinted in Calissi, *Counterpoint*, 433 (560a–561a), 457 (581a–582a).

31 **When the group took him out to the crime scene:** Interrogation of Edgar Smith, *State of New Jersey v. Edgar Smith*, reprinted in Calissi, *Counterpoint*, 456–57 (581a–582a).

31 **Eddie pointed to the spot:** Testimony of Gordon Graber, *State of New Jersey v. Edgar Smith*, reprinted in Calissi, *Counterpoint*, 299 (429a).

31 **A little over an hour later:** Testimony of Charles deLisle, *State of New Jersey v. Edgar Smith*, reprinted in Calissi, *Counterpoint*, 391 (521a); *Courier News* (Plainfield, NJ), March 7, 1957, 1.

32 **The announcement of the arrest:** *Bergen* [NJ] *Evening Record*, March 7, 1957, 1; *Herald-News* (Passaic, NJ), March 7, 1957, 1.

32 **Townspeople were quick to note:** *Bergen* [NJ] *Evening Record*, March 7, 1957, 9; *Herald-News* (Passaic, NJ), March 8, 1957, 2; *Paterson* [NJ] *Evening News*, March 8, 1957, 10.

33 **Adding further intrigue:** *Herald-News* (Passaic, NJ), March 8, 1957, 2; clinical record of Edgar H. Smith, Jr., CPL USMC, November 2, 1953, Tripler Army Hospital, APO 438.

33 **One former employer:** *Morning Call* (Paterson, NJ), March 8, 1957, 1; *Bergen* [NJ] *Evening Record*, March 7, 1957, 9; *Herald-News* (Passaic, NJ), March 8, 1957, 2; *Paterson* [NJ] *Evening News*, March 8, 1957, 10.

33 **But another account:** *Herald-News* (Passaic, NJ), March 7, 1957, 1.

34 **Patricia Smith was thunderstruck:** *Bergen* [NJ] *Evening Record*, March 8, 1957, 1; *Daily News* (New York), March 8, 1957, 3.

35 **Only the month before:** *Bergen* [NJ] *Evening Record*, March 8, 1957, 2; *Daily News* (New York), March 8, 1957, 3.

35 **"After murder, what?":** Reprinted in *Scranton* [PA] *Times-Tribune*, March 8, 1957, 3.

36 **She was buried:** *Scranton* [PA] *Times-Tribune*, March 8, 1957, 1.

37 **The service was conducted:** Ibid.

37 **Eddie's mother, Ann Chupak:** *Bergen* [NJ] *Evening Record*, March 8, 1957, 1, and March 9, 1957, 1.

38 **Edgar Smith was indicted:** *Bergen* [NJ] *Evening Record*, March 9, 1957, 1; *Morning Call* (Paterson, NJ), March 16, 1957, 13; *Bergen* [NJ] *Evening Record*, March 15, 1957, 1, 2.

38 **Both sides objected to the date:** *Bergen* [NJ] *Evening Record*, March 15, 1957, 2; *Herald-News* (Passaic, NJ), March 15, 1957, 1.

38 **The time crunch became:** *Bergen* [NJ] *Evening Record*, March 22, 1957, 1; John E. Selser obituary, *Bergen* [NJ] *Evening Record*, September 19, 1979, D-25.

38 **He got a three-week extension:** *Bergen* [NJ] *Evening Record*, April 12, 1957, 1.

39 **Selser retained a private investigator:** Andy Nicol, investigative report, March 25–May 10, 1957, WFBP, Box 152, Folder 6.

39 **Selser told Judge O'Dea:** *Bergen* [NJ] *Evening Record*, May 2, 1957, 2.

39 **As defense strategies go:** *Bergen* [NJ] *Evening Record*, May 14, 1957, 1 and 7.

39 **Guy Calissi was ready:** Ibid.

4. OPENINGS

41 **Ron Calissi took his seat:** This section is drawn from Ronald E. Calissi, *Counterpoint: The Edgar Smith Case* (Hackensack, NJ: Manor, 1972), 43–45.

44 **Slowly and methodically:** Opening remarks of Guy W. Calissi, *State of New Jersey v. Edgar Smith*, reprinted in Calissi, *Counterpoint*, 47–52 (177a–182a).

44 **John Selser was next:** Opening remarks of John E. Selser, *State of New*

Jersey v. Edgar Smith, reprinted in Calissi, *Counterpoint*, 52–62 (182a–192a).

46 **Guy Calissi interjected:** *State of New Jersey v. Edgar Smith*, reprinted in Calissi, *Counterpoint*, 62 (192a).

47 **Newspaper headlines that evening:** *Daily News* (New York), May 16, 1957, 1; *Asbury Park* [NJ] *Press*, May 16, 1957, 1; *Morning Call* (Paterson, NJ), May 16, 1957, 1; *Herald-News* (Passaic, NJ), May 16, 1957, 1.

47 **Myrna Zielinski was:** Testimony of Myrna Zielinski, *State of New Jersey v. Edgar Smith*, reprinted in Calissi, *Counterpoint*, 65–77 (195a–207a).

47 **Selser began his cross-examination:** Testimony of Myrna Zielinski, *State of New Jersey v. Edgar Smith*, reprinted in Calissi, *Counterpoint*, 77–86 (207a–216a).

47 **Next Calissi called Barbara Nixon:** Testimony of Barbara Nixon, *State of New Jersey v. Edgar Smith*, reprinted in Calissi, *Counterpoint*, 87–95 (217a–225a); author's interview with Barbara Nixon, April 2, 2019.

48 **Vickie's mother, Mary:** Testimony of Mary Zielinski, *State of New Jersey v. Edgar Smith*, reprinted in Calissi, *Counterpoint*, 95–105 (225a–235a).

48 **Over the next two days:** Testimony of the following law enforcement officials in *State of New Jersey v. Edgar Smith*, reprinted in Calissi, *Counterpoint*, included Captain Edmund Wickham, 118–63 (248a–293a); James W. Stewart, 201–12 (331a–341a); Russell Ridgway, 212–28 (342a–358a) and 748 (870a); Gordon Graber, 287–307 (417a–437a); Arthur Abrams, 337–41 (467a–471a); Carl De Marco, 345–63 (475a–494a); Vahe Garabedian, 364–71 (494a–501a); Ulric Fairbanks, 371–79 (501a–509a); Charles E. Smith, 387 (517a); Charles DeLisle, 388–91 (518a–521a); Henry Voss, 386–87 (517a–518a); Walter Spahr, 391–400 (521a–530a).

48 **When Calissi brought out:** Testimony of James W. Stewart, *Start of New Jersey v. Edgar Smith*, reprinted in *Counterpoint*, 209–10 (339a–340a); *Bergen* [NJ] *Evening Record*, May 17, 1957, 2.

48 **Two female jurors gasped:** *Daily News* (New York), May 17, 1957, 3.

49 **But he had himself under control:** Ibid.; *Bergen* [NJ] *Evening Record*, May 18, 1957, 1.

49 **At 3:30 that Friday afternoon:** Testimony of Donald Hommell, *State of New Jersey v. Edgar Smith*, reprinted in Calissi, *Counterpoint*, 305 (435a); *Bergen Evening Record*, May 18, 1957, 1.

49 Only that morning, he had told: *Daily News* (New York), May 17, 1957, 3.

49 As Hommell walked toward the stand: Testimony of Donald Hommell, *State of New Jersey v. Edgar Smith*, reprinted in Calissi, *Counterpoint*, 305–6 (435a–436a).

5. "I JUST THREW IT OUT THE WINDOW"

51 It rained hard: *Bergen* [NJ] *Evening Record*, May 20, 1957, 1.

51 One of the lucky ones: Mary Higgins Clark, *Kitchen Privileges: A Memoir* (New York: Simon & Schuster, 2001); Mary Higgins Clark, "Edgar Smith—The Human Copperhead," in *I, Witness: Personal Encounters with Crime by Members of the Mystery Writers of America*, edited by Brian Garfield (New York: Times Books, 1978), 245–56; author's interviews with Mary Higgins Clark, January 30 and May 12, 2015.

52 When Donald Hommell took the stand: Testimony of Donald Hommell, *State of New Jersey v. Edgar Smith*, reprinted in Ronald E. Calissi, *Counterpoint: The Edgar Smith Case* (Hackensack, NJ: Manor, 1972), 308 (438a); *Bergen* [NJ] *Evening Record*, May 20, 1957, 2.

52 Guy Calissi's direct examination: Testimony of Donald Hommell, *State of New Jersey v. Edgar Smith*, reprinted in Calissi, *Counterpoint*, 309 (439a).

52 The defense lawyer pressed Hommell: Ibid., 313 (443a).

53 Selser asked how many times: Ibid., 314–15 (444a–445a).

53 The adversarial relationship: Ibid., 318–19 (448a–449a).

53 Calissi took umbrage: Ibid., 321 (451a).

53 The lawyers sparred more: Ibid., 321–25 (451a–455a).

54 Selser returned to cross-examine: Ibid., 325–35 (445a–465a).

54 Selser then tried to ask: Ibid.; no dental records or other documentation could be found to determine whether Edgar Smith had protruding teeth.

55 Calissi had one last question: Ibid., 335–36 (465a–466a).

55 Before the day ended: Testimony of Raphael Gilady, *State of New Jersey v. Edgar Smith*, reprinted in Calissi, *Counterpoint*, 379–86 (509a–516a).

56 It was not clear to Calissi: *Bergen* [NJ] *Evening Record*, May 20, 1957, 1; testimony of the following law enforcement officials in *State of New Jersey v. Edgar Smith*, reprinted in Calissi, *Counterpoint*: Charles E.

Smith, 387 (517a); Charles DeLisle, 388–91 (518a–521a); Henry Voss, 386–87 (517a–518a); Walter Spahr, 391–400 (521a–530a).

56 **Calissi and Selser's sparring:** *State of New Jersey v. Edgar Smith*, reprinted in Calissi, *Counterpoint*, 403–09 (533a–539a).

56 **On the stand, under oath:** Testimony of Edgar Smith, *State of New Jersey v. Edgar Smith*, reprinted in Calissi, *Counterpoint*, 409–12 (539a–542a).

56 **As a rebuttal witness:** Testimony of Louis M. Kalstad, *State of New Jersey v. Edgar Smith*, reprinted in Calissi, *Counterpoint*, 412–14 (542a–544a).

57 **After more back-and-forth:** Ibid., 414–21 (544a–551a); *Bergen* [NJ] *Evening Record*, May 21, 1957, 6.

57 **Calissi wrapped up his prosecution:** *State of New Jersey v. Edgar Smith*, reprinted in Calissi, *Counterpoint*, 501–12 (623a–634a).

6. "EDDIE AND DON AREN'T FRIENDS ANYMORE"

59 **This was the moment:** *Bergen* [NJ] *Evening Record*, May 23, 1957, 1; Associated Press, reprinted in the *Long Branch* [NJ] *Daily Record*, 8.

59 **Edgar's wife and mother:** *Bergen* [NJ] *Evening Record*, May 23, 1957, 1.

59 **Selser first questioned Smith:** Testimony of Edgar H. Smith, *State of New Jersey v. Edgar Smith*, reprinted in Ronald E. Calissi, *Counterpoint: The Edgar Smith Case* (Hackensack, NJ: Manor, 1972), 512–65 (634a–687a).

60 **Selser then asked:** Ibid., 532–34 (654a–656a).

60 **Hommell got up abruptly:** *Bergen* [NJ] *Evening Record*, May 23, 1957, 1; *Paterson* [NJ] *Evening News*, May 23, 1957, 1.

61 **Reporters seemed to be:** *Rockland* [NY] *Journal-News*, May 23, 1957, 3; *Bergen* [NJ] *Evening Record*, May 23, 1957, 1; *Paterson* [NJ] *Evening News*, May 23, 1957, 1.

61 **The next day, it was Guy Calissi's turn:** Testimony of Edgar H. Smith, *State of New Jersey v. Edgar Smith*, reprinted in Ronald E. Calissi, *Counterpoint: The Edgar Smith Case* (Hackensack, NJ: Manor, 1972), 565–664 (687a–786a).

61 **Edgar mostly stayed composed:** Ibid., 645 (767a); *Bergen* [NJ] *Evening Record*, May 24, 1957, 1.

62 **Calissi asked if Edgar:** Testimony of Edgar H. Smith, *State of New*

Jersey v. Edgar Smith, reprinted in Calissi, *Counterpoint*, 645–46 (767a–768a).

62 **Selser finally objected:** Ibid., 646–47 (768a–769a).

62 **Next Selser called Rosella Wood:** Testimony of Rosella Wood, *State of New Jersey v. Edgar Smith*, reprinted in Calissi, *Counterpoint*, 670–80 (792a–802a); *Herald-News* (Passaic, NJ), May 24, 1957, 2.

63 **Patricia Smith took the stand:** Testimony of Patricia Smith, *State of New Jersey v. Edgar Smith*, reprinted in Calissi, *Counterpoint*, 691–716 (812a–838a); *Herald-News* (Passaic, NJ), May 24, 1957, 1.

63 **When Selser called Frank Gilg:** Testimony of Frank J. Gilg, *State of New Jersey v. Edgar Smith*, reprinted in Calissi, *Counterpoint*, 724–27 (846a–849a).

63 **It was clear to the audience:** *Rockland* [NY] *Journal-News*, May 25, 1957, 3.

64 **When Selser's final two witnesses:** *Rockland* [NY] *Journal-News*, May 25, 1957, 1; *Bergen* [NJ] *Evening Record*, May 25, 1957, 1.

64 **Edgar Smith's trial had many dramatic moments:** *Bergen* [NJ] *Evening Record*, May 27, 1957, 1.

64 **Ruth Starr Zeitler:** *Bergen* [NJ] *Evening Record*, May 24, 1957, 1, May 27, 1957, 1, and May 28, 1957, 1.

65 **He was a star:** *Bergen* [NJ] *Evening Record*, May 27, 1957, 2, and May 28, 1957, 1.

65 **Ronald Marrone went on:** *Bergen* [NJ] *Evening Record*, September 5, 1957, 6, and October 15, 1971, 2; obituary on Ancestry.com notes that Marrone died in Cropwell, Alabama, on March 8, 2016.

65 **The swift arrest and charging:** *Bergen* [NJ] *Evening Record*, May 27, 1957, 1.

66 **John Selser went first:** *State of New Jersey v. Edgar Smith*, reprinted in Calissi, *Counterpoint*, 783–806 (905a–928a).

66 **Calissi began his summation:** Ibid., 806–21 (928a–943a).

67 **The following morning:** Ibid., 822–55 (944a–977a).

7. "IT CAN'T BE"

69 **Guy Calissi was taken aback:** *Daily News* (New York), May 29, 1957, 3.

69 **After the group of ten men:** Cited in *State of New Jersey v. Edgar Smith*,

reprinted in Ronald E. Calissi, *Counterpoint: The Edgar Smith Case* (Hackensack, NJ: Manor, 1972), 855 (977a).

69 Edgar took it in: *Newsday*, May 29, 1957, 1; *Bergen* [NJ] *Evening Record*, May 29, 1957, 1.

69 Judge O'Dea told the jurors: *State of New Jersey v. Edgar Smith*, reprinted in Calissi, *Counterpoint*, 863–67 (985a–989a).

70 Later, Anthony Zielinski told reporters: *Bergen* [NJ] *Evening Record*, May 29, 1957, 1.

70 Calissi was beyond tired: Ibid., 1.

70 When a reporter: Ibid., 1.

70 Selser was appalled: Ibid., 2.

71 Just before he passed sentence: *State of New Jersey v. Edgar Smith*, reprinted in Calissi, *Counterpoint*, 863–67 (985a–989a).

8. PATRICIA

75 The last time Patricia Smith: *Bergen* [NJ] *Evening Record*, July 8, 1957, 1, and August 6 1958, 1.

75 She and Patti Ann fled: *Herald-News* (Passaic, NJ), August 15, 1958, 1.

75 Patricia was grateful: *Paterson* [NJ] *Evening News*, August 16, 1958, 3; *Herald-News* (Passaic, NJ), August 15, 1958, 2.

76 Patricia was, by the standards of the day: *Herald-News* (Passaic, NJ), August 15, 1962, 41; *Bergen* [NJ] *Evening Record*, June 2, 1958, 1, and March 2, 1962, 2.

76 Edgar's cell was on the upper tier: *Bergen* [NJ] *Evening Record*, June 2, 1958, 1, and March 2, 1962, 2.

76 The Death House kept the inmates: *Herald-News* (Passaic, NJ), July 20, 1957, 10; *Bergen* [NJ] *Evening Record*, June 2, 1958, 3.

77 For the Smiths' second wedding anniversary: *Bergen* [NJ] *Evening Record*, June 4, 1958, 1; *Morning Call* (Paterson, NJ), June 4, 1958, 1; *Daily Home News* (New Brunswick, NJ), June 8, 1958, 1; *Bergen* [NJ] *Evening Record*, June 9, 1958, 1.

77 On June 25, 1958: *State v. Smith*, 27 N.J. 433 (1958), Justia, https://law .justia.com/cases/new-jersey/supreme-court/1958/27-n-j-433-0.html; *Herald-News* (Passaic, NJ), June 26, 1958, 2.

78 **John Selser swiftly announced:** *Bergen* [NJ] *Evening Record*, July 30, 1958, 1.

78 **But after a clemency hearing:** *Bergen* [NJ] *Evening Record*, July 31, 1958, 1.

78 **Selser, meanwhile, dropped:** *Bergen* [NJ] *Evening Record*, August 6, 1958, 1, and August 7, 1958, 1.

78 **In his affidavit:** *Herald-News* (Passaic, NJ), August 14, 1958, 2; *Bergen* [NJ] *Evening Record*, August 7, 1958, 1, and August 11, 1958, 1.

79 **The next few days:** *Bergen* [NJ] *Evening Record*, August 15, 1958, 1; *Herald-News* (Passaic, NJ), August 14, 1958, 2.

79 **The fourteen-witness, two-day hearing:** *Bergen* [NJ] *Evening Record*, August 15, 1958, 1; *Herald-News* (Passaic, NJ), August 14, 1958, 1.

79 **A US army private:** *Herald-News* (Passaic, NJ), August 14, 1958, 2.

79 **Pelzer, the bar owner:** Ibid.; *Paterson Evening News*, August 14, 1958; and *Bergen* [NJ] *Evening Record*, August 15, 1958, 1.

80 **Judge O'Dea wasn't swayed:** *Bergen* [NJ] *Evening Record*, August 15, 1958, 1.

80 **Patricia Smith rarely commented:** *Herald-News* (Passaic, NJ), August 15, 1958, 23; *Paterson* [NJ] *Evening News*, August 15, 1958, 1.

81 **Both Ann and Patricia planned:** *Herald-News* (Passaic, NJ), August 16, 1958, 3.

82 **If Patricia didn't know then:** *Herald-News* (Passaic, NJ), August 18, 1958, 2.

82 **The Death House was a spooky place:** Ibid., 2.

83 **The hours ticked by:** *Bergen* [NJ] *Evening Record*, August 18, 1958, 2.

83 **A member of the New Jersey Legislature:** *Bergen* [NJ] *Evening Record*, August 19, 1958, 2, and August 20, 1958, 2.

84 **Patricia was only dimly aware:** *Paterson* [NJ] *Evening News*, August 19, 1958, 2.

84 **At around 3:00 p.m.:** Ibid.

84 **Judge Morrill had issued the stay:** *Bergen* [NJ] *Evening Record*, August 19, 1958, 1 and 2.

85 **Reporters pounced on the car:** *Paterson* [NJ] *Evening News*, August 19, 1958, 2; *Herald-News* (Passaic, NJ), August 19, 1958, 1.

85 **But as the news spread:** *Bergen* [NJ] *Evening Record*, August 20, 1958, 1 and 9.

86 In the fall of 1955: This section is sourced primarily from an affidavit Patricia gave to the Bergen County Prosecutor's Office in 2000 as part of its efforts to ensure that Edgar Smith would not be released from prison. The affidavit was included in Ronald Calissi's personal archives.

9. DIVORCES

89 With the swift conviction: *Paterson* [NJ] *Evening News*, August 18, 1958, 1; Ramsey High School 1959 yearbook on Ancestry.com.

89 The media coverage: *Paterson* [NJ] *Evening News*, August 18, 1958, 1, and August 19, 1958, 2.

90 Vickie's father, Anthony: *Bergen* [NJ] *Evening Record*, December 12, 1957, 1; *Paterson* [NJ] *Evening News*, December 18, 1957, 26.

90 Mary finally filed for divorce: *Zielinski v. Zielinski*, Superior Court of New Jersey, Chancery Division: Bergen County, Docket no. M-3587–58-R, filed August 5, 1959, WFBP, Box 152, Folder 7.

91 The divorce was granted: *Herald-News* (Passaic, NJ), October 2, 1959, 15.

91 After the decree, Mary moved: *Paterson* [NJ] *Evening News*, June 30, 1960, 13; *Record* (Bergen, NJ), July 1, 1960, 5; Mary Jane Zielinski obituary, *Scranton* [PA] *Times-Tribune*, January 5, 2002, 26; "Divorce Decree or Dismissal Coupon" in re: *Mary Fay[e] Zielinski v. George Self*, Pulaski County, Arkansas, July 29, 1964.

91 Anthony, meanwhile, remarried: *Record* (Bergen, NJ), March 30, 1977, 6, and January 20, 1983, 20.

91 In public Patricia Smith remained: *Paterson* [NJ] *Evening News*, May 5, 1959, 1; *Bergen* [NJ] *Evening Record*, November 23, 1959, 1.

92 "He didn't kill her": *Paterson* [NJ] *Evening News*, May 5, 1959, 1.

92 After Judge Morrill died: *Morning Call* (Paterson, NJ), March 14, 1961, 6.

92 "DEAREST SMITTY": *Record* (Bergen, NJ), June 16, 1960, 56.

93 Eventually Patricia got involved: *Reno Gazette-Journal*, June 28, 1962, 13, and January 1, 1963, 18; *Paterson* [NJ] *Evening News*, June 29, 1960, 11, and June 15, 1962, 1.

93 Love, however, couldn't quite make up: *Paterson* [NJ] *Evening News*, June 18, 1963, 19.

93 **Patricia was determined:** Author's interview with "Patti Hafford," September 10, 2019; EHS, letter to WFB, October 28, 1963, WFBP, Box 152, Folder 7.

93 **In the summer of 1962:** *Record* (Bergen, NJ), July 5, 1962, 3, and August 1, 1962, 2.

94 **Edgar had been on death row:** *Herald-News* (Passaic, NJ), August 1, 1962, 1 and 35; *Record* (Bergen, NJ), August 1, 1962, 2; Associated Press, reprinted in the *Daily Home News* (New Brunswick, NJ), August 15, 1962, 30.

94 **When one of the condemned men:** *Paterson* [NJ] *Evening News*, December 7, 1971, 12.

94 **Edgar was in legal limbo:** *Record* (Bergen, NJ), September 6, 1962, 1.

95 **The new year brought more convicted men:** *Paterson* [NJ] *Evening News*, March 4, 1964, 15.

95 **In the fall of 1962:** EHS, letter to WFB, October 28, 1963.

95 **He also obtained books:** *Ridgewood* [NJ] *Herald-News*, July 19, 1962, 1.

10. A "LIFETIME" SUBSCRIPTION

99 **When William F. Buckley, Jr., became interested:** This section is drawn primarily from John B. Judis, *William F. Buckley, Jr.: Patron Saint of the Conservatives* (New York: Simon & Schuster, 1988), with additional biographical information gleaned from Alvin S. Felzenberg, *A Man and His Presidents: The Political Odyssey of William F. Buckley, Jr.* (New Haven, CT: Yale University Press, 2018); Carl T. Bogus, *Buckley: William F. Buckley Jr. and the Rise of American Conservatism* (London: Bloomsbury Press, 2011); Richard Brookhiser, *Right Time, Right Place: Coming of Age with William F. Buckley Jr. and the Conservative Movement* (New York: Basic Books, 2009); Christopher Buckley, *Losing Mum and Pup: A Memoir* (New York: Twelve Books, 2009); and Nicholas Buccola, *The Fire Is Upon Us: James Baldwin, William F. Buckley Jr., and the Debate over Race in America* (Princeton, NJ: Princeton University Press, 2020).

99 **Also forthcoming was this 1980 assessment:** George Will, "Anniversary Salute," *National Review*, December 31, 1980.

102 **Less than two years:** William F. Buckley, Jr., "Why the South Must

Prevail," *National Review*, August 24, 1957, 146; Judis, *William F. Buckley, Jr.*, 138.

102 **There were giant paradoxes:** Judis, *William F. Buckley, Jr.*, 38.

103 **"I don't think I had":** Ibid., 44.

104 **That ability, more than a decade:** Author's interviews and conversations with Christopher Buckley, Aggie Dowd, Terry Teachout, and Sam Tanenhaus.

104 **It began with a newspaper column:** *Ridgewood* [NJ] *Herald-News*, July 19, 1962, 1; Donald G. M. Coxe, "Should Edgar Smith Be Executed?," *National Review*, October 8, 1963.

105 **Buckley wrote Edgar a letter:** WFB, letter to Ann Chupak, September 28, 1962, WFBP, Box 152, Folder 6; WFB, telegram to EHS, September 26, 1962, WFBP, Box 152, Folder 6; EHS, letter to WFB, October 9, 1962, WFBP, Box 152, Folder 6.

105 **Buckley sensed that Edgar's plight:** Author's interview with Donald G. M. Coxe, January 7, 2020.

105 **Though Coxe did not give up:** Ibid.

105 **Coxe's application:** WFB, letter to Ann Chupak, September 28, 1962, WFBP, Box 152, Folder 6; William F. Buckley, Jr., "The Approaching End of Edgar H. Smith, Jr.," *Esquire*, November 1, 1965, 116–21, 178–83.

106 *Cell 2455, Death Row:* Theodore Hamm, *Rebel and a Cause: Caryl Chessman and the Politics of the Death Penalty in Postwar California, 1948–1979* (Berkeley: University of California Press, 2001).

106 **Edgar Smith and William F. Buckley corresponded:** EHS, letters to WFB, October 17, November 27, and December 13, 1962, WFBP, Box 152, Folder 6; WFB, letters to EHS, October 30 and December 20, 1962, WFBP, Box 152, Folder 6.

107 **Buckley wrote again:** WFB, letter to EHS, January 18, 1963, WFBP, Box 152, Folder 6.

107 **Coxe got his approval:** Author's interview with Donald G. M. Coxe, January 7, 2020.

108 **Six months earlier:** *Record* (Bergen, NJ), December 28, 1960, 2, and January 23, 1960, 5.

108 **Edgar's latest appeal:** WFB, letters to EHS, July 25, August 13, August 30, and September 26, 1963, WFBP, Box 152, Folder 6; EHS, let-

ters to WFB, July 26, August 26, and September 10 and 13, 1963, WFBP, Box 152, Folder 6.

108 **Buckley, who was already leaning:** WFB, letter to EHS, September 26, 1963, WFBP Box 152, Folder 6; Coxe, "Should Edgar Smith Be Executed?"

109 **Coxe's piece did not garner:** Ibid.

109 **Edgar soon had another favor:** EHS, letter to WFB, October 14, 1963, and WFB, letter to EHS, October 17, 1963, WFBP, Box 152, Folder 6.

109 **Buckley began to be drawn in:** EHS, letter to WFB, October 21, 1963, WFBP, Box 152, Folder 6.

110 **Edgar then piled on:** EHS, letter to WFB, November 18, 1963, WFBP, Box 152, Folder 6.

11. "MY GOD, I WISH I COULD BE ABSOLUTELY CERTAIN"

111 **By 1964, William F. Buckley:** WFB, letter to EHS, March 25, 1964, and EHS, letter to WFB, March 25, 1964, WFBP, Box 152, Folder 6.

111 **Buckley's outrage at the treatment:** WFB, letter to EHS, March 25, 1964; and EHS, letter to WFB, June 24, 1964, WFBP, Box 152, Folder 6.

112 **Buckley had become more invested:** EHS, letter to WFB, February 17, 1964, and WFB, letter to EHS, March 3, 1964, WFBP, Box 152, Folder 6.

112 **In March, the court appointed:** EHS, letters to WFB, March 26 and April 3 and 8, 1964, WFBP, Box 152, Folder 6; *Record* (Bergen, NJ), March 17, 1964, 1.

112 **The habeas hearing took place:** EHS, letters to WFB, April 19 and May 10, 1964, WFBP, Box 152, Folder 6.

112 **Edgar was even more upset:** *Escobedo v. State of Illinois*, Supreme Court 378 U.S. 478, 84, S. Ct. 1758, 12.L. Ed.2d.977, argued April 29, 1964, ruled on June 22, 1964, https://www.law.cornell.edu/supremecourt /text/378/478.

113 **Since Edgar hadn't been allowed:** *State v. Smith*, 202 A.2d 669 (N.J. 1964), https://www.courtlistener.com/opinion/2187824/state-v-smith; EHS, letter to WFB, July 13, 1964, WFBP, Box 152, Folder 6.

113 **News that Buckley called:** *Wilmington* [DE] *Morning News*, June 11, 1964, 1; EHS, letter to WFB, June 14, 1964, WFBP, Box 152, Folder 6.

113 **Edgar's newest appeal:** *State v. Smith*, 202 A.2d 669 (N.J. 1964); EHS, letters to WFB, July 13 and August 6, 1964, and WFB, letter to EHS, July 22 and August 5, 1964, WFBP, Box 152, Folder 6.

114 **In August, though:** WFB, letters to EHS, August 10 and 18, 1964, and EHS, letter to WFB, August 20, 1964, WFBP, Box 152, Folder 6.

114 **Edgar responded more sharply:** EHS, letter to WFB, September 12, 1964, WFBP, Box 152, Folder 6.

115 **Then Edgar, for the first time:** Ibid.

116 **In his response, Buckley clarified:** WFB, letter to EHS, September 16, 1964, WFBP, Box 152, Folder 6.

116 **Communication slowed:** WFB, letter to EHS, October 21, 1964, and EHS, letter to WFB, October 16, 1964, WFBP, Box 152, Folder 6.

116 **Yet their friendship had become:** EHS, letters to WFB, October 22 and November 5, 1964, and WFB, letter to EHS, November 3, 1964, WFBP, Box 152, Folder 6.

116 **Edgar filed his Supreme Court brief:** EHS, letter to WFB, November 23, 1964, and WFB, letter to EHS, November 30, 1964, WFBP, Box 152, Folder 6.

117 **Buckley was later touched:** WFB, letters to EHS, December 16 and 22, 1964, and EHS, letter to WFB, December 18, 1964, WFBP, Box 152, Folder 6.

117 **The more serious matter:** Ibid.; EHS, letter to WFB, December 24, 1964, and WFB, letter to EHS, December 31, 1964, WFBP, Box 152, Folder 6; EHS, letter to WFB, January 31, 1965, WFBP, Box 153, Folder 1; *Record* (Bergen, NJ), January 30, 1965, 3.

12. MEETING IN TRENTON

119 **William F. Buckley arrived:** William F. Buckley, Jr., "The Approaching End of Edgar H. Smith, Jr.," *Esquire*, November 1, 1965, 116–21, 178–83; WFB, letters to EHS, February 8, 12, and 25, 1965, and WFB, telegram to EHS, March 16, 1965, WFBP, Box 153, Folder 1; Nicholas Buccola, *The Fire Is Upon Us: James Baldwin, William F. Buck-*

ley Jr., and the Debate over Race in America (Princeton, NJ: Princeton University Press, 2020), 244–45.

119 **What occupied Buckley's mind:** EHS, letters to WFB, March 12 and 17, 1965, and WFB, letter to EHS, March 10, 1965, WFBP, Box 153, Folder 1.

120 **When he got there:** Buckley, "The Approaching End of Edgar H. Smith, Jr."

120 **Granted entrance:** Ibid.

124 **Edgar wrote Buckley:** EHS, letter to WFB, March 19, 1965, WFBP, Box 153, Folder 1.

124 **The levity in Edgar's letter:** Ibid.

124 **Judge O'Dea, however, denied:** EHS, letter to WFB, April 13, 1965, WFBP, Box 153, Folder 1; Ann Chupak, letter to WFB, April 18, 1965, Box 153, Folder 2.

124 **Granting the stay on Good Friday:** EHS, letter to WFB, April 17, 1965, WFBP, Box 153, Folder 1.

124 **Then part of his habitual mask dissolved:** Ibid.

125 **Buckley was preparing:** WFB, letter to EHS, April 27, 1965, and EHS, letter to WFB, May 1, 1965, WFBP, Box 153, Folder 1.

125 **By May 13, Buckley had returned:** WFB, letter to EHS, May 13, 1965, WFBP, Box 153, Folder 1; John B. Judis, *William F. Buckley, Jr.: Patron Saint of the Conservatives* (New York: Simon & Schuster, 1988), 241.

125 **But he hadn't forgotten Edgar:** WFB, letters to EHS, July 6 and 23 and August 11, 1965, WFBP, Box 153, Folder 1.

126 **"I was totally flabbergasted":** EHS, letter to WFB, July 21, 1965, WFBP, Box 153, Folder 1.

126 **Edgar wrote again on August 1:** EHS, letter to WFB, August 1, 1965, and WFB, letter to EHS, August 5, 1965, WFBP, Box 153, Folder 1.

127 **Much to the annoyance:** WFB, letter to EHS, August 17, 1965, WFBP, Box 153, Folder 1.

13. WAITING FOR DEATH

129 **The *Esquire* issue:** *Paterson Morning Call* (Paterson, NJ), October 19, 1965, 1; *Record* (Bergen, NJ), October 19, 1965, 1; William F. Buckley,

Jr., "The Approaching End of Edgar H. Smith, Jr.," *Esquire*, November 1, 1965, 116–21, 178–83.

129 **Reactions to Buckley's piece:** Ibid.

130 **The most specific and pointed critique:** EHS, letter to WFB, October 22, 1965, WFBP, Box 153, Folder 1.

131 **Buckley did wonder why:** EHS, letter to WFB, November 4, 1965, WFBP, Box 153, Folder 1.

131 **Edgar did seem to understand:** Ibid.

132 **Buckley responded:** WFB, letter to EHS, October 27, 1965, WFBP, Box 153, Folder 1.

132 **Buckley could nitpick:** Ibid.

132 **Edgar assured Bill he was fine:** EHS, letters to WFB, November 1 and 9, 1965, and WFB, letter to EHS, November 3, 1965, WFBP, Box 153, Folder 1.

133 **Buckley did not need that assurance:** WFB, memorandum to legal defense fund contributors, January 7, 1966, WFBP, Box 152, Folder 2; WFB, letter to EHS, November 29, 1965, WFBP, Box 153, Folder 1.

133 **Buckley had also devoted:** The version titled "A Lonely Man Waits for Death" appeared in the *Daily Journal* (Franklin, IA), November 9, 1965, 2; titles for the column in other newspapers included "The Story of Edgar Smith," "In the Death House Is a Man Named Smith," and "The Death House—and Beyond."

134 **Buckley also mentioned the case:** EHS, letter to WFB, November 14, 1965, WFBP, Box 153, Folder 1.

134 **Two weeks after the column ran:** EHS, letter to WFB, November 23, 1965, WFBP, Box 153, Folder 1.

134 **Buckley was confused by the news:** WFB, letter to EHS, November 23, 1965, WFBP, Box 153, Folder 1.

135 **"Guess what?":** EHS, letter to WFB, April 2, 1966, WFBP, Box 153, Folder 5; *Miranda v. Arizona*, 384 US 436 (1966).

135 **Edgar had also heard rumors:** EHS, letter to WFB, August 4, 1966, WFBP, Box 153, Folder 5; *Millville* [NJ] *Daily*, April 29, 1966, 4.

135 **While waiting on a big move:** EHS, letter to WFB, April 2, 1966, WFBP, Box 153, Folder 5; *Miranda v. Arizona*, 384 US 436 (1966).

136 **"Eventually" was the key term here:** EHS, letter to WFB, July 7, 1966, WFBP, Box 153, Folder 5.

136 **Buckley, who had just returned:** WFB, letter to EHS, August 10, 1966, WFBP, Box 153, Folder 5; *Firing Line* broadcasts are archived at the Hoover Institution on War, Revolution and Peace at Stanford University and online at https://www.hoover.org/library-archives/collections/firing-line.

137 **He had hoped to cheer Edgar up:** EHS, letters to WFB, July 26 and August 14, 1966, WFBP, Box 153, Folder 5.

137 **Buckley also updated Edgar:** WFB, letter to EHS, August 11, 1966, WFBP, Box 153, Folder 5.

137 **Edgar said he would try:** EHS, letters to WFB, August 14, 30, and 31, 1966, and WFB, letter to EHS, August 18, 1966, WFBP, Box 153, Folder 5.

137 **Buckley had never:** WFB, letter to EHS, September 8, 1966, and EHS, letter to WFB, September 12, 1966, WFBP, Box 153, Folder 5.

138 **The bulk of their correspondence:** EHS, letter to WFB, July 10, 1966, WFBP, Box 153, Folder 5; William F. Buckley, Jr. "New York at the Police Squad," On the Right, July 19, 1966.

138 **The letter is worth considering:** EHS, letter to WFB, July 10, 1966, WFBP, Box 153, Folder 5.

139 **On December 29:** EHS, letter to WFB, December 30, 1966, WFBP, Box 153, Folder 5; WFB, letter to Lloyd McCorkle, January 3, 1967, WFBP, Box 154, Folder 1.

140 **Even with no screen:** WFB, letter to Lloyd McCorkle, January 3, 1967, WFBP, Box 154, Folder 1.

140 **Edgar couldn't have cared less:** EHS, letter to WFB, January 6, 1967, WFBP, Box 154, Folder 1.

140 **The answer, as would become evident:** EHS, letter to WFB, December 20, 1965, WFBP, Box 153, Folder 1.

14. LUNCH AT PAONE'S

143 **Sophie Wilkins was anxious:** SCW, letter to EHS, November 14, 1967, SWP, Box 24; SCW, letter to WFB, November 15, 1967, WFBP,

Box 46; SCW, letter to Sam Vaughan, September 5, 1978, SWP, Box 22, Folder 1.

143 **Sophie had first written to Buckley:** SCW, letter to WFB, October 28, 1965, WFBP, Box 78, Folder 11.

144 **Sophie had joined Alfred A. Knopf in 1959:** SCW, résumé, SWP, Box 23, Folder 15.

144 **Knopf was one of the most prestigious:** Charles McGrath, *Alfred A. Knopf, 1915–2015: A Century of Publishing* (New York: Alfred A. Knopf, 2015); Gay Talese, "Random House Will Buy Knopf in Merger," *New York Times*, April 17, 1960, 1; Sam Roberts, "William Loverd, Who Promoted Literary Giants, Dies at 78," *New York Times*, June 19, 2019; Douglas Martin, "Ashbel Green, Longtime Editor at Knopf, Dies at 84," *New York Times*, September 19, 2012; Peter B. Flint, "Harold Strauss, Editor, Dead; Brought in Japanese Literature," *New York Times*, November 30, 1975, 73.

145 **She had emigrated from Vienna:** Biographical/historical note, SWP.

145 **Sophie was on her third marriage:** Marriage record for Sophie Prombaum and Meyer Klein, July 5, 1934, New York, New York Extracted Marriage Index, 1866–1937; marriage record for Sophie Prombaum and Alvin Meyer, May 1, 1942, Virginia Department of Health, Virginia, Marriages, 1936–2014; SCW, letter to EHS, October 3, 1967, SWP, Box 24; biographical/historical note, SWP; SCW, letter to WFB, September 24, 1979, SWP, Box 8, Folder 2; SCW, letter to Barbara Ehrenreich, February 9, 1985, SWP, Box 10, Folder 2.

145 **By 1967, her decade-long union:** Author's interview with Adam Wilkins, November 2018.

146 **Sophie's personality and demeanor:** Author's interviews with Kathy Hourigan, October 4, 2018; Toinette Lippe, January 6, 2019; Nancy Nicholas, October 5, 2018; and Anne McCormick, January 14, 2019.

146 **Sophie sensed commercial opportunity:** SCW, letter to Erle Stanley Gardner, March 22, 1965, SWP, Box 10, Folder 12; EHS, letter to WFB, August 11, 1967, Box 154, Folder 1.

146 **What spurred Sophie:** SCW, letter to WFB, October 28, 1965, WFBP, MS 576, Series Part I, Box 46; SCW, letter to WFB, November 16, 1965; WFB, letter to SCW, November 22, 1965, WFBP, Box 78, Folder 11.

147 **Sometime after Edgar mentioned:** EHS, letter to WFB, May 27, 1967, WFBP, Box 67; Ann Chupak, letter to SCW, May 23, 1967, and SCW, letter to Ann Chupak, May 25, 1967, SWP, Box 24, Folder 1; SCW, letter to EHS, July 26, 1967, SWP, Box 24, Folder 2.

147 **By November, their strictly professional correspondence:** EHS, letter to SCW, October 11, 1967, SWP, Box 24, Folder 5; SCW, letter to EHS, October 17, 1967; EHS, letter to SCW, October 21, 1967.

147 **At Paone's, she expected:** SCW, letter to EHS, November 14, 1967, SWP, Box 24; SCW, letters to WFB, November 15 and 24, 1967, WFBP, Box 78, Folder 11; SCW, letter to WFB, June 3–6, 1988, SWP, Box 8, Folder 3.

147 **By the end of the lunch:** William F. Buckley, Jr., "Sophie Wilkins, R.I.P.," *National Review*, June 2, 2003, 14.

148 **"For me, it was":** SCW, letter to WFB, SWP, Box 8, Folder 3.

148 **Two decades later:** SCW, letter to WFB, July 4, 1998, SWP, Box 6, Folder 5; EHS, letter to SCW, October 11, 1967, SWP, Box 24, Folder 6.

15." THEY MUST THINK I AM HOUDINI"

149 **She'd learned from Ann Chupak:** SCW, postcard to EHS, December 27, 1967, WFBP, Box 154, Folder 1; Ann Chupak, letters to SCW, May 23 and 28 and June 11, 1967, SWP and SCW, letters to Ann Chupak, May 25 and June 13, 1967, SWP, Box 24, Folder 1.

150 **There was one more unexpected complication:** EHS, letter to SCW, July 24, 1967, SWP, Box 24, Folder 3.

150 **Edgar was also considering:** Ibid.

151 **As promised, Edgar's subsequent letter:** EHS, letter to SCW, July 24, 1967, SWP, Box 24, Folder 3.

151 **Edgar's letters met:** SCW, letter to EHS, July 28, 1967, SWP, Box 24, Folder 3.

151 **She also thought that getting an agent:** Ibid.; EHS, letter to SCW, August 5, 1967, SWP, Box 24, Folder 3.

152 **Sophie also made one early:** SCW, letter to EHS, July 28, 1967, SWP, Box 24, Folder 3.

152 **In other early letters:** EHS, letter to SCW, September 7, 1967, SWP, Box 24, Folder 5.

153 **"Hello, my wide-eyed, liberal friend":** EHS, letter to SCW, August 5, 1967, SWP, Box 24, Folder 4.

153 **Sophie had, in one:** SCW, letter to EHS, July 26, 1967, SWP, Box 24, Folder 3.

153 **Edgar walked the comments back:** EHS, letter to SCW, August 6, 1967, SWP, Box 24, Folder 4.

154 **After Sophie described:** SCW, letter to EHS, August 23, 1967, SWP and EHS, letter to SCW, August 31, 1967, SWP, Box 24, Folder 4.

154 **That was a prelude:** EHS, letter to SCW, September 5, 1967, SWP, Box 24, Folder 4.

154 **Sophie would later claim:** SCW, letter to WFB, July 4, 1998, SWP, Box 6, Folder 5.

155 **"Why are you so special?":** EHS, letter to SCW, September 5, 1967, SWP, Box 24, Folder 5.

155 **On October 5, Sophie wrote:** SCW, letter to EHS, October 5, 1967, and EHS, letter to SCW, October 5, 1967, SWP, Box 24, Folder 5.

155 **Three days later, on October 8:** EHS, letter to SCW, October 8, 1967, SWP and SCW, letter to EHS, October 9, 1967, SWP, Box 24, Folder 5.

156 **She knew the score:** SCW, letter to EHS, October 9, 1967, SWP, Box 24, Folder 5.

156 **Edgar was having none:** EHS, letter to SCW, October 11, 1967, SWP and EHS, letter to SCW, October 21, 1967, SWP, Box 24, Folder 5.

156 **Sophie, meanwhile, repeated:** SCW, letter to EHS, November 5, 1967, SWP, Box 24, Folder 6.

156 **The correspondence got hotter:** EHS, letters to SCW, November 11, 21, and 25, 1967, and SCW, letter to EHS, November 23, 1967, SWP, Box 24, Folder 6.

157 **Edgar joked:** EHS, letters to SCW, November 1 and 5, 1967, SWP, Box 24, Folder 6.

157 **When they did meet:** SCW, letter to EHS, November 12, 1967, SWP, Box 24, Folder 6.

16. BLOOD, NERVES, VIBRATIONS

159 **He was frustrated:** EHS, letter to SCW, September 7, 1967, SWP, Box 24, Folder 5.

159 **By October 3, Sophie's enthusiasm:** SCW, letter to EHS, October 3, 1967, SWP, Box 24, Folder 5.

159 **Three weeks later:** EHS, letter to SCW, October 28, 1967, SWP, Box 24, Folder 5.

160 **He instructed his mother:** EHS, letter to SCW, October 28, 1967, SWP, Box 24, Folder 5; SCW, memorandum, November 16, 1967, AAKR, Box 924, Folder 5.

160 **She felt the structure:** SCW, memorandum, November 16, 1967, WFBP, Box 57, Folder 1; SCW, letter to EHS, November 23, 1967, SWP, Box 24, Folder 6.

160 **Sophie was at last:** SCW, letter to EHS, November 12, 1967, SWP, Box 24, Folder 6; EHS, letter to SCW, November 11, 1967, SWP, Box 24, Folder 6.

161 **Then he appeared:** Ibid.

161 **Sophie felt awkward:** SCW, letter to EHS, November 12, 1967, SWP, Box 24, Folder 6.

161 **Edgar, however, had:** EHS, letter to SCW, November 11, 1967, SWP, Box 24, Folder 6.

162 **Sophie felt compelled:** SCW, letter to EHS, November 12, 1967, SWP, Box 24, Folder 6.

162 **But she determined:** SCW, letters to EHS, November 12 and 24, 1967, SWP and SCW, letter to Ann Chupak, December 3, 1967, SWP, Box 24, Folder 6.

162 **The mask behind which:** EHS, letter to SCW, November 25, 1967, SWP, Box 24, Folder 6.

163 **The dark cloud apparently lifted:** EHS, letter to SCW, December 2, 1967, SWP, Box 24, Folder 6.

163 **The correspondence deepened:** SCW, letter to EHS, December 8, 1967, SWP, Box 24, Folder 6.

163 **At Christmas, Edgar sent her:** EHS, letters to SCW, December 20, 22, and 28, 1967, SWP, Box 24, Folder 6.

164 **Sophie was flattered and thrilled:** SCW, letter to EHS, January 2, 1968, SWP, Box 24, Folder 7.

17. HATKIC

165 **Sophie Wilkins began the New Year:** SCW, letters to EHS, January 2, 3, and 6, 1968, SWP, Box 24, Folder 7; author's interview with Adams Wilkins, December 2018.

165 **"Your colors remind me":** SCW, letter to EHS, January 2, 1968, SWP, Box 24, Folder 8.

165 **Edgar was pressing her:** Ibid.; EHS, letter to SCW, December 28, 1967, SWP, Box 24, Folder 8.

166 **Sophie preferred to write:** Referencing SCW letter to EHS, January 6, 1968, SWP, Box 24, Folder 8: "My Eddie, by today you will have gotten my letters from 3 I, and the 2 from 4 I, and maybe the 4 pieces of mail I sent out to you yesterday!"

166 **Sophie, perhaps as a means:** Ibid.

167 **Sophie visited Edgar again:** EHS, letter to SCW, January 20, 1968, SWP, Box 24, Folder 8.

167 **Writing three days later:** SCW, letter to EHS, January 23, 1968, SWP, Box 24, Folder 8.

167 **More nicknames proliferated:** EHS, letters to SCW, February 8 and 25, 1968, SWP, Box 24, Folder 8.

167 **The nickname he preferred:** EHS, letter to SCW, February 26, 1968, SWP, Box 24, Folder 8.

167 **"Soitanly!":** EHS, letter to SCW, May 5, 1968, SWP, Box 25, Folder 2.

168 **Bubbling under the professions:** EHS mentioned the "hatkic" letters in a letter to SCW, February 28, 1968: "Epic on the way to Steve, with some trepidation on my part." SWP, Box 24, Folder 8.

168 **But there was no page limit:** The "hatkic" epics that have survived run well past a dozen pages each.

168 **Though the first such "epic":** EHS, reference to letter to SCW, February 8, 1968, SWP, Box 24, Folder 8.

169 **It isn't clear:** EHS, letter to SCW, January 20, 1968, SWP, Box 24, Folder 8.

169 **Edgar had made a point:** Ibid.

169 **Many years later:** SCW, letter to WFB, March 9, 1973, SWP, Box 6, Folder 4.

169 **One characteristic example:** EHS, letter to SCW, April 20, 1968, SWP, Box 25, Folder 8.

171 **And on Edgar went:** Ibid.

171 **Sophie, in later years:** SCW, letter to WFB, July 4, 1998, SWP, Box 6, Folder 5.

18. MARCH TO PUBLICATION

173 **In January 1968, Sophie wrote:** SCW, memorandum, January 24, 1968, SWP, Box 23, Folder 15.

174 **Then she passed:** Angus Cameron, memorandum, February 1968, SWP, Box 23, Folder 15.

174 **In early February, Sophie spoke:** Robert Lescher, letter to SCW, February 7, 1968, SWP, Box 25, Folder 1; WFB, letter to EHS, September 13, 1967, WFBP, Box 154, Folder 1.

174 **Over the next nine pages:** Robert Lescher, letter to SCW, February 7, 1968, SWP, Box 25, Folder 1.

175 **Sophie visited Edgar on February 8:** EHS, letter to SCW, February 8, 1968, SWP, Box 25, Folder 1.

175 **Edgar took the agent's comments:** Ibid.

176 **Change was in the air:** Henry Raymont, "Knopf Hires 3 Top Aides of Simon & Schuster; Gottlieb, Chief Editor, Leaving with Anthony Schulte and Nina Bourne," *New York Times*, January 6, 1968, 26.

176 **She had allies:** Author's interview with Kathy Hourigan, October 4, 2018; SCW, letter to EHS, February 21, 1968, SWP, Box 25, Folder 1.

177 **Before Sophie could formally present:** Arthur Abelman, letter to SCW, February 26, 1968, AAKR, Box 924, Folder 5; SFL, letter to EHS, March 8, 1968, SWP, Box 25, Folder 1; EHS, letter to WFB, March 3, 1968, WFBP, Box 154, Folder 1.

177 **"Every time I try to write or think":** EHS, letter to SCW, March 7, 1968, SWP, Box 25, Folder 1.

177 **Then he went in for the kill:** Ibid.; EHS, letter to WFB, March 6, 1968, WFBP, Box 154, Folder 1.

177 **Sophie attempted to soothe:** SCW, letter to EHS, March 9, 1968, SWP, Box 25, Folder 1.

178   **The spring proved to be vital:** Robert Gottlieb, letter to SCW, March 17, 1968, AAKR and SCW, letter to Robert Gottlieb, March 18, 1968, AAKR, Box 924, Folder 5.

178   **When Sophie floated the idea:** EHS, letters to SCW, March 28 and April 1, 1968, SWP, Box 25, Folder 2.

179   **He also joked:** EHS, letter to SCW, March 28, 1968, and SCW, letter to EHS, March 29, 1968, SWP, Box 25, Folder 2. In addition, the author relayed this anecdote to Tommy Trantino in an interview in 2019; he laughed and said he did not recall the exchange but did remember SCW fondly (and EHS less so).

179   **Edgar made one more impassioned case:** EHS, letter to SCW, April 1, 1968, SWP, Box 25, Folder 2.

180   **Whatever he thought:** Ibid.

180   **Perhaps that's why:** EHS, letter to SCW, April 4, 1968, SWP, Box 25, Folder 2.

180   **Sophie seemed taken aback:** SCW, letter to EHS, April 6, 1968, SWP, Box 25, Folder 2.

180   **Soon Edgar sent Sophie another:** EHS, letter to SCW, April 20, 1968, SWP, Box 25, Folder 8; EHS, letter to SCW, April 28, 1968, SWP, Box 25, Folder 2.

180   **But Sophie didn't seem to mind:** Signed contract, AAKR, Box 924, Folder 5. For the history of "Son of Sam" laws, see "1105. The First Amendment Problems of 'Son of Sam' Laws," Criminal Resource Manual 1101–1199, Department of Justice Archives, https://www .justice.gov/archives/jm/criminal-resource-manual-1105-first-amen dment-problems-son-sam-laws.

181   **Sophie was also preoccupied:** SCW, letter to EHS, May 9, 1968, SWP, Box 25, Folder 3.

181   **Edgar asked if his mother could attend:** Ibid.

181   **There was another surprise guest:** WFB, letter to EHS, March 27, 1968, WFBP, Box 154, Folder 2.

182   **Sophie's presentation:** SCW, letter to EHS, May 9, 1968, SWP, Box 25, Folder 3; Anthony Schulte, letter to SCW, May 10, 1968, WFBP, Box 57, Folder 1; Anthony Schulte, letter to WFB, May 11, 1968, WFBP, Box 276, Folder 9.

182 **Sophie, of course, expressed:** SCW, letter to WFB, May 10, 1968, WFBP, Box 57, Folder 1.

183 **After the meeting:** SCW, letter to EHS, May 10, 1968, SWP, Box 25, Folder 3.

183 **Five days later:** EHS, letter to SCW, May 14, 1968, SWP, Box 25, Folder 3.

183 **She visited again:** EHS, letter to SCW, May 26, 1968, SWP, Box 25, Folder 3; EHS, letter to WFB, May 14, 1968, WFBP, 276, Folder 9.

183 **That proved to be:** EHS, letter to SCW, May 28, 1968, SWP, Box 25, Folder 3.

184 **He wrote Sophie on May 29:** EHS, letter to SCW, May 29, 1968, SWP, Box 25, Folder 3.

184 **She, in turn, apologized:** SCW, letter to EHS, May 26, 1968, SWP, Box 25, Folder 3.

184 **Sophie kept herself abreast:** SCW, letter to EHS, June 23, 1968, SWP, Box 25, Folder 3.

185 **Buckley was delighted:** WFB, letter to EHS, May 23, 1968, WFBP and EHS, letter to WFB, May 25, 1968, WFBP, Box 276, Folder 9.

185 **Buckley finally read:** WFB, letter to EHS, May 29, 1968, SWP, Box 25, Folder 3.

185 **The note confused Edgar:** Ibid.

185 **Sophie's next visit:** EHS, letter to SCW, June 16, 1968, SWP, Box 25, Folder 3.

186 **Sophie read that letter:** SCW, letter to EHS, June 18, 1968, SWP, Box 25, Folder 3.

186 **They patched things up:** The Editors, "September Books," *Publishers Weekly*, June 3, 1968, 73; SCW, letter to EHS, June 26, 1968, and EHS, letter to SCW, June 27, 1968, SWP, Box 25, Folder 3.

186 **Capote, however, did read:** SCW, letter to EHS, July 10, 1968, SWP, Box 25, Folder 4.

187 **Edgar replied right away:** EHS, letter to SCW, July 11, 1968, SWP, Box 25, Folder 4; William F. Buckley, Jr., "The Protracted Life of Edgar Smith," *Life*, February 1979, 54–71.

187 **Otherwise, Edgar spent:** *Witherspoon v. Illinois*, 391 U.S. 510 (1968), decided by the Supreme Court on June 3, 1968; WFB letter to EHS,

July 11, 1968, SWP and EHS, letter to SCW, July 22, 1968, SWP, Box 25, Folder 4; SMU, letter to EHS, July 29, 1968, WFBP, Box 154, Folder 2

188 **On August 2, Sophie received:** EHS, letter to SCW, August 4, 1968, SWP, Box 25, Folder 4.

19. THE BREACH

189 **July 1968 was a good month:** SCW, letter to EHS, July 25, 1968, SWP, Box 25, Folder 4.

189 **Edgar also received:** SMU, letter to EHS, July 29, 1968, SWP, Box 25, Folder 4; EHS, letter to SCW, August 3, 1968, and EHS, letter to WFB, August 3, 1968, WFBP, Box 276, Folder 9.

190 **But the very next day:** EHS, letter to SCW, August 4, 1968, SWP, Box 25, Folder 4.

190 **Edgar told Sophie:** Ibid.

191 **Sophie, upon receiving the letter:** SCW, letter to SFL, August 6, 1968, SWP, Box 25, Folder 4.

191 **She followed up with Lichtenstein:** Ibid.

192 **Then she set about:** SCW, letter to EHS, August 6, 1968, SWP, Box 25, Folder 4.

192 **Until the matter was sorted out:** Ibid.

192 **A few days later:** SCW, letter to EHS, August 8, 1968, SWP, Box 25, Folder 4.

193 **Sophie wrote to Steve Lichtenstein again:** SCW, letter to SFL, August 7, 1968, SWP, Box 25, Folder 4.

193 **If Edgar did go ahead:** Ibid.

194 **That same Wednesday:** EHS, letter to SCW, August 7, 1968, SWP, Box 25, Folder 4.

194 **The entire letter must have been:** Ibid.

194 **The letter gained him no traction:** SCW, letter to EHS, August 8, 1968, SWP, Box 25, Folder 4.

195 **Sophie wondered if her reaction:** Ibid.

195 **Yet within two weeks:** SCW, letter to EHS, August 25, 1968, SWP, Box 25, Folder 4.

195 **Edgar at last realized:** EHS, letter to WFB, August 8, 1968, WFBP, Box 276, Folder 9.

195 **A few days later:** WFB, letter to EHS, August 15, 1968, WFBP, Box 276, Folder 9; SCW, letter to WFB, August 13, 1968, SWP, Box 25, Folder 4.

196 **Buckley hadn't understood:** John B. Judis, *William F. Buckley, Jr.: Patron Saint of the Conservatives* (New York: Simon & Schuster, 1988), 288–93.

196 **"It is quite true":** WFB, letter to EHS, August 15, 1968, WFBP, Box 276, Folder 9.

196 **Edgar's mood also improved:** EHS, letter to WFB, August 19, 1968, WFBP, Box 276, Folder 9.

197 **A week later, on August 26:** WFB, letter to EHS, August 26, 1968, WFBP, Box 276, Folder 9; SCW, to EHS, August 27, 1968, SWP, Box 25, Folder 4.

197 **Neither Sophie nor Edgar, it seemed:** SCW, letter to EHS, August 10, 1968, SWP, Box 25, Folder 4.

197 **A long letter:** EHS, letter to SCW, August 9–10, 1968, SWP, Box 25, Folder 4.

197 **For Buckley had read:** WFB, telegram to EHS, August 10, 1968, WFBP, Box 154, Folder 1; EHS, letter to SCW, August 9–10, 1968, SWP, Box 25, Folder 4.

198 **Edgar also wrote:** SCW, letter to EHS, August 14, 1968, and SCW, letter to SFL, August 17, 1968, SWP, Box 25, Folder 4.

198 **Sophie couldn't help admitting:** SCW, letter to SFL, August 17, 1968, SWP, Box 25, Folder 4.

198 **Edgar, however, would remain:** SCW, letter to EHS, September 4, 1968, SWP, Box 25, Folder 5.

20. *BRIEF AGAINST DEATH*

200 **Naturally, local newspapers reached out:** *Morning Call* (Paterson, NJ), September 5, 1968, 42.

200 **Edgar was curious:** EHS, letters to SCW, September 3 and 5, 1968, SWP, Box 25, Folder 5.

201 **Edgar was pleased with the reviews:** Ruth Blum, "Smith: Killer?

Genius?," *Sunday News* (Ridgewood, NJ), September 22, 1968, 1; Mark Howat, "Death Row's Smith Raises Some Doubts," *Record* (Bergen, NJ), September 4, 1968, 1; Christopher Lehmann-Haupt, "Books of the Times; Life and Times of a Victim," *New York Times*, September 3, 1968, 41; Ross MacDonald, "Eddie's Story," *New York Times Book Review*, September 22, 1968, 8; WFB, letter to EHS, September 5, 1968, WFBP, Box 276, Folder 9.

201   **Edgar also looked forward:** EHS, letters to SCW, September 3 and 5, 1968, SWP, Box 25, Folder 5.

201   **After Edgar watched his friend:** EHS, letter to WFB, September 4, 1968, WFBP, Box 276, Folder 9.

201   **Buckley also appeared:** SFL, letter to EHS, September 6, 1968, SWP, Box 25, Folder 5; transcript of WNEW program, September 5, 1968, WFBP, Box 154, Folder 2.

202   **Buckley dismissed the judgment:** Transcript of interview by Lloyd Dobyns, WNEW, September 5, 1968, WFBP, Box 154, Folder 2.

202   **Edgar's postpublication letters:** EHS, letters to SCW, September 3 and 5, 1968, SWP, Box 25, Folder 5.

202   **Sophie reacted to the book's publication:** SCW, letter to EHS, September 7, 1968, SWP, Box 25, Folder 5.

203   **The day before, Sophie had returned:** EHS, letter to SCW, September 14, 1968, and SCW, letter to EHS, September 15, 1968, SWP, Box 25, Folder 5.

203   **By October 10, two days after:** SCW, letter to EHS, October 10, 1968, SWP, Box 25, Folder 6; WFB, letter to EHS, October 11, 1968, WFBP, Box 276, Folder 9.

203   **A week later, Sophie and Buckley rejoiced:** SCW, letter to WFB, October 18, 1968, WFBP, Box 276, Folder 9.

203   **The good book news helped alleviate:** WFB, letter to EHS, October 5, 1968, WFBP, Box 154, Folder 2; SMU, letter to EHS, October 29, 1968, SWP, Box 25, Folder 6.

204   **It turned out that the Supreme Court:** SFL, letter to EHS, October 30, 1968, WFBP, Box 276, Folder 9; EHS, letter to SCW, November 5, 1968, SWP, Box 25, Folder 6.

204   **Then came the big shock:** SCW, letter to EHS, November 12, 1968, SWP, Box 25, Folder 6.

204 **Edgar was understandably ecstatic:** EHS, letter to SCW, November 12, 1968, SWP, Box 25, Folder 6.

205 **Buckley saw no reason:** WFB, telegram to EHS, November 12, 1968, WFBP, Box 154, Folder 2; WFB, letter to EHS, November 18, 1968, SWP, Box 25, Folder 6.

205 **Umin went even further:** SMU, letter to EHS, with comments by SCW, November 12, 1968, WFBP, Box 154, Folder 2.

205 **With the clock restarted:** EHS, letter to SCW, November 13, 1968, SWP, Box 25, Folder 6.

206 **He also implored Steve Lichtenstein:** WFB, letter to SFL, December 16, 1968, WFBP, Box 154, Folder 2.

206 **Edgar also wondered:** EHS, letter to SCW, November 13, 1968, SWP, Box 25, Folder 6.

206 **As 1968 drew to a close:** EHS, letter to SCW, December 8, 1968, SWP, Box 25, Folder 6.

206 **"I am reimpressed":** SCW, letter to EHS, December 20, 1968, SWP, Box 25, Folder 6.

21. ROGUE'S WAKE

209 **For Sophie Wilkins, 1968 had been:** SCW, letter to EHS, November 22, 1968, SWP, Box 25, Folder 6.

209 **Edgar, however, didn't share:** EHS, letter to SCW, December 22, 1968, SWP, Box 25, Folder 6; EHS, letter to WFB, March 10, 1969, WFBP, Box 152, Folder 8.

210 **In 1957, Juliette had been living:** Juliette Scheinman, letter to SCW, undated (ca. 1969), SWP, Box 25, Folder 6; author's interview with Bill Scheinman, November 16, 2019.

210 **Her life had changed:** Author's interview with Bill Scheinman, November 16, 2019; *Record* (Bergen, NJ), June 22, 1961, 13; Juliette Scheinman obituary, *New York Times*, September 18, 2013; Tom Wolfe, "Radical Chic: That Party at Lenny's," *New York*, July 29, 1970, https://nymag.com/docs/07/05/070529radical_chic.pdf.

211 **The two women went out:** Juliette Scheinman, letter to SCW, undated (ca. 1969), SWP, Box 25, Folder 6. SCW lived at 211 West 106th Street, and Scheinman lived on West End Avenue near Lincoln Center.

211 **"Watch your step":** SCW, comments, relayed in a letter from EHS to WFB, January 19, 1969, WFBP, Box 152, Folder 8.

212 **Her love of Bloomingdale's:** Author's interview with Bill Scheinman, November 16, 2019; EHS, letter to WFB, January 19, 1969, WFBP, Box 152, Folder 8; WFB, letters to EHS, January 17 and February 10, 1969, WFBP, Box 152, Folder 8.

212 **Edgar's increased attention:** EHS, letter to SCW, December 22, 1968, SWP, Box 25, Folder 6; EHS, letter to WFB, January 28, 1969, WFBP, Box 152, Folder 8.

213 **Conditions on death row:** Undated ad for Sears portable typewriter with EHS handwriting indicating that he now had one of his own; SWP, Box 25, Folder 7.

213 **But then his progress:** EHS, letter to SCW, January 5, 1969, SWP, Box 25, Folder 7.

213 **Sophie also decided:** Author's interview with Adam Wilkins, December 21, 2018; SCW, letter to EHS, January 7, 1969, SWP, Box 25, Folder 7; SCW, letter to WFB, January 27, 1969, WFBP, Box 67, Folder 1; EHS, letter to WFB, April 26, 1969, WFBP, Box 152, Folder 8.

214 **What Sophie didn't know:** EHS, letters to WFB, January 12 and February 20, 1969, WFBP, Box 152, Folder 8.

214 **Sophie's letters, meanwhile:** SCW, letter to EHS, January 16, 1969, SWP, Box 25, Folder 7.

214 **A week later, on January 23:** SCW, letter to EHS, January 23, 1969; SWP, Box 25, Folder 7.

215 **Sophie claimed:** Ibid.

215 **Edgar, too, had reached:** EHS, letter to SCW, January 26, 1969, SWP, Box 25, Folder 7.

215 **They did not keep the change:** SCW, letters to WFB, January 27 and February 8, 1969, WFBP, Box 67, Folder 1; EHS, letter to WFB, January 31, 1969, WFBP, Box 152, Folder 8; WFB, letter to SCW, February 4, 1969, WFBP, Box 67, Folder 1.

216 **She begged to differ:** SCW, letter to WFB, January 24, 1969, WFBP, Box 67, Folder 1.

216 **Edgar also saw the value:** Correspondence between EHS and SCW, SWP, Box 25, Folders 7–10.

216 **The timing also likely coincided:** SCW, letter to WFB, April 2, 1969, WFBP, EHS, letter to WFB, April 5, 1969, and WFB, letter to EHS, April 15, 1969, WFBP, Box 67, Folder 1; EHS, letter to WFB, April 30, 1969, WFBP, Box 152, Folder 8.

216 **After prison officials intercepted:** EHS, letter to Juliette Scheinman, June 8, 1969, included with materials provided by the Bergen County Prosecutor's Office opposing EHS's bid for parole, 2000.

217 **The loss of uncensored mail transmission:** EHS, letter to WFB, April 30, 1969, WFBP, Box 152, Folder 8.

217 **What with the many months:** EHS, letters to WFB, April 30 and May 5, 1969, WFBP, Box 152, Folder 8.

217 **After the confiscated letter fracas:** EHS, letter to WFB, June 18, 1969, WFBP, Box 154, Folder 2; Judge O'Dea, ruling, June 5, 1969, and his later revocation, June 15, 1969, WFBP, Box 152, Folder 8.

218 **The following month:** Walter H. Waggoner, "George H. Barlow, U.S. Judge, 58," *New York Times*, March 6, 1979, B6; Orin Kerr, "Judge Leonard I. Garth: 1921–2016," *Washington Post*, September 26, 2016; EHS, letter to WFB, July 23, 1969, WFBP, Box 152, Folder 8.

218 **Despite the reduction:** SCW, memorandum, January 23, 1969, SWP, Box 25, Folder 2.

219 **William F. Buckley told Edgar:** WFB, letter to SCW, March 26, 1969, WFBP, Box 67, Folder 1; WFB, letter to EHS, September 17, 1969, and EHS letter to WFB, September 10, 1969, WFBP, Box 152, Folder 8.

219 **And was *A Reasonable Doubt*:** EHS, letter to WFB, June 1, 1969, WFBP, Box 152, Folder 8.

219 **Juliette Scheinman also read:** EHS, letters to WFB, September 10 and 14, 1969, WFBP, Box 152, Folder 8.

220 **What Edgar may have suspected:** SCW, editorial letter, October 1969, and Robert Gottlieb, rejection letter, October 24, 1969, SWP, Box 25, Folder 9.

220 **But Gottlieb wasn't ready:** Robert Gottlieb, rejection letter, October 24, 1969, SWP, Box 25, Folder 9.

220 **Since Knopf didn't want to commit:** EHS, letters to WFB, October 25 and 29, 1969, WFBP, Box 152, Folder 8; Jack Geoghegan, letter to Robert Lescher, November 12, 1969, SWP, Box 25, Folder 10;

Robert Lescher, letter to EHS, November 14, 1969, WFBP, Box 155, Folder 6.

220 **The company was so enthusiastic:** EHS, letter to WFB, November 12, 1969, and WFB, letter to EHS, November 13, 1969, WFBP, Box 152, Folder 8; Jack Geoghegan, letter to Robert Lescher, November 12, 1969, SWP, Box 25, Folder 10.

221 **Edgar was fine with that suggestion:** EHS, letter to Robert Lescher, November 15, 1969, WFBP, Box 79, Folder 2; EHS, letter to Jack Geoghegan, November 21, 1969, and EHS, letter to Robert Lescher, December 5, 1969, WFBP, Box 155, Folder 6.

221 **It was a good way to close:** EHS, letter to WFB, December 4, 1969, WFBP, Box 152, Folder 8.

221 **He had alienated Sophie romantically:** WFB, letter to EHS, December 1, 1969, WFB, telegram to EHS, December 17, 1969, and EHS, letter to WFB, December 28, 1969, WFBP, Box 152, Folder 8.

22. *A REASONABLE DOUBT*

223 **Edgar Smith felt frustrated:** EHS, letters to WFB, February 11 and 19, 1970, WFBP, Box 154, Folder 2; SMU, letter to Judge George H. Barlow, February 6, 1970, WFBP, Box 260, Folder 2239; SMU, letter to Judge George H. Barlow, February 14, 1970, SMU, letter to EHS, February 20, 1970, EHS, letter to Judge George H. Barlow, February 25, 1970, SFL, letter to EHS, February 27, 1970, and EHS, letter to SFL, February 28, 1970, WFBP, Box 155, Folder 7.

223 **Barlow wrote back:** Judge George H. Barlow, letter to SMU, March 3, 1970, WFBP, Box 155, Folder 7.

224 **Umin successfully angled for:** SMU, letter to EHS, March 10, 1970, WFBP, Box 260, Folder 2239; EHS, letter to WFB, April 2, 1970, WFBP, Box 154, Folder 2.

224 **Edgar ended up spending:** EHS, letter to WFB, April 17, 1970, WFBP, Box Box 154, Folder 2.

224 **But, he admitted to Buckley:** EHS, letter to WFB, April 19, 1970, WFBP, Box 154, Folder 2.

225 **Edgar, wearing his new suit:** *Sunday News* (Ridgewood, NJ), April 19, 1970, 1; EHS, letter to WFB, May 2, 1970, WFBP, Box 154,

Folder 2; EHS, letter to WFB, April 21, 1970, WFBP, Box 155, Folder 7.

225 **Edgar was back in court:** EHS, letter to SMU, May 3, 1970, and EHS, letter to Frances Bronson, May 11, 1970, WFBP, Box 155, Folder 7; EHS, letter to WFB, May 11, 1970, WFBP, Box 154, Folder 2.

225 **Though Steve Umin argued valiantly:** EHS, letters to WFB, May 11 and August 5, 1970, WFBP, Box 154, Folder 2.

226 **Edgar's legendary imperturbability:** EHS, letters to WFB, September 26 and October 3, 1970, WFBP, Box 154, Folder 2.

226 **Smith's screed understandably caused:** WFB, telegram to EHS, October 7, 1970, WFBP, Box 154, Folder 2; SMU, letter to WFB, October 7, 1970, and WFB, letter to SMU, October 22, 1970, WFBP, Box 155, Folder 7.

227 **True, the friendship between:** Author's interview with David Quammen, December 28, 2018; SCW, letter to WFB, June 12, 1970, WFBP, Box 275, Folder 2411.

227 **Sophie and Bill's championing:** SCW, letter to Henry Robbins, June 5, 1970, WFBP, Box 155, Folder 7; SCW, letter to WFB, May 18, 1970, WFB, letter to SCW, June 3, 1970, and EHS, letter to SCW, June 4, 1970, WFBP, Box 154, Folder 2; *Record* (Bergen, NJ), July 24, 1970, 9; *New York Times*, July 23, 1970, 27.

227 **Perhaps Sophie's work:** EHS, letter to WFB, September 13, 1970, WFBP, Box 154, Folder 2.

227 **Sophie, however, felt:** SCW, letters to WFB, April 14 and May 18, 1970, WFBP, Box 275, Folder 2411.

227 **Edgar Smith's first novel:** EHS, letter to WFB, July 26, 1970, WFBP, Box 154, Folder 2.

228 **Steve Umin's colleague:** David Webster, letter to EHS, July 31, 1970, WFBP, Box 155, Folder 7; WFB, letter to EHS, August 6, 1970, and EHS, letter to WFB, Box 154, Folder 2.

228 **The public reception:** Allan Hubin, "Criminals at Large," *New York Times Book Review*, October 4, 1970, 14; Anonymous, "A Reasonable Doubt," *Kirkus Reviews*, August 1, 1970; EHS, letter to Agatha Schmidt, August 13, 1970, WFBP, Box 155, Folder 7.

229 **The capper was a blurb:** EHS, letter to WFB, August 28, 1970, WFBP, Box 154, Folder 2.

229 **With so much publicity:** EHS, letter to WFB, WFBP, Box 154, Folder 2; Steven M. Umin, letter to WFB, August 4, 1970, and WFB, letter to Jack Kroll, August 13, 1970, WFBP, Box 155, Folder 7.

229 **"There is, to begin with":** EHS, letter to Albert C. Wagner, August 3, 1970, WFBP, Box 155, Folder 7.

230 **The letter didn't work:** SMU, letter to EHS, August 4, 1970, WFBP, Box 155, Folder 7; EHS, letters to WFB, October 3 and 22, 1970, WFBP, Box 154, Folder 2; Richard Lingeman, "From the Pen of Edgar Smith," *New York Times Book Review*, December 13, 1970, 8; *Record* (Bergen, NJ), November 8, 1970, 117.

230 **Edgar enjoyed the praise:** EHS, letter to WFB, September 29, 1970, WFBP, Box 154, Folder 2.

230 **Good legal news came unexpectedly:** WFB, telegram to EHS, October 7, 1970, EHS, letters to WFB, December 2 and 31, 1970, WFBP, Box 154, Folder 2.

23. BID FOR A NEW TRIAL

231 **Beginning on January 18, 1971:** *Bulletin* (Philadelphia), January 17, 1971, XB-3; *Record* (Bergen, NJ), January 19, 1971, 24.

232 **The Newark courtroom:** *Record* (Bergen, NJ), January 19, 1971, 24; WFB, letter to EHS, January 18, 1971, and EHS, letter to WFB, January 23, 1971, WFBP, Box 154, Folder 3; author's interview with Bill Scheinman, November 16, 2019; *Herald-News* (Passaic, NJ), February 1, 1971, 2; SCW, letter to EHS, January 20, 1971, WFBP, Box 275, Folder 2412.

232 **The press, not only:** *Herald-News* (Passaic, NJ), January 19, 1971, 1; *Daily News* (New York), January 19, 1971, 7; *Record* (Bergen, NJ), January 19, 1971, 1.

232 **The day before the hearing:** *Bulletin* (Philadelphia), January 17, 1971, XB-3.

232 **When Knight asked:** Ibid.

233 **On the first day:** *Record* (Bergen, NJ), January 19, 1971, 24; *Paterson* [NJ] *Evening News*, January 19, 1971, 1.

233 **The prosecutors had made:** Ibid.

233 **It was up to Judge Gibbons:** *Record* (Bergen, NJ), January 19, 1971, 24; *Herald-News* (Passaic, NJ), February 11, 1971, 4.

233 **Gibbons, a slender man:** Ibid.

234 **The hearing often seemed:** *Record* (Bergen, NJ), January 19, 1971, 24; *Paterson* [NJ] *Evening News*, January 19, 1971, 1; *Herald-News* (Passaic, NJ), February 11, 1971, 4.

234 **Fred Galda, then an assistant prosecutor:** *Herald-News* (Passaic, NJ), January 19, 1971, 2; *Record* (Bergen, NJ), January 19, 1971, 24.

234 **Walter Spahr, flown in:** *Herald-News* (Passaic, NJ), January 19, 1971, 2, and January 20, 1971, 2; *Paterson* [NJ] *Evening News*, January 20, 1971, 1; *Record* (Bergen, NJ), January 20, 1971, 7.

235 **Spahr, sporting a blue sports jacket:** Ibid.

235 **The next day, Judge Gibbons:** *Herald-News* (Passaic, NJ), January 21, 1971, 1; *Record* (Bergen, NJ), January 21, 1971, 1.

236 **The tape was cued up and played:** Ibid.

236 **Judge Gibbons had to adjourn:** *Record* (Bergen, NJ), January 24, 1971 11, and January 25, 1971, 20; EHS, letter to WFB, January 30, 1971, WFBP, Box 154, Folder 3.

237 **The hearing resumed:** *Herald-News* (Passaic, NJ), February 1, 1971, 2; *Record* (Bergen, NJ), February 2, 1971, 9.

237 **The following day:** *Herald-News* (Passaic, NJ), February 3, 1971, 2; *Record* (Bergen, NJ), February 3, 1971, 7.

237 **Calissi was then cross-examined:** Ibid.

238 **When it restarted:** *Record* (Bergen, NJ), February 9, 1971, B4; *Herald-News* (Passaic, NJ), February 10, 1971, 6; *Paterson* [NJ] *Evening News*, February 10, 1971, 43.

238 **Edgar, accompanied by two guards:** EHS, letter to WFB, February 11, 1971, WFBP, Box 154, Folder 3.

238 **When asked about his statement:** *Herald-News* (Passaic, NJ), February 10, 1971, 6; *Paterson* [NJ] *Evening News*, February 10, 1971, 43; *Record* (Bergen, NJ), February 10, 1971, 1.

239 **Fitzpatrick, on cross, pressed Edgar:** Ibid.

239 **Edgar was the last:** *Record* (Bergen, NJ), February 10, 1971, 1; *Herald-News* (Passaic, NJ), February 11, 1971, 3; *Central New Jersey Home News*, February 11, 1971, 57.

239 **Webster and Umin were optimistic:** SMU, letter to WFB, January 27, 1971, WFBP, Box 260, Folder 2239; Edgar Smith, "A Pre-Posthumous Conversation with Myself," *Esquire*, June 1, 1971, 14–20.

239 **On May 14:** *Paterson* [NJ] *Evening News*, May 14, 1971, 1; *Record* (Bergen, NJ), May 14, 1971, 1.

24. CONVICTION OVERTURNED

241 **Steve Lichtenstein had the honor:** *Asbury Park* [NJ] *Press*, May 15, 1971, 1; EHS, letter to Frances Bronson, May 18, 1971, WFBP, Box 244, Folder 2083.

241 **To Buckley, he quipped:** EHS, letter to WFB, May 14, 1971, WFBP, Box 154, Folder 3.

241 **Ann declined to speak:** *Record* (Bergen, NJ), May 16, 1971, 2; Frances Bronson, letter to SCW, May 18, 1971, WFBP, Box 275, Folder 2412.

242 **Bergen County prosecutor Robert Dilts:** *Paterson* [NJ] *Evening News*, May 14, 1971, 1; *Herald-News* (Passaic, NJ), May 20, 1971, 1.

242 **A Bergen *Record* reporter:** *Record* (Bergen, NJ), May 16, 1971, 2.

243 **He told the reporter:** Ibid.

243 ***Miami Herald* reporter Ann Wilder:** *Miami Herald*, reprinted in the *Record* (Bergen, NJ), June 27, 1971, 1.

243 **Then there was the whole business:** *Record* (Bergen, NJ), August 12, 1964, 3; *Wilmington* [DE] *Morning News*, August 12, 1964, 1.

243 **But the judge:** *Wilmington* [DE] *Morning News*, February 11, 1965, 1.

244 **Hommell emphasized that Edgar's story:** *Miami Herald*, reprinted in the *Record* (Bergen, NJ), June 27, 1971, 1.

244 **Hommell's bitterness and preoccupation:** *Greenville* [SC] *News*, January 12, 1979, 2. Hommell did not respond to repeated interview requests by email and telephone for this book.

244 **At a June 8 hearing in Newark:** *Record* (Bergen, NJ), June 8, 1971, 2, and June 9, 1971, 1; WFB, letter to EHS, June 1, 1971, and draft document of Smith's eventual appearance on *Firing Line*, June 9, 1971, WFBP, Box 154, Folder 3.

245 **The following morning:** *Central New Jersey Home News*, June 9, 1971,

1; *Herald-News* (Passaic, NJ), June 10, 1971, 1; *Record* (Bergen, NJ), June 10, 1971, 1.

245 **The Bergen *Record* ran:** *Record* (Bergen, NJ), June 10, 1971, 1; *Herald-News* (Passaic, NJ), June 10, 1971, 1; EHS, letter to WFB, June 11, 1971, WFBP, Box 154, Folder 3; EHS, letter to Frances Bronson, June 15, 1971, WFBP, Box 244, Folder 2083.

245 **He hoped the book:** EHS, letter to SMU, June 23, 1971, and EHS, letter to Robert Lescher, July 13, 1971, WFBP, Box 244, Folder 2083; EHS, letter to SCW, July 27, 1971, SWP, Box 20, Folder 15.

245 **He was far more interested:** EHS, letters to WFB, March 6, 1971, April 23 and 30, 1971, and June 23 and 29, 1971, WFBP, Box 154, Folder 3.

246 **On August 2:** *Paterson* [NJ] *Evening News*, August 3, 1971, 1; *Record* (Bergen, NJ), August 3, 1971, 1; EHS, letter to SMU, August 5, 1971, WFBP, Box 244, Folder 2083.

246 **Edgar kept sending:** EHS, letters to SMU, August 5, 8, 24, and 30, 1971, SFL, letter to SMU, August 18, 1971, and SMU, letter to EHS, August 26, 1971, WFBP, Box 260, Folder 2239.

247 **Buckley, too, was taken aback:** WFB, letter to SMU, August 31, 1971, WFBP, Box 260, Folder 2239.

247 **Umin responded with gratitude:** SMU, letter to WFB, September 10, 1971, WFBP, Box 260, Folder 2239.

247 **Edgar's ire against his lawyer:** *Record* (Bergen, NJ), October 12, 1971, 1.

247 **As Edgar's life took:** SCW, letter to EHS, July 18, 1971, SWP, Box 20, Folder 15; EHS, letter to WFB, June 27, 1971, WFBP, Box 154, Folder 3.

248 **Sophie was devastated:** Ibid.; SCW, letter to WFB, March 9, 1971, and SCW, letter to WFB, November 2, 1971, SWP, Box 7, Folders 1–3; SCW letter to EHS, July 18, 1971, SWP, Box 20, Folder 15.

248 **Her depression didn't lift:** SCW, letter to WFB, November 2, 1971, SWP, Box 7, Folders 1–3.

248 **Sophie once described:** SCW, letter to WFB, November 29, 1971, WFBP, Box 275, Folder 2412.

249 **The mood in Bergen County:** *Record* (Bergen, NJ), October 15, 1971, 2 and 18.

249 **Which was why Edgar pressed:** EHS, letters to WFB, September 11

and 17, 1971, and WFB, letters to EHS, September 14 and October 11, 1971, WFBP, Box 154, Folder 3.

249 **His lawyers believed:** EHS, letters to WFB, October 24 and 31, 1971, and November 9 and 15, 1971, and WFB, telegrams to EHS, November 3 and 12, 1971, WFBP, Box 154, Folder 3.

249 **He grumbled and griped:** Ibid.; EHS, letter to SCW, October 28, 1971, SWP, Box 20, Folder 15; SMU, letter to EHS, November 15, 1971, WFBP, Box 260, Folder 2239.

250 **He was especially disgruntled:** EHS, letter to WFB, November 22, 1971, WFBP, Box 154, Folder 3.

250 **All of which led:** Ibid.; Edgar Smith, *Getting Out* (New York: Coward, McCann & Geoghegan, 1973), 239.

25. *NON VULT*

253 **On December 6, 1971:** *Record* (Bergen, NJ), December 6, 1971, 1.

253 **The courtroom was packed:** *Record* (Bergen, NJ), December 7, 1971, 1; *Bulletin* (Philadelphia), December 7, 1971, 1; *New York Times*, December 7, 1971, 1.

253 **When Edgar, dressed in a dark suit:** Edgar Smith, *Getting Out* (New York: Coward, McCann & Geoghegan, 1973), 226–29; *Record* (Bergen, NJ), December 7, 1971, 1.

254 **Edgar's voice was nearly inaudible:** Ibid.

254 **Judge Pashman then handed down:** *New York Times*, December 7, 1971, 1.

255 **Two vehicles—a limousine:** Author's interview with Jack Carley, May 13, 2020; *Record* (Bergen, NJ), December 7, 1971, 1.

255 **Edgar answered some of the questions:** Smith, *Getting Out*, 236–37.

256 **Buckley took off his jacket:** Ibid.

256 **Buckley and Edgar agreed:** William F. Buckley, Jr., "The Protracted Life of Edgar Smith," *Life*, February 1979, 54–70.

256 **The limousine arrived:** Smith, *Getting Out*, 238.

256 **The audience was friendly:** Author's interview with Bill Scheinman, November 16, 2019; SCW, letter to WFB, December 13, 1971, WFBP, Box 275, Folder 2412.

257 **As planned, the direct Q and A:** "The Edgar Smith Story: Part I" and "The Edgar Smith Story: Part II," *Firing Line*, taped December 6, 1971, https://digitalcollections.hoover.org/objects/6207 and https://digital collections.hoover.org/objects/6208.

257 **Edgar swiveled his chair:** "The Edgar Smith Story: Part II," *Firing Line*, taped December 6, 1971, https://digitalcollections.hoover.org /objects/6208.

258 **When the taping ended:** Smith, *Getting Out*, 238.

258 **His nearest and dearest were there:** SCW, letter to Patricia Buckley, December 9, 1971, WFBP, Box 275, Folder 2412.

258 **At 2:30 a.m., Edgar borrowed:** Smith, *Getting Out*, 239.

259 **The limo dropped Ann off:** Ibid.

26. FREEDOM'S FIRST DAWN

261 **No one should have been:** Author's interview with Bill Scheinman, November 6, 2019; Associated Press, reprinted in *Press & Sun-Bulletin* (Binghamton, NY), November 7, 1971, 20.

261 **She had been a faithful correspondent:** EHS, letter to SCW, May 30, 1971, SWP, Box 25, Folder 6; EHS, letter to WFB, May 31, 1971, WFBP, Box 154, Folder 3.

262 **Late the next morning:** This section is drawn primarily from Hans Knight, "Smith Enjoys First Day of Freedom After 14½ Years on Death Row," *Bulletin* (Philadelphia), December 7, 1971, WFBP, Box 79, Folder 5.

265 **Sophie Wilkins waited:** SCW, letter to WFB, December 13, 1971, WFBP, Box 275, Folder 2412.

265 **To judge from the lack:** EHS, letter to WFB, February 18, 1971, WFBP, Box 154, Folder 2.

265 **Buckley, naturally, didn't take kindly:** WFB, letter to EHS, March 4, 1971, and EHS, letter to WFB, March 7, 1971, WFBP, Box 154, Folder 2.

265 **Still, Sophie and Edgar had managed:** Ibid.; WFB, letter to SCW, December 28, 1971, WFBP, Box 275, Folder 2412.

266 **A week after Edgar's release:** SCW, letter to WFB, December 14, 1971, WFBP, Box 275, Folder 2412.

267 **The key, she wrote:** Ibid.

27. THE CELEBRITY CONVICT

269 **John Selser, the lawyer:** *Sunday Press* (Asbury Park, NJ), December 19, 1971, D1.

270 **Selser reflected on why:** Ibid.

270 **Steve Umin, whose legal work:** Author's interview with Jack Carley, May 13, 2020; SMU, letters to WFB, June 26, 1972, and February 6, 1973, and SMU, telegram to WFB, October 16, 1973, WFBP, Box 260, Folder 2239.

270 **Edgar had much to figure out:** EHS, letter to WFB, January 26, 1972, WFBP, Box 244, Folder 2083; *Record* (Bergen, NJ), December 29, 1971, 1.

271 **He spent Christmas with his mother:** Author's interview with Jack Carley, May 13, 2020; author's interview with Christopher Buckley, May 4, 2020.

271 **Two days before the end of 1971:** *Record* (Bergen, NJ), December 29, 1971, 1.

271 **Edgar said he experienced moments:** Ibid.

272 **The day before Lombardi's article:** Author's interview with Aggie Dowd, May 12, 2020.

273 **William F. Buckley knew:** WFB, letter to Ann Chupak, December 14, 1972, Box 114, Folder 497.

273 **Edgar had written to Buckley:** EHS, letter to WFB, January 26, 1972, WFBP, Box 244, Folder 2083.

274 **After that, correspondence:** EHS, postcards to WFB, June 27 and July 4, 1972, WFBP, Box 244, Folder 2083.

274 **Buckley wrote to Edgar in July:** WFB, letter to EHS, July 18, 1972, WFBP, Box 244, Folder 2083.

274 **Edgar's Upper West Side apartment:** Author's interview with Bill Schcinman, November 16, 2019; EHS, letter to WFB, January 26, 1972, WFBP, Box 244, Folder 2083.

275 **Shortly after Edgar's release:** This section is drawn from author's interview with Bill Scheinman, November 16, 2019.

28. COUNTERPOINT

277 **Edgar Smith brushed off:** *Record* (Bergen, NJ), December 6, 1972, 1, and January 23, 1977, 8. Eileen Conlon did not respond to multiple attempts to reach her.

277 **He embraced his literary fame:** For his talk show appearances, see *Ridgewood* [NJ] *Herald-News*, Thursday, January 13, 1972, 50; *Star Tribune* (Minneapolis), March 5, 1972, 223; *Daily News* (New York), April 27, 1972, 110; *Paterson* [NJ] *Evening News*, May 25, 1972, 23 and February 3, 1973, 34; and transcript of interview with Arlene Francis, WOR, May 25, 1972, WFBP, Box 244, Folder 2083. For Robert Dilts, see *Herald-News* (Passaic, NJ), February 2, 1972, 1; *Paterson* [NJ] *Evening News*, April 7, 1972, 5; and *New York Times*, March 7, 1972, 39.

278 **Ronald Calissi watched:** Ronald E. Calissi, *Counterpoint: The Edgar Smith Case* (Hackensack, NJ: Manor, 1972), 43–47; *Record* (Bergen, NJ), May 8, 1972, 25.

278 ***Counterpoint* had run so long:** *Paterson* [NJ] *Evening News*, June 14, 1972, 46.

279 **Edgar commented publicly:** Agatha Schmidt, letter to WFB, July 17, 1972, WFBP, Box 244, Folder 2083; *Record* (Bergen, NJ), January 28, 1973, 20, and February 4, 1973, 120; *Washington Post Book World*, January 21, 1973, 4.

279 **Waltz also suggested:** John J. Geoghegan, letter to *Washington Post Book World*, February 4, 1973, 2.

279 **William F. Buckley, to whom:** SMU, letter to WFB, February 6, 1973, and WFB, letter to SMU, February 23, 1973, WFBP, Box 260, Folder 2239; WFB, letter to SCW, March 14, 1973, SWP, Box 7, Folders 1–3.

280 **Edgar found himself back:** *Record* (Bergen, NJ), August 30, 1973, C-24; *Paterson* [NJ] *Evening News*, August 30, 1973, 25.

280 **During the two-and-a-half-hour hearing:** Ibid.; *Paterson* [NJ] *Evening News*, August 31, 1973, 21; *Record* (Bergen, NJ), August 31, 1973, 12.

280 **But he returned to court:** *Herald-News* (Passaic, NJ), November 14,

1973, 9; *Record* (Bergen, NJ), November 14, 1973, 54; *Paterson* [NJ] *Evening News*, November 14, 1973, 1 and 6.

281 **Some months after his release:** Ann Chupak, letter to Frances Bronson, November 30, 1973, Frances Bronson, letter to Ann Chupak, December 3, 1973, Ann Chupak, letter to WFB, June 20, 1974, and WFB, letter to Ann Chupak, June 28, 1974, WFBP, Box 114, Folder 497; WFB, letter to EHS, February 20, 1974, WFBP, Box 244, Folder 2083.

29. PAIGE

283 **Paige Hiemier resembled:** *Record* (Bergen, NJ), July 11, 1988, 3; *Los Angeles Times*, July 5, 1989; EHS, letter to WFB, February 5, 1975, WFBP, Box 244, Folder 2083.

283 **Paige was a prodigy:** EHS, letter to WFB, February 5, 1975, WFBP, Box 244, Folder 2083; *Record* (Bergen, NJ), September 6, 1972, 2.

284 **She was shy and introverted:** *Record* (Bergen, NJ), June 3, 1969, 13.

284 **She met Edgar:** *Record* (Bergen, NJ), March 11, 1988; EHS, letter to WFB, February 5, 1975, WFBP, Box 244, Folder 2083.

284 **She claimed she had never talked:** *Record* (Bergen, NJ), July 11, 1988, 3.

284 **Her choice of boyfriend:** Ibid.; EHS, letter to WFB, February 5, 1975, WFBP, Box 244, Folder 2083.

285 **Just before Paige left:** Author's interview with Ron Calissi, January 9, 2015; author's interview with Paige Hiemier, March 4, 2018.

285 **Paige and Edgar moved:** Edgar H. Smith and Paige Hiemier, marriage record, December 31, 1974, California marriage index, 1960–1985, on Ancestry.com; *Daily News* (New York), February 4, 1975, JL5.

286 **Ann Chupak had written:** Ann Chupak, letter to WFB, June 20, 1974, WFBP, Box 114, Folder 497.

286 **Buckley wrote her back:** WFB, letter to Ann Chupak, June 28, 1974, WFBP, Box 114, Folder 497.

286 **Eileen had continued:** Ann Chupak, letter to WFB, June 20, 1974, WFBP, Box 114, Folder 497.

287 **Buckley knew the score:** WFB, letters to Ann Chupak, November 25, 1974, and January 30, 1975, WFBP, Box 114, Folder 497.

287 **Buckley finally heard from Edgar:** EHS, telegram to WFB, December 19, 1974, Box 244, Folder 2083.

287 **Buckley supposed that Edgar's:** WFB, letter to Ann Chupak, January 30, 1975, WFBP, Box 114, Folder 497.

288 **Edgar wrote again in February:** EHS, letter to WFB, February 5, 1975, WFBP, Box 244, Folder 2083.

288 **Edgar, in his telling:** Ibid.

288 **From then on, Edgar:** EHS, letter to WFB, February 28, 1975, WFBP, Box 244, Folder 2083.

289 **Buckley took some time:** WFB, letter to EHS, February 18, 1975, WFBP, Box 244, Folder 2083.

289 **After that exchange:** For more on Buckley's advocacy of Gary Mc-Givern and Charles Culhane, described in detail in the footnote, see *Daily Freeman* (Kingston, NY), March 14, 1975, 1 and 11, March 16, 1975, 1, and March 27, 1975, 11; William F. Buckley, Jr., "A Sentence Bent by Politics," On the Right, January 22, 1986; and Gary McGivern and Marguerite Culp Papers 1967–2003, Lloyd Sealy Library, John Jay College of Criminal Justice, New York.

290 **Buckley flew to California:** EHS, letter to WFB, March 4, 1975, and WFB, letter to EHS, March 26, 1975, WFBP, Box 244, Folder 2083.

290 **When Paige went:** William F. Buckley, Jr., "The Protracted Life of Edgar Smith," *Life*, February 1979, 54–70.

290 **At the end of the night:** WFB, letter to EHS, March 26, 1975, and EHS, letter to WFB, February 5, 1975, WFBP, Box 244, Folder 2083.

291 **Paige wrote to Buckley:** Paige Hiemier, letter to WFB, April 1975, and WFB, letter to Paige Hiemier, April 16, 1975, WFBP, Box 244, Folder 2083.

291 **After their reunion:** EHS, letters to WFB, March 30, May 18, June 9, 17, and 30, July 8 and 24, and September 2 and 17, 1975, and WFB, letters to EHS, April 22, April 29, May 9, June 17, July 15, August 6, and October 1, 1975, WFBP, Box 244, Folder 2083.

292 **Soon Edgar wasn't working:** EHS, letters to WFB, September 17 and October 6, 1975, WFBP, Box 244, Folder 2083.

292 **Edgar described Paige's health issues:** Ibid.; WFB, letter to EHS, November 3, 1975, WFBP, Box 244, Folder 2083.

292 **The truth, which Paige revealed:** William M. Schmidt, Office of the Bergen County Prosecutor, "Objection to the Parole of Edgar Smith," July 31, 2000; *Los Angeles Times*, July 5, 1989, 17.

293 **He did receive a litany:** EHS, letter to WFB, March 30, 1975, WFBP, Box 244, Folder 2083.

293 **The last straws came:** Testimony of Gerald Warren, *The People of the State of California v. Edgar Herbert Smith, Jr.*, Superior Court of California, County of San Diego, Docket no. A17321, 387–400.

30. RAGE, REVIVED

298 **Lefteriya Ozbun finished her shift:** This section is drawn primarily from *The People of the State of California v. Edgar Herbert Smith, Jr.*, Superior Court of California, County of San Diego, Docket no. A17321. Ozbun's testimony begins on page 30 of the court transcript prepared as part of EHS's appeal of his conviction to the Fourth Appellate District, Court of Appeal for the State of California.

299 **Before Lisa could react:** Testimony of Lefteriya Ozbun, *State of California v. Edgar H. Smith, Jr.*, 46–47.

299 **Lisa knew with utter clarity:** *Los Angeles Times*, July 5, 1989, San Diego County section, 2.

299 **She started to struggle:** Testimony of Lefteriya Ozbun, *State of California v. Edgar H. Smith, Jr.*, 48–52.

300 **Lisa managed to get:** Ibid., 53.

300 **People rushed toward her:** Ibid., 54–58.

300 **Then the driver snapped out:** Testimony of Frank Hobdy, *State of California v. Edgar H. Smith, Jr.*, 120–32; testimony of Darwin Ozbun, *State of California v. Edgar H. Smith, Jr.*, 80–84.

300 **The ambulance ferried Lisa:** Testimony of Morton C. Jorgensen, *State of California v. Edgar H. Smith, Jr.*, 107–19.

301 **Lisa was in intensive care:** *Daily News* (New York), October 8, 1976, 3; *Record* (Bergen, NJ), November 14, 1976, A-16.

301 **When the police ran:** Testimony of Johnny Boulden, *State of California v. Edgar H. Smith, Jr.*, 174–90.

31. ON THE RUN

303 **Betty Lovell's telephone rang:** Testimony of Betty Lovell, *State of California v. Edgar H. Smith, Jr.*, 256–70.

304 **Sandler had known Edgar:** Testimony of Herbert Sandler, *State of California v. Edgar H. Smith, Jr.*, 166–74.

305 **Shortly after midnight:** Testimony of Barbara Fenity, *State of California v. Edgar H. Smith, Jr.*, 144–60.

305 **While Barbara was at work:** Testimony of Stephen Jordan, *State of California v. Edgar H. Smith, Jr.*, 160–66.

306 **Edgar picked up Barbara:** Testimony of Barbara Fenity, *State of California v. Edgar H. Smith, Jr.*, 144–60.

306 **William F. Buckley heard:** Author's interview with Christopher Buckley, May 4, 2020; author's interview with Jack Carley, May 13, 2020; WFB, letter to SMU, 260, Folder 2239.

306 **Buckley also called:** Author's interview with Christopher Buckley, May 4, 2020.

307 **Meanwhile, Edgar actually *was*:** Police investigative notes, *State of California v. Edgar H. Smith, Jr.*, October 13, 1976; author's interview with Geoffrey Norman, March 16, 2021.

308 **By that time:** Ibid.

308 **Edgar called Barbara Fenity:** Testimony of Barbara Fenity, *State of California v. Edgar H. Smith, Jr.*, 144–60.

308 **At some point:** Testimony of Edgar Smith, *State of California v. Edgar H. Smith, Jr.*, 432–42.

309 **The phone at the *National Review* offices:** William F. Buckley, Jr., "The Return of Edgar Smith," On the Right, November 20, 1976.

32. ARRESTED AGAIN

311 **Five FBI agents arrived:** *Record* (Bergen, NJ), October 14, 1976, A-1 and A-5; testimony of Edgar H. Smith, *State of California v. Edgar H. Smith, Jr.*, 432–42.

312 **Edgar was arraigned:** *Record* (Bergen, NJ), October 14, 1976, A-1, and October 17, 1976, A-4.

312 **After a preliminary hearing:** Abbreviated court minutes, *State of California v. Edgar H. Smith, Jr.*, November 16, 1976; *Daily News* (New York), November 17, 1976, JL 5.

312 **Once that news became public:** WFB, letter to Ann Chupak, November 29, 1976, WFBP, Box 114, Folder 497.

313 **The judge finally decided:** Abbreviated court minutes, *State of California v. Edgar H. Smith, Jr.*, November 19, 1976; *Paterson* [NJ] *Evening News*, November 20, 1976, 1.

313 **At the bail hearing:** Ibid.

313 **The point was moot:** William F. Buckley, Jr., "The Return of Edgar Smith," On the Right, November 20, 1976.

313 **Paige was determined:** Paige Smith, letter to WFB, October 28, 1976, and WFB, letter to Paige Smith, November 8, 1976, WFBP, Box 244, Folder 2083.

314 **When her family told her:** Jack Carley, letter to WFB, November 29, 1976, WFBP, Box 244, Folder 2083.

314 **Paige telephoned Jack Carley:** Ibid.; Paige Smith, letter to Jack Carley, November 24, 1976, WFBP, Box 244, Folder 2083.

314 **Paige paid a high price:** *State of California v. Paige Dana Smith*, Docket no. A19239; *Paterson* [NJ] *Evening News*, January 29, 1977, 3; *Record* (Bergen, NJ), January 30, 1977, 3.

314 **Paige surrendered:** *Record* (Bergen, NJ), January 30, 1977, 3, and July 13, 1977, 3; *State of California v. Paige Dana Smith*, Docket no. A19239.

315 **Her supervisor, Sherry Ryan:** Letter from Sherry Ryan, *State of California v. Paige Dana Smith*, Docket no. A19239.

315 **Paige's criminal conviction:** Order dismissing accusation against probationer, July 28, 1982, *State of California v. Paige Dana Smith*, Docket no. A19239.

33. "THE SAGA OF A BAD MAN"

317 **Edgar Smith's trial began:** *The People of the State of California v. Edgar Herbert Smith, Jr.*, Superior Court of California, County of San Diego, Docket no. A17321.

317 **In unflinching detail, she described:** Testimony of Lefteriya Ozbun, *State of California v. Edgar H. Smith, Jr.*, 30–80.

317 **Neely called several more witnesses:** *State of California v. Edgar H. Smith, Jr.*, testimony of Barbara Fenity, 144–60; testimony of Herbert Sandler, 166–74; testimony of Betty Lovell, 265–70; additional witness testimony, 174–256.

317 **Ryan called a handful:** Testimony of Edgar H. Smith, *State of California v. Edgar H. Smith, Jr.*, 276–320.

318 **His testimony proved to be astonishing:** Ibid.; *Record* (Bergen, NJ), March 29, 1977, A-1 and A-5.

318 **He said his life:** *Record* (Bergen, NJ), March 29, 1977, A-1 and A-5.

319 **On cross-examination:** Testimony of Edgar H. Smith, *State of California v. Edgar H. Smith, Jr.*, 321–87.

319 **The lawyers made their closing arguments:** *State of California v. Edgar H. Smith, Jr.*, 410.

319 **The next morning:** *Record* (Bergen, NJ), March 31, 1977, 1; *Herald-News* (Passaic, NJ), March 31, 1977, 1; *State of California v. Edgar H. Smith, Jr.*, 411–17.

320 **Judge Harelson asked:** *State of California v. Edgar H. Smith, Jr.*, 411–17.

320 **On March 31, Edgar didn't arrive:** *State of California v. Edgar H. Smith, Jr.*, 418–20.

320 **Judge Harelson found Edgar:** Ibid., 423; *Record* (Bergen, NJ), April 1, 1977, 1.

321 **The court finally reconvened:** *State of California v. Edgar H. Smith, Jr.*, 452–77.

321 **Then Edgar tried another tack:** Ibid.; *Herald-News* (Passaic, NJ), April 26, 1977, 1.

322 **He carried on:** *State of California v. Edgar H. Smith, Jr.*, 452–77; *Record* (Bergen, NJ), April 26, 1977, 1.

323 **Judge Harelson clearly agreed:** *State of California v. Edgar H. Smith., Jr.*, 473–77.

323 **In Bergen County, some people celebrated:** *Record* (Bergen, NJ), April 26, 1977, 1.

323 **The original prosecutor, Guy Calissi:** *Herald-News* (Passaic, NJ), March 30, 1977, 1.

323 **Guy's son Ron:** *Ridgewood* [NJ] *Herald-News*, March 31, 1977, 6.

324 **Edward Fitzpatrick, the prosecutor:** *Herald-News* (Passaic, NJ), April 3, 1977, 27.

324 **The *Paterson Evening News* tracked down:** *Paterson* [NJ] *Evening News*, March 31, 1977, 23; *Record* (Bergen, NJ), March 30, 1977, 1.

324 **The Bergen *Record*'s April 4 editorial:** *Record* (Bergen, NJ), April 4, 1977, 40.

34. "USED AND BETRAYED"

325   **William F. Buckley had wanted:** William F. Buckley, Jr., "The Return of Edgar Smith," On the Right, November 20, 1976; author's interview with Jack Carley, May 13, 2020.

325   **Buckley did not buy:** William F. Buckley, Jr., "The Saga of Edgar Smith, Part III," On the Right, April 19, 1977.

326   **The next month, Buckley:** *Herald-News* (Passaic, NJ), May 4, 1977, 13.

326   **For once, Buckley:** Ibid.

326   **He faced more pointed criticism:** Associated Press, reprinted in *Daily American* (Somerset County, PA), August 29, 1977, 9.

326   **Buckley would be more eloquent:** William F. Buckley, Jr., "The Protracted Life of Edgar Smith," *Life*, February 1979, 54–70.

327   **But it had become plain:** Ibid.

327   **Edgar learned of the *Life* article:** EHS, letter to WFB, January 28, 1979, SWP, Box 6, Folder 4.

327   **He sent his soon-to-be ex-wife:** EHS, letter to Paige Smith, February 1, 1979, SWP, Box 6, Folder 4.

328   **He was particularly incensed:** EHS, letter to WFB, January 28, 1979, SWP, Box 6, Folder 4.

328   **And he wasn't done:** Ibid.

328   **Bill responded on February 23:** WFB, letter to EHS, February 23, 1979, WFBP, Box 78, Folder 1–2.

329   **Edgar sent Paige a copy:** Paige Smith, letter to WFB, February 16, 1979, WFBP, Box 78, Folder 1–2.

329   **Buckley responded to Paige's letter:** WFB, letter to Paige Smith, March 1, 1979, Box 78, Folder 1–2.

330   **Nearly a year after the attack:** *Lefteriya Lisa Ozbun and Darwin Ozbun v. Edgar Herbert Smith, and Does 1 Through 150, Inclusive*, Superior Court of the State of California, County of San Diego, Docket no. 405162, complaint filed September 30, 1977.

330   **Edgar and the Ozbuns' lawyer:** EHS, motion to dismiss the Ozbuns' lawsuit, November 10, 1980; document scheduling a trial for August 16, 1982.

330 **But Ozbun kept fighting:** *Los Angeles Times*, July 5, 1989, San Diego County section, 2.

331 **She felt grateful to be alive:** Ibid.

35. A STRANGE TRIANGLE

335 **As far as William F. Buckley was concerned:** Author's interview with Jack Carley, May 13, 2020; author's interview with Christopher Buckley, May 4, 2020.

335 **His son, Christopher, provided some insight:** *Boston Globe*, May 23, 1982, A-13.

336 **Sophie became Buckley's de facto first reader:** William F. Buckley, Jr., "Sophie Wilkins, R.I.P.," *National Review*, June 2, 2003, 14; WFB, letter to SCW, March 14, 1973, SWP, Box 6, Folder 3.

337 **The 1979 publication:** SCW, letter to WFB, August 1979, SWP, Box 7, Folders 1–3.

337 **Buckley and Sophie also commiserated:** WFB, letter to SCW, July 11, 1981, SWP, Box 7, Folders 1–3.

337 **Then, out of the blue:** EHS, letter to WFB, June 3, 1998, SWP, Box 7, Folders 1–3; Edgar Smith, *A Tale of Old San Francisco: A Historical Account of the Tragic Life of William B. Sheppard, Born in Ireland 1827, Hanged in San Francisco 1854* (Reno, NV: Sejanus Press, 1998), introduction.

337 **Edgar's literary agent, Bob Lescher:** Robert Lescher, letter to WFB, July 15, 1980, WFBP, Box 78, Folders 1–2.

338 **Buckley sent a copy:** WFB, memorandum to Sophie Wilkins, Steve Umin, and Jack Carley, June 24, 1998, WFB, letter to SCW, June 24, 1998, and SCW, letter to WFB, July 4, 1998, SWP, Box 7, Folders 1–2.

338 **After Edgar received:** EHS, letter to WFB, June 3, 1998, SWP, Box 7, Folders 1–2.

339 **He wrote that he felt some urgency:** Ibid.

339 **In May 2003:** Buckley, "Sophie Wilkins, R.I.P."

340 **Sophie had been far happier:** Author's interview with Adam Wilkins, December 21, 2018; correspondence between SCW and WFB, 1983–2003, SWP, Boxes 6–8.

340 In the fall of 2002: Buckley, "Sophie Wilkins, R.I.P."

340 They were a strange triangle: SCW, letter to WFB, July 4, 1998, SWP, Box 7, Folders 1–2.

36. VACAVILLE

341 Edgar Smith thought: EHS, letter to Henry Goldman, July 1977, reprinted in *Record* (Bergen, NJ), March 2, 1978, C-11; *Edgar H. Smith v. Edwin Miller et al.* (1989), Civil no. 90–0225-E-BTM, United States District Court for the Southern District of California, summary judgment granted September 5, 1992; Mike Kelly, letter to Ronald Calissi, December 7, 1989, Ronald A. Calissi personal papers.

341 But the last forty years: Psychiatric evaluation reports included with California Bureau of Prisons Parole Board documents, 1986, 1988, 1992, 1994, 1999, and 2000, obtained by the author, 2014.

342 Interviews with the press: *Record* (Bergen, NJ), February 19, 1978, 1; Edward H. Smith, Jr., "Edgar Smith Looks Back," *Record* (Bergen, NJ), March 2, 1978, C-11; February 24, 1982, marriage record to Beverley Bevan, listed in the California Marriage Index, 1960–1982, on Ancestry.com; reference to Travel Plus in the transcript for EHS's 1987 parole hearing; Beverley Bevan, death notice, listed in the Social Security Death Index, 1936–2007, on Ancestry.com.

342 "I don't think Edgar": *Los Angeles Times*, July 5, 1989, R-17.

342 Paige sought to rebuild her life: Paige Hiemier, letters to the State of California Board of Parole Hearings, 1988 and undated (likely early 1990s); conversation and email correspondence with the author, 2018; *Record* (Bergen, NJ), July 11, 1988, 3.

342 She could not outrun: William M. Schmidt, Office of the Bergen County Prosecutor, "Objection to the Parole of Edgar Smith," July 31, 2000; *Record* (Bergen, NJ), April 6, 2009, L-1.

343 When Edgar was up for parole: *Record* (Bergen, NJ), April 6, 2009, L-1.

343 Patricia Horton had tried: Author's interviews with "Patti Hafford" and "Jennifer Hafford," September 10 and 21, 2019.

343 But Patti wasn't interested: Author's interview with "Patti Hafford," September 10, 2019.

344 **The Haffords, along with Patti:** Patricia and Gene Hafford, divorce record, March 25, 1981, King County, Washington; author's interview with "Patti Hafford," September 10, 2019.

344 **Patti had few complaints:** Author's interviews with "Patti Hafford" and "Jennifer Hafford," September 10 and 21, 2019; "Patricia Hafford," death record, June 6, 2009, Social Security Death Index, on Ancestry .com.

345 **Jennifer, by then in her thirties:** Interviews with "Jennifer Hafford," by the author, September 21, 2019, and by Rosemarie Ho, April 6, 2021.

347 **Edgar Smith's final parole hearing:** State of California Board of Parole Hearings, High Desert State Prison, Susanville, California, April 23, 2009.

347 **He'd waived his parole hearings:** State of California Board of Parole Hearings, stipulations in 2007 and 2008.

347 **He argued:** State of California Board of Parole Hearings, High Desert State Prison, Susanville, California, April 23, 2009.

348 **In his final parole hearing:** Ibid.; author, letter to EHS, December 10, 2014, and EHS, reply to the author, December 19, 2014.

349 **Stiebel, who died in 2002:** Steve Behrens, "The Liberal Behind Buckley's Talk Show, Warren Steibel, Dies at 76," *Current*, February 11, 2002, Internet Archives Wayback Machine, https://web.archive.org /web/20120204091616/http://www.current.org/people/peop020 3steibel.html; Craig Unger and Sharon Churcher, "Film Deal for Fast-Talking Slayer," *New York*, May 11, 1981, 13.

349 **Edgar closed with a question:** EHS, letter to the author, December 19, 2014.

349 **I took his final question first:** Author, letter to EHS, January 1, 2015.

350 **Edgar's next letter:** EHS, letter to the author, February 10, 2015.

350 **Instead, I sent a list:** Author, letter to EHS, March 9, 2015.

350 **The tone was blistering:** EHS, letter to the author, April 6, 2015.

351 **Edgar Smith died:** Paul W. Valentine, "Edgar H. Smith, Death Row Inmate Whose Release Was Championed by William F. Buckley Jr., Dies at 83," *Washington Post*, September 23, 2017; author's interview with "Patti Hafford," September 10, 2019.

351 **Edgar's death went unnoticed:** David Stout, "Edgar Smith, Killer

Who Duped William F. Buckley, Dies at 83," *New York Times*, September 25, 2017.

351 **Edgar had outlived so many:** Aside from previously sourced obituaries: Paul Vitello, "Robert Lescher, Editor and Literary Agent, Dies at 83," *New York Times*, December 8, 2012; Steven M. Umin, obituary, *Washington Post*, February 19, 2012; Jay Levin, "Ronald Calissi, Bergen County Public-Safety School Head and 'Larger than Life' Figure, Dies at 69," *Record* (Bergen, NJ), September 26, 2016; Deborah Fredericks, email to the author, May 11, 2017.

351 **Paige Hiemier had been reluctant:** Paige Hiemier, email to the author, May 11, 2017; author's conversation with Paige Hiemier, March 4, 2018.

352 **Patti, Edgar's daughter:** Author's interviews with "Patti Hafford" and "Jennifer Hafford," September 10 and 21, 2019.

CODA: 1948

353 **Kathy Bell began the walk home:** This section is drawn largely from a police report written up by the New Milford, New Jersey, police department, case no. I-555, December 6, 1948, WFBP, Box 276, Folder 9; Ronald E. Calissi, *Counterpoint: The Edgar Smith Case* (Hackensack, NJ: Manor, 1972), 1009–17; and Kathy Bell's interview with the Bergen County Prosecutor's Office, included as part of William M. Schmidt, Office of the Bergen County Prosecutor, "Objection to the Parole of Edgar Smith," July 31, 2000.

356 **Edgar Smith told:** Edgar Smith, *Brief Against Death* (New York: Alfred A. Knopf, 1968), 48–49; William F. Buckley, Jr., "The Approaching End of Edgar H. Smith, Jr.," *Esquire*, November 1965, 116–21, 178–83.

356 **Outraged, Kathy told:** Calissi, *Counterpoint*, 1009–17.

357 **Nearly three decades later:** William M. Schmidt, Office of the Bergen County Prosecutor, "Objection to the Parole of Edgar Smith," July 31, 2000.

358 **Kathy Bell died in 2008:** Kathy Bell, obituary and Social Security record. Her married last name is being withheld to protect the family's privacy.

Bibliography

SELECTED WORKS BY EDGAR H. SMITH, JR.

Brief Against Death (New York: Alfred A. Knopf, 1968)

A Reasonable Doubt (New York: Coward-McCann, 1970)

71 Hours (written as Michael Mason; New York: Coward, McCann & Geoghegan, 1972)

Getting Out (New York: Coward, McCann & Geoghegan, 1973)

A Tale of Old San Francisco (Reno, NV: Sejanus Press, 1998)

SELECTED WORKS BY WILLIAM F. BUCKLEY, JR.

God and Man at Yale (Chicago: Henry Regnery Company, 1951)

McCarthy and His Enemies: The Record and Its Meaning (with L. Brent Bozell, Jr.; Chicago: Henry Regnery Company, 1954)

Up From Liberalism (Lanham, MD: Rowman & Littlefield Publishers, 1959)

"The Approaching End of Edgar H. Smith, Jr.," *Esquire*, November 1, 1965

The Unmaking of a Mayor (New York: Viking Press, 1966)

Cruising Speed: A Documentary (New York: Putnam, 1971)

Saving the Queen: A Novel (New York: Doubleday, 1976)

Stained Glass: A Novel (New York: Doubleday, 1978)

"The Protracted Life of Edgar Smith," *Life*, February 1979.

Overdrive: A Personal Documentary (New York: Doubleday, 1983)

Miles Gone By: A Literary Autobiography (Chicago: Regnery Publishing, 2004)

WORKS BY OTHERS ON BUCKLEY

Carl T. Bogus, *Buckley: William F. Buckley Jr. and the Rise of American Conservatism* (London: Bloomsbury Press, 2011)

Richard Brookhiser, *Right Time, Right Place: Coming of Age with William F. Buckley Jr. and the Conservative Movement* (New York: Basic Books, 2009)

Nicholas Buccola, *The Fire Is Upon Us: James Baldwin, William F. Buckley Jr., and the Debate over Race in America* (Princeton, NJ: Princeton University Press, 2019)

Carol Buckley, *At the Still Point: A Memoir* (New York: Simon & Schuster, 1996)

Christopher Buckley, *Losing Mum and Pup: A Memoir* (New York: Twelve Books, 2009)

Priscilla L. Buckley, *Living It Up with National Review: A Memoir* (Dallas, TX: Spence Publishing Company, 2005)

Lee Edwards, *William F. Buckley, Jr.: The Maker of a Movement* (Wilmington, DE: Intercollegiate Studies Institute, 2010)

Alvin S. Felzenberg, *A Man and His Presidents: The Political Odyssey of William F. Buckley, Jr.* (New Haven, CT: Yale University Press, 2017)

John B. Judis, *William F. Buckley, Jr.: Patron Saint of the Conservatives* (New York: Simon & Schuster, 1988).

Charles Lam Markmann, *The Buckleys: A Family Examined* (New York: William Morrow & Company, 1973)

William F. Meehan III (ed.), *Conversations with William F. Buckley, Jr.* (Jackson: University Press of Mississippi, 2009)

Kevin M. Schultz, *Buckley and Mailer: The Difficult Friendship That Shaped the Sixties* (New York: W. W. Norton & Company, 2015)

OTHER WORKS

Ronald E. Calissi, *Counterpoint: The Edgar Smith Case* (Hackensack, New Jersey: Manor Book Company, 1972)

Harry Camisa and Jim Franklin, *Inside Out: Fifty Years Behind the Walls of New Jersey's Trenton State Prison* (Windsor, NJ: Windsor Press & Publishing, 2003)

Jerome B. Falk, Jr., "Review: *Brief Against Death*," *California Law Review* 57, no. 3 (May 1969): 830–35

Brian Garfield (ed.), *I, Witness: Personal Encounters with Crime by Members of the Mystery Writers of America* (New York: Times Books, 1978)

Theodore Hamm, *Rebel and a Cause: Caryl Chessman and the Politics of the Death Penalty in Postwar California, 1948–1979* (Berkeley: University of California Press, 2001)

Lona Manning, "The Great Prevaricator," *Crime Magazine*, 2003 (last updated October 10, 2009, accessed at http://www.crimemagazine.com /great-prevaricator-0)

David Quammen, *To Walk the Line: A Novel* (New York: Alfred A. Knopf, 1970)

Gary Rosenshield, "Crime and Redemption, Russian and American Style: Dostoevsky, Buckley, Mailer, Styron, and Their Wards," *The Slavic and East European Journal* 42, no. 4 (Winter 1998): 677–709

Index

Abbott, Jack Henry, 337
Abelman, Arthur, 177
Adan, Richard, 337
Agnew, Spiro, 253
Alfred A. Knopf publishing
    company. *See also* Wilkins,
    Sophie
    anticipating Edgar's arrival,
        264–265
    Bourne, Nina, 176, 264
    Gottlieb, Robert, 146,
        176–178, 198, 219–220,
        247, 264
    management changes,
        176
    ownership changes, 144
Alioto, Joseph, 290
Anderson, Willie, 25
Ansonia Independent Demo-
    crats, 210
appeals. *See also* plea deal; stay
    of execution
    clemency hearing, 78
    on convict's constitutional
        rights violated, 84–85
    evidentiary hearing, 230

habeas corpus hearing,
    112–113, 223, 225
legal defense fund for (*see*
    legal defense fund)
to New Jersey governor,
    78
to New Jersey Supreme
    Court, 77–78, 113–114
new trial hearing, 79–80
Pelzer affidavit, 78–79
Third Circuit Court of Ap-
    peals, 108, 230, 245–246
to US Supreme Court,
    78–79, 112–113, 116,
    204–205
"The Approaching End of Ed-
    gar H. Smith, Jr." (Buck-
    ley), 127, 129–130
Atkins, Susan, 347

bail revocation, 244–245
Baldwin, James, 119
Barlow, George, 217–218, 223,
    230
Bell, Kathy, 353–358
Belli, Melvin, 116

Bergen *Record*
  on Bergen County citizen's
    mood, 248–249
  Calissi, Ron interview, 278
  on Edgar's admission of guilt,
    324
  on Edgar's arrest, 32
  on Edgar's divorce announce-
    ment, 94–95
  on evidentiary hearing, 236
  Getting Out review, 278–279
  Gilroy interview, 32
  on *non vult* pleading, 253
  Selser interview, 323
  Smith, Paige interview, 343
Bernstein, Leonard, 210
Bevan, Beverley, 342
Black Panthers, 210
Bloomingdale's, 262–263
Bonham, James, 37
Bonham, John, 37
Bourne, Nina, 176, 264
Bowerman, Robert, 290n
Bozell, L. Brent, Jr., 100
Bozell, Patricia, 102–103
Brennan, William J., Jr., 79,
  84–85, 124
Brewer, Marie, 79
Brief Against Death (Smith)
  attorney's manuscript review,
    177–178
  Bell in, 356
  Buckley's opinion of, 197
  Calissi's opinion of, 200, 278
  Capote's review of, 186–187
  compared to Selwyn Raab,
    173
  copy editor's changes,
    190–191
  defense fund donations from
    sales of, 211
  Edgard depicted in, 199
  Edgar's penchant for conjec-
    ture, 174–175
  editor for (*see* Wilkins, So-
    phie)
  editorial meeting on, 178
  editorial memo for, 173
  as evidence at evidentiary
    hearing, 239
  excerpt in *Saturday Evening
    Post*, 189
  finished copies of, 188–189
  Hommell depicted in, 199
  introduction to, 181–182
  Knopf formally accepts,
    180–181
  literary contract for, 180–181
  manuscript comments,
    151–152, 173–176
  media promotions for,
    201–202
  New Jersey Author Award
    for, 203
  praise for, 197–198
  Publishers Weekly on, 186
  reviews of, 200–202
  sales conference presentation,
    181–182
  sales figures, 203
  sequel to, 245
  Spahr depicted in, 234
  success of, 5
  title change to, 178–180

Vickie depicted in, 199, 358
WNEW's five-part special,
201
Bronson, Frances, 231–232,
241, 309
Bryson, Sandra, 347–348
Buckley, Christopher, 270–271,
306–307, 335, 350, 350n
Buckley, Pat, 119, 258, 258n
Buckley, William F., Jr.
Alioto and, 290
American conservative movement and, 1, 99–100
"The Approaching End of
Edgar H. Smith, Jr.," 127,
129–130
Belli and, 116
Brief Against Death and,
181–182, 197, 201–202
at Cambridge University
debate, 119
on capital punishment, 116
Capote and, 187
Carley and, 325, 337–338
Catholicism's influence on,
102
Chupak and, 285–287, 312
criminal justice system, views
on, 25
criticism for supporting Edgar, 325–327
Cruising Speed, 248
debate brilliance, 100,
102–103
at Democratic National Convention, 196
Edgar's correspondence with

(*see* Buckley-Smith correspondence)
Edgar's relationship with (*see*
Buckley-Smith relation-
ship)
education, 103
Esquire article on Edgar's
case, 125–126
father's influence on, 100–102
feeling "used and betrayed,"
325–327
Firing Line and, 136, 255–
258
Fitzpatrick's criticism for,
323–324, 325
God and Man at Yale, 100
learning of Edgar-Sophie
relationship, 168–169
Lichtenstein and, 205
"A Lonely Man Waits for
Death" article, 133–134
loyalty to friends, 103–104,
139
McCarthy and His Enemies,
100
as Morris County Bar As-
sociation featured speaker,
326
as *National Review* founder,
1, 99–100
neoconservative movement
and, 1
at *non vult* pleading, 253
opinion on *Getting Out*,
279
outrage at death row prisoner's treatment, 111

Buckley, William F., Jr.
(*continued*)
paying lawyers directly,
246–247
A Reasonable Doubt, assessment of, 218–219
at Republican National Convention, 196
On the Right column, 4,
133–134, 313
run for New York City mayor,
125
Selser and, 269
setting up legal defense fund,
111–112
Smith, Paige and, 291, 329
teenage reputation, 103
Umin and, 226, 335–336,
337–338
at University of California
debate, 290
Vidal and, 196
Wilkins relationship with (*see*
Buckley-Wilkins relationship)
at Young Americans for Freedom convention, 326
Buckley, William F. "Will," Sr.,
100–102
Buckley-Smith correspondence.
See also Buckley-Smith
relationship
addressing William as a
"friend," 115
on attorney's comments to
Murder in Mahwah,
177

on blood saturated bra,
130–131
complaining about Sophie,
184–185
on Death House recreation
restrictions, 196
on death row visit, 123–124
on defense fund coffers, 137
on depression setting in,
136–137
on Edgar's apparent "serenity," 114–116
on Edgar's exposure to outside world, 224
on Edgar's financial state,
288
Edgar's flattery, 110
on Edgar's innocence, 114
on Edgar's own grievances,
292–293
on Edgar's revolving door of
jobs, 291–292
Edgar's urgency to apologize,
338–339
on Edgar-Sophie relationship, 168–169, 265
Esquire article on Edgar's
case, 127, 129–130, 132
on first name basis, 116
on Juliette Scheinman,
211–212
on legal strategy, 246
on Lichtenstein hire, 126
on loss of uncensored mail
transmission, 216–217
on mayoral run, 132–133
on new trial legal issues, 131

on *New Ultrecht* project-in-
progress, 184
pace of, 125
on Paige's health issues, 292
on police brutality, 126,
138–139
on release predictions, 132
repairing breach between
themselves, 287–289
ruptured friendship, 281
sharing case particulars,
106–107
on Sophie-Edgar relation-
ship, 195–196
on stay of execution timing,
124–125
on Supreme Court brief,
116–117
on *A Tale of Old San Francisco*
manuscript, 337–338
on Umin, 225–226
update as free man, 273–274
William being drawn in,
109–110
on writ of certiorari, 205
Buckley-Smith relationship
aftermath of Edgar's arrest
and, 325
beginnings of, 104–105
belief in Edgar's innocence,
4, 133
Buckley's advocacy for, 1–3
committed to freeing Edgar,
111
complexity of, 8
Death House visits, 119–123,
134–135, 139–140

defense fund (*see* legal defense
fund)
Edgar's gifts to William,
221
Edgar's imperturbability and,
113–114
Edgar's legal defense team
and, 205–206
on first name basis, 116
introducing Sophie to Edgar,
140
Life magazine article,
326–328
at University of California
debate, 290
visit restrictions, 120–121
Williams feeling "used
and betrayed" by Edgar,
325–327
Buckley-Wilkins relationship
Edgar as fugitive and, 306
Edgar as their shared experience, 147–148, 265–267,
337–338
Edgar's freedom and, 273
growing closer over the decades, 335–337
hospital visits, 340
lunch meetings, 143, 147
Quammen and, 226–227
Sophie expressing jealousy to,
215–216
Sophie self-justifying racy
sagas to Edgar, 192
Sophie-Edgar relationship
and, 195, 227
Sophie's depression and, 248

Buckley-Wilkins relationship
    (*continued*)
  Sophie's eulogy, 339
  thank you letter, 182
Bundy, Ted, 345

Cain, James M., 5, 228–229
California Medical Facility,
    Vacaville, California, 7
Calissi, Beverly, 42
Calissi, Carolou, 42
Calissi, Elaine, 42
Calissi, Guy, Jr., 42
Calissi, Guy W.
  on *Brief Against Death*, 200,
    278
  children, 42
  criminal justice system, views
    on, 323
  daily morning routine, 42
  death, 116
  on death penalty, 43
  on Edgar's admission of guilt,
    323
  Edgar's arrest and, 30, 32
  Edgar's grand jury indict-
    ment and, 38
  Edgar's lawsuit against, 341
  Edgar's trial, 52–53, 55,
    61–62, 78
  at evidentiary hearing,
    237–238
  Marrone and, 65
  nightly ritual, 42
  on Pelzer affidavit, 78–79
  personality, 43
  post-trial, 70

presenting closing argument,
    66–67
  Selser's adversarial relation-
    ship with, 53, 56
  speculating on Zielinski
    murderer, 18
  trial preparation, 39
  Zeitler and, 64–65
Calissi, Ron, 41–43, 277–278,
    285, 323, 341, 356
Cambridge University, 119
Cameron, Angus, 173–174
capital punishment. *See also*
    criminal justice system;
    death penalty
  Buckley debating Belli on,
    116
  Edgar as keynote speaker on,
    277
  Edgar's book idea on, 136
  Edgar's *National Review* offer
    on, 111
  jury selection and, 187
  losing public support, 5
Carley, John "Jack," 225, 256,
    257, 314, 325
Carson, Johnny, 201
Cell 2455, Death Row (Chess-
    man), 106
Chessman, Caryl, 105–106, 229
Chrys Cross Company, 279–
    280
Chupak, Alex (Edgar's stepfa-
    ther), 20
Chupak, Ann (Edgar's mother)
  background, 20
  Buckley and, 285–287, 312

Conlon and, 286
on Edgar's financial state,
    285–286
on Edgar's innocence, 37
at Edgar's sentencing, 75
at evidentiary hearing, 231
'final goodbye' to Edgar, 84
at *Firing Line* taping, 256
Goldwater and, 134
at habeas corpus hearing, 225
hiring Edgar's defense at-
    torneys, 37, 75
at Knopf/Random House
    sales conference, 181
media comments, 81
at *National Review*'s annual
    dinner, 134
opinion on Death House, 77
overturned conviction reac-
    tion, 241
Smith, Patricia and, 75, 77
on stay of execution, 124
verdict reaction, 69
Wilkins and, 147, 149–150,
    162, 286
at Zielinski trial, 59
Clark, Mary Higgins, 3, 51–52
Clark County District Court,
    Nevada, 311
clemency hearing, 78
Cleveland Container Corpora-
    tion, 91
Comstock, Robert, 85
Conlon, Eileen, 277, 281, 286,
    314
Connor, Joan, 93–94
Copperman, Louis, 263

Counterpoint (Calissi), 42, 278,
    356
Coward-McCann, 220–221
Coxe, Donald, 2, 105, 107–109
crime of opportunity, descrip-
    tion of, 297
criminal justice system. *See also*
    capital punishment; death
    penalty
    Buckley's opinion of, 25
    Calissi's opinion of, 323
    Edgar trying to game the,
        359
    guilty plea, as strategic re-
        sponse to, 269
    persons of color and, 1–2
    public views on, 138, 249
Cruising Speed (Buckley), 248
Culhane, Charles, 290n
Cuomo, Mario M., 290n
Curley, Robert, 33–34, 80, 104,
    197–198
Curran, Claire, 35–36

Death House
    Buckley's impression of,
        120–122
    executions at, 93–94
    inhumanity of, 111
    prison cells, description of, 76
    recreation yard usage, 196
    television sets as welcome
        distraction, 95
death penalty. *See also* capital
    punishment; criminal jus-
    tice system
    Calissi's opinion of, 43

death penalty (*continued*)
Chessman advocating abolition of, 106
conversations on necessity
of, 5
Haines' opinion of, 83
jury pool and, 187
New Jersey abolishing,
248–249
A Reasonable Doubt and, 5
repeal of, 229n
seeking of, in Edgar's case,
41, 323
defense fund. *See* legal defense
fund
Delaware juvenile reformatory,
113
deLisle, Charles, 237
Democratic National Convention, 196
Dilts, Robert, 242, 242n, 277
Dobyns, Lloyd, 201
Dowd, Aggie. *See* Schmidt,
Agatha

Edmonds, Arthur, 120, 231
Ehrenbeck, Arthur, 30, 235
Endicott, Leslie, 357
Ernst, Joseph, 93–94
Escobedo, Danny, 112–113
Escobedo v. Illinois, 112–113
Esquire magazine, 4, 6, 125–
126, 127, 129, 230
evidentiary hearing. *See also*
appeals
audio recording of original
interrogation, 235–236

Barlow rules for, 230
Brief Against Death as evi-
dence, 239
Calissi testimony, 237–238
Edgar's custom tailored suit
for, 231
Edgar's testimony, 238–239
Ehrenbeck testimony, 235
federal court of appeals order,
5–6
Galda testimony, 234
Garabedian testimony, 234
Gilroy testimony, 233–234
Graber testimony, 234
prosecution for, 232–233
psychiatrists' testimony,
236–237
ruling, 239
Scheinman at, 231
Spahr testimony, 234–235
Umin at, 239
Wilkins at, 231
execution stay, 78, 84–86, 85n,
114, 124
The Executioner's Song (Mailer),
336

Fairbanks, Ulric, 29
FBI (Federal Bureau of Investi-
gation), 309, 311
Federal Kidnapping Act of
1932, 106n
Fenity, Barbara, 305–306, 308,
317, 327
Ferber, Catherine, 79
Firing Line television show, 136,
255–258

Fitzpatrick, Edward, 232–233, 235, 239, 323–324
Fuller, Vincent, 205
Furman v. Georgia, 229n

G. P. Putnam's Sons, 248
Galda, Fred, 28–31, 41, 64, 234
Garabedian, Vahe, 28, 234
Garth, Leonard, 217–218
Garvey, Jerry, 254–255, 256
Gaudielle, Joseph, 37–38
Geoghegan, Jack, 220, 279
Getting Out (Smith), 6, 259, 278–279
Gibbons, John J., 230, 233, 239, 244
Gilady, Raphael, 18, 29–30, 55–56, 130
Gilg, Frank, 63
Gilmore, Gary, 336
Gilroy, Joe
    Bergen *Record* interview, 32
    Edgar and, 19, 20–22
    evidentiary hearing testimony, 233–234
    Hommell and, 22–23
    police statement, 25
    talking about Vickie's murder, 22–24
    Zielinski trial testimony, 48–49
Ginsberg, Allen, 290n
Gloekler, Emily, 12
God and Man at Yale (Buckley), 100
Goldwater, Barry, 116, 134

Gottlieb, Robert, 146, 176–178, 198, 219–220, 247, 264
Graber, Gordon, 28, 48, 234
Green, Ashbel, 144
Gregg v. Georgia, 229n
Greski, Anthony, 244–245

habeas corpus hearing, 112–113, 223–225. *See also* appeals; evidentiary hearing; plea deal
Hafford, Gene, 93, 343
Hafford, Patricia. *See* Smith, Patricia Horton
Haines, C. William, 83
Hammett, Dashiell, 146
Harelson, Gilbert, 317, 320–321
hatkic epics, 168
Hauptmann, Bruno, 121
Heimier, Paige. *See* Smith, Paige Heimier
Hicks, Robert, 75, 78, 94
High Desert State Prison, 343
Hobdy, Frank, 300
Hoffert, Emily, 138
Hommell, Donald
    at Delaware juvenile reformatory, 113
    as depicted in *Brief Against Death*, 199
    Gilroy and, 22–23
    overturned conviction reaction, 243–244
    post-trial, 70
    preoccupation with money, 244

Hommell, Donald (*continued*)
talking about Vickie's murder, 22–24
in Vero Beach, Florida, 243
Zielinski, Myrna and, 15
at Zielinski trial, 49, 52–55, 59–60
Horne, Alistair, 103
Horton, Patricia Ann. *See* Smith, Patricia Horton
Hourigan, Kathy, 176, 187–188
Hout, Paul R., 280
Howat, Mark, 200
Hubin, Allen, 228
Hudson, Myrtle, 108
Hudson, Ralph, 84, 108, 120
Huerta Márquez, José Victoriano, 100
Hundemann, Theodor, 79

In the Belly of the Beast (Adan), 337
"Interview with Myself" (Smith), 229–230
Irwin, Donald J., 137

Jahos, Evan, 242n
Jalisco Auto Body Shop, 304
Jennifer (Patti Ann's daughter), 344–347, 352
Johnson, Geraldine Horton, 21, 34–35
Johnson, Lyndon, 116
Jordan, Stephen, 305
Jorgensen, Morton, 300
Judis, John, 101

Juvenile and Domestic Relations Court, Bergen County, 355

Kalstad, Louis, 30, 56
Kane, Peter S., 37
Kearney, Steven, 357
Kelly, Mike, 343
Kintner, Janet, 311–312
Kirkus, 228
Kissinger, Henry, 326
Klein, Meyer, 145
Knight, Hans, 232
Knopf, Alfred A., 144. *See also* Alfred A. Knopf publishing company
Koshland, William, 197
Kromka, S. C., 16–17

Learsy, Carol, 270–271
legal defense fund, 4, 111–113, 126, 137, 143, 150, 211, 290n
Lehmann-Haupt, Christopher, 200
Lescher, Robert, 174–175, 220, 230, 245, 337
Lichtenstein, Stephen F.
Buckley imploring help from, 205
delivering Edgar/Sophie sagas, 168
as Edgar's lawyer, 94, 126–127
leaving the case, 112
on overturned conviction, 241

promoting *Brief Against
Death*, 201
reviewing Edgar's manu-
script, 159
Wilkins and, 190–191, 193
Life magazine article, 326–327
Lindbergh, Charles, Jr., 106n
Lindsay, John, 139n
Lingeman, Richard, 229–230
Lippe, Toinette, 176
"Little Lindbergh Law," 106n
Lock the Lock (Trantino), 178–179
Lombardi, Frank, 253, 271–272
"A Lonely Man Waits for
Death" (Buckley), 133–134
Los Angeles Times, 330–331
Lovell, Betty, 303, 317
Loverd, William, 144

Macdonald, Ross, 5, 200
Mailer, Norman, 186, 336
Malkin, Captain, 121–123
Marrone, Ronald, 64–65, 249
Mason, Michael (pseudonym),
71 Hours, 6, 245. *See also*
Smith, Edgar
Matawan Regional High
School, 232
McCarthy and His Enemies
(Bozell and Buckley), 100
McGivern, Gary, 290n
Metropolitan Correctional
Center, San Diego, 311
Meyer, Alvin, 145
Meyner, Robert W., 78, 83
Miami Herald, 243
The Mike Douglas Show, 6

Millbrook School, 103
Miranda v. Arizona, 135, 233
Morrill, Mendon, 84
Morris County Bar Association,
326
Murder in Mahwah manuscript.
See Brief Against Death
(Smith)

National Review
annual dinner, 134
"Blacks as inferior race" opinion piece, 102
Coxe joining team, 105
Edgar's first visit to offices of,
263–264
Edgar's fondness for, 4, 95
Edgar's lifetime subscription
to, 105
founder of, 1, 99–100
Neely, Richard, 312–313, 317,
319, 322
neoconservative movement, 1,
99–100
New Jersey Author Award citation, 203
New Jersey District Court, 204
New Jersey Supreme Court,
77–78, 83, 113–114, 124
new trial. *See* evidentiary hearing; habeas corpus hearing;
plea deal
New Ultrecht project-in-
progress. *See A Reasonable
Doubt*
New York *Daily News*, 301
New York Times, 253, 257

New York Times Book Review, 228, 229–230

Nicol, Andrew, 39, 131–132

Nixon, Barbara, 12, 14–16, 47

Nixon, Richard, 99, 217–218

non vult pleading, 6–7, 249–250, 253–254. *See also* plea deal

Norman, Geoffrey, 257, 273, 307

O'Dea, Arthur J. *See also* Zielinski trial

appointing Selser, 38

approving lie detector test, 39

approving sodium amytal proposal, 39

denying Buckley second visit, 126–127

denying Coxe's application to see Edgar, 105

denying Edgar's new trial bid, 80, 112, 124

granting Buckley visiting privileges, 117, 134

reaction to jury's verdict, 69–70

receiving complimentary copy of *A Reasonable Doubt*, 228

On the Right column, 4, 133–134, 313

Ozbun, Darwin, 298, 300, 329–330

Ozbun, Lefteriya "Lisa"

abduction of (*see* Ozbun abduction)

emergency surgery, 300–301

fighting against Edgar's parole, 330–331

filing lawsuits against Edgar, 329–330

Los Angeles Times interview, 330–331

New York *Daily News* interview, 301

trial (*see* Ozbun trial)

Ozbun abduction. *See also* Ozbun trial

arraignment, 311–312

arrests in, 311

attempted murder of, 6

bail hearing, 312–313

Bronson and, 309

Buckley calls FBI, 309

Buckley's concern for son Christopher, 306–307

Edgar at LAX airport, 306

Edgar at West Point, 308

Edgar in Las Vegas, 309

Edgar in New York City, 307

Edgar in Philadelphia, 308

Edgar on the run, 303–309

FBI arrest, 309, 311

Fenity and, 305–306, 308

Jordan and, 305

kidnapping with intent to rob, 298–300

Lisa describing ordeal, 301

Lovell and, 303

Pancer and, 304, 307–308

police confiscating car, 304

Sandler and, 303–304

Ozbun trial

arraignment, 311–312

bail hearing, 312–313
closing arguments, 319–320
Conlon testimony, 314
Edgar as bruised and bat-
tered, 319
Edgar's testimony, 317–319
Lisa's testimony, 317
mentally disordered sex offender strategy, 321–322
preliminary hearing, 311–312
rape motive, 318–319
sentencing, 7, 321–323
verdict, 320–321

Pancer, Michael, 304, 307–308
parole applications
Bell and, 356–357
denial of, 341
final hearing, 347–348
Ozbun fighting against,
330–331
psychiatric evaluations and,
341
Smith, Paige and, 342–343
Pashman, Morris, 253–254
Passaic *Herald-News*, 33–34,
244–245, 323–324
Paterson Evening News, 12, 28,
76, 89, 92, 278, 324. *See also*
Curley, Robert; Rosenthal,
Pierce I.
Pearl Harbor attack, 103
Pelzer, Herbert, 78, 79–80
Pelzer affidavit, 78–79
Philadelphia *Bulletin*, 232, 253,
257
Playboy magazine, 6, 257

plea deal. *See non vult* pleading
police brutality, 138–139
Publishers Weekly, 186

Quammen, David, 226–227

Random House, 144
RCA, 144
A Reasonable Doubt (Smith)
Buckley's assessment of,
218–219
Cain's review of, 228–229
Coward-McCann agree to
publish, 220–221
death penalty and, 5
editorial letter on, 219
Lescher's opinion of, 220
literary reviews of, 228
manuscript progress, 189,
204, 213
media promotions for,
229–230
as new project-in-progress,
183–184
public reception of, 228–229
release of, 227–228
revised version of, 218–219
Scheinman's opinion of, 219
Wilkins' opinion of, 218
working title for, 183
Zielinski's fictional avatar in,
358–359
Republican National Convention, 196
Richter, William, 75, 78, 84,
94
Ridgewood *Herald-News*, 104

Ridgway, Russell, 48
Rockefeller, Charles "Rocky,"
   20–21, 25
Rosenthal, Pierce I., 28
Rule, Ann, 344
Ryan, Sherry, 314–315
Ryan, Thomas, 312, 314–315,
   317, 320

San Diego Union, 293
Sandler, Herbert, 303–304, 317
Saturday Evening Post, 189
Saveriano, Tony, 25
Schaefer, Adolph, 69
Schanz, Charles, 12, 33
Scheinman, Bill, 256, 274–275
Scheinman, Juliette
   background, 210–211
   Bloomingdale's shopping
      spree, 262–263
   breaking off relationship, 275
   celebrating Edgar's birthday,
      238
   Edgar's blossoming relation-
      ship, 274–275
   Edgar's erotic letters, 216
   on Edgar's freedom, 261–262
   at Edgar's release party, 258n
   at evidentiary hearing, 231
   at *Firing Line* taping, 256
   at habeas corpus hearing, 225
   as official girlfriend, 224
   prison visiting privileges, 211,
      217
   A Reasonable Doubt assess-
      ment, 219
   Wilkins friendship, 211

Scheinman, William X., 210,
   219
Schmidt, Agatha, 228–229,
   231–232, 272–273
Schulte, Anthony, 176, 178,
   182, 201
Seeger, Pete, 290n
Self, George, 79
Selser, John E.
   acquittal motion, 57
   appealing execution, 78
   Bergen *Record* interview, 323
   Buckley and, 269
   Calissi's adversarial relation-
      ship with, 53, 56
   on Edgar's innocence,
      269–270, 323
   as Edgar's lawyer, 38
   on Edgar's original convic-
      tion, 270
   Edgar's testimony, 59–60
   Hommell's testimony and,
      53–54
   O'Dea and, 38
   presenting closing argument,
      66
   on time of death, 130
   verdict reaction, 70–71
71 Hours (Mason), 6, 245
Shapiro, Karl, 339
Sheppard, William B., 337
Smith, Charles, 30
Smith, Edgar
   attention from women,
      212
   background, 19–20
   Bell and, 353–358

Buckley's correspondence
with (*see* Buckley-Smith
correspondence)
Buckley's relationship with
(*see* Buckley-Smith relationship)
death of, 350–352
on death row (*see* Smith,
Edgar, death row)
describing "the perfect murder," 87
failing health, 1
as free man (*see* Smith, Edgar,
as free man)
Gilroy and, 19, 20–21
as local paper correspondent,
33–34
marriages (*see* Chupak, Ann;
Smith, Paige Heimier;
Smith, Patricia Horton)
mother (*see* Chupak, Ann)
Ozbun, Lisa and (*see* Ozbun
abduction)
parole (*see* parole applications)
personality, 20
praise for *National Review*,
4, 95
prison (*see* Smith, Edgar,
death row; Smith, Edgar,
life imprisonment)
publications (*see* Smith, Edgar, writings of)
Scheinman and (*see* Scheinman, Juliette)
Selser and (*see* Selser, John E.)
townspeople's characteriza-
tion of, 32–33
transformation into a national
cause, 1–2
at Trenton State Prison (*see*
Smith, Edgar, death row)
Umin and, 187, 203, 225–
226, 245–247, 270
Vickie's murder (*see* Zielinski
murder; Zielinski trial)
Wilkins' correspondence with
(*see* Wilkins-Smith correspondence)
Wilkins' relationship with (*see*
Wilkins-Smith relation-
ship)
Smith, Edgar, death row
announcing divorce, 94–95
contraband items discovery,
217
Coxe interview/article,
107–109
Curley's article on, 104
daily routine, 76–77
depression setting in,
136–138
Edgar's last request, 82–83
family visit to, 82–83
family's 'final goodbye,'
83–84
first time out of, 224–225
improved conditions on,
212–213
in legal limbo, 94
losing access to *National
Review*, 95
overturned conviction reaction, 241
release from, 254–255

Smith, Edgar, death row
(*continued*)
second wedding anniversary
celebration, 77
thirst for reading, 95
Smith, Edgar, as free man
bank loan default, 280–281
at Buckley's Christmas party,
270–271
cross-country road trip, 274
as DEA informant, 291
Death House flashbacks, 271
embracing literary fame, 277
Firing Line taping, 255–258
first full day of, 262–264
first night as, 258–259
formal release, 254–255
landlord dispute, 279–280
Lombardi and, 271–272
party in honor of, 258–259
refuge in Manhattan hotels,
270
revolving door of jobs,
291–293
Smith, Edgar, life imprisonment. *See also* Smith,
Edgar, death row
author's correspondence with,
348–350
Bevan marriage, 342
dying in prison, 350–352
failing health, 347
at High Desert State Prison,
343
meeting granddaughter, 345
press interviews, 341–342
seeing grown daughter, 345

suing Calissi, 341
suing Paige, 341
Smith, Edgar, writings of
Brief Against Death (*see Brief
Against Death*)
commissioned book reviews,
230
convincing self of writing
capabilities, 135–136
elected to US chapter of
PEN, 227
Getting Out, 6, 259, 278–279
"Interview with Myself,"
229–230
Murder in Mahwah (*see Brief
Against Death*)
New Jersey Author Award
citation, 203
New Ultrecht (*see A Reasonable
Doubt*)
novel writing project, 213
PEN America nomination, 5
pseudonym for (*see* Mason,
Michael)
publisher rejections, 288–289
A Reasonable Doubt (*see A
Reasonable Doubt*)
A Tale of Old San Francisco,
337–338
thriller manuscript, 230
Warren and, 293
Smith, Paige Heimier (wife)
background, 283–284
Bergen *Record* interview, 343
Buckley and, 291, 329
Calissi, Ron and, 285
Carley and, 314

criminal conviction, 314–315
dating Edgar, 284
on Edgar's death, 351
at Edgar's hearings/trial,
    313–314, 319–320
Edgar's incendiary letter to,
    327–329
Edgar's lawsuit against, 341
on Edgar's parole,
    342–343health issues, 292
Horton resemblance, 283
indictment against, 314
Lovell and, 303
marrying Edgar, 285
rebuilding life without Edgar,
    342
Ryan and, 314–315
Sandler and, 304
Smith, Patricia Horton (wife)
    background, 20
    breaking free from Edgar,
        343
    Chupak and, 75, 77
    death of, 344
    divorce, 93
    doubts on Edgar's innocence,
        92
    as dutiful, devoted wife,
        76–77, 91–92
    on Edgar describing "the
        perfect murder," 87
    on Edgar's arrest, 34
    Edgar's letter to, 81–82
    at Edgar's sentencing, 75
    'final goodbye' to Edgar, 84
    media interviews, 92
    meeting Edgar, 86

prison visiting privileges, 35
public comments, 80–81, 85
second husband Gene, 93, 343
sexual relations of, 86–87
testimony, 63
verdict reaction, 69
at Zielinski trial, 59, 63
Smith, Patti Ann (daughter),
    20, 35, 75, 343–347, 351,
    352
Smith, Richard (brother)
    background, 20
    'final goodbye' to Edgar, 84
    at habeas corpus hearing, 225
    at *National Review*'s annual
        dinner, 134
    nicknaming Edgar, 156
    overturned conviction reac-
        tion, 241
Sokol, Albert, 30
Spahr, Walter, 30, 200, 234–
    235, 237
Springstead, Harold, 232–233
St. John the Evangelist Roman
    Catholic Church, 36
stay of execution, 78, 84–86,
    85n, 114, 124
Steaming to Bamboola (Buckley),
    335
Steibel, Warren, 255, 349
Stewart, James, 38, 48
Strauss, Harold, 144
Sturdivant, Fred, 84, 93
Sullivan, Ronald, 253, 257–258

A Tale of Old San Francisco
    (Smith), 337–338

Third Circuit Court of Appeals, 108, 230, 245–246

Today show, 201

Toth, Stephen, 112

Trantino, Tommy, 178–179

Tremont, Jane, 209, 213–214

Trenton State Prison. *See* Death House; Smith, Edgar, death row

Trilling, Lionel, 145

Umin, Steven M.
  in advisory capacity, 205
  Buckley and, 226, 335–336, 337–338
  death of, 336n
  Edgar and, 187, 203, 225–226, 245–247, 270
  at evidentiary hearing, 239
  at habeas corpus hearing, 223–225
  on Supreme Court brief, 203–205

United States v. Jackson, 106n

US Supreme Court
  declining hearings of Gibbon's decision, 247
  execution stay filing, 78–79
  granting writ of certiorari, 204–205
  habeas corpus hearing, 112–113
  Miranda rulings, 135, 233

Vidal, Gore, 196

Villarosa, Dave, 24

Voss, Henry, 30

Wachenfeld, William A., 78

Wagner, Albert C., 229

Waldeck, Addison, 29

Walters, Barbara, 201

Waltz, Jon, 279

Ward, Joseph, 311

Warren, Earl, 125

Warren, Gerald, 293

Webster, David, 228, 237, 239

Weil, Gotshal & Manges, 177

White, Byron, 204

Wickham, Edmund, 17, 48

Wilder, Anne, 243

Wilkins, Adam, 8

Wilkins, Sophie
  background, 144–145
  belief in Edgar's innocence, 146, 266–267
  Buckley introducing Edgar to, 4
  Buckley's relationship with (*see* Buckley-Wilkins relationship)
  Chupak and, 147, 149–150, 162, 286
  death of, 339
  depression of, 248
  donating to Edgar's defense fund, 143
  on Edgar's character, 336
  Edgar's correspondence with (*see* Wilkins-Smith correspondence)
  Edgar's relationship with (*see* Wilkins-Smith relationship)
  at evidentiary hearing, 231

at *Firing Line* taping, 256
happy at end of life, 339–340
Knopf firing of, 247–248
Knopf management changes
    for, 176
Lichtenstein and, 190–191,
    193
overturned conviction reac-
    tion, 241
personality, 146
pushing to be Edgar's editor,
    146–147
A Reasonable Doubt, opinion
    on, 218
Shapiro and, 339
suffering dramatic life rever-
    sals, 247–248
Wilkins, Thurman, 145–146,
    150, 171, 213, 247, 339
Wilkins-Smith correspondence
    acknowledging each other's
        importance, 206
    on approval list as "friend,"
        150
    beginnings of, 147
    on *Brief Against Death*, 159,
        160, 190–192, 202
    changed tone in, 153
    decreased frequency in,
        215–216
    deepening into danger-
        ous emotional territory,
        162–164
    on Edgar's artwork, 165
    Edgar's bona fides, 152
    Edgar's feelings poured out
        in, 197

elaborate postscripts, 167–168
"epics" delivered as legal cor-
    respondence, 168
erotically charged letters,
    169–172, 180
expressing overt interest in
    each other, 153–154
on fiction project, 150–151
hatkic epics, 168
having to keep it clean, 168
intimate fantasies, 154–155
letter exchange frequency,
    152
loss of uncensored mail trans-
    mission, 216
love declarations, 163–164
on love letters' secrecy, 148
on *Murder in Mahwah* manu-
    script, 151–152, 178–180
on need for a literary agent,
    150–151
on *New Ultrecht* project-in-
    progress, 184
photo exchange, 155–156
post-book publication letters,
    202
on power as masculine inter-
    est, 153
on professionalism, 149
on self-putdowns, 155–156
soothing Edgar's wounded
    ego, 177–178
Sophie ending things,
    214–215
Sophie suspending friend-
    ship, 192–195
Sophie's bona fides, 151

Wilkins-Smith relationship
  Buckley learning of, 168–169
  differentiating between love
    and friendship, 166
  disconnect between Edgar's
    writing and in person,
    165–166
  Edgar's first day of freedom
    and, 264–266
  feelings for one another, 164
  as just an 'affair of the mind,'
    171–172
  nicknames for each other,
    156, 167
  in-person visits, 157, 160–
    162, 166–167, 175–176, 180
  sniping at one another,
    183–186
  Sophie pulling back emotion-
    ally, 213
  Sophie seeking change in,
    209
  Sophie suspending friend-
    ship, 192–195
  Sophie's romantic jealousy,
    213–214
Will, George, 99
Williams, Edward Bennett,
  187n
Williams & Connolly, 187
Witherspoon v. Illinois, 187
WNEW, 201
Wolfe, Tom, 210
Wood, Rosella, 62–63
writ of certiorari, 204–205
Wylie, Janice, 138

Yeager, Howard, 121, 123
Young Americans for Freedom
  Convention, 326

Zeitler, Ruth Starr, 27, 64–65,
  66–67, 249
Zielinski, Anthony (father)
  on Edgar's admission of guilt,
    324
  extreme cruelty to Mary
    Faye, 90–91
  filled with rage and grief,
    90–91
  overturned conviction reac-
    tion, 242–243
  remarriage, 91
  searching for Vickie, 15–18
  verdict reaction, 70
  Vickie's complaints about, 11
  at Vickie's funeral, 37
Zielinski, Henry (uncle), 36–37
Zielinski , Jolie (baby), 37
Zielinski, Joseph (uncle), 36–37
Zielinski, Mary Faye (mother),
  11, 15–18, 37, 48, 89–91
Zielinski, Mary Faye (sister), 11,
  16, 36, 79
Zielinski, Myrna, 11, 14–15, 47
Zielinski, Victoria "Vickie"
  background, 11–12
  as depicted in *Brief Against
    Death*, 199
  education, 12
  fictional avatar of, 358–359
  murder of (*see* Zielinski
    murder)

Nixon friendship, 12, 14
personality, 12–13
relationship with her father,
11
Zielinski murder
blood saturated bra, 130–131
Curran capturing town's
mood of, 35–36
Edgar murder charge, 31–32
Edgar on day of, 21–22
Edgar's activities following,
23–25
Edgar's confession (see plea
deal)
finding body, 17–18
funeral, 36–37
overview, 3
physical evidence, 27–28
police investigation, 25,
28–32
search for body, 16–17
theories on, 131–132
Vickie's activities on day of,
14–15
Zielinski trial. See also appeals
Calissi, Ron at, 41–42
Calissi and Selser sparring at,
53, 56
defense strategies, 39
defense's case, 59–64
Edgar's cross-examination,
61–62
Edgar's police statement as
evidence, 57
Edgar's reaction to evidence,
48

Edgar's testimony, 3, 56,
59–60
evidence presented at, 48
execution date set, 78
Gilady testimony, 55–56
Gilg testimony, 63
Gilroy testimony, 48–49
grand jury indictment, 38
Hommell testimony, 49,
52–55, 59–60
jury instructions, 67
jury selection, 39
Kalstad testimony, 56
law enforcement officials'
testimonies, 48
newspaper headlines on,
46–47
Nixon testimony, 47
opening statements, 44–46
preparation, 37–39
prosecution's case, 48–57
Selser moves for acquittal, 57
sentencing, 71
Smith, Patricia testimony, 63
time of death approximation,
55, 55–56n, 130
verdict, 67, 69
Wood testimony, 62–63
Zielinski, Mary Faye testimony, 48
Zielinski, Myrna testimony,
47
Zigarelli, Joseph, 236–237
Zimmerman, Thomas L., 355